EVALUATION
A Practical Guide
for Teachers

EVALUATION
A Practical Guide
for Teachers

Terry D. TenBrink
University of Missouri, Columbia

BRIAR CLIFF COLLEGE
LIBRARY
SIOUX CITY, IOWA

McGraw-Hill Book Company
New York St. Louis San Francisco Düsseldorf
Johannesburg Kuala Lumpur London Mexico
Montreal New Delhi Panama Paris São Paulo
Singapore Sydney Tokyo Toronto

EVALUATION
A Practical Guide
for Teachers

1 2 3 4 5 6 7 8 9 0 MAMM 7 9 8 7 6 5 4

Library of Congress Cataloging in Publication Data

LB
3051
.T33

TenBrink, Terry.
    Evaluation: a practical guide for teachers.

    Includes bibliographies.
    1. Educational tests and measurements. I. Title.
LB3051.T33   371.2′7   73-20434
ISBN 0-07-063497-1

This book was set in Vladimir by University Graphics, Inc. The
editors were Robert C. Morgan, Alison Meersschaert, and David
Dunham; the designer was Pencils Portfolio, Inc.; the production
supervisor was Bill Greenwood. The drawings were done by
Vantage Art, Inc.
The Maple Press Company was printer and binder.

To my wife, Betty,
and my children, Sue, Jill, and Doug

CONTENTS

FOCUS

This book is designed to help pre-service and in-service teachers understand the basic principles of evaluation and to provide them with step-by-step procedures for the evaluation process. A balanced treatment of criterion-referenced and norm-referenced measurement includes (1) the rationale for selecting techniques appropriate for specific instructional purposes, (2) directions for construction and use of criterion-referenced and other teacher-made evaluation instruments, and (3) use of evaluation results to make sound educational judgments and decisions. Throughout the text, evaluation is presented as an important step toward more effective instruction.

The book's organization follows a model of the evaluation process which was developed to help students understand how evaluation can be useful in dealing with practical classroom problems. The model is first presented in the form of a flowchart that illustrates the important procedures involved in evaluation. It emphasizes the basic principles of measurement and their application to specific evaluation problems.

Chapters 1 and 2 examine the principles underlying all evaluation procedures and introduce the model of the evaluation process. Understanding these principles, students will have a rationale for the specific procedures involved in the planning, construction, and use of various evaluation techniques. The traditional concepts of reliability and validity and the problem of dealing with measurement error are discussed in practical terms.

Chapters 3 through 9 explain each step of the evaluation process and discuss the procedures involved in planning for and effecting classroom evaluation. A unique feature of this text is a thorough treatment of the use of evaluation as a basis for making judgments and decisions (Chapters 7 and 8). Chapter 9 explains some useful ways to summarize and report evaluation results to parents, administrators, and others.

Chapters 10 through 14 describe step-by-step procedures for selecting and constructing all major information-gathering instruments. Emphasis is placed on those instruments the teacher is most likely to find useful in the classroom. For example, Chapter 12 is devoted to projects and assignments, a major source of information about students.

To make this text understandable and easy to use, learning objectives are specified at the beginning of each chapter and exercises are provided throughout. These learning aids will reinforce major ideas and give students feedback about how well they understand what they have read. (Answers to all exercises are provided in Appendix B.)

Important information is frequently summarized and highlighted in ruled boxes. This material will allow the student to preview each chapter efficiently. In addition, these important concepts and principles can be readily located for review and class discussion.

Throughout the text statistical concepts are explained where they are needed. A more comprehensive treatment is then provided in Appendix A, along with an explanation of computational procedures.

My greatest debt of gratitude is to my students. Over a period of five years they have reacted to ideas, read preliminary drafts, and provided invaluable feedback.

I also wish to acknowledge the help of many of my colleagues who read and criticized this text, section by section. I am especially indebted to William Mehrens, Natalie Sproull, and Martin Wong, who provided helpful suggestions for the improvement of clarity, accuracy, and organization.

I would feel especially negligent if I did not acknowledge the help of my editors, Robert C. Morgan, who gave encouragement and valuable suggestions, and Alison Meersschaert, who provided extensive critique of the manuscript—evidence that publishers can be helpful to their authors.

A special note of thanks goes to Mary Wiles, who worked diligently throughout the typing of the manuscript and who ably withstood pressures and deadlines which were not under her control.

Finally, I wish to thank my family for their patience and encouragement.

Terry D. TenBrink

EVALUATION
A Practical Guide
for Teachers

PART ONE

CONCEPTS IMPORTANT TO AN UNDERSTANDING OF THE EVALUATION PROCESS

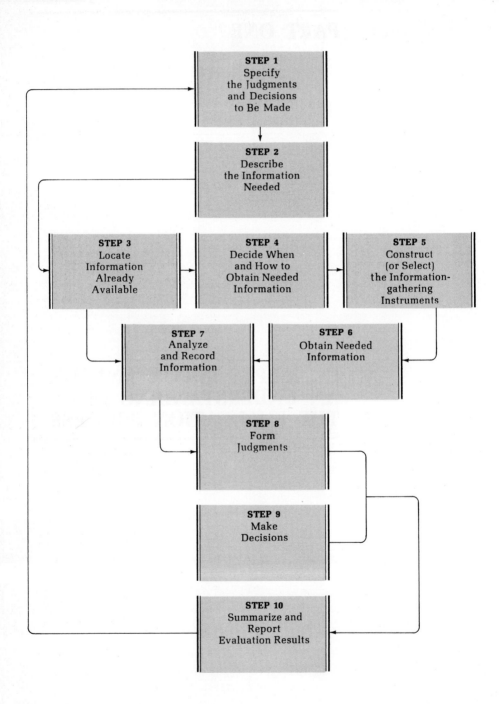

CHAPTER 1

The Evaluation Process: A Model for Classroom Teachers

This book is based upon the premise that evaluation is an important part of the teaching-learning process. It provides you with a model of the evaluation process which has been especially designed to meet the needs of the classroom teacher. The notion that evaluation, properly used, can aid learning has been applied directly in this text. At the beginning of each chapter you will be told what you are expected to learn. Then, throughout each chapter, periodic exercises are provided which have been designed to help you evaluate your progress.

This first chapter introduces you to the model of the evaluation process which will be used as a basis for the organization of the book.

After you have read this chapter, you should be able to

1. Define evaluation.
2. Briefly describe the interdependence among decisions, judgments, and information.
3. Recall the three major stages in the evaluation process.
4. Use the flowchart representing a model of the process of evaluation
   (*a*) to locate the important steps in that process and (*b*) as a guide to the organization of this book.

Evaluation is one of those words which has taken on many meanings. It seems to mean something a little different to each person. Take a few seconds and try a simple experiment. Jot down the first few words which come to your mind when you think of the word *evaluation.* Do not think a long time about it. Just write down the first thing that comes to your mind. Now compare your response with the responses found in Table 1.1. The lists in Table 1.1 represent the responses I obtained when I asked groups of pre-service and in-service teachers to do this experiment. Each list begins with the responses that occurred most often and ends with those that occurred least often.

Notice that the most popular response for both groups was "tests." But testing is not evaluating. Another popular response was "grading." This response comes very close to the meaning of *evaluation,* yet evaluation is more than just grading. It is true that the process of evaluation *involves* such things as tests, grades, quizzes, etc. However, none of these concepts clearly defines *evaluation.* Notice that two of the responses are related to the negative aspects of evaluation "unfairness" and "invasion of privacy." These responses bear witness to the

TABLE 1.1

Frequently occurring responses of pre-service and in-service teachers to the question, "What comes to your mind first when you hear the word *evaluation?*

Pre-Service Teachers	In-Service Teachers
Tests	Tests
Grades	Measurement
Achievement	Grades
Unfair	Accountability
Judgment	Invasion of privacy

popularity of the many issues centering around the *improper use* of evaluation, but they serve more to distort than to clarify its meaning. Furthermore, because of the popularity of discussions on the misuse of evaluation procedures, it is easy to lose sight of the fact that *evaluation is an important and exciting part of the teacher's daily activities.*

Evaluation is an important part of what the teacher does because, without some kind of evaluation, it would be almost impossible to teach. Good teachers are constantly seeking better ways to present material and more efficient ways for the students to learn. In order to do this, they must know a great deal about their students. They need to know something about their abilities, their past achievements, their interests, their strengths, and their weaknesses. Consequently, teachers are continuously seeking answers to questions of the following type: "Which concepts shall I teach first?" "Why is Martha having trouble with long division?" "How can I get my students to *want* to study this material?" "How long will it take to complete this unit?" "What kind of assignment would help the students the most?"

One might legitimately judge a teacher's effectiveness by how well he is able to answer the above kinds of questions. Evaluation helps the teacher to answer these questions. In fact, you will soon see that evaluation can be thought of as the process by which those kinds of questions *are* answered.

Evaluation is an exciting part of the teacher's activities because of the challenge the above questions pose *and* because of the satisfaction that comes from meeting that challenge and successfully answering the questions. But before you can fully appreciate how evaluation can play such an important role in teaching, you must understand that evaluation involves much more than testing and assigning grades. The process of evaluation involves many concepts. Even the experts are not in complete agreement as to exactly which activities should properly be included in the process of evaluation.[1] But this book has *not* been written for the experts who would debate at length about the details of the evaluation process. Rather, it has been written for the teacher who will evaluate. Consequently, we will begin with a simple definition of the term *evaluation* and, from that definition build a working model of the process of evaluation. This model should follow logically from our simpler definition and, when it is completed, it should meet the requirements given below.

A Model of the Process of Evaluation Should Do the Following:

1. Clearly specify each step in the process of evaluation
2. Be applicable to all types of evaluation problems
3. Be easy to understand and easy to use

---

[1] Read, for example, the various opinions expressed at a recent symposium: M. C. Wittrock and David E. Wiley (eds.), *The Evaluation of Instruction — Issues and Problems,* Holt, Rinehart and Winston, Inc., New York, 1970.

EVALUATION DEFINED

Stated most simply, to evaluate is to place a value upon—to judge. In education, that usually means judging a student, a teacher, or an educational program. Teachers make numerous judgments in the process of evaluating the educational achievement of their students. One common kind of judgment is the letter grade. Through the grading process a teacher makes public, as it were, his judgments about a student's achievement. However, grading is only one form of judgment. Actually, teachers are constantly evaluating. Daily they judge the progress of their students' work, the appropriateness of assignments, the readiness of their students to approach a new task, etc. Figure 1.1 presents a list of questions which illustrate these kinds of judgments. Notice that many of the judgments which the questions in Figure 1.1 represent do serve to help the teacher do a better job of teaching.

Some of the questions in Figure 1.1 are easy to answer, some are more difficult. Some affect only a single person, others affect many people. Some are eventually written down and reported, others are never even spoken aloud. Some are used by the teacher to make decisions, while others serve to help other people make decisions. Some of these judgments are about students, some about teachers, and some about the educational program. Together, they form an integral part of the teaching-learning process. In fact, it is difficult to imagine educa-

FIGURE 1.1. Questions illustrating the kinds of judgments which are typical of those made daily by teachers.

1. How well can Johnny read?
2. How long will it take the third graders to complete the seat work I've assigned?
3. Would Mary be able to serve successfully as a group leader?
4. How well have the students in my third hour science class learned the symbols for the basic elements we discussed?
5. What are the chances that Lisa could learn to play the flute?
6. Of the three spelling books recommended by the administration, which one would best meet the needs of our inner-city elementary classrooms?
7. How interested are my advanced math students in investigating number systems with a base other than 10?
8. Did my students develop any new interests as a result of the career day activities?
9. Zelda has the lead in the class play and needs extra practice time. Can she miss four of her English classes in the next two weeks without getting too far behind the rest of the class?
10. Which word attack skills have not yet been mastered by David?

tion occurring at all without these kinds of judgments being made. Educational evaluation, then, could be defined as a process of making the judgments which must be made in order for education to work.

Notice that this definition emphasizes the fact that evaluation is a *process* of making judgments. Evaluation is not a single act. It involves a series of activities, a number of steps. This will become obvious to you if you think about what you do when you make judgments. Suppose, for example, that you were asked to evaluate the writing style of this book, to judge it as easy to read or difficult to read. After you realized what kind of judgment was being called for, your next step would probably be to determine what kind of information you would need in order to make that judgment. It might be something as simple as the number of words you were able to read per minute or as complex as the number of unfamiliar words divided by the total number of words. It might be something highly objective, such as the number of questions you could answer on a multiple-choice test. Or perhaps it would be something very subjective, such as the kind of feeling you get when you read it. In any case, having decided upon the kind of information you need, you would then try to obtain that information (e.g., keep track of the number of words that you read per minute). Once you obtain the needed information, it will become necessary for you to interpret it. You will need to decide, for example, reading how many words per minute indicates an easy-to-read book and reading how many words per minute indicates a hard-to-read book. Once this point has been reached, you are finally ready to pass judgment—to evaluate.

On the basis of the above discussion we might alter our definition of evaluation to read something like the following: "Evaluation is the process of obtaining information and using it to make judgments."

According to the above definition, evaluation involves *obtaining information and making judgments.* Many experts have defined evaluation in just this way (Stake, 1967). Others, however, would add one further step, the step of making decisions (Alkin, 1966; Scriven, 1967). Although one might argue convincingly that evaluation is complete once a judgment has been made, it is easy to see the logic of adding this last step. Once a judgment has been made, it is usually used to influence the outcome of some decision(s). Each of the questions listed in Figure 1.1 may eventually lead to at least one decision. The judgment that Johnny is a slow reader may be used by the teacher to help him decide what reading group to place Johnny in. It may also help the teacher in his decision about the kinds of materials to assign Johnny in his other work. Furthermore, it may be useful in making decisions about how much independent work should be assigned to Johnny.

Sometimes the judgments made by one person may be used to help someone else make a decision. The judgments of each of the elementary teachers about the value of a particular spelling book may be used by the administration in deciding whether or not to purchase that book. The music teacher's judgment about Lisa's ability to learn to play a flute may influence her parents' decision to sign her up for lessons. The administrator's and peers' judgments about a certain teacher's skills may be used by the school board in their decision to increase that teacher's salary.

Recognizing the importance of evaluation's role in decision making, let us revise once more the definition of evaluation:

> Evaluation is the process of obtaining information and using it to form judgments which in turn are to be used in decision making

This final definition emphasizes the fact that evaluation is a process which utilizes *information* to make *judgments* and *decisions.*

Educational decisions are made on the basis of judgments, and judgments, in turn, are made on the basis of information. The interdependence of these three concepts (decisions, judgments, and information) essentially defines *evaluation.* A clear understanding of each of these concepts and their interdependence is prerequisite to any understanding of the details of the process of evaluation.

Decisions: The Ultimate Goal of Evaluation

It has already been pointed out that the final activity in evaluation is decision making. Evaluation's ultimate goal, its reason for existing, is to make decisions possible.

What is a decision? Cronbach (1971, p. 448) defines a decision as *"a choice between courses of action."*

A student chooses to attend one college over many; the college decides to accept him.

A teacher assigns an essay to his class—he has chosen that kind of assignment over other possible ones.

Elroy is advanced to a new reading group. The teacher helps him select a book to read on his own.

Gregory Walner changes the tenth-grade lab assignment because his students were unable to successfully complete the last one he assigned them.

Decisions always call for some action. A choice is made to *do* this rather than that, to say this instead of that, to *maintain* status quo instead of changing, to *assign* this, to *select* him, to *engage* in that, to *reject* them.

Judgments: An Important Outcome of Evaluation

Information is obtained and interpreted and a judgment is formed. The judgment is an important outcome of information gathering because judgments are the major considerations in decision making. Judgments, unlike decisions, do not call for action. Instead, they are estimates of present condition or predictions of future performance.

> G. A. Hibalski is judged to be academically able.

> A teacher makes the judgment that his students are capable of doing the work he has assigned them.

> A book is judged to be appropriate for Elroy to read (it is easy to read and particularly interesting to young boys).

> It is Walner's judgment that his students could not be successful at the assignment he had planned.

Information: The Essential Ingredient in Evaluation

Information provides the data base for making judgments. Information which is useful for making educational judgments takes many forms. It can be quantitative or qualitative; general or specific; about people, materials, programs, or processes. However, no matter what form it takes, information is the essential ingredient in evaluation. Without some kind of information, valid judgments and decisions are virtually impossible to make. *With* appropriate and accurate information, judgments which will lead to sound decisions *can* be made.

> A student is judged to be academically able because he has a B+ average for his last two years of high school.

> Many students have voluntarily read essays placed on a table in the back of the room. The teacher therefore concludes that his students enjoy reading essays.

> Walner's students failed an earlier assignment which he considered prerequisite to the one he was about to assign. He therefore judges his students to be incapable of successfully completing the assignment.

The above discussion highlights the fact that the process of evaluation involves a series of interrelated activities. Judgments and decisions cannot be made until information is obtained. But it does little good to obtain information until you know what kinds of judgments and decisions need to be made. And the kinds of judgments and decisions to be made determine not only what kind of information is needed but also how and when it should be obtained. It is important, then, to be able to distinguish between judgments on the best information available.

Try the exercise below to see how well you remember what you have read so far.

EXERCISE 1.1

1. Which of the following terms is most inclusive?
   a. Testing

>   *b.* Evaluating
>   *c.* Grading
> 2. Evaluating is a process of obtaining _____ and using it to form
> _____, which are in turn to be used in _____.
> For each statement in items 3 through 8, indicate whether it is an example
> of:
>   *a.* A decision
>   *b.* A judgment
>   *c.* Information
> 3. "I am going to promote Jana to third grade."
> 4. "George got ten out of fifteen spelling words wrong."
> 5. "Mary is a slow reader."
> 6. "The history book is difficult to understand."
> 7. "The class discussion went over poorly."
> 8. "We will now begin Unit III."

A MODEL OF THE EVALUATION PROCESS

The model of evaluation I am about to propose is an idealized plan of action. It sets forth in detail each step in the process of evaluation. Ideally, each time you have judgments or decisions to make, you will follow these steps. *Occasionally,* this will be possible. Whenever a very important and formal decision must be made (e.g., deciding which textbook to adopt or which student should receive a scholarship), it would be worth the effort to carefully, systematically carry out each step. Most of the time, however, the steps in the model will not be carried out in every detail. Often, important steps will be omitted or completed out of sequence.

The value of a model such as this is that it *does* provide an ideal. Once you understand what *should* be done, you will be aware of any deviation from that ideal. You will also know what the probable consequence of any deviation will be. Some of the multitude of judgments and decisions teachers make daily are of less consequence than others. It may be expedient in those cases to be less rigorous in carrying out the evaluation procedures. Nevertheless, anytime evaluation occurs, the evaluator goes through three stages in the process of getting from the point of recognizing a need for evaluation to the point where a judgment or decision is made.

First, he gets ready to evaluate. This may simply be a momentary recognition of the fact that a judgment or decision must be made. Or, it may involve a fairly elaborate plan, executed very carefully in an attempt to ensure well-formed judgments and payoff decisions.

Second, he obtains the information he needs. Often this means remembering a couple of experiences and a few isolated facts. Sometimes it means giving standardized tests, carrying out systematic observation, and obtaining the opinion of others.

Finally, he makes the judgments and decisions. Again, this can be done very informally in a matter of seconds or very formally over a period of several days, weeks, or months.

These three stages in the evaluation process form the basic structure of our evaluation model. Take a moment to compare these stages with our earlier definition of *evaluation.* The model (represented at this point by the three stages) should follow logically from the definition.

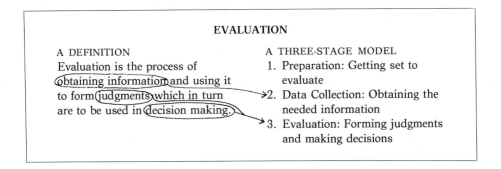

The definition essentially says (1) obtain information and (2) make judgments and decisions. That corresponds fairly well with stages 2 and 3. How about the first stage? Why is the preparation stage necessary?

One obvious reason for the preparation stage is that we must first recognize the need to make judgments and decisions before we will feel any need to obtain information. Of course, teachers often obtain information about their students without having anything but the vaguest notion about how that information will be used.

> I give tests because that's what teachers do. . . And the school expects you to. . . . And I gotta give grades.

The above quote from an elementary teacher suggests a second good reason for the preparation stage: unless you know what *kind* of information is needed, it will be difficult to obtain what *is* needed (that is, stage 2 involves getting *needed* information). Just any old information will not do. It must be the kind of information needed in order to make specific judgments and decisions.

Let us take a closer look at these three stages. Each stage involves a number of important steps. Each step is an important part of the evaluation process. The model will be presented in the form of a flowchart. When it is completed, you should be able to use the chart to guide you through any evaluation task.

Stage 1: Preparation

Figure 1.2 presents the steps in the preparation stage. Each step is discussed briefly here as a way of introducing the model of the evaluation process. In later chapters, each step will be treated in detail.

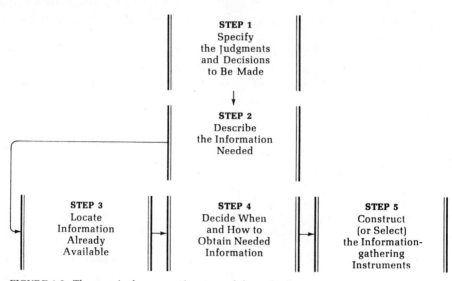

FIGURE 1.2. The steps in the preparation stage of the evaluation process.

Step 1: Specify the kind of judgments and decisions to be made. The importance of indicating which decisions are to be made cannot be overemphasized. M. C. Alkin includes this step in his definition of *evaluation*. He defines *evaluation* as "the process of ascertaining the decision areas of concern, selecting appropriate information, and collecting and analyzing information in order to report summary data useful to decision makers in selecting among alternatives" (Alkin, 1969, p. 2). Unless we specify the decisions which are to be made, it is difficult to determine accurately what kind of information is needed. A brief example might help you to see how a statement of the decision(s) to be made can make it easier to determine the kinds of information needed.

Miss Hurlon, a high school speech teacher, has been getting information about the ability of the students in her classes for about six weeks. At this point, a memo comes to her attention reminding her that she must choose approximately ten students to take part in a speech contest in the spring. She is faced with specific decisions to make. She must decide which students should take part in the contest and which students would perform best at each of several types of speeches. The information she gathers about her students now becomes more specific, more directly related to the decisions to be made. Now she has a very definite need for the information.

Once the decisions have been identified, the required judgments can be specified. The speech teacher's decisions about whom to send to the speech contest require several kinds of judgments. She must make judgments about the skills of her students, about how much free time they have to practice for the contest, and about the competition these students will have to face. By specifying the judgments which will influence her decisions, Miss Hurlon can more easily determine what information she will need.

Often, the decisions that must be made are determined first, and then the judgments needed to make those decisions. However, as a teacher thinks through a given evaluation task, he will sometimes think first of judgments which must be made and secondly of the kind of decisions for which the judgments can be used. There is such a close relationship between judgments and decisions that it is difficult to think of one without the other. Therefore it does not make sense to try to first think of *all* the decisions to be made and then all the judgments. Rather, the required judgments and decisions are determined at approximately the same time. This will become clearer when you read Chapter 3, where the procedures for determining judgments and decisions will be discussed in detail.

Step 2: Describe the information needed. The more accurately you can describe the information needed, the better you will be able to select the method best suited for obtaining it. A brief example will serve to illustrate this point.

G. H. Fallow, a high school English teacher, has just completed a unit of modern American poetry. Twelve poems were studied in depth, and now G. H. wants to find out what his students have learned.

How should he get that information? Should he use an essay test or a multiple-choice test? Maybe a true-false test would do just as well. The essay would be easier to construct, but the multiple-choice test would be easier to grade. More true-false questions could be asked in an hour than any other kind of questions, and so that might be an appropriate kind of test to use.

G. H. recalled that his old high school English teacher always gave fill-the-blank and matching tests on poems they had studied.

What should he do?

G. H.'s struggle to choose a test format is very typical. Typical also is the kind of reasoning he is using to arrive at a selection — although it is true that some of the differences between essay and objective-type tests are *not* the kinds of differences which are most important when selecting one particular test over another. Each of the types of tests teachers have available for use in the classroom are best suited for getting a particular kind of information. How much easier it would be for G. H. to select an appropriate test if he knew exactly what kind of information he wanted about his students. He could then select the best kind of test to obtain that information. Suppose, for example, he wanted information about how well the students have been able to memorize the names of the authors of each of the poems studied. A matching test might be most appropriate. On the other hand, an essay test would be more appropriate if he needs information about how well the students can synthesize what they have learned, defending the modern poem as true poetry.

Suppose that G. H. also wants to know something about the attitudes his students have toward modern poetry. Now he might not use a test at all but some other information-gathering technique. In any case, it will be easier for G. H. to select an appropriate information-gathering technique if he can adequately describe the information he needs. The procedures for describing information are discussed in Chapter 4.

Step 3: Locate information already available

Some information is useful for forming many different kinds of judgments.

Some information is obtained routinely in most educational settings.

Some information is dutifully recorded in cumulative folders.

When "some" information is available, *and* it is the kind of information you need, *and* it is likely to be fairly accurate, *use it!* The beginning of Chapter 5 tells you how to locate information which has already been obtained.

Step 4: Decide when and how to obtain needed information.   Throughout the remainder of the book it will become increasingly apparent that it is important to obtain information at the right time and under the right conditions. It is often useful to set up a schedule for obtaining information. This schedule would specify both when and how the information is to be obtained.

> A science teacher sets a date for a test and tells the students to come prepared to answer essay questions without the aid of their books or class notes.
> A band director tells his students that during the following week he will listen to each member sight read a new piece of music.
> As the first graders learn the sounds of letters and letter combinations, their teacher makes plans to obtain information about how well the pupils *can* form various sounds as well as how well they *do* form them in normal conversation. The plans call for tests to be given periodically and for systematic observation to be made of the pupils' conversations.

In the above examples, the teachers have planned well. They determined the kind of information-gathering technique to be used (essay test, performance test, observation), and they specified when the information would be obtained (during the following week).

Although it is not always necessary, it is often helpful also to specify in advance some system for recording the information you hope to obtain. The second part of Chapter 5 deals with the various activities involved in making plans for obtaining information.

Step 5: Construct (or select) the information-gathering instruments to be used.   There are at least four types of information-gathering techniques available to the classroom teacher (testing, observing, making inquiry, and analyzing projects and assignments). The third part of Chapter 5 offers several suggestions for constructing teacher-made instruments and for selecting appropriate standardized ones. In Part Three (Chapter 10 through 14), specific information is given about each of several information-gathering instruments. Step-by-step procedures are provided for the construction of specific teacher-made instruments and for the selection of particular kinds of standardized instruments.

Stage 2: Data Collection

There are two steps in this stage: (6) obtaining the information and (7) analyzing and recording that information.

Step 6: Obtain the needed information. Step 6 is explained briefly at the beginning of Chapter 6. General rules for using each of the four information-gathering techniques are discussed. More detailed information on the use of each of the wide variety of instruments can be found in Chapters 10 through 14.

Step 7: Analyze and record information. After the information has been obtained, it must be analyzed to obtain evidence of its accuracy and then recorded so that it can be used in forming judgments. The remainder of Chapter 6 deals with those procedures. It should be noted that before you use any information located in step 3, it should *also* be analyzed. Consequently, one sometimes goes from step 3 (locating available information) to step 7 (analyzing and recording information). If we add steps 6 and 7 to the model, it will look like the diagram in Figure 1.3.

FIGURE 1.3. The steps in the preparation stage and the data-collection stage of the evaluation process.

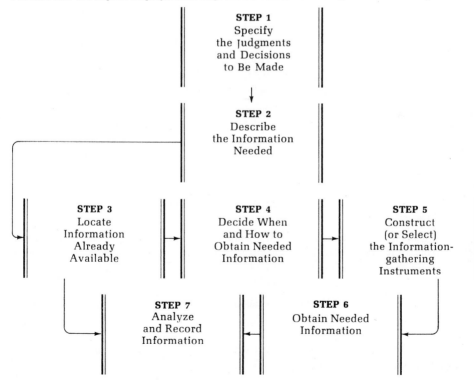

Stage 3: Evaluation

In the third stage of the evaluation process, judgments and decisions are made (steps 8 and 9) and the results of evaluation are summarized and reported (step 10).

Step 8: Form judgments.   Forming judgments which can be used in decision making is a relatively simple process. One begins by comparing the information he has (e.g., test scores) with some referent. On the basis of this comparision, estimative judgments and/or predictive judgments are formed. These judgments can then be used in making decisions.

Suppose, for example, we have given kindergartners a test to measure readiness for number concepts. Sally gets twenty-seven correct. We compare this score to the scores of other kindergarten pupils (our referent) and discover that a score of 27 is well above average. Consequently, we judge Sally to be very good with numbers (an estimate) and we feel that she has an excellent chance to succeed in first-grade arithmetic (a prediction).

These judgments could *help* us make decisions. (Should Sally go on to first grade? Which arithmetic group should Sally be placed in?)

Chapter 7 describes step-by-step procedures for forming judgments from various kinds of information.

Step 9: Make decisions.   Making decisions is a more complex process than that of forming judgments. Some very good guidelines have been formulated for making administrative, personnel, and curricular decisions (see, for example, Griffiths, 1959; Cronbach and Gleser, 1965; Alkin, 1970). However, the concepts appropriate for administrative decisions (utility, cost benefit, and cost effectiveness) are unnecessarily cumbersome for the classroom teacher. Each day the teacher makes a multitude of decisions. Many of these are virtually impossible to analyze in terms of dollars and cents (or other measures of cost). Nevertheless, it would be helpful if the teacher had some guidelines to help him make decisions.

It makes no sense to carefully, systematically obtain evaluative information and then turn around and make decisions haphazardly. A system for making classroom decisions ought to have the following characteristics:

Simplicity: It should be easy to use and should not consume a great deal of the teacher's time.

Flexibility: It should be useful for complex decisions involving many alternative courses of action (e.g., Which language arts series should be used in kindergarten through sixth grade?) as well as simple decisions involving few alternative courses of action (e.g., Whom should I select to send to the speech contest?).

Objectivity: It should help the decision maker to be more objective in his choice among alternatives.

A decision, you will recall, is a choice among alternative courses of action. A system for decision making should help to highlight the similarities and dif-

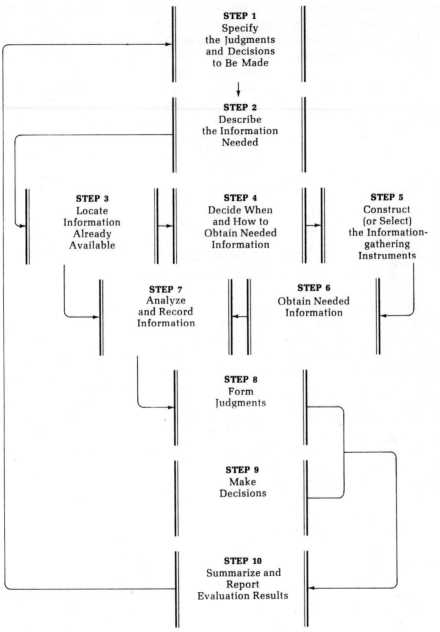

FIGURE 1.4. The evaluation process.

ferences among the various alternatives so that a choice might be more easily made. Such a system will be presented in Chapter 8.

Step 10: Summarize and report the results.   Very often teachers are asked to report their evaluation to others. Parents, teachers, administrators, and the students themselves all have an interest in the teacher's findings. The report card is a familiar system for reporting the results of evaluation. Parent-teacher conferences, letters, and the cumulative folder are other ways in which the results of evaluation can be reported. Below are some of the questions teachers most frequently ask about reporting evaluation results.

> Who has a right to the results of evaluation?
>
> How should grades be assigned?
>
> Are grades necessary?
>
> What do I do in a parent-teacher conference?
>
> What should be placed in the cumulative folder?
>
> How do I handle a parent's telephone request for information about his child?

These and other important questions will be answered in Chapter 9.

In Figure 1.4 the last three steps have been added to the model. Notice that there is an arrow leading from step 10 back to step 1. It is not unusual at all for a summary of the judgments and decisions you have made to point up the need for further judgments and decisions, and thus the whole process starts all over.

The basic procedures to be followed throughout these ten steps are discussed in Chapter 3 through 9. The specific problems associated with the construction and use of each of the major information-gathering instruments is then treated in Chapter 10 through 14.

All the procedures discussed in this text rest upon a few basic principles. These principles are explained in Chapter 2. Throughout the text you will read about various statistical procedures. When you feel that you need a more detailed explanation or you wish to learn the computational procedures involved, you may wish to read Appendix A: Statistics.

SUMMARY

1. Evaluation is valuable to the classroom teacher because it helps him to answer important questions about his students and about his instructional procedures.
2. Evaluation is the process of obtaining information and using it to form judgments which in turn are to be used in decision making.
3. A decision is a choice among alternative courses of action.
4. Judgments are estimates of present condition or predictions of further performance.
5. Information is the essential ingredient in evaluation because it provides the data base for making judgments.

6. Evaluation is a process involving ten steps. There are three major stages in the process: *(a)* the preparation stage, *(b)* the data-collection stage, and *(c)* the evaluation stage.
7. The ten steps in the evaluation process are as follows:
   a.   Specify the judgments and decisions to be made.
   b.   Describe the information needed.
   c.   Locate information already available.
   d.   Decide when and how to obtain needed information.
   e.   Construct (or select) the information-gathering instruments to be used.
   f.   Obtain the needed information.
   g.   Analyze and record information.
   h.   Form judgments.
   i.   Make decisions.
   j.   Summarize and report evaluation results.

References

Alkin, Marvin C.: "Evaluation Theory Development," *Evaluation Comment,* 2, 1969, Center for the Study of Evaluation, University of California, Los Angeles.

———: "Evaluating Net Cost-Effectiveness of Instructional Programs," in M.C. Wittrock and David E. Wiley (eds.), *The Evaluation of Instruction: Issues and Problems,* Holt, Rinehart and Winston, Inc., New York, 1970.

Cronbach, Lee J.: "Test Validation," in Robert L. Thorndike (ed.), *Educational Measurement,* 2d ed., American Council on Education, Washington, D.C., 1971.

——— and Goldine C. Gleser: *Psychological Tests and Personnel Decisions,* University of Illinois Press, Urbana, Ill., 1965.

Griffiths, Daniel E.: *Administrative Theory,* Appleton Century Crofts [educational division], Meredith Publishing Company, New York, 1959.

Scriven, M.: "The Methodology of Evaluation," *American Educational Research Association Monograph Series on Curriculum Evaluation,* no. 1, Rand McNally & Company, Chicago, Ill., 1967.

Stake, R. E.: "The Countenance of Educational Evaluation," *Teachers College Record,* vol. 68, 1967.

Wittrock, M. C., and David E. Wiley (eds.): *The Evaluation of Instruction Issues and Problems,* Holt, Rinehart and Winston, Inc., New York, 1970.

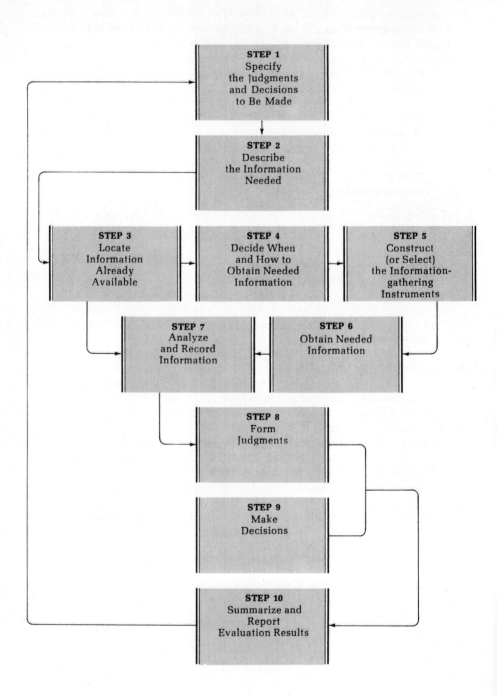

STEP 1
Specify
the Judgments
and Decisions
to Be Made

STEP 2
Describe
the Information
Needed

STEP 3
Locate
Information
Already
Available

STEP 4
Decide When
and How to
Obtain Needed
Information

STEP 5
Construct
(or Select)
the Information-
gathering
Instruments

STEP 7
Analyze
and Record
Information

STEP 6
Obtain Needed
Information

STEP 8
Form
Judgments

STEP 9
Make
Decisions

STEP 10
Summarize and
Report
Evaluation Results

CHAPTER 2

The Basic Principles
of Evaluation

This text is essentially a "how to do it" book. From Chapter 3 to the end, it will provide you with numerous steps to take and procedures to follow. You will more readily understand these procedures if you understand the principles upon which they are based. Most of the procedures you will read about in this book have been devised by measurement experts who were guided by a set of basic principles derived from measurement theory.

In this chapter these basic principles of measurement are expanded to include a set of rules which will be applicable to the entire process of evaluation. The rules which result should be practical aids, useful at each step in the process of evaluation.

More specifically, a thorough understanding of these principles should help you to meet the objectives outlined below.

When given a description of evaluation in process, you should be able to

1. Identify the potential sources of error.
2. Describe the procedures for minimizing that error.
3. Select and describe the most appropriate methods for estimating that error.
4. Explain briefly how the information obtained could be used even though it may not be completely accurate.

The principles of measurement and evaluation will make more sense to you if you understand the assumptions which underlie them.

SOME UNDERLYING ASSUMPTIONS

The basic principles developed in this chapter rest upon certain assumptions about the characteristics of individuals and what occurs when they are observed. These assumptions are simple, straightforward, and logical. Nevertheless, the complexity of measurement and the dos and don'ts of evaluation rest upon them.

Assumption 1: Individuals Have Measurable Abilities

In measurement theory, this assumption means that individuals have true scores. When we set out to measure a person's intelligence, we assume that he has some real amount of intelligence which differs from the amount other individuals have. Whether we are measuring height or weight, intelligence or personality, arithmetic skills or speaking ability, we assume that the individuals we are observing have some amount of the ability being measured. The information from the observations we make is used to estimate the individual's true ability or true score.

Assumption 2: Observation Contains Error

In measurement theory, this means the observed score is not equal to the true score. We have just assumed that each person *has* a true score for any given characteristic we observe. Now we are making the assumption that the score obtained from the observation of an individual is not the same as his true score. In other words, we err when we measure. You can easily demonstrate the reality of this assumption by taking a yardstick and measuring someone many, many times. Try to be as accurate as you can. Suppose you measure to the nearest

$\frac{1}{32}$ inch. Each time you measure, you are likely to get a different number. Your measurements (observed scores) of this individual's height will vary considerably. Obviously, the person's height is not changing as you measure and therefore many of the measurements you make are in error. If this kind of error occurs when we measure physical characteristics, then error surely must occur when we measure psychological characteristics. In fact, psychological measurements are much less direct and are subject to even greater error.

Assumption 3: An Observed Score Is Made Up of a True Score Plus an Error Score

In measurement theory this assumption is often written algebraically as $X = t + e$; where X stands for a person's observed score, t equals his true ability or true score, and e equals his error score. It should be recognized, at this point, that an error score can be either negative or positive. Sometimes when we measure, we obtain a score which is larger than the person's true score. In this case, the error score would be positive and would add to the true score, thus increasing the observed score. With equal frequency, we obtain scores which are less than a person's true score. In such a case, the error score would be negative and would subtract from the true score. This can be illustrated by placing hypothetical values in the algebraic formula given above. However, remember that they must always be hypothetical. We really never know for certain what a person's true score is or exactly how much error is involved in any given measure. Later, we will be dealing with procedures for *estimating* a person's true score and his error score, but we will never know exactly the degree of error made in any given case. *The true score will always remain unknown.*

Nevertheless, suppose we do know that Zelda's true IQ is 110. We measure her IQ, get a score of 115, and place these numbers in the formula.

$$X = t + e$$
$$115 = 110 + 5$$

The error would be a $+5$ which, added to a true score of 110, gives us the observed score, 115. Had we obtained an observed score of 105, the error would be -5.

$$X = t + e$$
$$105 = 110 + (-5)$$

At this point in our discussion, it is more important for you to realize that error occurs than it is for you to understand how we can estimate that error. Once you know what kinds of errors occur in evaluation and something about what causes error to occur, then you will be in a better position to understand the basic principles of measurement. These principles center around the problem of error. They serve as rules for identifying, preventing, and estimating error as well as for living with any error which cannot be accounted for.

The error we have just described is referred to as *measurement error,* and it decreases the accuracy of the observed score. Measurement error can be thought of as inconsistency. From one measurement to the next, the measures do not agree; they are not consistent. The measurement term used to describe this inconsistency is *unreliability. Reliability,* then, is a term describing the consistency that *does* exist in measurement, the freedom from measurement error. Any observation about an individual will be somewhat unreliable — it will contain some measurement error. We must learn to cope with that error in evaluation in order to make the most appropriate decisions. A highly inaccurate score is of little value in evaluation.

However, because a great deal of emphasis in measurement theory is placed upon measurement error (unreliable scores) it is easy to forget the fact that even if an observed score is perfectly reliable, it could still be useless to the evaluator. A highly reliable arithmetic score does us very little good if information is needed about a person's reading ability. An arithmetic score from a test measuring the knowledge of decimals is of little use in an evaluation of the ability to compute the area of various geometric shapes. The information we obtain through measurement must be not only reliable but also appropriate. It must be the kind of information needed. When a test yields the kind of information needed, it is considered to be a *valid* test and the information obtained *valid* information. *Validity* is the measurement term used to describe the appropriateness of an information-gathering instrument or of the information which has been obtained. When the information obtained is not the kind of information needed, it is said to be *invalid.* Using invalid information will lead to errors in judgment just as surely as using unreliable information.

In a real sense, then, there are two kinds of error: the kind which is traditionally associated with measurement error (unreliability) and that kind which occurs because the information is not appropriate for the judgments and decisions which must be made (invalidity).

Whenever we obtain information, some error will occur. The basic principles of evaluation are designed to help you cope with this problem of error. These principles state that

1. Sources of error can be identified.
2. Error can be minimized.
3. Error can be estimated.
4. Error can be "lived with."

PRINCIPLE 1: SOURCES OF ERROR CAN BE IDENTIFIED

The first important principle that should guide your evaluation activities is the principle that many sources of error can be identified. If sources of error can be identified, an attempt can be made to prevent the error from occurring (i.e., we may be able to remove or reduce the effects of any given source of error). A brief description of the major sources of error should be helpful. As you read through the remainder of the book, you will see many more specific examples of the kinds of error which are to be discussed in the next few pages. Try to commit these major sources to memory. This will be valuable to you when you begin watching for error in your own evaluation procedures.

Sources of Error within the Information-gathering Instrument

There are a number of factors within tests and other information-gathering instruments which contribute to error. These factors can contribute to unreliability and/or invalidity.

Inappropriate content. Obviously, if information is needed about a student's understanding of modern math concepts, questions in a test to yield that information should be math questions. Even more specifically, they should be questions dealing with concepts of modern math rather than concepts of traditional math. Furthermore, if a representative sample of different concepts is not included in the test questions, then the information gained will be in error. Inappropriate content contributes to invalidity.

The difficulty of the items. If test items are too difficult or too easy, the information gained might be in error. Reliability is affected by the difficulty of the items. If items are too easy or too hard, they will likely yield unreliable information. If Daryl gets all the items correct on an American history test, we do not know what his true ability is. For example, we do not know how many items he would have gotten correct if the items had been more difficult.

To some extent, validity can also be affected by the difficulty of the items in a test. For example, a test on which several persons obtain perfect scores (a test which is too easy) will yield information which is inappropriate (not valid) for certain kinds of judgments and decisions. If norm-referenced judgments are to be formed and selection decisions made, information from a very easy test would be inappropriate. If a test is very easy, many persons are likely to obtain the same or nearly the same scores. Therefore it becomes very difficult to distinguish among persons on the basis of their scores. When a test is too hard, it would be difficult to make the comparisons called for by norm-referenced judgments because most persons would probably score low and it would again be difficult to distinguish various levels of ability.

Other factors besides the difficulty of the subject matter can influence the level of difficulty of a given item. For example, the reading level of an item can make the item more difficult. When this is true, the information obtained will reflect not only the subject matter being tested but also the individual's ability to read. If a measure of reading ability is not the primary purpose of the test, then the information gained will not be valid.

Ambiguity.   The accuracy of information depends to a large extent upon how clear, concise, and understandable the elements in an information-gathering instrument are. If the directions are unclear and the students are really not certain how they are to respond to the items, then the reliability and also the validity of the information obtained will be reduced. Furthermore, any single ambiguous item will also decrease the reliability of the information obtained. If a student is unsure of what a question is asking or uncertain about the meaning of the possible responses he might make, confusion will occur and the information obtained will be in error.

Amount of information.   The length of a test, the time spent observing, and the number of questions on a questionnaire all affect the reliability and the validity of the information obtained. A test must, for example, be long enough so that a large sample of the information needed can be obtained and so that some consistency in responses can be ascertained.

Sources of Error within the Information-gathering Process

Error arises not only because of problems associated with the design of the information-gathering instrument but also because of problems associated with its *use.*

Test administration.   For example, if the person administering a test gives unclear directions, unreliable and invalid information can result. Of course, error can also occur because the conditions under which a test was given were poor. For example, if a test is being given in a room where there are numerous distractions (e.g., people walking through the room or lawn mowers running outside the window), the accuracy of the scores may be affected.

Scoring and recording.   Another obvious source of error within the information-gathering process is that of scoring and recording information. It is very easy to make simple errors in computation, in transferring data, etc. These factors also contribute to the amount of error in the information which is to be used for making judgments and decisions.

Sources of Error within the Individual Being Evaluated

For each individual being evaluated, there are many factors which may contribute to error. A discussion of a few of the major ones will serve to set the stage for further discussions in later sections. These factors are particularly important when information is to be used in making decisions about a single individual.

Trait instability. Human traits and psychological characteristics fluctuate from day to day as well as from month to month and year to year. These fluctuations are a major source of measurement error. Some traits, such as IQ, are fairly stable over long periods of time. However, many of the characteristics which we measure in education fluctuate a great deal, even changing from one day to the next. Particularly subject to fluctuations are traits of personality, attitudes, and interests. Because so many human characteristics do change over time, it is important to obtain information about those characteristics as closely as possible to the time when the information is to be used in decision making.

Response to the evaluation task. The way in which an individual responds to a test (or any other evaluation task) can cause error. For example, a student's attitudes toward a test may influence his score. If he does not care at all, his score will reflect this. If he cares too much and becomes overly anxious, his score will also be in error.

Besides the student's attitude, his understanding of what is expected of him is crucial. If he does not understand the directions, if he is unclear as to whether or not he should guess, or if he does not realize he is supposed to do his best, then his score will be in error.

Response set is another source of error within the individual being evaluated. Response set is a tendency on the part of an individual taking a test to respond in a consistent fashion. Some individuals, for example, tend to take many more chances at guessing than others. Some individuals find it difficult to work slowly and accurately and always work for speed. Many people are set to respond to essay questions in a way which is often inefficient and therefore can add error to their score. A person's tendency to guess or not to guess can be considered a response set. Furthermore, guessing itself is a source of error. Any given person's score may be higher or lower than it ought to be depending upon whether his luck is good or bad on the items on which he guessed.

Test-taking ability. The test-taking ability of students is another source of error. Some students are better at taking tests than others. Suppose that Mike and Jerry have equal ability in mathematics but Mike is more adept at taking tests. On a given math achievement test, Mike's score might be higher than Jerry's— not because they differ in terms of the ability being measured but because one of them is better able to take tests.

Health. A final factor within the individual being evaluated is his general health. Although the student's general health is not always easily determined by the teacher, it is an important factor in the accuracy of any evaluation which the teacher makes. If an individual is ill, tired, or emotionally upset, he will not perform up to standards and his score will not be an accurate reflection of his true ability.

EXERCISE 2.1

For each of the sources of error listed below, jot down examples from your own experiences (e.g., think of times when you were quite certain your own test score was in error).

1. Within the test (instrument error)
2. Within the testing situation (process error)
3. Within the individual being tested (individual error)

PRINCIPLE 2: ERROR CAN BE MINIMIZED

Perhaps the most important principle of evaluation is the principle that error can be minimized. The old adage "It is better to do a thing right than to explain why you did it wrong" certainly applies to evaluation procedures. It is true that some error will occur no matter how carefully one measures. Some error occurs by chance and some error is due to minor fluctuations in the measurement conditions which are almost impossible to control. Nevertheless, much of the error described in the above discussion can be prevented. The more error we can prevent, the more likely it is that we will obtain information which is valid and reliable. There are three important rules for minimizing error and ensuring valid, reliable information.

Rules for Ensuring the Relevance and Validity of Information

Rule 1. Relate everything you do to your reason for evaluating.

Rule 2. At every step in the process of evaluation, be clear, concise, and consistent.

Rule 3. Always obtain a representative sample of the information needed.

When these three rules are properly understood, many of the detailed instructions for selecting, constructing, and using evaluation techniques become common sense. If you understand these rules, you will have little need to memorize long lists of procedures for minimizing error. Everything you do in evaluation can be "tested" against these rules. If *none* of these rules is violated, your procedures are probably adequate. If *any one* of them is violated, your procedures are inadequate and the information you obtain will likely contain more error than it should.

Relate All Evaluation Activities to the Reason for the Evaluation

Obviously, this rule is designed primarily to help you obtain valid information. Remember, for information to be valid it must meet the purpose for which it is intended. If we are going to compare the performance of several students, for example, we must have information which is comparable from student to student.

If estimates are going to be made about the ability of chemistry students to design an experiment, then information is needed about that ability and not about their knowledge of chemical terms or formulas.

The question of whether or not certain information (e.g., test scores) is valid cannot be answered until a further question is asked: "valid for what?" Unless you have a specific purpose in mind for evaluative information, there is no way you can ascertain its validity. By the same reasoning, whenever you set out to obtain valid information, you must set out to obtain information which is *valid for some purpose.* Whether you are selecting a test or contructing one, whether you are administering a test or scoring it—at every step in the process of evaluation, it is important to be aware of the reason you are evaluating. Surely it makes sense that in order to obtain the information needed for a given purpose you must know what kind of information is useful for that purpose. The more precisely you can describe the information you need, the easier it will be to obtain it. If a teacher needs to make judgments about what his students have learned, he must know as precisely as possible what they were supposed to have learned (and what they might possibly have learned that they were not supposed to).

Be Clear, Concise, Consistent

At all times, avoid ambiguity and inconsistency! If a student does not understand what he is expected to do, how can we judge his ability to do it? If we confuse a student by writing tests or test items which are unclear or unnecessarily lengthy, we will be measuring the level of his confusion rather than the level of his achievement. It is equally important to be consistent in the way we obtain information, because a lack of consistency makes any interpretation of the information difficult if not impossible.

A common synonym for *reliability* is *consistency.* In fact, you will see that the techniques for estimating reliability rely heavily upon the notion of consistency. If there is a lack of consistency in the way the information was obtained from individual to individual, then meaningful comparisons among the individuals, cannot be made. This is why it is not advisable to compare the scores of students who have taken different IQ tests. This is also why students' scores on a classroom test should not be compared unless all had the same set of questions, the same set of instructions, and the same amount of time to complete the test.

Now, suppose that all tenth grade history students were given the same essay question about the Civil War but each *perceived* the question to mean something different. A question which can be interpreted to have more than one meaning would be an ambiguous question.

Consider this essay question: "What are the important events leading up to the Civil War?"

What does this question mean? Is it asking only for the events which caused the war? Or, is it asking for *all* the important events just prior to the war? How early in history should one begin in his answer? Are only events of a political nature to be considered?

Notice how the ambiguity of the above question could cause different people to answer it in different ways. This would have the same effect as giving each student a different question. Inconsistency would occur, reliability would decrease, and the students' scores could not be compared.

Ambiguity in an item could also invalidate the item. The information obtained from a test containing ambiguous items would be very difficult to interpret. A student whose answer on an item differed from what the teacher expected would probably get the item wrong. But how does the teacher interpret that information? It could be that the student did not know the answer. It could also be that the student *did* know the answer but was answering an essentially different question than the one the teacher was asking (or thought he was asking). How can one judge the validity of information when the nature of the information cannot be ascertained?

Obtain a Representative Sample of Information

When taking the driving test for your driver's license, you probably had to drive several blocks. Perhaps you were taken on a route which led you to the top of a hill. There you may have been asked to stop, turn right, shift lanes, turn left, and pull into a parallel parking space. The tester takes you on a drive which is long enough for him to obtain a representative sample of your driving skills. A representative sample is obtained because the tester watches you respond to a variety of situations like those you will have to respond to in day-to-day driving. This maximizes the validity of the driving test. It allows the tester to make sure that you carry out all procedures correctly.

If you were trying to judge a marksman's ability with a rifle, you would not try to do so on the basis of watching him shoot one shot. If someone's spelling ability is to be judged, he must spell more than one word. To assess the math skills of eighth graders, one would want them to try more than a single math problem.

How much information is adequate? How many questions must a test include? What is a representative sample? A sample which is representative of the population has the attributes outlined below.

Attributes of a Representative Sample

1. The individuals in the sample are like the individuals in the population.
2. Any summary of information obtained from a sample should match a summary of the same information obtained from the population.

There is no way that you can obtain information about everything your students know or are able to do. You cannot ask every possible question about a given subject. Consequently, whether you want to or not, each time you obtain information you are obtaining a sample—a sample of knowledge, a sample of attitudes, a sample of behavior. The question then, is not to sample or not to sample but *how* to sample. What procedures can you follow which will produce a representative sample?

Before answering this question, we ought to take a moment to answer a more basic one: "What is a representative sample?" A sample which is representative of the above attributes only makes sense if you understand the relationship between the population and a sample. Let us define a population as all knowledge, all aspects of a given skill, all spelling words in a spelling book, all seventh graders in a school system, etc. A sample, then, is some proportion of that population. Notice that both the population and the sample are made up of numerous individuals (as used here, *individuals* refers to persons as well as to objects, ideas, facts, etc.). All the individuals in a given population are members of that population by virtue of the fact that they share common characteristics or attributes. For example, if we define as our population of interest the citizens of the United States presently living, then anyone who has citizenship and is alive is a member of the population. If we define our population as all the facts contained in a given physics book, then any fact in that book is a member of the population. We might broaden that population to include all facts about physics known to man, and then our population would be exceedingly larger.

A sample is composed of some number (but not all) of the members of the given population. Any individual who or which does not possess the given characteristics or attributes which define the population should not be in the sample which is supposed to represent that population. That is why a test question which asks for facts other than those the test was supposed to measure in the first place should not be in the test. The fact asked for by that test question is not a member of the sample because it does not have the characteristics which define the members of the population.

So a representative sample is one which accurately reflects the population of interest. But how does one obtain a representative sample? What are the steps that must be taken?

A Preview of the Process of Obtaining a Representative Sample.

1. Describe the population.
2. Describe a representative sample.
3. Choose an appropriate sampling technique.
4. Obtain the sample.

Describe the population.   First, you need some approximation of the size of the population. Next, you need to determine what kind of individuals are in that population. Finally, it is necessary to know the approximate proportion of each kind of individual in the population.

Suppose, for example, that we wish to know whether or not the students in a given school district favor a twelve-month school year. The population could be defined as all the students in the school district. We may know that there are approximately 10,000 students in the school district. However, these 10,000 students could be categorized in a number of ways: (1) early elementary, later elementary, junior high, high school; (2) from an inner-city, rural, or urban background; (3) lower, middle, or upper socioeconomic class, etc.

Finally, we would try to determine the proportion of students in each category that we feel is important. For example, half of the students may be from the lower socioeconomic class, 40 percent from the middle class, and only 10 percent from the upper class.

In the above example, the individuals of interest were people. Frequently, the teacher faces the problem of defining a population of knowledge rather than a population of people. Suppose, for example, a teacher wished to know how well all his eighth graders could spell. He could not possibly ask them to spell *every* word in the English language. Therefore he is faced with the problem of obtaining a *sample* of their spelling ability. If we define the population as all English words, then the words we choose to have the students spell must be a representative sample of that population. How might we define the population? The total number of words could be thought of as approximately equal to those words contained in the *Oxford English Dictionary* (note that the actual number of words is not always necessary when estimating the size of the population as long as some indication of its size is available to help you visualize the total population your sample is supposed to represent). How does one describe all the words in the English language? Are there any subgroups (i.e., different kinds of words to be spelled)? Yes, there are a number of ways in which all the words in the English language could be categorized. Many of these categories would make useful descriptive labels for defining the various kinds of individuals (in this case, words) found in the population. For example, the words in the English language differ considerably according to their frequency of use, and one might classify words in the population on the basis of this variable. Another way in which words in the language could be categorized is according to those which are spelled phonetically and those which cannot be spelled phonetically. If we have some indication of proportion of words occurring in the various categories of each of these schemes, then we might more accurately be able to build a sample of the various kinds of words found in the English language.

It should be noted that it is not necessary to describe all the categories which could be used to define the population. One needs to select only those categories which would be important when obtaining the kind of information that you need. If you want information about how well the students can spell, then those various ways of categorizing the words in the English language which might make a difference in how easily they are spelled should be considered.

The above situations are formidable tasks indeed, but they do illustrate the fact that populations (even very large ones) can be described in such a way that obtaining a representative sample becomes a manageable job.

Describe a representative sample. If you have done a good job of describing the population, the task of describing the sample needed is an easy one. It is simply a matter of reiterating the important variables which characterize the population and if possible indicating the probable proportion of individuals from the population that should be included in the sample. One other step which must be taken is to indicate the size of the sample (note that this will also tell you the approximate *number* of individuals needed for each of the categories defined).

Choose an appropriate sampling procedure. Numerous sampling procedures are utilized by educational researchers and psychometricians. However, the classroom teacher can get along well with two basic techniques used individually or in combination. The first sampling procedure is simple but powerful. It is called *random sampling. Random sampling* refers to the process of drawing a random sample of individuals from some population. It is the old "throw all the names in the hat and draw one out" procedure.

A random sample is one in which every individual in the population has an equal chance of getting into the sample. This is a very good procedure because it eliminates any bias. However, it has a very serious drawback: Every individual in the population must be identified and given an opportunity to be selected. When sampling knowledge or behavior, it is usually impractical if not impossible to identify *all* individuals in the populations. For example, how can one identify all the facts known about English grammar or everything a student knows or should know about the Civil War? It is equally difficult to identify all possible questions that could be asked about a democratic form of government or all the possible story problems calling for simple multiplication skills. Populations of student behaviors or of behavioral situations are equally difficult to describe in such a way that every individual person, object, or fact could be identified.

There are only a few cases where the population of knowledge can be specified clearly enough so that every individual, fact, or idea can be identified. For example, it is not difficult to identify all of the spelling words in a given spelling book or all of the vocabulary words learned in a given semester. Bones in the body, nerves in the nervous system, phonemes in the English language, states and their capital cities, and other *finite* lists of facts represent the kind of knowledge which can be so specified. The teacher can obtain a random sample of these kinds of facts. When this is true, the teacher needs only to put each fact on a piece of paper, put all of them in a box or other container, and then draw out some sample number of them to use as test items.

Except for these few lists of finite facts, most of the things a teacher wishes to obtain information about cannot be readily sampled through a random sampling procedure. Consequently, another procedure must be used. An exceptionally useful one is called *quota sampling*. Quota sampling, as the name implies, is the process of building a sample by "filling quotas" (i.e., by getting a certain proportion of individuals with this characteristic, a certain proportion of them with some other characteristic, etc.) until you have a sample which has groups of individuals *in the same proportion* as those known or hypothesized to be in the population.

The problem with random sampling is that all the individuals in a population cannot usually be easily identified and given an equal chance to occur in the sample. The problem with quota sampling is that there frequently is not a representative sample of individuals selected for each category. But these problems can be overcome to some extent by combining quota and random sampling. Suppose, for example, we were going to build a test utilizing this procedure. The steps we would take would be as follows:

1. Decide on the various kinds of information you wish to measure.
2. Determine the number or proportion of items you wish to use for each category.
3. Obtain or construct as many items as possible which would measure the information described by each category.
4. From the items in each category, select a random sample equal in size to the number of items needed.

Following this procedure would give you a better chance of getting a representative sample of items in each category because you selected randomly from all those that you could possibly obtain—given the time and energy you have as a teacher.

PRINCIPLE 3: ERROR CAN BE ESTIMATED

If some estimate can be made about the amount of error in measurement data, that estimate can be used to temper judgments and improve decision making. Before discussing the procedures for estimating error, it might be worthwhile to review the concept of error. The notion of error was expanded to include not only measurement error (unreliability) but also the kind of error which occurs when the information does not serve its intended purpose (invalidity). There are a number of sources of error, not the least of which is chance. Error due to chance cannot be eliminated. No matter how carefully we follow the rules for the prevention of error, the information we obtain will always contain some error. Another way to express this phenomenon is to say that no score, no evaluative information, is completely reliable or perfectly valid. The concern of the evaluator is that he does have information which is as reliable and as valid as possible.

What can he do to get some idea about how much error has occurred?

There are two major strategies which can be employed in an effort to answer this question. The first strategy is to obtain empirical evidence. If you want to know how much consistency there is in the results of a certain test, check it out. Compare, for example, the results obtained at two different times and see how much consistency there is from the first to the second measure. A great deal of consistency suggests high reliability, very little consistency suggests low reliability. If you want to know how well test scores meet their intended purpose, check them out. Suppose, for example, the results of a reading readiness test are supposed to predict success in learning to read. A comparison of the test results with later performance in learning to read will provide evidence of the validity of the readiness scores. If they predict poorly, predictive validity is in question.

The second strategy is to look for clues. Sometimes it is not possible (or at least not economical) to use the first strategy. Empirical evidence is occasionally hard to obtain.

Would circumstantial evidence do?

Yes. Often that is all that is available and it is better than no evidence at all.

So if you notice that a child is sick, that is a clue: the results might not be accurate. When you find that the results of a test do not agree with all the other information you have, that is a clue: perhaps the information is in error.

A more detailed analysis of these two strategies will help to clarify the distinction between them and at the same time serve to point out how and when each is to be used.

REMEMBER

The idea is to obtain all the data we can about the error in any information so that we can use that information to best advantage when making judgments and decisions. The first strategy is to obtain empirical evidence.

In the next few pages we will describe a variety of techniques for estimating the reliability and validity of evaluative information. Throughout the discussion we will often refer to test results. The basic strategy of obtaining empirical evidence of reliability and validity can be used with any kind of evaluative information. However, in order to obtain the precise numerical estimates discussed in this section, measurement results must be used (i.e., numbers must be available). Consequently, the discussion in this section is particularly applicable to the results of tests and other measurement techniques. The strategy of searching for clues, on the other hand, will prove to be particularly valuable when more subjective information-gathering techniques have been used.

Reliability

Up to this point, we have described reliability as freedom from measurement error, and we have equated it with consistency. The more consistent test results are, the more reliable they are. To obtain empirical evidence of the reliability of test scores, then, one simply needs to demonstrate the consistency of those scores. However, there are a number of ways in which scores can be thought of as being consistent. Consequently, there are different kinds of reliability estimates. Test results can be reliable in one sense and not in another. The particular kind of reliability estimate needed will depend upon the kind of judgments and decisions for which the results will be used.

Stability: consistency over time. The procedure for estimating stability (often referred to as test-retest reliability) is very simple. The same test is given at two different times to the same individuals and the results of the two administrations are compared (i.e., analyzed for consistency). If the results are stable over time, then there will be some consistency in the way the individuals score from the first to the second testing. Those individuals who score high the first time the test is given would be expected to score high when the test was given again. By the same token, those who scored low on the test the first time it was given would be expected to score low the second time.

Suppose that in November Miss Gray tests the ability of each of the seventh graders to sing on pitch. Those who perform well (i.e., get a high score) will be included in the choral group for the Christmas pageant. Miss Gray recognizes the importance of the stability of the test scores. If the scores are not stable for at least a few weeks, then those whose ability to sing on pitch was very good in November may or may not be good in December. If the scores are stable for at least a few weeks, then she can count on the students she had selected in November performing the same way in December.

One might argue that this test-retest procedure has little or no value because, if the results are inconsistent from the first to the second testing, there is no way of knowing what the source of the error was. Suppose the results Miss Gray obtains in November do not hold up through December. Is the error originating in the test, the administration of the test, or within the individuals? Miss Gray cannot be certain. How can she know if the test was at fault (instrument error) or if she administered it poorly (administrative error)? Maybe the ability to sing on pitch is simply not a stable trait (individual error). The point is that it does not matter where the error came from. It is there. Consequently, the results are not very useful for decisions which will be acted upon some few weeks after original testing.

At this point, our description of the analysis made of Miss Gray's results indicates a somewhat subjective process. One merely looks over the results to see whether those who tended to score high on the first testing tended to score high again, whether those who scored low on the first testing also scored low on the second testing, etc. This procedure, of course, will yield a rough estimate of reliability of the results, and that is valuable as an indicator of how far you can trust those results. A more thorough analysis yielding a rather precise statement of the *amount* of consistency which exists from the first to the second testing would be far more useful. Measurement experts use a statistic called the *correlation coefficient* to help them accomplish this goal. It is fairly easy to compute (although somewhat time-consuming), and you may find out how to do so by referring to Appendix A.

It would be worthwhile to digress a little at this point to briefly discuss the correlation coefficient. It is a numerical description of the relationship between two sets of scores which have been obtained from the same group of individuals.[1] The size of a correlation coefficient can vary from 0 (representing no correlation) to 1 (representing perfect correlation) and can be either negative or positive. A positive correlation means that the individuals who score high on one set of scores tend to score high on the other set of scores and individuals who score low on one set tend to score low on the other. A negative correlation means that individuals who score high on one set of scores tend to score low on the other and vice versa. In other words, a negative correlation means that there is an *inverse* relationship between the two sets of scores. This is the kind of relationship which exists, for example, between athletic ability and golf scores. People who have high athletic ability are likely to have low golf scores (a low score in golf is a good score). The correlation between athletic ability and golf scores would be high but negative.

A correlation coefficient is generally designated by an *r*. Subscripts are often used to indicate which two measures have been correlated (e.g., $r_{ab} = .87$ means that measure a has correlated with measure b and the resulting coefficient was .87). The *strength* of the relationship is indicated by the size of the number (the closer to 1, the stronger; the closer to 0, the weaker). The sign ($+$ or $-$) indicates the *direction* of the relationship ($+$ indicates a positive relationship and a $-$ indicates an inverse one). Now, let us return to our discussion of reliability. Further details about the correlation coefficient, including formulas for computing it, can be found in Appendix A.

When a correlation coefficient is used to estimate consistency over time, it is called a *coefficient of stability*. Coefficients of stability vary greatly in size

---

[1] Technically, it is a measure of the linear relationship (see Appendix A).

depending on characteristics being measured and the time between the first and second testing. Achievement scores and aptitude scores tend to be more stable than personality scores, for example. Coefficients of stability computed for standardized aptitude tests often exceed .90. As the time between testings increase, the coefficient of stability tends to decrease.

Equivalence: consistency across different forms.   Give two forms of the same test to a group of individuals. Correlate the two sets of scores obtained. The reliability coefficient which results is called a *coefficient of equivalence.* It is sometimes also referred to as *equivalent-form* or *alternate-form reliability.* Obviously, this type of reliability is important when different forms of a test are to be used (e.g., when a teacher gives alternate forms of a test to every other student so that it will be less tempting to cheat or when a makeup test has to be given to students who were absent on test day). Many standardized tests have at least two forms, and estimates of equivalency are often reported in the manuals which accompany these tests.

Equivalence and stability.   When we use alternate forms across a time span, we gain the advantages of equivalent forms and test-retest reliability. This method of estimating reliability is probably the best method because it accounts for more of the sources of error than any other single method. This is particularly true when there is a fairly long time limit between the administration of the two forms (e.g., a year or more). When the time span between the administration of the alternate forms is short, equivalency is being estimated. When the time span is long, both equivalency and stability are being estimated.

Internal consistency: consistency across different parts of a test.   This method of estimating reliability is very popular because it requires only *one administration* of only *one form* of a test. The two most commonly used methods for estimating the internal consistency of a test are (1) the split-half method and (2) the Kuder-Richardson method. The split-half method is much like the alternate forms method with no time span between the administration of the forms. The estimate of reliability obtained from this method is usually an overestimate. When a test is timed so that many students are unable to complete the test, the split-half reliability will be an especially high estimate. For a purely speeded test (simple items only, designed to find out how fast students can work), a split-half reliability coefficient would be completely meaningless.

The split-half estimate of reliability is obtained by comparing the two sets of scores which result from splitting a test in half and scoring each half separately. Usually this means scoring the odd-numbered items separately from the even-scored items. The two sets of scores can then be correlated. The coefficient which results would be an estimate of the reliability of each of the two "half-tests." In order to obtain an estimate of the whole test, a statistical correction must be made. The formula used to make this correction is called the Spearman Brown correction formula and is presented in Appendix A.

Most standardized test publishers use the Kuder-Richardson method for estimating internal consistency. This method utilizes formulas developed by

Kuder and Richardson. The formulas are designed to yield a coefficient which is inflated less than those obtained with the usual split-half method. The coefficient obtained is equivalent to the average of the coefficients you might get if you split a test in half every way possible (first and last halves, odd and even items, random sorting of items into piles, etc.).

Teachers rarely use these formulas to estimate the reliability of their own classroom test results. However, when important decisions rest upon the results of a classroom test, it is desirable to have an estimate of reliability. Consequently a simplified version of one of the KR formulas (KR 21) appears in Appendix A. Using this formula, a teacher can estimate the reliability of the results of any test which is scored on the basis of the number correct. Only very basic computational skills are needed.

Scorer (interjudge) reliability: consistency across raters. A special problem arises when observational techniques are used for obtaining information. Two observers watching the same performance or rating the same product may not agree on what they see or hear. When observational techniques are used, a major source of error is the observer. An estimate of the consistency of the results obtained from two or more observers gives a measure of that source of error. When more than one person scores a number of papers, a major source of error is in the scoring. Scorer reliability is designed to estimate that source of error.

The method for estimating interjudge reliability is simple. Two or more observers obtain information about the same group of individuals at the same time, and the information obtained by one observer is compared with the information obtained by another observer. A large amount of agreement means high interjudge reliability, a small amount of agreement means low reliability. When correlation is used to make the comparison, the resulting coefficient gives us a numerical estimate of the degree of consistency between observers. When more than two observers are compared, more sophisticated techniques must be used. These require analysis of variance procedures. If you are interested in finding out more about these procedures, you may wish to read Cronbach's (1970) measurement text, which is listed in the bibliography at the end of this chapter.

EXERCISE 2.2

For each of the following situations, indicate the kind of reliability estimate that would be most appropriate. Use the following key:

    a. Coefficient of stability
    b. Coefficient of equivalence
    c. Internal consistency
    d. Scorer reliability

1. A teacher wishes to estimate the reliability of the results of his midterm exam. He only has one form of the test and does not want to give it more than once.

2. The speech department wants to know if the ratings they make during the speech contests are reliable.
3. The tenth grade algebra teacher wishes to know if the results of the ninth grade general math exam still constitute reliable information (one year after they were obtained).
4. Mr. Tombsy has two classes of ninth grade social studies. He used a different form of the same test for each group. He wants to know if the two forms are essentially measuring the same thing.
5. Mrs. Gorjey wants to use the information she has about her students' writing ability to predict their success as news reporters for the school paper.
6. Which test results are most reliable?

   Test A ($r_{aa} = .72$)

   Test B ($r_{aa} = .83$)

   Test C ($r_{aa} = .91$)
7. Which *correlation* is strongest?

   a. $r_{ab} = -.81$

   b. $r_{ac} = -.32$

   c. $r_{ad} = +.47$

   d. $r_{ae} = +.78$
8. Gallager made an error when calculating the correlation between the results of two tests. Which one of the following coefficients is most likely *not* correct?

   a. $r_{xy} = -.20$

   b. $r_{xz} = +.30$

   c. $r_{zt} = +.87$

   d. $r_{wx} = +1.3$

Validity

Valid information is appropriate information. It is the kind of information which serves the purpose intended.

What purpose *does* evaluative information serve?

The immediate purpose served by evaluative information is the formation of judgments. You will recall from the discussion in Chapter 1 that judgments can be classified as either estimates or predictions. We can check the validity of information by "testing it" to see if the judgments it leads to are correct. Because test results are used to make different kinds of judgments, different methods for estimating the validity of those results have been devised.

Most evaluative judgments used in educational decision making fall into two types: those where present ability is being judged (estimates) and those where future performance is being judged (predictions). Thus validity estimates should help answer the following questions:

1. How well does the information I have help me to judge present ability?
2. How well does the information I have help me to judge future performance?

Question 1 is typically answered by a method of estimating validity called *concurrent validity,* and a method called *predictive validity* helps to answer question 2. Concurrent and predictive validity are really the specific instances of a more general approach to validity estimates called *criterion-related validity.* The term *criterion-related* refers to the fact that a criterion is selected so that the results of a test can be validated by comparing them to those obtained with a criterion measure. For example, the validity of the IQs obtained from group IQ tests are often judged against the scores obtained from some individual IQ test. Scores from the Stanford-Binet test often serve as a criterion. If the scores of some group test compare favorably with those obtained with the Binet, then they are said to be valid.

Concurrent validity. When judgments are to be made estimating present ability or performance, concurrent validity is usually used. The procedure to be followed is simple and logical. From the same group of individuals, obtain two sets of information at the same time, or *concurrently.* One set of information would be the scores of the test to be validated. The second would be the measure of performance being estimated. These two sets of information could then be compared. If test scores are a valid measure of the performance we are estimating, then the test scores should compare favorably with some other measure of that performance. For example, scores from a test designed to estimate arithmetic ability could be validated by comparing them to scores obtained from some other test of arithmetic ability which had been given at about the same time. The other measure might be arithmetic grades, another arithmetic test, or any other acceptable measure of arithmetic ability.

So the results of a test are validated by checking them out. If they rank the students the same way they would be ranked by other measures of the performance being estimated, then the results are said to be valid.

By now, you have undoubtedly guessed that the comparison usually made is a statistical one and the statistic used is the *correlation coefficient.* It is referred to as a *validity coefficient,* and the higher the coefficient, the higher the validity. Validity coefficients are usually lower than reliability coefficients and, even for standardized tests, they range from very low (in the .20s and .30s) to very high (in the .90s).

Suppose we try another example. Mr. Sargo has been using scores from an English test to select students for his journalism class. Are these scores valid? This question cannot really be answered until the question "Valid for what?" is answered. Mr. Sargo wants to know if these scores allow him to make accurate judgments about the writing ability of the students. In other words, are they valid for estimating writing ability? Those with high scores will be judged to have good writing ability; those with average scores, average ability; and those with low scores, low ability. Now the problem is defined. If those who tend to have high English test scores also tend to have good writing ability and those with low English test scores tend to have poor writing ability, then the validity of the English test scores will have been established. They will have been "proved" to be valid for estimating writing ability.

So, as the next term begins, Mr. Sargo gives the new group of prospective journalism students the English test. But this time he also gives them a short writing assignment. He then compares the results of the two sets of information. As expected, those students getting high English test scores are the ones who do the best writing, and those who write poorly receive the low English test scores. To obtain a more precise estimate of the concurrent validity of the English test scores, he correlated them with the writing scores. The correlation coefficient was .56, not too bad.

Perhaps Mr. Sargo has chosen a poor criterion measure (his judgments of the students' writing skills). Maybe if a different measure (perhaps something a little more reliable) were used, the results would be even better. Consequently he obtains from the English department's test files a standardized test which had been proved to be a valid and reliable measure of writing skill. He gives the students this test also. Then he correlates the results of this test with the results of the English test. This time the correlation coefficient was .69, slightly better. In either case, Mr. Sargo feels reasonably certain that his English test is a fairly valid measure of writing ability and he decides to continue using it to select students for his journalism class.

Predictive validity.   Mr. Sargo was satisfied that the English test results seemed to be fairly valid for estimating *present* writing ability. However, he now began to wonder whether they would be valid for predicting how well the students would be able to write by the end of the journalism course. He had noted that some students improved their writing skills a great deal with a semester's instruction, while others improved very little through the semester. Sometimes a student who wrote poorly on the first or second assignments would turn out to be one of the best writers by the end of the semester.

And so the stage has been set for a predictive validity study.

Mr. Sargo already has the English test results (obtained at the beginning of the semester). Suppose he now waits until the end of the semester and obtains measures of the students' writing ability at that time. Then he can correlate the results of the English test with each of the two measures of writing ability (his own measure and the standardized measure). The English test would have been given at the beginning of the semester and the other two measures at the end. If the English test results are valid predictors of writing skill after one semester's instruction, then the correlations should be high. Mr. Sargo does this and obtains a correlation coefficient of .08 between the English test and his judgments of writing ability and one of .17 between the English test and standardized test of writing skill. These validity coefficients are very low and suggest that although the concurrent validity of the English test scores is fairly high (when writing ability is used as the criterion), the predictive validity is low (using the same criterion but at a later time).

You can see, again, why the question, "Are the results of a given test valid?" cannot be answered unless a further question is first answered: "Valid for what?" *Test results can be valid for one kind of judgment and invalid for another.*

Construct validity. Criterion-related validity is used to determine whether measurement results can be used successfully to make judgments (estimates or predictions) of a specified criterion. The results will obviously differ depending upon the criterion selected, (e.g., teacher's judgment of writing ability versus standardized test of writing ability) as well as on the kind of judgment being made (an estimate or a prediction). Now, what does one do if he is interested in estimating a general ability, one not related to a *single* criterion?

In the above example, for instance, Mr. Sargo defined writing ability quite specifically: first, as the ability it took to get a good score when writing a journal article and, secondly, as the ability to score high on the standardized test of writing skills he used. But, if writing ability can be defined quite specifically in these two ways, how many more ways are there to measure this ability? Perhaps writing ability is a rather general ability which exhibits itself in a wide variety of situations.

If it is, can it be measured by a single test?

Intelligence seems to be such a diffuse general ability, and we try to measure *it* with single tests.

Reading comprehension, anxiety, social adjustment, study skills, and foreign language aptitude represent a few more of the many general traits or abilities that psychologists have identified and tried to measure. These general traits or abilities are called *constructs*. Whenever scores from any single measure are used to make judgments about the "amount" of the trait a person possesses, a different validity question arises. The general question is: "Do the results from this single measure [e.g., the writing skills test] produce valid, estimative judgments about the amount of the trait [e.g., the writing ability] an individual possesses?" The answer can be found in construct validation.

How does one validate the measurement of a construct?

Although construct validity is more involved than criterion-related validity, the basic idea is again simple and logical: obtain some results and see if they do what they are supposed to. In this case they are "supposed to" estimate a trait which exhibits itself in numerous ways. Therefore, we need numerous criteria with which we can compare our test results. The selection of the various criteria is usually determined by some "theory" about the construct supposedly being measured. Thus, according to the theories of intelligence, IQ exhibits itself in numerous verbal skills, in problem-solving ability, in school achievement, etc. The results of an IQ test can be said to have high construct validity if they are shown to be related to all or to most all of the criteria that the theory says they should be . . . *if* the theory is right.

Suppose the test results do not act as the theory says they should? Are the test results invalid? Or is the theory wrong? It is difficult to tell. When this occurs, it's "back to the drawing board" for the researcher. The problem is one a teacher rarely faces. However, it does point out one of the limitations of validity coefficients that teachers should be aware of. If the criterion (or in the case of construct validity, several criteria) are not selected properly, the estimates of the validity will be meaningless. Even if a teacher never computes a reliability or validity coefficient, he will need to use and interpret one from time to time. Therefore he should be aware of the major uses of reliability and validity coefficients.

EXERCISE 2.3

Write brief, concise answers to each of the following questions.

1. Briefly define validity.
2. The question "Is the information valid?" cannot be answered until another question is first answered. What is that other question?
3. Why do we need different ways to estimate validity?
4. For what kinds of judgments is concurrent validity most important? Predictive validity? Constructive validity?

Uses of Reliability and Validity Coefficients

Let us review quickly the logic behind the computation of reliability and validity coefficients. We begin with a need for scores which will lead to accurate judgments. We decide the scores must, first of all, be free from measurement error (be reliable) and that they must, second, meet their intended purpose (be valid). Different sources of measurement error will cause different kinds of inconsistencies. Therefore we set up situations where these inconsistencies will show up and then obtain a measure of how much consistency does in fact show up.

A measure of whether results are valid or not is obtained similarly. We use the scores as intended (i.e., make judgments with them) and then see if the judgments hold true. In other words, we look for evidence that the information has done what we wanted it to. A simple logical procedure, *yet one which defeats its own purpose.*

Did you notice?

Remember Miss Gray?

Miss Gray needed results which would be consistent over time, so that when she measured in November she could use the results to make decisions about performance in December. *But,* in order to find out whether or not she would have to measure again in December, she obtained a measurement in December. She defeated her own purpose.

Remember Mr. Sargo?

Mr. Sargo wanted to use the results of an English test to estimate writing ability. This way he would not have to take the time to score writing assignments. But in order to find out if the results of the English test could be used instead of the results of a writing assignment, he had to give and score the writing assignment. He defeated his own purpose.

Often, in order to check out a set of results to see if they are OK, we defeat our own purpose in the process. It is like drinking a cup of hot chocolate to see if it is too hot for your little sister to drink. You decide it is not too hot but it is gone. Of course, if you can get more from the pan and you can assume it will be the same temperature as the cup you tested, then all is not lost.

And herein lies the genius of the reliability and validity coefficients. If you can get more results from a test and you can assume they will be as reliable and as valid as the results you checked out, then all is not lost. Once the reliability and validity of a test has been established, you can be reasonably certain that each time it is used the results will be similarly reliable and valid. Of course, this assumes that you will administer the test under similar conditions and to the same kind of individual.

Judging the value of a test. Reliability and validity coefficients are important criteria for judging the value of a test. If it has been demonstrated that a test has yielded reliable and valid results before, it is likely that it will yield reliable and valid results again. Of course, this will be particularly true if the test is used exactly the same way both times. Therefore published tests are standardized and teachers are urged not to deviate from the standard set of instructions for administering and scoring them.

Besides their usefulness in the selection of tests, reliability and validity coefficients are also used to arrive at two very valuable statistics: the standard error of measurement and the standard error of estimate. These statistics are the main statistical tools for interpreting test scores. The formulas for computing these statistics can be found in Appendix A.

The standard error of measurement. Reliability coefficients are used in computing standard errors of measurement. While reliability indicates *freedom* from error, the standard error of measurement estimates the amount of error which *does* exist. Whereas reliability is used as an estimate of the accuracy of the measurement results as a whole, the standard error of measurement is used as an estimate of the accuracy of the results for a given individual.

The basic idea behind the use of the standard error of measurement is very simple. Remember our earlier discussion? Measurement error occurs when a person's obtained score differs from his true score. Suppose a certain test has a standard error of measurement of two points ($Se = 2$). Intuitively, what this means is that the average distance between the observed score and the true score is estimated to be 2 points.[2]

So if Randy's obtained score is 84, what is his true score? If we are willing to assume that we probably did not make any greater error in Randy's score than the average amount of error, then we could argue that Randy's true score is no more than 2 points (plus or minus) from his observed score of 84. In other words, his true score probably lies somewhere between 82 and 86 ($84 \pm 2 = 82$ to 86).

The standard error of estimate. The validity coefficient is used in com-

---

[2] This is not absolutely true but it is a reasonable way of interpreting the standard error. Actually, 68 percent of the time the true score will be included in a range determined by one *Se* unit below and one *Se* unit above the observed score.

puting the *standard error of estimate* (sometimes referred to as the *standard error of prediction*). While validity indicates how free from error our judgments are, the standard error of estimate estimates the amount of error we do make when we make a judgment. Whereas validity is used as an estimate of the accuracy of making certain kinds of judgments, the standard error of estimate is used as an estimate of the accuracy of a specific judgment for a given individual.

Again, the basic idea is simple. In fact, it is the same as the idea behind the procedures for using the standard error of measurement. However, instead of indicating how far off the obtained scores are from the true scores, the standard error of estimate indicates how far off the estimated or predicted scores will be from the scores actually obtained. A couple of examples should help to clarify this point.

An algebra aptitude test is given near the end of the eighth grade and the results are used to select those who should take algebra in the ninth grade. The school counselor, using a prediction formula based upon the predictive validity of the algebra aptitude test, predicts Marvin's ninth grade algebra achievement. He predicts that Marvin will score a 92 on the achievement test given at the end of ninth grade. How far off will his prediction be? The standard error of estimate, based upon the predictive validity coefficient of the aptitude test, is 6.5. The interpretation of the standard error of estimate is similar to the interpretation of the standard error of measurement. Consequently, the counselor is reasonably certain that Marvin's actual achievement test score will probably fall somewhere between 87.5 and 96.5.

Debbie transfers to your fourth grade class from another school district. Her cumulative folder shows that a recent reading comprehension test had been given (we will call it test A). Her grade equivalent score was 5.6. How does this compare with the reading comprehension level of your students? They were also given a reading test recently (let us call it test B). The average grade placement score for your class was 4.9.

The school counselor, knowing the correlation between tests A and B (and the standard deviations of the two tests),[3] was able to estimate Debbie's test B score from her test A score. Her grade equivalent score of 5.6 on test A was estimated to be approximately equal to a grade equivalent of 5.1 on test B. In other words, it was estimated that if Debbie had taken test B instead of test A (but at the same time that she took test A), her test B grade equivalent score would have been 5.1. The accuracy of this estimative judgment is indicated by the size of the standard error of estimate. Suppose the standard error of estimate based upon the correlation between test A and test B (essentially, a concurrent validity coefficient) was .5 grade equivalent points. The counselor could be reasonably certain that Debbie's test B grade equivalent would be somewhere between 4.6 and 5.7 (5.1 $\pm$ .5).

---

[3] Standard deviation is discussed in Appendix A.

We have just discussed the techniques used to obtain empirical evidence of the amount of error which exists in measurement. A second strategy for estimating error is to watch for clues.

Teachers typically do not take the time to obtain formal evidence of the reliability and/or validity of their tests. Except for full-length exams (of one hour or more) given at midterm or at the end of the semester, it is probably not worth the effort anyway. Given the small number of students in the typical classroom, any statistical estimates are not likely to be very stable. The few times when it would be valuable for a teacher to obtain reliability and validity estimates of his test results are discussed in Appendix A.

Teachers, furthermore, obtain a great deal of the information they need through nonmeasurement procedures. Information of this kind does not lend itself to statistical manipulations and therefore reliability and validity estimates are impractical in these situations also.

Nevertheless, it is valuable for teachers to at least be able to recognize gross error when it occurs. Thus they might be able to avoid making erroneous judgments and decisions. It is easy to understand the procedures involved in learning to watch for clues. However, to make this approach to the estimation of error work, practice is required. Initially, the teacher must make a conscious effort to watch for clues which point to error. Before long, it will become a habit, a natural part of the teacher's classroom activities. This is a skill which can be developed only with practice in the classroom.

Our search for error should begin with the sources of error: the information-gathering instrument itself, the information gathering process, and the individual being tested. Clues which signal potential error can be discovered before, during, and after any information-gathering session.

Clues Prior to Testing

The information-gathering instrument itself is a major source of error. However, an advantage of searching the instrument for potential sources of error is that the search can be made *prior* to its use. Sometimes defects in an information-gathering instrument can be corrected before it is used (e.g., faulty directions or a typing error in one of the questions). When sources of error are found which cannot be easily corrected, the test can be rejected and a different instrument used or a note of the problem can be made and the results interpreted accordingly.

Content validity. A careful analysis of the items in a test to see if they seem to be dealing with appropriate content can give you some idea about the validity of an instrument. This procedure is particularly valuable as a way of assessing the validity of achievement tests. Suppose you are teaching seventh grade

English and standardized achievement tests are to be given to all junior high students. You examine the items to get some idea about how valid the test is as a measure of the skills in English which you expected your students to achieve. After comparing the content of the items with the goals you had set for your class, you discover that many of the items measure things which you had not taught. Furthermore, many of the things you expected your students to achieve were not measured by the test. You conclude (quite correctly) that the English subtest has low validity as a measure of how well your students achieved what was expected of them. This kind of validity estimate is called *content validity.* Notice that this is an estimate of validity based upon an analysis of test items and does not give you the empirical evidence of validity which you get from examining the test results. Nevertheless, content validity is a useful and important method for estimating validity. It is particularly valuable when you have clearly described the information you need. Then you will be able to decide more easily whether or not the test will give you the kind of information you need.

Obvious ambiguity. In the process of analyzing a test, ambiguity in the directions as well as in the items themselves can sometimes be spotted. If the meaning of any part of an information-gathering instrument is ambiguous, the results are likely to be in error. Teacher-made tests often suffer from ambiguity, and they should always be checked for this source of error. Having a fellow teacher read and interpret a test is a useful way of discovering potential unreliability of results due to ambiguity. A fellow teacher should be able to read your instructions and tell you what the students are expected to do. If he is fairly familiar with the subject matter, he should also be able to answer most questions correctly. Those answered incorrectly can be discussed. It could be that he simply does not know the answer. But it could also be that he misunderstood the question. When that occurs, the question is probably ambiguous.

Teachers' tests are not the only instruments that suffer from ambiguity. Although most standardized tests are quite free from this source of error, many published but nonstandardized, instruments do contain ambiguity. Questions found in the teachers' manuals or at the end of a chapter in a textbook are often poorly written. Many workbooks, mimeographed work sheets, and test exercises supplied by educational publishers are also poorly constructed. Particularly troublesome are the worksheets designed to give practice in reading and language art skills. The pictures in these exercises are often unclear, poorly drawn, or inappropriate for the skill being tested. Notice, for example, the pictures in the worksheet illustrated in Figure 2.1. The pupils are instructed to circle the pictures of things which begin with the "w" sound. There are a number of pictures, however, which are potentially ambiguous (i.e., they are likely to be called by different names). For example, *tent* is a highly likely label for the picture of the wigwam. And, how about the picture of the world? Could it be just as legitimately called a *globe?*

Previous evidence. Another clue about how valid and/or reliable test results will be is the information about how reliable and valid the results were

Distraction.   If there is a great deal of distraction or if there are unusually long or dramatic disturbances, students might not perform up to expectations. A jackhammer going full blast just outside the window, a fire alarm, a fire in the building across the street, long announcements over the intercom and other such disturbances can affect the results of a test. Normal traffic noises, the choir singing on the next floor up, or the usual office girl's entry to pick up attendance slips—interruptions like these are probably not very disturbing (especially if they are everyday occurrences that the students have gotten used to). These "normal" distractions rarely affect test results to any significant degree. It should be noted, however, that some students are much more easily distracted than others. When the students are having to block out disturbances throughout a test, part of the differences in the scores may be due to ability to concentrate and not to knowledge of the material being tested.

Look for Clues after the Test Has Been Given

There are a number of ways to obtain clues *after* evaluative information has been gathered. Clues can be found in what the students say, in the test results themselves, and in the evidence left behind (e.g., in the test booklets or on the answer sheets).

Clues from the students.   Inevitably, students will complain about tests, particularly if they find them to be difficult. Although student complaints are often unjustified, students will occasionally raise legitimate points. It is usually worthwhile to examine the complaints of students. Treat these complaints as clues that could lead to sources of error. For example, students often complain that the test did not cover the material they studied. If that *is* true, then they either studied the wrong things or the test measured the wrong things. A little further investigation may reveal the truth. In fact, one of the biggest problems with teacher-made tests is that they do not measure an appropriate and adequate sample of the material which was taught. Much of this problem can be avoided if the teacher uses clearly defined instructional goals to guide the evaluation procedures as well as the teaching activities.

When students read into the questions something different from what was intended, it may be that the questions are ambiguous. Although you cannot take at face value the student's descriptions of what they thought an item meant, you can treat this student's "misunderstandings" as a clue. A search for further evidence through item analysis can help to resolve the issue (see Chapter 10).

Clues from the Test Results

Whenever the results of a test deviate significantly from the expected outcome, they should be questioned. Suppose that a very bright class performs poorly on a test. A number of things could cause this to happen: the teacher may have done a poor job of teaching, the students may not have studied, enough time may not have been allotted for the students to learn the material, or the test may have been poorly constructed and/or poorly administered.

Go back and reexamine the test items. Compare them to the instructional goals. Search for possible ambiguities.

Talk to the students. Ask them what they feel the trouble was. Try to find out whether or not they misunderstood the instructions, find out if they felt pressed for time.

Look at the items themselves. Were a lot of "easy" items as well as "difficult" items missed? Did only the poorer students miss the "easy" items or did some of the better students also miss these items?

If an item was missed equally often by the students who scored well on the test as a whole and by those who scored low on the test, the item was not functioning properly. A large number of these kinds of items would indicate a relatively large amount of measurement error.

Another clue that test scores may be in error comes from the range of the scores. If all the students scored within a few points of each other, the reliability of the results will probably be very low. It should be noted that if all the students obtained the same score on a test, interstudent comparison could not be made. If you want to know which of two students has the most ability, there must be enough range in the test scores to allow the differences in ability to be reflected in different scores.

Clues Left Behind

Occasionally, after the test is completed, you can find clues left behind by the students. The scratch paper they used during the test, the test booklets, and the answer sheets themselves can contain clues which indicate possible error. I have seen standardized test booklets, for example, which contained numerous drawings, sketches, and doodles—suggesting that the student was probably not working diligently on the test itself. An examination of the answer sheet will often reveal the fact that only a few items were completed or that the answers seemed randomly selected. Caution should be exercised in interpreting clues of this kind, but if the results do not jibe with other information which is available about the student, then they probably are in error and should be interpreted accordingly.

PRINCIPLE 4: ERROR CAN BE "LIVED WITH"

No matter how carefully and systematically we obtain information, some error will always occur. However, because there are ways to estimate the amount of error which has occurred (or at least to recognize gross error when it does occur), we can live with this problem. Even though information does contain error, it can still be used if it is carefully interpreted. Of course, the smaller the error, the more useful the information and the more reliable the judgments formed from that information. This is why tests are such valuable sources of information. Other things being equal, they yield more accurate information more efficiently than any other information-gathering technique. Before information can be used for making judgments and decisions, it should be verified (checked to see if it is true). The three rules discussed below serve as general guidelines, the specific applications of which will be discussed in Chapter 7.

Rule 1: Hedge

A sophisticated form of hedging is the interpretation of scores that we discussed earlier. Using the standard error of measurement, we interpret a score by indicating a band or range within which we feel confident the true score lies. In other words, we do not accept an observed score as "truth." We hedge. We say that the observed score is an estimate of the true score which is accurate within certain limits.

To hedge is to avoid committing oneself. A firm commitment should not be made on the basis of a single test score. When making a decision, for example, one should not make a commitment to a particular course of action on the basis of one piece of information. Put off making a commitment. Delay making a decision until further information can be obtained and the "truth" of the information can be substantiated. Rule 2 provides the first step in the process of substantiating the truth of any evaluative information.

Rule 2: Hypothesize

You know that any single piece of evaluative information will not be perfectly accurate. However, if you have obtained it carefully, doing everything possible to keep error to a minimum, the information is likely to be fairly accurate and probably useful. At best, you can estimate the accuracy using reliability and validity estimates. At least, you can be cognizant of clues which point to possible sources of error. In any case, you cannot be certain. But if you hedge, giving yourself a little time, you can test the accuracy of the information you have. Suppose you assume that the information you have is perfectly accurate. Now answer the following question:

> What would that information lead you to hypothesize about the behavior of the individual(s) for whom you have the information?

The answer to this question will leave you with hypotheses which you can subsequently confirm or reject in light of further information. Let us examine a couple of examples.

Duane, a second grader, got 95 percent of the items correct on a test of word-attack skills. Only two of his classmates got higher scores than he did. If this score is an accurate reflection of Duane's true ability to use word-attack skills, then the following hypotheses would seem reasonable:

In other, similar tests, Duane will also perform near the top of the class.

When reading new material orally, Duane should have little trouble sounding out unfamiliar words.

Julie scored 18 out of a possible 50 points on the midterm in her tenth grade algebra class. The class average was 32 points. Assuming this score to be an accurate estimate of her algebra ability, we might hypothesize the following:

Other tests and quizzes, given prior to the midterm, were also very low.

Informal discussion with Julie should reveal a lack of understanding of basic concepts and rules.

If, in fact, Duane's and Julie's scores are fairly free from error, then the above hypotheses should be confirmed. If, on the other hand, we test the above hypotheses and find that we must reject them (i.e., they do not hold true), then we have evidence that the scores were not accurate and could not be trusted for important judgments and decisions. So, once we have formulated hypotheses on the basis of the information we have, the next step is to test the hypotheses to see if they hold true. Which leads us to rule 3: confirm or reject the hypotheses.

Rule 3: Confirm

When you obtain evidence that the hypotheses based upon a test score hold true, you confirm the accuracy or "truth" of that score. In the above examples, the hypotheses were "tested" by obtaining further information (or examining previously attained information). The "other" information could be classified into one of two types: that information obtained with a similar test (replication) and that information obtained with different procedures (supplementation).

Replication. One method for testing the "truth" of information is replication (obtaining information under similar circumstances). The first way to obtain a replication is to give an alternate form of a test.

The results of Meloney's achievement tests appear to be inaccurate. Give her an alternate form of the same test and compare the results.

Bernie's IQ suggests he can do better work than he has been doing. Perhaps the IQ is wrong. Give him another form of the same IQ test and see if he gets approximately the same score.

The second way to obtain a replication of test results is to give similar tests measuring approximately the same things. For example, instead of an alternate form of the IQ test which had been given to Bernie, a different IQ test could be given. Obviously, direct comparisons of the two scores cannot be made as they can when alternate forms of the same test are used. However, the additional information can provide some evidence about the accuracy of the original information.

Supplementation. Another method for testing the "truth" of information is supplementation. Supplement the present information with other information obtained under different circumstances. This is the procedure used to test the second hypothesis about Duane's word-attack abilities. The original information was obtained from a test of word-attack abilities. The original information hypothesis that he should have little trouble reading orally. An observation of his oral reading skills provides a different circumstance for obtaining information about Duane's word-attack skills and leads to the confirmation or rejection of the above hypothesis.

It should be noted, at this point, that if two pieces of information do not agree, you have no way of knowing which is probably most accurate. No way, that is, unless you have some evidence that one of the two is more likely to contain error than the other (e.g., a test usually contains less error than a teacher's observations, a highly reliable standardized test usually yields more reliable scores than a teacher-made test, midterm test scores are probably more accurate than quizzes). In any case, it is usually worthwhile to obtain many different kinds of information, all related to the same skill or ability, before any important decisions are made.

EXERCISE 2.4

1. Describe the major uses of reliability and validity estimates.
2. There are two ways to estimate the amount of error in measurement: *(a)* obtain empirical evidence and *(b)* watch for clues. How do these two methods differ? How are they alike? When should each be used?

SUMMARY

1. The basic principles of evaluation are designed to help you cope with the problem of error. These principles may be stated as follows: *(a)* sources of error can be identified, *(b)* error can be minimized, *(c)* error can be estimated, and *(d)* error can be "lived with."
2. There are many sources of measurement error within the information-gathering instrument, the information-gathering process, and the individual being evaluated.

3. By applying three general rules to evaluation techniques, error can be minimized and validity and reliability assured. The three rules are *(a)* relate everything you do to the reason you are evaluating; *(b)* at every step in the process of evaluation, be clear, concise, and consistent; and *(c)* always obtain a representative sample of the information needed.
4. In a representative sample, the individuals are like the individuals in the population. A summary of information obtained from a representative sample will match a summary of the same information obtained from the population.
5. There are two basic strategies for estimating the amount of measurement error: *(a)* obtain empirical evidence of reliability and validity and *(b)* watch for clues which indicate that error may have occurred.
6. Reliability is an estimate of freedom from error and can be thought of as consistency.
7. *Validity* refers to the fact that evaluative information is appropriate for making particular judgments and decisions which have been anticipated.
8. Validity and reliability estimates are useful for *(a)* judging the value of a test and *(b)* calculating the standard error of estimate and the standard error of measurement.
9. Clues which indicate measurement error can be found *(a)* prior to testing, *(b)* during testing, and *(c)* after testing.
10. There are three things that can be done even though some error exists: *(a)* hedge, *(b)* form hypotheses, and *(c)* confirm or reject the hypotheses.

References

Cronbach, Lee J.: *Essentials of Psychological Testing,* 3d ed., Harper & Row, Publishers, Incorporated, New York, 1970.

Suggested Readings

The following texts contain particularly good discussions of the basic principles of measurement:

Mehrens, William A., and Irvin J. Lehmann: *Measurement and Evaluation in Education and Psychology,* Holt, Rinehart and Winston, Inc., New York, 1973, unit II.

Nunally, Jum C.: *Educational Measurement and Evaluation,* 2d ed., McGraw-Hill Book Company, 1972, New York, part I.

Thorndike, Robert L., and Elizabeth Hagen: *Measurement and Evaluation in Psychology and Education,* 3d ed., John Wiley & Sons, Inc., New York, 1969, chap. 6.

For an especially thorough and up-to-date treatment of validity and reliability, read:

Cronbach, Lee J.: "Test Validation," in Robert L. Thorndike (ed.), *Educational Measurement,* 2d ed., American Council on Education, Washington, D.C., 1971.

Stanley, Julian C.: "Reliability," In Robert L. Thorndike (ed.), *Educational Measurement,* 2d ed., American Council on Education, Washington, D.C., 1971.

PART TWO

STEPS IN THE
EVALUATION PROCESS

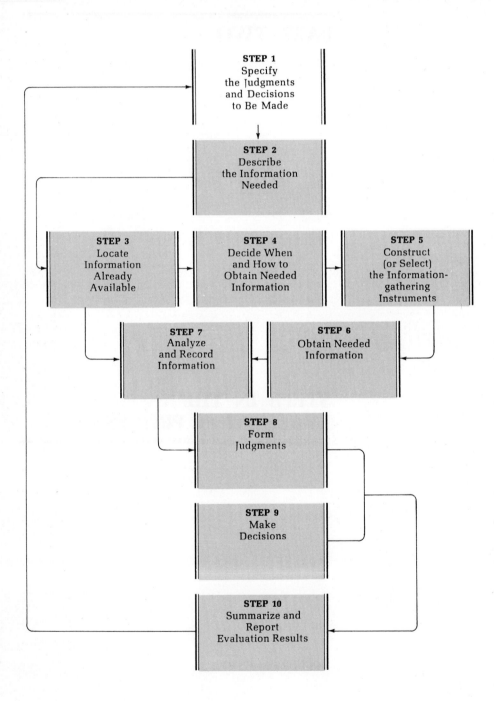

CHAPTER 3

Specifying the Judgments and Decisions to Be Made

A Funny Thing Happened to Me
on the Way to the Classroom.

As I rounded a corner in the hall, Educator approached me and said,

"*Goest thou to teach?*"

"*Ah, truly,*" said I.

"*Knowest thou the outcome of thine instruction?*"

"*My goals are clearly perceived.*"

"*And behaviorally stated?*" said he.

"*And behaviorally stated,*" said I.

"*May thine instruction bring forth the expected learning outcomes.*"

And on another day not long thereafter, I, burdened with lengthy examinations for the accounting of my students, confronted Assessor. He spoke:

59

"Goest thou to test?"
"Ah, truly," said I.
"And wilt thou measure learning outcomes?"
"Indeed, and a proper sampling of them, sir!"
"May thine examinations objectively assess."
But as I turned to go, Evaluator appeared.
"Goest thou to evaluate?"
"It seemeth so," said I.
"Knowest thou the outcome of thine evaluation?"
"Outcome, sir? Meanest thou the scores my students shall receive?"
"Nay, but the use to which these scores shall be put."
For with them thou wilt surely make judgments and decisions grave."
So new to me was this line of questioning, I began to tremble. For tests are to give, and to score, and to neatly record. But to make grave decisions. . . ? And even if it were so, to know *in advance* what decisions I might make? Truly Evaluator is a troublemaker. . . . "Knowest thou the outcome of thine evaluation?" How absurd.

And yet, it is not absurd at all to wish to know, *before* you begin a task, what you ultimately hope to accomplish. Nor is it absurd to specify, before you set out to obtain information, how you plan on using it. Certain kinds of decisions require certain kinds of judgments. And the kind of information which is useful for one type of judgment may be useless for another. Furthermore, the nature of the judgments and decisions one hopes to make determines when and under what conditions the information is obtained.

Which is to say that tests are to give, and to score, and to neatly record, *and* to help in making judgments and decisions. But, that is what this chapter is all about.

By the time you have finished reading this chapter, it is hoped that you will have learned to

1. Think first of judgments and decisions which must be made and *then* of the information needed and the procedures for obtaining it.
2. Accept the idea that, when anticipated judgments and decisions are clearly described, the next steps in the evaluation process will be easier.

Furthermore, when given a set of questions which teachers often ask themselves as they attempt to improve their instruction and help their students to learn, you should be able to

3. Indicate which questions call for judgments and which for decisions.
4. Think of similar questions you might ask if you were the teacher.

5. Fully describe each decision.
6. Determine the most important judgments which would help the teacher to make those decisions.
7. Fully describe each judgment.
8. Determine at least some of the kinds of decisions which could be made from the judgments.

A systematic approach to the task of describing anticipated judgments and decisions will make that task much easier. One such approach might be to begin with the questions teachers would naturally ask themselves about their instruction and their students' learning. The first step would then be to determine whether such a question called for a judgment to be formed or a decision to be made.

If a decision was being called for, then it should be described (answering a few simple questions about the nature of the decision is all that is necessary). Once a decision is described, one can determine what judgments will be needed in order to make that decision. Now the judgments can be described (again, answers to a few simple questions will suffice).

If a teacher asks a question which calls for a judgment, then the first step would be to describe that judgment. Next, one could determine what kinds of decisions might be made easier once that judgment had been made. Those decisions could then be described.

This whole process has been diagramed as a flowchart (see Figure 3.1). Examine this flowchart carefully, because it contains all the major concepts treated in this chapter. An understanding of these concepts is important. You will recall that one of the major rules for minimizing error is to relate everything you do to the reason for the evaluation (i.e., to the judgments and decisions you anticipate making). In order to be able to apply this rule, you must be able (1) to specify what judgments and decisions you wish to make and (2) to describe them as precisely as possible.

BEGIN WITH QUESTIONS

Judgments and decisions almost always begin as questions. Whenever a teacher asks himself a question about what is going on in his classroom, it is likely that the answer he arrives at will be either a judgment or a decision.

Teachers are continuously asking themselves questions about their student's progress and their own effectiveness. They want to know what to teach, how to teach, how to motivate, what to test, when to test, how to reach a certain student, etc. It would be valuable if they could learn to recognize these questions

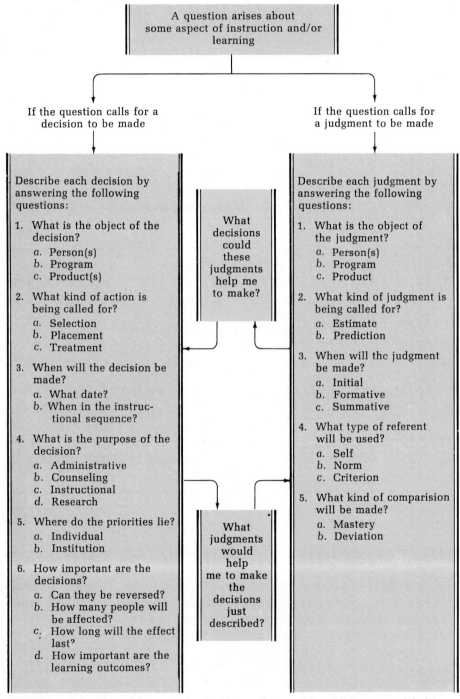

FIGURE 3.1. A flowchart of the process involved in specifying anticipated judgments and decisions.

as stimulants to judgments and decisions and then set out to make those judgments and decisions as systematically as possible. Just being aware of the fact that you *are* judging and that those judgments *will* be used to make decisions can help to make you more conscious of the many things which influence decision making. That can lead to more objective decisions, better teaching, and improved learning.

If a question can be answered by a statement which calls for action to be taken, a decision is needed. If the question can be answered by a statement which estimates present condition(s) or predicts future performance, a judgment is being sought.

EXERCISE 3.1

Consider the following questions asked by classroom teachers. For each question, decide whether it would be answered by a call to action (a decision) or by an estimate of present condition or prediction of future performance (a judgment).

1. What time during the day should I have reading?
2. Are my third graders ready to begin cursive writing?
3. How long will it take Ruth to finish her report on Benny Goodman?
4. Does Doug read faster than most third graders?
5. Shall I give a test on Friday or on the following Monday?
6. Which of the students will probably have the most trouble with this course?
7. Will Susan be able to complete Algebra I successfully?
8. Shall I mark the students down for turning their papers in late?
9. Should Jill be moved to the first-chair position in the trombone section?

Items 1, 5, 8, and 9 are all questions which call for action to be taken. The remaining items represent questions which are answered with statements of present condition (estimates) or future performance (predictions). If you thought that any of those questions were calling for action to be taken, you probably are sensitive to the fact that well-formed judgments lead quite naturally to decisions. Consequently, you may have responded to a projected *use* of the answer to the question rather than to the answer itself. For example, item 2 poses the question: "Are my third graders ready to begin cursive writing?" The answer to this question (yes, they are ready or no, they are not ready) estimates the present condition of the third graders. Therefore, the question is answerable by a judgment. Now, the obvious next step is to *use* this answer to make a decision (I will begin a unit in cursive writing or I will not begin a unit in cursive writing). It is certainly valuable to be able to see not only the judgments which are implied by the questions we ask as teachers but also the decisions which those judgments lead one to make. Nevertheless, it is also important to be able to distinguish between judgments and decisions. When you can do that, you can then proceed to a careful description of those judgments and decisions. Furthermore, once you have carefully described the judgments and decisions you hope to make, it will be easier for you to get the information needed in order to make them.

DESCRIBE THE DECISIONS TO BE MADE

An important goal of this chapter is to enable you to describe educational decisions fully.[1] One way to do this is to answer the six simple questions outlined in the flowchart in Figure 3.1. Let us examine each of these questions in turn.

What Is the Object of the Decision?

Educational decisions are usually made about individual students. For example, Ryker is selected for band and assigned to first trombone, third chair. Milner is promoted to fifth grade. Eloise is given extra work to complete before she is allowed to move to the next level in reading.

However, the individual student is not and should not be the only object of educational evaluation. Teachers, materials, learning activities, teaching methods, lesson plans, objectives, tests, curricula, virtually any "person, place, or thing" can be the object of educational decisions. The basic process of evaluation is the same no matter what the object of the decisions to be made. However, some of the particular techniques for obtaining information and interpreting it will vary according to what or who is being decided upon. Therefore, it is important to indicate what or who is being decided upon.

What Kind of Action Is to Be Taken?

The categories *selection, placement, and treatment* seem to describe fairly well the "courses of action" representative of educational decisions. These categories are not completely distinct and some decisions may not fit neatly into any of them. Nevertheless, they do provide a useful way to describe educational decisions.

Selection decisions. When the alternative courses of action are *accept* or *reject,* the decision is referred to as a *selection decision.* Selection decisions are the kinds of decisions in which an individual is (or some few individuals are) selected out from the rest. Selection implies that not all individuals being decided upon will be chosen. There may be many individuals to select from, but in each case the decision is either accept or reject; there are no other alternatives. Sup-

---

[1] See the suggested readings at the end of this section for references to various schemes for classifying decisions. Many of the ideas used to develop the classification scheme for this section have been borrowed from these sources.

pose, for example, a student is trying to select a college to attend. He may have many colleges to choose from, but for each college there are only two possible courses of action: accept or reject.

Typical selection decisions are made by institutions: a medical school screens hundreds of applicants, accepting or rejecting each one; a high school selects one new biology teacher from among several who applied; the Ford Foundation decides to fund some projects and not to fund others.

Selection decisions can be made at many different levels within an institution: A coach selects some boys for the basketball team and rejects others. An English department selects new textbooks for freshman English. A school superintendent chooses a new principal for the middle school.

A classroom teacher makes numerous selection decisions: Miss Vappy selects a film to be shown in her biology class. Mr. Veltopal selects some of the exercises in the math book and rejects others. The band director selects his music carefully. Marlene Offendorp selects George as editor and five other students as feature writers. A first grade teacher selects Melodie as "teacher's helper."

Even individual students can make selection decisions: Farlo decides to go to Artville Junior College instead of either of the other two colleges which had accepted him. A freshman in high school chooses baseball rather than track as his spring sport. Mary decides to sign up for Miss Vappy's class rather than Mr. Parlon's because she heard that Miss Vappy gives high grades.

Placement decisions. A second kind of "action to be taken" is that of placement. Placement decisions are the kinds of decisions that are made when an individual who has been accepted is placed in time or space. To be placed in time is to be placed at some point in a sequence of events, activities, or programs: George is placed at the third grade level in reading. There are twenty levels in the eighth grade program; Mary is placed at level fourteen. Eloise tests out of most of the freshman courses and begins college as a second-semester freshman.

To be placed in space is to be placed in a particular place or within a particular group: within a given third grade, students are placed into four different reading groups. A decision is made to place Laura in a special reading program, Wilbur in a speech correction class, and Sally in a learning disabilities class. Sometimes, being assigned to a particular place also means being assigned to a particular point in a sequence. For example, being placed in an advanced math class is an assignment to a place and to a point in a sequence. At other times, being placed in a particular place may have nothing to do with the sequence of instruction. For example, I may have two reading groups reading at the same level (point in the sequence), but each group consists of students with similar interests. Or two groups may start out at the same point in the instructional sequence, but one may be expected to advance much faster. Consequently, students may be placed in a group on the basis of aptitude rather than achievement.

Placement decisions involve a choice among numerous courses of action, not just between acceptance or rejection. Placement decisions are the kinds of decisions which are made *after* a selection decision has been made. Once an individual is accepted into a program, he must be placed within that program (i.e., placed into some group and /or at some point in the sequence of activities that constitute the program).

Treatment decisions. Treatment decisions are made about individuals once they have been accepted into and properly placed within a program. Developing lesson plans for a unit in social studies, assigning a chapter to read, and providing individual study kits for those who need vocabulary enrichment are all activities which call for treatment decisions.

Treatment decisions are easily confused with placement decisions, because to be placed at a certain academic level often means that a given treatment will take place. The reason for this seeming overlap in these two types of decisions is that treatment decisions can be made for all the individuals at a given level (or within a given group). When this occurs all individuals placed together will be *treated* alike. However, even though two individuals have been placed at the same point in an instructional sequence, they still might profit most from different treatments. For example, all the third graders in the advanced reading group will not necessarily get the same reading assignments or even work on the same reading skills. Treatment decisions, then, can be made for a group of individuals or for a single individual.

EXERCISE 3.2

For each decision listed below, decide whether it is a selection, placement, or treatment decision.

1. To choose the members of the student council.
2. To decide on a new textbook.
3. To assign the third graders to reading groups.
4. To assign the questions at the back of Chapter 5.
5. To put George in a slower math group.
6. To choose four students to go to the science fair.
7. To decide how to introduce the students to the concept of conservation.
8. To have Eloise begin on page 72.
9. To pick two discussion leaders.
10. To assign a term paper to the eleventh graders.

When Will the Decision Be Made?

It is important to know when a decision will be made, because the information upon which the judgments and decisions are based should be obtained as close to the time of the decision as possible. The time of a decision can be considered in terms of the calendar (by Tuesday, the fifteenth, I need to decide whom to send to the speech contest) or in terms of the instructional process (*before, during,* or *after* instruction).[2] Listed below are examples of decisions made prior to, during, and after instruction.

Examples of Decisions

Prior to instruction:

      To select learning outcomes
      To choose learning materials
      To select learning activities
      To decide when to test

During instruction:

      To continue the discussion tomorrow
      To skip the planned assignment
      To watch the news report about the attempted assassination
      To have Alice work the supplementary problems

After Instruction:

      To use the same textbook next year
      To spend more time on unit one next time
      To recommend George for advanced calculus
      To recommend Peter for summer school

What Is the Purpose of the Decision?

It is helpful to know the purpose served by the decisions to be made. Will they serve an administrative purpose, a counseling purpose, an instructional purpose, or a research purpose?

Administrative decisions. Decisions which primarily serve administrative purposes are decisions which affect the total operation of an administrative unit (e.g., a citywide system, an inner-city high school, a suburban elementary school). Decisions dealing with the allocation of resources, the selection of curricula, and the formation and maintenance of a staff are all examples of administrative decisions.

Counseling decisions. Decisions serving a counseling purpose would be those decisions which help students make vocational and educational choices as well as those which guide the student toward better study habits, better social relationships, or better mental health.

Instructional decisions. The vast majority of the decisions made in any educational institution are instructional decisions. Instruction (particularly if

---

[2] We use the term *instructional process* here, and throughout the book, to refer to both the teaching *and* the learning activities. Both teacher and learner behaviors are important, but of course the ultimate goal of teaching is student learning.

conceived of as the process of guiding learning) is the main function of education, and numerous instructional decisions are made daily. Decisions about which learning outcomes can reasonably be expected, which learning activities should be used to help the student achieve those outcomes, where in a learning sequence a student should be placed, and which motivational techniques should be tried are all examples of decisions that serve an instructional purpose.

Research decisions. A final reason for educational decisions is research. The educational researcher makes decisions about which hypotheses to test, who should be included in the sample, and which treatments are likely to cause learning to occur most efficiently. The educational researcher seeks to explore systematically the kinds of questions that teachers are asking informally: Which learning strategies work best for particular kinds of learning? What kinds of learning outcomes can most easily be attained through programmed instruction? Is there one best sequence for presenting the basic math concepts? What effect do low grades have on a student's continued achievement?

Where Do the Priorities Lie?

Is the decision being made based upon the values and needs of the individual? Or is the decision an institutional decision, based upon the values and needs of the institution? In an *individual decision,* the choice of possible actions to be taken is unique (i.e., it is likely not to occur again). When, for example, an individual selects a college to attend, he is not likely to have to make that same decision again. An *institutional decision,* on the other hand, is one in which a large number of comparable decisions are to be made. When a college accepts or rejects a given student, that is only one of many similar decisions. The individual selecting a college or a career has a great deal at stake and can afford very little error. A college selecting an individual, however, has a lot less at stake. If a single individual is accepted when he should have been rejected — or vice versa, the institution does not suffer a great deal. Institutional decisions can therefore be made on the basis of a set of rules which will "on the average" yield the fewest errors. These rules can be applied to all the decisions of the same kind. The admission policy of an institution exemplifies a set of these kinds of rules and their use in institutional decision making.

Do teachers ever make institutional decisions? Whenever the needs of the class or the school influence a decision more strongly than do the needs of the individual, we might consider that to be an institutional decision. Sometimes it is imperative that the needs of the class as a whole be given greater consideration than the needs of any individual student in that class. For example, almost all the students in the class have mastered the skills needed in order to understand a film you plan on showing. You decide to show it even though two or three individuals are not ready and will probably have trouble understanding it. Sometimes the needs of the institution (e.g., budgetary needs) force themselves upon situations. In such cases the needs of individuals must be forgotten or compromised.

For example, the creative writing class could probably be taught best if writing assignments were turned in and analyzed by the teacher daily. However, the class has 40 students and the teacher has four such classes. With approximately 160 students, the teacher cannot analyze everyone's writing every day. He must decide on a compromise solution even though it may not be the most efficient way for the individuals in the class to learn.

At this point I do not wish to debate the moral issues involved, but I do wish to point out the fact that when you make decisions, you must be aware of which values are most strongly affecting those decisions.[3]

How Important Are the Decisions?

The decisions teachers make daily will range in importance according to the seriousness of the consequences of those decisions. It is important, therefore, to be aware of the importance of any decision you make. You will not have time or money to use the best and most thorough information-gathering technique for each bit of information you need about your students. This means you will have to make some choices after gathering some information very carefully under the best of conditions and gathering other information under less desirable conditions. Furthermore, you must be ready to reverse your decisions when other information, demonstrating that you should, becomes available.

Criterion 1: Reversibility. One criterion which could be used for judging the importance of an educational decision is reversibility. If a decision cannot be reversed once it has been made, then the utmost care must be taken in making that decision and the information obtained should be as accurate as possible.

The decision to pass or fail a student is virtually an irreversible decision, and these kinds of decisions are the most important. The information needed to make these kinds of decisions must be as accurate as possible no matter what the cost. Some of the kinds of decisions we make as teachers are not irreversible, however, and perhaps they are a little less important. For example, we like to think that once we have put a certain student in a slow reading group that he can move out of that group if he demonstrates that he is more capable than we thought or if he improves his reading ability. Although, in theory this is true, for the most part these kinds of grouping decisions have a very lasting effect upon the student and upon the teacher's subsequent attitudes toward that student.

Criterion 2: How many people will be affected? Another criterion which is useful in helping one to decide about the importance of an educational decision is how many persons are affected. Some of our decisions affect only one person and others affect many people. Those affected may be your students only, all the students in the school, or—sometimes—perhaps the entire community may be affected by the decisions we make.

Many a high school principal has, for example, made the decision to give the

[3] A more complete discussion about how our values affect the outcomes of our decisions can be found in Chapter 8.

students a long enough noon hour so they can leave the building and go out in the community, and disaster has resulted. The students, having had more time than they needed to eat their lunch, began to loiter in stores, wander through town getting in trouble, and the entire community as well as the students themselves were affected. Teachers are often faced with similar kinds of decisions (e.g., whether or not they should take their students on field trips and under what conditions these trips should be taken). The selection of leaders for various positions within the school is another example of the kind of decision which affects many people. Not only the people who have been chosen are affected but also those who might have been chosen but were not. Of course, so are those who must work under this duly chosen leader.

Criterion 3: Length of time the effect will last.   A third criterion that can be used in assessing the importance of an educational decision is that of how long the effect of the decision will last. Some decisions are irreversible and last virtually forever. Other decisions, although reversible at some point in time, may last a relatively long time and are, therefore, quite important. Once a textbook has been selected, you usually cannot change texts again for at least a year. Compare the importance, then, of making the choice of a textbook with that of choosing a filmstrip to be shown once, a movie to be borrowed from a neighboring school, or a mimeographed sheet to be handed out. The effects of the choice of these materials would be short-lived, and if a decision turned out to be a bad one, the effects would not last too long. Of course, in the choice of materials, we must consider not only how long we will be required to use the materials but also how long the effect of the materials will be felt by the students. Other things being equal, the longer the effect of a decision, the more important it will tend to be and the more necessary it will be to obtain information which is as accurate as possible.

Criterion 4: Importance of the learning outcomes(s).   A final criterion for judging the importance of a decision is the importance of the learning outcomes for which the decision is appropriate. The vast majority of the educational judgments and decisions teachers make are related to their instructional goals. Decisions are made about the selection of these goals, the appropriate means for helping the students to attain them, and what to do once they have attained them. Some instructional goals are very important because they are prerequisite to the attainment of other goals. It is sometimes useful to establish minimum-level goals as well as goals which go beyond that minimum level. It is important for everyone to reach the minimum-level goals. The assessment of these goals must be accurate and therefore must be made on the basis of information gathered with the best techniques available.

DESCRIBE THE JUDGMENTS TO BE FORMED

Judgments, like decisions, can readily be described by answering a few simple questions. As we discuss each question, keep in mind the fact that our goal is to find out enough about the anticipated judgments so that we will be able to obtain the needed information at the right time and under the right conditions.

What Is the Object?

Like the decisions we make, our judgments can be made about any "person, place, or thing." What or whom we pass judgment on is partially determined by the object of the action anticipated by the decisions to be made. If, for example, you must decide upon the fate of one of your students, then you will make judgments about that statement. *However,* decisions are usually made on the basis of numerous judgments. Furthermore, the object of those judgments is not always the same as the object of the decision. Suppose you are trying to decide which reading group to place Donna in. Surely you would have to make some judgments about Donna (her reading ability, her interest level, her social maturity). But you would also find it valuable to make judgments about the ability of the others in the group (those Donna will have to keep up with) and about the difficulty of the materials to be used.

What Kind of Judgment Will Be Made?

Earlier we defined a judgment as an estimate of present condition *or* a prediction of future performance. It is important to distinguish between estimates and predictions, but sometimes the distinction is difficult to make. Take, for example, item 2 from Exercise 3.1:

2. Are my third graders ready to begin cursive writing?

Is the answer to this question an estimate or a prediction? If you said, "prediction," you are *wrong.* Suppose the answer to the question were, "Yes, my third graders are ready." That answer is a statement of condition estimating the level of readiness for a new task. Will the third graders succeed at this new task? Probably. But—note carefully—when we say, "they *probably* will succeed," *then* we have made a *predictive* judgment. That predictive judgment, in this case, *depended* upon the prior estimate of their readiness. Of course, the ultimate reason for asking that kind of question in the first place was that a decision could be made (to begin or not to begin cursive writing).

In order to form an estimate, the information used must have a known (or at least hypothesized) relationship to potential behavior or ability. In order to serve as the basis of a prediction, the information must have a known (or at least hypothesized) relationship to actual performance under certain conditions. Suppose, for example, you wish to estimate your students' ability to learn. You could use scores from an intelligence test which you hypothesized were related to a general ability to learn. However, if you now want to use those IQs for predicting academic performance in a public school classroom, you need further information.

Now you must know the relationship between IQ and actual performance in a classroom situation (where motivation, teaching procedures, and many other factors also affect that performance). An estimate of a person's academic aptitude may be high and yet, given additional information (e.g., the student is not motivated), the prediction may be that he will not do well in school at all.

This distinction should become clearer as you read. In Chapter 7 there will be a fuller discussion about the relationship between estimates and predictions. For now, a little practice in distinguishing between estimates and predictions will help you prepare for later discussion. Exercise 3.3 has been designed to give you that practice.

EXERCISE 3. 3

For each question, decide whether an estimate or a prediction is being asked for.

1. How long will it take Ruth to finish her report?
2. Does Mary understand the concept of freedom?
3. How well do you understand the concept of prediction?
4. Will you get at least ten of these items correct?
5. How well can Martha use a dictionary?
6. Will Wilbur pass the midterm in history?
7. What are Tular's chances of passing French?
8. How good are Laura's phonetic skills?
9. Will Susan be able to complete Algebra I successfully?
10. What is the probability that I will be able to finish the unit on the Bill of Rights by May 1?
11. How much do my students know about the Civil War?
12. Have my students reached the goals I set for them?

When Should the Judgment Be Made?

A child starts school at five years of age. At that point he begins to accumulate test scores and grades. As the student goes through school, each teacher follows the same pattern: assignments, quizzes, and tests are given. They are scored, recorded, summed, and averaged. Each score is added on to the rest until the end of the marking period arrives, final judgments are made, and grades are given. Three marking periods (sometimes four) make a year, and a grand average is computed. These grades are accumulated in a folder especially designed for that purpose. Periodically, these cumulative folders are analyzed and a student is given a cumulative grade-point average (GPA). And if, upon completion of high school, his GPA is high enough, this student may enter college, where he will again accumulate grade points. Twenty years after he began school we find our student, a full-grown man, working toward the completion of a Ph.D. and a final, glorious grade-point average.

With that kind of tradition, it is no wonder that it is difficult to conceive of educational judgments occurring at any other time than at the conclusion of instruction. But difficult or not, we must recognize the importance of forming judgments before instruction begins (initial judgments) and during instruction (formative judgments) as well as upon the completion of instruction (summative judgments).

Initial judgments.   The importance of initial judgments is easy to see when we recognize the many decisions which a teacher must make when planning for instruction. Decisions made prior to instruction rest heavily upon initial judgments. It should be remembered that our initial judgments are often incorrect. It is necessary, therefore, to be willing to alter our judgments as the instructional process begins.

Formative judgments.   Formative and summative evaluation are terms introduced by Scriven (1967) to distinguish between final evaluation of a curriculum and evaluation for the purpose of ongoing improvement of a curriculum. These concepts have now been generalized to application beyond curriculum evaluation. Benjamin Bloom, for example, applies the terms to the evaluation of student outcomes. Formative observations, according to Bloom, serve the following purposes: "to determine the degree of mastery of a given learning task and to pinpoint the part of the task not mastered" (Bloom, 1971, page 617).

Formative judgments are especially important in making placement and treatment decisions. Learning to monitor the pogress of your students continuously will be one of the most challenging aspects of teaching. It is essentially a process of making formative judgments.

Summative judgments.   *Summative evaluation* refers to evaluation made at the conclusion of instruction—at the end of the course or some substantial part of it. When students have had all the time the educational structure will allow them to reach the instructional goals, then comes the final judgment. How far have the students come? Which goals did they reach? Which skills have they mastered? These are the kinds of questions which typically lead to summative judgments. Summative judgments, although based at least in part on the past, are oriented toward *future* decisions. Grades, for example, are used by next year's teachers, by future potential employers, by placement bureaus, etc.

How Should the Judgment Be Made?

Recently there has been a great deal of emphasis on *criterion-referenced measurement.* There seems to be a battle waging between the advocates of criterion-referenced measurement and those of *norm-referenced mesaurement.* At this point, let me briefly define the important terms in this controversy. Then we will take a closer look at those concepts in an attempt to get a better understanding of the process of forming judgments. I hope to demonstrate that these terms are really interrelated concepts which are useful in describing the alternative kinds of judgments which can be made from evaluative data and that they are not really "conflicting" concepts at all. In fact, *both* norm-referenced and criterion-referenced approaches are of value to the classroom teacher.

Criterion-referenced measurement is an attempt to interpret test results in terms of clearly defined learning outcomes which serve as the criteria (or referents) for forming judgments. Norm-referenced measurement is an attempt to interpret test results in terms of the performance of some group. The group is called a norm group because its performance serves as the norm (or referent) for forming judgments.

As you can tell from the above definitions, the difference between criterion-referenced and norm-referenced evaluation is *not,* first of all, a difference in the kinds of tests which are used.[4] Rather, the difference lies in the way the test results are interpreted, i.e., *in the way they are used to form judgments.* An examination of how judgments are formed should help to validate this point.

Basically, the process of forming judgments involves comparing evaluative information to some referent. The type of referent used *and* the kind of comparison made are two of the factors which distinguish one type of judgment from another. A third factor, whether the judgment is an estimate or a prediction, was discussed earlier. In a moment, you will see how these three factors are related, but first let us discuss the procedures for selecting an appropriate referent and choosing a method for comparing information to that referent.

What Type of Referent Will Be Used?

The most common referents are (1) the individuals own performance, (2) the performance of a group of similar individuals, and (3) a performance criterion. A different type of judgment is being made each time you use a different type of referent. An understanding of each of these types of referents will help you to select those which are most appropriate for the judgments and decisions you anticipate making. However, before discussing each of the types of referents, let us examine a little more closely this notion of a referent.

A referent is that which is referred to when making a judgment; it takes the form of a *score,* a *value,* or a *description of performance.*

Example of a Score Used as the Referent

Jerry correctly pronounced sixteen sight vocabulary words. This was compared to a score of only seven correctly pronounced words when he tried to read the same list last week. He has gained a great deal.

---

[4]Virtually any kind of test can be used to make any kind of judgment. However there are *some* differences in the way you should design a test depending upon which type of judgments you plan on making. These differences will be discussed in Chapter 13.

The referent in this example is a score (the number of words correctly pronounced). You will recognize this as a self-referenced judgment, but scores can be used as referents in all types of judgments.

Example of a Value Used as a Referent

Mrs. Jardin's fourth grade class took a test of map reading skills. She felt that they were very good at map reading because their average score was twice that of the average of all fourth graders in that school district.

Mrs. Jardin has made a judgment about the performance of her class by comparing it to the performance of all fourth grade classes in the school district that took the same test. What is the referent? The average score of all the fourth grade classes in the district served as the referent of Mrs. Jardin's judgment. This time the referent was a *value* arrived at by computing the average performance of a group of similar students.

Note that the referent in this example is not all the fourth graders in the school district. Rather, it is the average of the scores obtained by those fourth graders. The referent is a value placed upon the performance of the fourth graders in the school district. These fourth graders serve as a reference group (or norm group, as it is more commonly called), but the comparison is made to the *average of their performance* and not to fourth graders themselves.

Example of a Description Used as a Referent

A checklist of Mary's activities during class discussion becomes more meaningful when compared to the checklists obtained about her peers during the same discussion periods.

In this case, the referent is not a single score or a given value but a *description* of how the other students performed on the same task that Mary did. In making this comparison, the teacher might find it valuable to summarize the kinds of responses made by the class as a whole and then to use this summary as a referent for making judgments about Mary's performance. This is a norm-referenced judgment. The next example illustrates the use of a description in a criterion-referenced judgment.

Example of a Description Used as a Referent

The results of a criterion-referenced mathematics test are compared to a chart which describes the behaviors being measured. Each test item supposedly measures particular learning outcomes. Judgments are made about which objectives a student has not yet mastered (and which he has) by comparing the items he missed with a description of the objectives those items were measuring.

Again, we have in this example a referent which is a description of performance. When a student misses a large number of items measuring the same objective, the judgment is made that he has not mastered the objective.

A referent, then, is information in the form of a score, a value, or a description. But more important than the form of the referent is the type of referent used. The three major types of referents will now be discussed.

Self-referenced judgments. Self-referenced judgments are made by comparing the information you have about an individual to some other information you have about *that same individual.* Using information about the individual himself as a referent is very useful for making judgments about improvements, gains, attitude changes, etc.

When you are comparing two pieces of information about a single individual, everything should be the same except for a single characteristic. If, for example, you are considering how much a student has improved in a given skill, then the same test (or some alternative form of it) should be given twice. The conditions under which the test was given, the time the student is given to take the test, etc., should all be held constant. If you are trying to compare a student's performance on two different kinds of tasks, then they should both be given at the same time under similar conditions, and the only thing that should differ would be the type of task being given.

Self-referenced judgments must be made on the basis of reliable instruments. Test-retest and alternate form reliability are especially important because the judgments are frequently ones in which the same information is obtained over time or across different forms of the same test.

Finally, a referent for use in self-referenced judgments should be in the same format as the information that will be compared with it. This means that the percentage of items correct should be compared with the percentage of items correct. Descriptions of performance during a speech should be compared to descriptions of performance during a speech. Combined results of several rating scales should be compared with the combined results of several rating scales. To try to compare a raw score with a percentage score is no less ridiculous than trying to compare a verbal description to a numerical value.

Norm-referenced judgments. Norm-referenced judgments are made by comparing the information you have about an individual with information about a group of similar individuals. Whenever you use as a referent, information about the performance of some group of individuals *on the same task,* you are making norm-referenced judgments. This kind of referent allows you to compare the information you have about someone's performance with similar information about the performance of others. Whenever you wish to know how well an individual performed in comparison with his peers, norm-referenced judgments are appropriate. These kinds of comparisons are inevitable. More importantly, they are necessary. Selection decisions would be virtually impossible to make without norm-referenced judgments. How do you choose one individual over another without comparing them?

Prediction also relies heavily upon norm-referenced comparisons. It is very helpful, when trying to predict success, to know how an individual compares with those he will compete with for that success. Of course, not all success arises out of competition, but much of life *is* competitive. And, if we *do* want to predict how a person will perform in a competitive situation, we must make the appropriate norm-referenced judgments.

Many placement decisions are also made, at least partially, on the basis of norm-referenced judgments. When we assign an individual to a particular place in an educational program, we usually take into consideration how he compares with others who will be placed with him.

An important requirement of norm-referencing is that the individuals in the norm group are *like* the individuals being judged. Whenever this requirement is not met, faulty judgments will result. A very common example of this can be found when teachers interpret standardized achievement test scores. The teachers in urban, middle-class schools are often delighted that their students score above grade level on achievement tests. However, the grade equivalent which is obtained from the standardized test is made by comparing the students' scores with those of students throughout the United States. The average ability of the students in the middle class schools is considerably higher than the average for all the schools in the United States combined. Consequently, it should be expected that those students would do better than the reference group on a whole. By the same token, students in lower socioeconomic and inner-city schools usually have an average ability level somewhat less than that of the nation as a whole. Furthermore, the students may have had less than the usual degree of success in school up to the time of testing, and it is therefore difficult for them to achieve as much as the average student their age. Consequently, teachers handling such students should not be surprised if they find them scoring below the "national average."

A second criterion for a referent which is used in norm-referenced judgments is that the conditions under which the referent was obtained should not differ from the condition under which the original information was obtained. In other words, if I give my students an achievement test and give them a longer time to answer the items than the test manual calls for, the conditions under which the information was obtained and those under which the referent was obtained are not the same. Therefore, a meaningful comparison cannot be made. Most standardized tests are given under "ideal" conditions; any time that the test is administered under something less than ideal conditions, the information obtained is difficult to interpret.

A third criterion for a referent to be used in norm-referenced judgments is that it be based upon information which contains a minimal amount of error. If the referent is a score (or a value obtained from some summarization of scores) derived from a test which is unreliable, then it is not very meaningful to compare some score with that referent. The reason for this is obvious. To compare information with a highly inaccurate referent is to make judgments which will be highly inaccurate.

Finally, a referent to be used in norm-referenced judgments should be up to date. If we are going to compare an individual's performance with that of some norm group, then the information obtained from that norm group should be fairly recent. A referent can become outdated very quickly. Suppose, for example, you are trying to judge a student's achievement in a given subject matter. If you compare a student's scores obtained in April with the scores which his peers obtained in February, the interpretation would be faulty. The student who took the test in April had two more months of opportunities to achieve.

Criterion-referenced judgments.   A criterion-referenced judgment is made by comparing the information you have about an individual with some performance criteria—some descriptions of expected behavior. These criteria are usually specified in terms of behaviorally stated instructional objectives. As you will see in a moment, it is best if these objectives are arranged so as to describe various *levels* of achievement. But let us begin our discussion of criterion-referenced judgments by examining a brief explanation of this concept as it was proposed by Robert Glaser (1963).

> Underlying the concept of achievement measurement is the notion of a continuum of knowledge acquisition ranging from no proficiency at all to perfect performance. An individual's achievement level falls at some point on this continuum as indicated by the behaviors he displays during testing. The degree to which his achievement resembles desired performance at any specified level is assessed by criterion-referenced measures of achievement or proficiency. The standard against which a student's performance is compared . . . is the behavior which defines each point along the achievement continuum. [Glaser, 1963, page 520]

The first sentence in the above quote says that we can think of achievement as ranging from no proficiency at all to perfect proficiency. That seems reasonable. Picture it this way:

No   Perfect
proficiency   proficiency

Next, Glaser says that we can assume that an individual's level of achievement lies somewhere on that continuum. This also seems reasonable. Picture it this way:

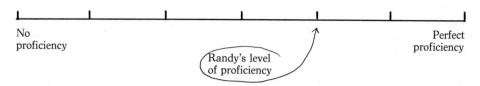

Then comes the clincher: "as indicated by the behaviors he displays during testing." You can begin to see what must be done in order to make criterion-referenced judgments. You begin with an assumed (or theoretical) continuum of achievement. Next, you observe an individual's behaviors during testing. From those behaviors you obtain an indication of his level of proficiency. In other words, you obtain the individual's level of proficiency on a continuum of achievement which has been defined by the testing situation:

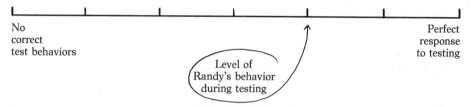

Now, you use the level of the individual's behavior during testing as an *estimate* of the individual's level of proficiency on the assumed continuum of achievement.

Notice that what has been described so far is essentially the process of making an estimative judgment. The judgment is made by *comparing* the person's level of behavior with the criterion behaviors which lie along an achievement continuum as defined by some test. At this point, no judgment was made about the level of proficiency needed before the student could move on to the achievement of other goals. That would be a predictive judgment and would require further information (e.g., what is the relationship between a specified level of proficiency and performance on the next task in the instructional sequence). Both predictive and estimative judgments can be made using a criterion-referenced approach.

Decisions about where students should be working in an instructional sequence or program (placement decisions) and what kinds of assignments should be given particular students (treatment decisions) are both aided greatly by criterion-referenced judgments.

The referent(s) used when making criterion-referenced judgments should be directly related to some statement(s) of behavior. Information about how well a student has achieved may take the form of test scores, descriptions from rating scales, etc. However, no matter what form the information takes, it should ultimately be phrased in terms of the kinds of test items or the types of behaviors which were observed. Thus you can check to see if the kinds of test items that were missed were measuring the particular behaviors which were stated to be important in the referent(s). If the referent is stated as a behavioral objective, then a comparison of how well a student performed on test items designed to measure that objective is a meaningful comparison.

The objectives represented by each referent should be clearly observable or testable. When this condition is met, then the observations we have made or the tests we have given will yield information which can in fact be meaningfully compared with these referents.

EXERCISE 3.4

1. How are self-referenced, norm-referenced, and criterion-referenced judgments alike? How are they different?
2. When constructing a test designed to help you make criterion-referenced judgments, you should base the test on clearly defined behavioral objectives. Why?

What Kind of Comparison Will Be Made?

Judgments are either estimates of present condition or predictions of future performance. When we judge our students, we are either estimating their present level of performance or predicting what their future level of performance will be. In self-referenced judgments, that level is defined in terms of how a person's performance compares to *his own* performance at a different time or under different circumstances. In norm-referenced judgments, that level is specified in terms of the level of performance achieved by *some norm group.* In criterion-referenced judgments, that level is defined in terms of some *performance criterion* (i.e., a description of the *expected* level of performance). But there are different ways to describe how a performance compares to a referent. In other words, different *kinds* of comparisons can be made.

Mastery judgments.   One kind of comparison is simply to indicate whether the observed performance falls above or below the level indicated by the referent. In this kind of comparison the referent is used as a cutoff score and the resulting judgment could be referred to as *mastery judgment.* When a person's performance is at a higher level than that indicated by the referent, he is said to have achieved mastery of the performance or skill being measured. If it is at a lower level than the level of the referent, he has not achieved mastery. With the increase in the popularity of mastery learning, we are seeing more and more of these kinds of judgments being made by teachers.

Examples of Mastery Judgments
A history teacher sets 80 percent as a cutoff score for his tests. Anyone who does not attain this level studies some more and keeps trying until he has "mastered" the material.

A science teacher includes, on each test, twenty-five items which are considered to be mastery items. Anyone *not* getting all twenty-five items correct must take that part of the test over again.

The Dolch word list is a list of basic sight vocabulary words. These are words that beginning readers must learn to recognize "on sight" without taking the time to sound them out phonetically. Many reading teachers test individuals periodically until they have mastered the entire list (only 100 percent performance is considered mastery).

When making these kinds of judgments, one must have good evidence for the fact that the cutoff score really does represent a point which separates mastery from nonmastery. What is so magical, for example, about getting 80 percent of the history test items correct? What makes 80 percent that much better a performance than 79 percent or 75 percent? In Chapter 7, the procedure for establishing a cutoff point will be discussed. At this point you are simply trying to determine whether or not you wish to make mastery judgments. There are a number of factors to consider.

First of all, mastery judgments usually imply a minimal standard of performance at a given level of performance. No one ever completely masters a subject. The question is, "Has the student mastered the material at some given level?" Some performances and skills are easier to judge in this manner than others. For example, math skills are easier to judge as having been mastered than creative writing skills. The sciences *generally* lend themselves to mastery judgment better than the arts. Furthermore, the lower levels of performance in a given area are easier to evaluate for mastery than are the upper levels. The simple basic skills of any subject matter lend themselves to mastery judgments. The complex, advanced skills do not.

Secondly, mastery judgments can be made with a self-, norm-, or criterion-referenced approach. Because the level of performance is *absolute* in criterion-referenced and relative in self- and norm-referenced approaches, a criterion-referenced approach is normally best for making mastery judgments. It may make sense in some cases to say that a student has mastered a skill when he surpasses the average performance of some norm group (e.g., "You will have mastered penmanship when you surpass the average performance of third graders."). However, it usually makes more sense to say that a student has mastered a skill when his performance surpasses the performance as described by some specified criterion (e.g., "You will have mastered penmanship when your performance surpasses that of the examples of page 17 of your penmanship book.").

Finally, mastery judgments should be made when meaningful decisions rest upon whether or not some level of performance has been mastered. If mastery at one level of performance is *clearly prerequisite* to performance at the next-higher level, mastery judgments are important. There are, of course, many instructional decisions which rest upon mastery judgments. Whenever these kinds of decisions are called for, mastery judgments should be made (and they should probably be criterion-referenced).

Deviation Judgments. In mastery judgments, we indicate whether an observed performance falls above or below some referent which has been designated as a cutoff point. In deviation judgments, we indicate *how far* an observed score *deviates* from some referent which has been chosen as a reference point.

Frequently, we are concerned about how far a student has progressed toward mastery. Sometimes we are concerned about how far a student has progressed *beyond mastery.* This kind of judgment can be made by setting up an achievement continuum, devising a criterion-referenced test measuring each point along that continuum, and then finding out what level of performance the student has reached—that is, how far he deviates from either end of that continuum or how far he deviates from some point on the continuum called mastery.

When selection decisions must be made, we are concerned about how far a student's performance deviates from the performance of his peers. This can be done by making a norm-referenced judgment in terms of some deviation score (e.g., performed better than 80 percent of his peers).

Deviation judgments are also valuable when trying to indicate how much a student has gained over some period of time. You will recognize this as a deviation judgment made with a self-referenced approach.

Three Factors Important in Forming Judgments

By way of review, let us examine once again the three factors which distinguish one type of judgment from another. The first factor could be called a *time factor.* Estimates are distinguished from predictions on the basis of time: estimates judge *present* (or past) performance and predictions judge *future* performance.

The second factor we considered was the type of referent used. Is the referent based upon information about the person being judged? Then it is a self-referenced judgment. Is the referent based upon information about persons similar to the one being judged? Then it is a norm-referenced judgment. Is the referent based upon performance criteria? Then it is a criterion-referenced judgment.

The third factor which distinguishes one type of judgment from another is the type of comparison made. If the referent is used as a cutoff score, a mastery judgment is being formed. If the deviation from the referent is determined along a scale or continuum, a deviation judgment is being formed.

Each of these three factors can be identified in any judgment. Thus it is possible, for example, to form estimates which are norm-referenced mastery judgments; predictions which are norm-referenced mastery judgments; estimates which are criterion-referenced mastery judgments; etc. Figure 3.2 illustrates the twelve types of judgments which can be formed when these three factors are considered.

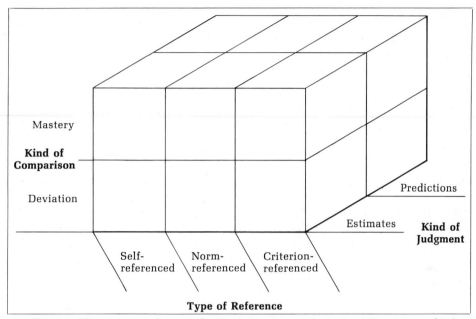

FIGURE 3.2. Three important factors in forming judgments and the twelve different types of judgments which result.

EXERCISE 3.5

Read each of the judgments listed below. Then decide if it is:
   a. An estimate or a prediction
   b. Self-referenced, norm-referenced, or criterion-referenced
   c. a mastery judgment or a deviation judgment
1. Jerry reads better than half of the kids in his class.
2. Peter will make more progress now that he has glasses.
3. George has mastered the ability to recite the times tables without error (through 12 × 12).
4. Mary finally mastered the art of singing on key. She now sings on key as often as the other girls in her section.
5. Sally will do above-average work in school.
6. The whole class can now correctly prepare a slide for use on the microscope.

SUMMARY

1. It is important to know, *before* you set out to obtain information, how you plan on using it.
2. The need for information usually begins as a question in the mind of the teacher. If the question asks what action should be taken, a decision is being called for. If the question asks about the past, present, or future condition of individuals, a judgment is being called for.

3. When describing decisions to be made, you should seek to answer the following questions: *(a)* What is the object of the decision? *(b)* What kind of action is to be taken? *(c)* When will the decision be made? *(d)* What is the purpose of the decision? *(e)* Where do the priorities lie? and *(f)* How important are the decisions?

4. The major types of decisions are defined by the action to be taken. They are *(a)* selection decisions, *(b)* placement decisions, and *(c)* treatment decisions.

5. The importance of decisions is determined by using the following criteria: *(a)* reversibility, *(b)* number of persons affected, *(c)* length of time the effect will last, and *(d)* the importance of the learning outcomes involved.

6. A referent is that which is referred to in making judgments and takes the form of a score, a value, or a description.

7. The referent in self-referenced judgments is a person's own performance at a different time or on a different task.

8. The referent in norm-referenced judgments is the performance of some norm group.

9. The referent in criterion-referenced judgments is a description of expected or desired performance. It takes the form of a behavioral objective or a group of behavioral objectives arranged as an achievement continuum.

10. Mastery judgments compare an individual's performance with a cutoff point. Performance which exceeds that defined by the cutoff point is considered mastery. Performance which is below the level defined by the cutoff point is considered nonmastery.

11. Deviation judgments place a value on a person's performance in terms of how far it deviates from either end of some continuum of performance, how far it deviates from the performance of others, or how far it deviates from mastery.

References

Bloom, Benjamin S., Thomas J. Hastings, and George F. Madaus: *Handbook on Formative and Summative Evaluation of Student Learning,* McGraw-Hill Book Company, New York, 1971

Glaser, Robert: "Instructional Technology and the Measurement of Learning Outcomes — Some Questions," *American Psychologist,* vol. 18, pp. 519–521, 1963.

Schriven, M.: "The Methodology of Evaluation," *American Educational Research Association Monograph Series on Curriculum Evaluation, no. 1,* Rand McNally and Company, Skokie, Ill., 1967.

Suggested Readings

The following references deal with decision making:

Griffiths, Daniel E.: "A Taxonomy Based on Decision-Making," in Daniel E. Griffiths (ed.), *Developing Taxonomies of Organizational Behavior in Educational Administration,* Rand McNally and Company, Chicago, 1969.

Mehrens, William A., and Irvin J. Lehmann: *Measurement and Evaluation in Education and Psychology,* Holt, Rinehart and Winston, Inc., New York, 1973, chap. 1.

Stufflebeam, D. I., W. A. Foley, W. J. Gephart, E. G. Guba, R. I. Hammond, H. O. Merriman, and M. M. Provus: *Educational Evaluation and Decision Making.* F. E. Peacock Publishers, Inc., Itasca, Ill., 1971.

The following references on criterion-referenced measurement and mastery learning should be helpful resources to anyone interested in these very current topics:

Block, J. H. (ed.): *Mastery Learning: Theory and Practice,* Holt, Rinehart and Winston, New York, 1971.

Bloom, Benjamin S.: "Learning for Mastery," *Evaluation Comment,* Center for the Study of Evaluation, vol. 1, no. 2, 1968.

Gronlund, N. E.: *Preparing Criterion-Referenced Tests for Classroom Instruction.* The Macmillan Company, New York, 1973.

Popham, James W. (ed.): *Criterion-Referenced Measurement—An Introduction.* Educational Technology Publications, Englewood Cliffs, N.J., 1971.

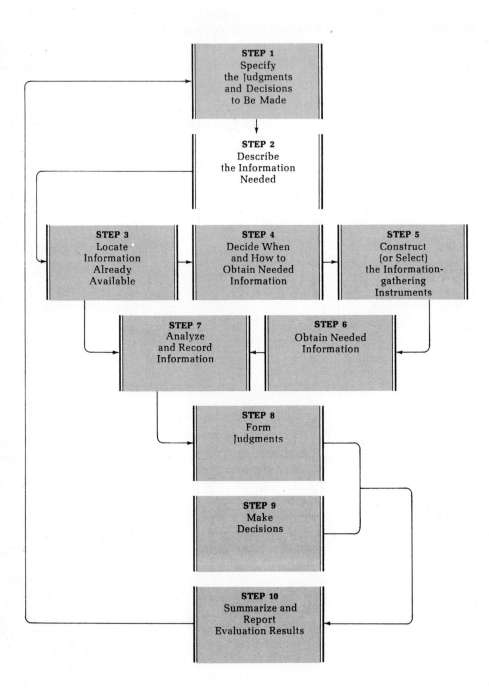

| STEP 1 Specify the Judgments and Decisions to Be Made |
| STEP 2 Describe the Information Needed |

| STEP 3 Locate Information Already Available | STEP 4 Decide When and How to Obtain Needed Information | STEP 5 Construct (or Select) the Information-gathering Instruments |

| STEP 7 Analyze and Record Information | STEP 6 Obtain Needed Information |

| STEP 8 Form Judgments |

| STEP 9 Make Decisions |

| STEP 10 Summarize and Report Evaluation Results |

CHAPTER 4

Describing the Needed Information

This chapter explains the second step in the evaluation process: "Describe the needed information." The more clearly you can describe information, the more easily you will be able to make the appropriate preparations for obtaining it. In order to locate needed information that is already available, you must know what kind of information you are looking for. In order to decide on the best time, place, and method for obtaining information, you need to know what the needed information is like. In order to construct valid information-gathering instruments, you must have a precise description of the information that those instruments should provide. There are at least four different ways to describe information. Each method provides you with a slightly different but equally useful description of evaluative information. This chapter has been written to help you learn to use all four methods.

87

This chapter should help you to

1. Describe the important dimensions of any needed information by answering four simple questions.
2. Develop a list of instructional goals which have been stated in observable terms.
3. Construct a table of specifications which could be used as a guide to test construction.
4. Construct an achievement continuum which would define the levels of attainment.

PROCEDURE 1: DESCRIBE THE IMPORTANT DIMENSIONS OF THE NEEDED INFORMATION

The answers to the following four questions will help you in the selection, construction, and use of tests and other information-gathering techniques:

1. What is the information about?
2. What kind of behavior is to be observed?
3. How specific must the information be?
4. How accurate must the information be?

What Is the Information About?

This question can be answered most easily by referring to your answer to the earlier question "Who or what is the object of the judgments and decisions you anticipate making?" Sometimes we need information about textbooks, filmstrips, a teaching method, an assignment—"things" instead of people. Information about the content, cost, length, and availability of "things" is important information in judging their value.

How much does the new English literature series cost? What pieces of literature are included? What is included in the teachers' manuals? These would be important questions to ask when trying to judge the value of a series of textbooks.

However, even more important than information about the books themselves would be information about students' responses to the books. How easy are the books for students to read? Are the pieces of literature appealing to the students who will be reading them? How well do students learn from these books? What kind of knowledge, skills, and interests will students who read these books develop? Most of the information we need in educational evaluation is information about responses people make to their environment. There are a number of ways to categorize human behavior. In particular, we are interested in the ways to classify learning behaviors.

What Kind of Behavior Is to Be Observed?

In recent years a number of schemes have been developed for classifying behavior. These have proved to be particularly valuable for determining the *kind* and *level* of learning we might expect from our students. As you study these schemes, remember that they were developed as models. Theoretically, any learned behavior should fit into one or more of these schemes. It turns out, however, that it is easier to think of examples of behaviors to fit each category than it is to begin with a behavior and try to fit it into one of the categories. There is some disagreement, for example, among teachers when they try to categorize a given behavior (Bloom, 1971, page 120). The real value of attempting to categorize behaviors lies in the fact that when you are finished, you have a careful description of the behavior you are interested in obtaining information about. That description should be invaluable in the construction and/or selection of an information-gathering technique. Even if you do not agree completely with a fellow teacher on how to categorize a given behavior, your categorization will help you to see more clearly what it is you are trying to evaluate.

A taxonomy of educational goals. A very popular scheme for classifying behaviors resulted from the efforts of a team of experts headed by Benjamin Bloom. In the early 1950s these educators set out to classify educational goals. They conceived of a taxonomy having three major domains: cognitive, affective, and psychomotor. The taxonomy of the cognitive domain was published in 1956 (Bloom, 1956). In 1964, the affective domain was completed (Krathwohl et al., 1964). Although Bloom and his colleagues have not yet developed a taxonomy of the psychomotor domain, one was developed by Simpson (1966). These various taxonomies have been designed to aid educators in classifying educational goals. They are, in fact, taxonomies of human behaviors and can be useful in classifying the kinds of responses people make to their environment. Condensed versions of the cognitive, affective, and psychomotor domains are given below.

Cognitive Domain

Knowledge. At the lowest level of the cognitive domain are goals that Bloom and others have called the knowledge level. This is the level of memorization of facts, and the goals which measure this level call for the student to be able to list, to recall, or to recognize facts that have been given. Examples of goals at this level would be the recall of the important dates of the Civil War, the ability to say the multiplication tables, and the ability to recognize the Presidents by name when given their pictures.

Comprehension. The next-highest cognitive goal is comprehension. At this level the student is able not only to parrot information that has been given but also to demonstrate that he understands that information. Perhaps the easiest way to measure whether or not this understanding occurs is to ask the student to restate the information "in his own words." Sometimes comprehension can be measured by asking the student to illustrate the information he has learned using examples which have not been used in the classroom or the text-book.

Application. The next-highest level in the cognitive domain is that of application. At this level the student must not only understand the facts which he has been called upon to learn but also be able to apply them to a new situation. For example, it is one thing for a student to memorize the rule that "When two vowels go a-walking, the first does the talking." It is something else to be able to understand that rule in such a way that he can rephrase it in his own words. It is still a higher level of complexity when the student is capable of *applying* that rule to a new situation. For example, one might call upon the student to sound out the word *heat,* using the rule which he has just learned. If the student has never been taught the word *heat* before, then this would be a good test of the application level. There are a number of situations in the classroom where rules are taught and the students are expected to be able to apply these rules in problem-solving situations. Often, when we test for this kind of knowledge, however, we simply test at the memorization level or at best at the comprehension level. If we simply ask a student to memorize the rule or event and give it back to us in his own words, we have still not tested his ability to apply that rule.

Analysis. The next level in this taxonomy of the cognitive domain is the analysis level. At this level the student is called upon to analyze the information he has received into its component parts. This is the kind of learning we expect of our students when we ask them to take a poem and break it down into its grammatical elements or into its logical parts. Other examples of this kind of behavior are the analysis of a chemical compound into its separate elements, the analysis of a newspaper article by separating it into fact and opinion, or the analysis of a speech into its major topics and subtopics.

Synthesis. A still higher level of cognitive behavior is exhibited when someone can combine a number of bits of information, synthesizing them into a new whole. This level of cognitive functioning allows the student to be able to read a number of stories about the Civil War and synthesize the facts from them into a set of opinions which he holds about war and its causes. Whenever someone synthesizes information from a variety of sources and reaches conclusions of his own, he is operating at this high level of the cognitive domain. According to Bloom and his colleagues, there is only one level of cognitive functioning which is higher than the synthesis level.

Evaluation. When a person has reached this level in cognitive functioning, he is able to make some evaluation about a given work, a piece of information, a story, a work of art, etc. To be able to analyze a poem into its component parts (analysis level) is a lower order skill than being able to take all the bits of information, such as the affective tones and qualities of a poem, and synthesize these into some fuller understanding of the poem (synthesis level). However, a still higher level of cognitive functioning is reached when the student is finally able to take all this information and make a value judgment about the poem. When a person is called upon to evaluate a piece of work cognitively, he is operating at the uppermost level of the cognitive domain.

Affective Domain

Receiving (attending).   This lowest level of the affective domain is characterized as a sensitivity to certain phenomena and stimuli. We first become aware of a certain stimulus, then we become willing to attend to it. Finally, we exercise control as we select what we attend to.

Responding.   At this level a person is *actively* attending. We would say of a student who has reached this level, "He is showing an interest in. . . ."

Valuing.   One step beyond an expression of interest is to actually feel that a thing, phenomenon, or behavior has worth. This level is characterized by a positive attitude toward and the placing a value upon.

Organization.   A learner begins to value many things in greater or lesser degrees. As he does so he begins to develop a *system* of values. Organizing values into a system characterizes this high level of affective behavior.

Characterization by a value or a value complex.   Organization of values has occurred. A system of values has been internalized. Now at this highest level, a person's behavior "gives him away." He is characterized by some internalized value or system of values. He acts according to what he believes.

Psychomotor Domain

Perception.   The first step in learning to perform a motor act is to become aware of what that act involves. You must perceive the objects, qualities, or relations which exist.

Set.   This second level is like the second step in the child's "get ready, get set, go" chant. A person completes this level when he is mentally, physically, and emotionally ready to perform the motor act under consideration.

Guided response.   At this level, the person is beginning to learn the motor skill. He goes through the motions under the guidance of someone else. Imitation and trial-and-error are the two major subcategories at this level.

Mechanism.   The motor response has been learned and now, at this level, becomes habitual. The learner experiences a degree of confidence and, although he may not have reached perfection, his execution could be considered skillful.

Complex overt response.   This is the level of the polished performer. Here the individual can perform complex movement patterns. The performance is smooth and efficient. There is little wasted time or energy. The person going through this stage resolves any uncertainties until a smooth performance is automatic.

Gagné's Model of Levels of Learning

Another popular taxonomy of learning has been proposed by Gagné (1970). A brief and somewhat simplified description of Gagné's taxonomy follows. The reader is urged to read the original sources referred to at the end of this chapter for a fuller understanding of the kinds of learning proposed by Gagné. This brief explanation of Gagné's model is offered so that you might see the possibility of using his scheme as a way of classifying the kind of information which you may wish to evaluate. This scheme, like Bloom's taxonomy of the cognitive domain, will be particularly useful when evaluating learning which is primarily cognitive as opposed to affective or psychomotor. Gagné distinguishes eight different types of learning, as follows:

1. **Signal learning.**   The individual responds in a diffuse, general way to a signal.
Example: Children learn to quiet down when the teacher raises her hand.
2. **Stimulus-response learning.**   The learner acquires an association between a stimulus and a precise response.
Example: Imitation of vocal sounds.
3. **Motor chaining.**   The learner acquires a chain of two or more stimulus-response connections.
Example: Learning to print the letters of the alphabet.
4. **Verbal association.**   Learning verbal chains.
Example: Learning the letters of the alphabet in order.
5. **Discrimination learning.**   The learner is able to correctly identify each of two or more highly similar stimuli.
Example: Learning to distinguish between blue and green, or the letters *b* and *d.*
6. **Concept learning.**   The learner makes a common response to two or more very different stimuli which belong to the same class.
Example: Classifying plants, forms of government, types of laws, etc.
7. **Rule learning.**   The learner can apply a rule to a new situation.
Example: Phonetic rules, spelling rules, rules of mathematical relations, etc.
8. **Problem solving.**   The learner combines two or more previously acquired rules to form a new capability.
Example: Solving proofs for geometric theorems.

Other Ways to Classify Behavior

Maximum versus typical performance.   A common way to classify standardized tests is by dividing them into two main groups: those that yield information about a person's maximum performance and those that yield information about a person's typical performance. The goal of a maximum performance test is to obtain information about how well a person *can* do under ideal conditions. The testing conditions are carefully controlled and the student is told "do your best." Measures of achievement and aptitude exemplify maximum performance tests. Personality measures, interest inventories, and attitude scales, on the other hand, yield typical performance information. These measures are designed to tell us what a person typically *does* do rather than what he can do. The type of information-gathering instrument we select, the way we use that instrument, and the interpretation we make of the results all depend, in part, on whether we are interested in information about a person's maximum or his typical performance.

Expected versus unexpected learning outcomes.   Often, the task of educational evaluation turns out to be a task of answering questions like the following:

What should be learned?

Which students are ready to learn?

What will be the most appropriate teaching and learning activities?

What materials would cause learning to occur most rapidly?

How much have the students learned?

Which skills can effectively be taught next?

Teachers make more judgments and decisions about the outcomes of learning than they do about anything else. The above list of questions simply serves to illustrate that fact. Anything that can be done to describe the outcomes of learning clearly will be extremely useful in deciding how to find out whether or not the learning occurred. Behavioral objectives stated in observable terms serve as precise statements of the kind of information needed to make judgments and decisions about learning outcomes. The author hopes that that will become quite evident by the time you have finished reading this section. For now, it is important for you to realize that learning outcomes can, and often should be, specifically stated.

However, a distinction should be made between *expected* and *unexpected* learning outcomes. Statements of educational goals specify what it is that the students are expected to learn. Surely this is important information when you are attempting to evaluate a student's progress, a teacher's effectiveness, or a program's value. Equally important is information about unexpected outcomes. It is important to know whether or not the students in a high school biology class acquired the knowledge and learned the skills the teacher expected them to learn. It is also valuable to know whether or not the students gained any knowledge or skills beyond what the teacher expected. Did any of the students turn to outside resources in the process of doing assignments and learn more from these sources? Were the experiments exciting enough to some of the students that they went beyond them to experiments of their own at home? These kinds of unexpected outcomes are pleasant surprises when they occur.

Not so pleasant, yet just as important to find out about, are the possible negative side-effects of learning. For example, it would be valuable, though disconcerting, to find out that all your fifth graders learned how to read a map perfectly but in the process came to hate geography! It would also be important to know that although the marching band members learned their march routines to perfection, they sacrificed a great deal in both technique and quality of tone.

How Specific Must the Information Be?

How specific should evaluative information be? This question can be answered best by referring to the judgments and decisions for which the information will be used. Sometimes we may have very specific decisions in mind when we are obtaining information. An algebra teacher wants to know which principles his students have mastered so he can decide on the next set of assignments.

A physical education teacher must select fourteen students to participate in a balance act; he needs information about how well his students can perform specific balancing skills. A kindergarten teacher tries to find out which vowel sounds her students produce incorrectly so that she can provide the appropriate corrective exercises.

On other occasions, we may have only a general decision area in mind when we obtain information. Then, the information we obtain will of necessity be general, perhaps useful for a number of related judgments and decisions.

How Accurate Must the Information Be?

Generally speaking, as the accuracy of the needed information increases, so does the cost of obtaining that information. It takes extended planning, skillful construction of the information-gathering techniques, and careful use of those techniques to obtain highly accurate information.

It will be valuable for you to weigh your estimate of how accurate the information must be against the cost of obtaining information which is that accurate. The more important decisions may require the most accurate information possible, no matter what the cost. For some less important decisions you may decide to sacrifice some accuracy because you have limited time or funds.

EXERCISE 4.1

Review the concepts you just read by answering the following questions:

1. What four questions should be answered in any attempt to describe the information needed for evaluation?
2. What are the three major domains in the taxonomy of Bloom et al.?
3. Although most of the information we obtain will be about expected learning outcomes, sometimes the _____ outcomes are also important.
4. As the accuracy or information increases, so does _____.
5. What is the value of carefully describing the information needed for evaluation?

PROCEDURE 2: DEVELOP A LIST OF INSTRUCTIONAL GOALS

This section is devoted to the procedures for clearly specifying anticipated learning outcomes in observable terms.

There has been much debate over the value of goals which state learning outcomes in observable terms.[1] Consequently, let us look briefly at the major issues in this debate before dealing with the procedures for writing such goals.

---

[1] Several articles dealing with this debate are referenced in the bibliography at the end of this chapter.

The Value of Instructional Goals

A number of worthwhile books, articles, and pamphlets have been written describing instructional goals. The terminology varies from author to author. Some refer to learning outcomes, others to behavioral objectives, and still others to instructional goals. In each case the idea is the same: decide where you want your students to be and what you want them to be able to do as a result of particular learning activities. Next, describe those student behaviors in explicit, observable terms. Take, for example, one of the goals of this chapter:

> By the time you have finished studying this chapter, you should be able to list several ways in which instructional goals can be used by the classroom teacher.

This example can be used to illustrate a number of important aspects of instructional goals. First of all, it does specify what behavior is expected: *"to list."* Secondly, it describes the subject matter content: *"ways in which goals can be used by the teacher."* These two elements are virtually always found in well-defined statements of anticipated learning outcomes. Their importance cannot be overemphasized, and we will discuss them more thoroughly later. Notice, however, that the above example defines more than the student behavior and the subject matter content. In this goal, a time element is stated: *"by the time you finish studying this section."* Whether stated explicit or not, statements of instructional goals always presuppose some time element. Therefore many instructional goals begin with the following kind of phrase: "By the end of this unit," "By the end of this semester," or "By the time the students finish this six-week marking period they will be expected to. . . ." These statements reflect the fact that goals indicate not only what is to be expected of the students but also how *soon* it can be expected of them.

Technically, more than time alone is involved in this concept. There is not only the implication that a certain time will elapse between where the student now is and where we would like him to be but there is also the implication that the student must engage in certain activities in order to reach those goals. Consequently, we say that upon completion of reading a certain chapter, having seen a particular film, or having completed a given learning package, the student is expected to exhibit certain changes in behavior.

As soon as we introduce the notion of experiences (either formal or informal) which must occur before goals can be reached, we must also introduce the notion of sequence. It should be recognized rather early in the development of instructional goals that certain goals can be met satisfactorily only if a number of prerequisite goals have been accomplished. This notion, of course, leads us to the establishment of priorities. But at this point, the task of establishing useful goals becomes time-consuming and difficult, and we might well ask: "Do these goals need to be specified in the manner in which many of the experts are now suggesting? Must goals be explicitly stated? Is the complexity of the process overpowering? Is it worth the effort?"

Actually, the complexity of the process of stating goals in observable terms is only one of a number of "objections to objectives." We will discuss each of the major objections briefly and then attempt to demonstrate that, despite these objections, well-defined goals can be useful to the classroom teacher.

Objections to educational objectives.   Defining goals in observable terms can become a rather complex, time-consuming activity. However, the really important question is whether or not it is worth it. There is increasing evidence to indicate that better instruction can result from the use of objectives (see, for example, McNeil's study of student teachers, 1967). Furthermore, carefully specified goals for small educational units have made possible some rather valuable innovations in evaluation procedures. Because specific learning outcomes can be defined, programmed instruction and individualized study programs can be efficiently evaluated. Formative evaluation and criterion-referenced measurement are workable concepts *because* both short-term and long-range goals can be specified in observable terms.

It is especially interesting to note that individualized learning programs are developed and evaluated on the basis of goals which are established for each program. This fact is interesting because one of the major objections to behavioral objectives is that they hamper the process of individualizing instruction. It is argued that the educational goals should differ for each student because of the differences in interests, ability, past experiences, etc. Although it is true that all individuals may not be striving for the same short-term goals at the same time, it is also true that most long-range goals are appropriate for all students (with the possible exception of certain exceptional children). For example, in a reading readiness program there are a number of learning outcomes which we expect of all pupils before they begin a formalized reading program. The readiness program is designed, among other things, to help the child learn to (1) identify each letter of the alphabet when he sees it and be able to produce its name and (2) differentiate among the various short and long vowel sounds when heard in isolation and in context. These and other goals are the same for all the pupils. The individual differences become important in the kinds of activities each pupil engages in as he attempts to reach the goals. When the goals are clearly established, then the teacher can devise numerous methods for helping the pupils reach them. Then too, the teacher can devise ways to find out if and when an individual has reached them.

Closely related to the above objection is the one which states that behavioral objectives curtail spontaneity. Some critics (e.g., Atkin, 1968) argue that if a teacher has zeroed in on the accomplishment of certain goals, he will not be able to make use of the unplanned but powerfully potential learning situations which arise spontaneously from the classroom activities. As students we used to call this "getting the teacher sidetracked." As teachers, we call it "capitalizing on the interests of the moment." If a teacher has clear-cut goals in mind, he might very well "capitalize" on those spontaneous activities which would serve as alternate paths to the goals. However, without clear-cut goals, these spontaneous situations may very well turn out to be nothing more than sidetracks—sidetracks where significant learning may or may not occur. Clearly defined goals should not keep the teacher from "sidetracking," but they should help him to use the sidetrack more efficiently for accomplishing worthwhile goals.

It is important for teachers to be aware of the limitations of establishing goals and, even more important, they should be careful not to misuse them. A very common misuse of instructional goals is the practice of writing goals which are trivial (note that this is also a common misuse of objective tests). Trivial learning outcomes are generally much easier to phrase in observable terms than are some of the more important outcomes. "To list in writing the causes of the Civil War" comes off the pen fairly easy. To write an observable behavior for the following goal is much more difficult: "To understand the social, economic, and political factors which bring about civil war." One such behavior might be: "when given descriptions of the social, economic, and political factors at work in two different pseudo-countries, the student should be able to identify the country most likely to experience a civil war in the next five years."

Obviously, a number of behaviors might be considered as indicants of an understanding of the factors causing civil war. Some would be better indicators than others. For purposes of instruction as well as evaluation, all the behaviors characteristic of persons who have reached a goal need not be specified. All that is needed are enough observable behaviors so that a judgment can be made as to whether or not the goal has been reached.

Uses of Instructional Goals

There are a number of ways in which instructional goals can be used. They can be used to serve instruction and learning as well as evaluation. These practical uses for instructional goals make them "worth the effort."

Using goals in lesson planning.   There are numerous ways in which clearly defined goals can be used by the teachers in developing lesson plans. For example, they can be helpful when selecting textbooks, producing visual aids, determining the most effective sequence of learning activities, and deciding which assignments suggested by the teacher's manual would be most appropriate.

Using goals in evaluation.   Goals are helpful in selecting tests, constructing tests and other evaluation techniques, obtaining information, and using that information to make judgments and decisions.

Clearly defined goals can also be valuable when scheduling information-gathering sessions. For example, a list of goals can be used to determine *when* information is to be gathered. Tests should be given when the goals are to be reached (e.g., "at the end of this unit").

The kinds of judgments we make and the criteria we use for making those judgments are both determined in part by the goals we have established. For example, the goals a first grade teacher has set for reading are important to the success of the pupils in the second grade reading program. Learning the alphabet is a goal which is prerequisite to using an index or a dictionary. Phonetic rules must be learned *before* independent reading can become a reality.

Using goals to summarize and report evaluation results. The instructional goals which you establish for your students can serve as extremely useful guides when you establish a plan for reporting information. It is certainly helpful to parents to get a list of goals which their child has reached. A number of examples of this type of reporting are given in Chapter 9.

Goals are useful to the learner. Because educational goals are extremely useful as guides to the teacher in developing teaching plans and evaluation plans, it is easy to forget that these goals will also be useful to the students when they are deciding how to study. If we expect a student to be able to meet the goals we have set for him, we ought at least to put those goals before him. High school teachers and junior high school teachers can type up these goals and hand them out to their students. If a student has a set of goals before him as he studies, he can plan his studying accordingly. If the goals call for the application of knowledge and the transfer of knowledge to new situations, the student can establish a learning strategy in which he tries to think of situations where he can apply the knowledge he is acquiring. If, on the other hand, the goals are to memorize information or make associations between two different kinds of information, he can readjust his study techniques. He might spend more time simply repeating over and over or perhaps establishing mnemonic devices to help him recall.

Elementary school pupils can also use instructional goals effectively. In fact, even first graders and kindergarteners can understand the idea that there are certain goals that they are expected to reach. It would be helpful, therefore, to put these goals before them in any way possible. The elementary school children who are old enough to read could also be given mimeographed sheets containing the goals. However, it should be remembered that these younger children cannot keep large numbers of goals in mind at one given time. Neither can they work toward goals over a long period of time. Therefore they must be presented with goals on a short-term basis. They must be given goals which can be reached rather quickly.

One of the ways to keep goals before elementary school children is to place the goals on the blackboard. Goals for the week can be placed alongside those for the day. As the students take part in each of the various learning activities for the day, the teacher can call attention to the goal which they are striving for through the particular experience they are engaged in. For example, if the teacher has set as a goal of the week that the students should be able to learn fifteen new vocabulary words in their reading series, he puts this on the blackboard for them to see. Then, each day, he will also write on the board, "Today we will learn the following new words: . . . ." As the students take part in the reading activities, they will understand that the reason they are doing that, among other things, is to learn those new words. Furthermore, on the blackboard or on some chart in the room, the teacher might state long-term goals such as: "By the end of the first term we will be able to read with expression." Now as the children come to reading class the teacher may from time to time announce to his students something like the following: "Today we are going to practice more on reading for expression so that we can reach the goal we have set for ourselves by the end of the semester. We are particularly interested in learning to pause when we see a comma. So let's remember to concentrate on this during our lesson today."

Sometimes goals can best be communicated to the students orally, but they will need to be stated over and over as a reminder of what is expected. This, of course, is especially true when we have very young children who cannot read.

EXERCISE 4.2

It will be of help to you to remember what you just read if you summarize the pros and cons of educational objectives. List the "objections to objectives," then the answers to those objections, and finally the major uses of objectives (instructional goals).

DEVELOPING A LIST OF INSTRUCTIONAL GOALS

We have already indicated that developing a list of well-defined goals is somewhat time-consuming. Nevertheless, the value of these goals to the teacher, the evaluator, and the learner make it worth the effort. Furthermore, there are a number of things which can make the task easier. First of all there are an increasing number of sources where teachers can locate goals which are already stated in observable terms. The teacher can select goals from these sources which seem to fit his particular situation. A particularly valuable source of well-defined goals is the behavioral objective exchange directed by James Popham.[2] By contributing observable objectives to the exchange, you become eligible to withdraw objectives which may suit your needs. There are also a number of sources where teachers can find goals that can be used if they are rewritten to conform to the standards set down in the next section of this chapter. Two of the most common of these sources are the course syllabi supplied by the school and the teacher's manuals accompanying the subject matter textbooks. Other sources include teacher magazines, subject matter journals, and college textbooks used in "methods" courses.

Secondly, it must be realized that the goals for a full year do not have to be developed all at once. A well-organized teacher who has a well-developed set of goals, a complete set of audiovisual aids and carefully written test items is a teacher who has worked a number of years to develop these. Good teaching aids,

[2] W. James Popham, "The Instructional Objectives Exchange: New Support for Criterion-Referenced Instruction," *Phi Delta Kappan,* 1970, vol. 52, no. 3, pp. 174–175.

good time-saving devices, and good instructional goals all take time to develop. Each year some of the work is done, each year revisions are made. Gradually, over a period of two or three years, the beginning teacher becomes an experienced teacher. Part of the value of that experience is that he has been able to develop a number of classroom tools which aid him in teaching and evaluating.

Finally, it is often possible and valuable for groups of teachers to cooperate in the development of a usable list of objectives. All the teachers teaching in the same grade or teaching the same subject might profitably combine their efforts. This could lead to greater agreement from teacher to teacher within a given grade. Furthermore, a better sequencing of goals across grades, within a given subject matter, could result from this combining of efforts.

Although teachers need not personally write all their goals, they should be able to develop their own lists of goals—"borrowing" where applicable, rewriting where necessary, and writing their own when needed.

Teachers should be able to:

1. Identify a well-defined, observable goal and evaluate its usefulness to their own situation.
2. Recognize a poorly written goal and rewrite it to meet the criteria of a well-defined goal.
3. Write a well-defined goal of their own.

The next three sections are designed to help you attain these skills. Reading this material should give you the knowhow. Practicing now, and again when you teach, will turn this knowhow into skill.

Identifying Well-defined Goals

There are certain characteristics which make well-defined goals easy to identify. If a goal is to be a useful classroom goal, it should have the characteristics outlined below.

A useful classroom goal should:

1. Be Student-oriented
2. Describe a learning outcome
3. Be explicit
4. Be observable

Well-defined goals are student-oriented. To say that goals should be student-oriented means that the emphasis must be upon what the *student* is expected to do and not on what the teacher will do.

Examples of Well-defined Goals

Pupils should be able to say the names of the vowels and produce the short and long sounds of each. Pupils should be able to write down their observations of a simple experiment, stating what was done and what happened. *Students* sould be able to solve long division problems using at least two different methods.

Sometimes teachers formulate goals which emphasize what the teacher is expected to do. These teacher-oriented goals are of limited value and should be avoided. In trying to help his pupils obtain the first goal in the above examples, a teacher might "play a record which introduces the vowels by name, giving examples of the long and short sounds each makes." Although this may be a worthwhile activity, it should be thought of as only one teacher activity which could help the pupils reach an important goal.

Well-defined goals describe a learning outcome. Remember, we are interested in goals, not experiences or activities. To say that the students "will practice their multiplication tables" or "write their spelling words ten times" is *not* to have specified learning outcomes. Rather, these are activities designed to help the student reach some goals. Yes, they are student-oriented activities, but they are not outcomes. Goals, specifying outcomes which might result from the above activities, could be worded this way:

Examples of Goals Describing Learning Outcomes

When presented the multiplication facts (through 10×10) on flash cards, students should be able to respond to each fact correctly within five seconds. Students will be able to spell without error at least 90 percent of the words in their spelling book.

Well-defined goals are explicit. In order to serve its intended purpose, a goal should be clearly, unambiguously stated, indicating quite specifically what the student is expected to be able to do.

Examples of Explicit Goals

The third grade pupils should be able to write a personal letter, correctly placing the heading, the greeting, the body, the closing, and the signature.

The second graders should be able to list at least three ways in which all neighborhoods are alike and four ways in which neighborhoods can differ.

By the time the students finish the semester of office practice, they should be able to describe in a sentence or two each of the required and optional parts of a business letter.

Note that each of the above examples contains a very explicit verb (to write, to place correctly, to list, to describe) and some object of the verb (a letter, the heading, ways in which neighborhoods differ, the parts of a business letter). These two aspects of goals help to make them explicit—look for them in any goals you might consider.

Examples of Educational Goals Ranging from Very General to Very Specific

Students should be able to read with understanding.   Very general

When given a story to read, students should be able to answer questions about the content of the story.

When given a short story, students should be able to identify the passages which describe the personality traits of the main characters.   Somewhat specific

Students should be able to identify the passages which describe the personality traits of the main character in *Catcher in the Rye.*

Students should be able to identify at least five passages from *Catcher in the Rye* which illustrate Holden's lack of confidence in himself.

Students should be able to recognize the five passages (cited in handout no. 3) which illustrate Holden's lack of confidence in himself.   Highly specific

Notice that the best goals in these examples lie somewhere in the middle of the continuum. When goals become too specific, they lose much of their value as a guide to study and become little more than test questions to be answered. Goals which are too specific generally encourage poor study habits. Students will tend to learn enough to meet the specific goal but not enough to meet the more general ability implied in the specific goal. The value of getting students to be able to identify passages from *Catcher in the Rye* which illustrate descriptions of personality traits lies in the fact that this ability will transfer to other short stories as well.

Well-defined goals depict observable behaviors. This characteristic of instructional goals is what makes them translatable into test items. It is virtually impossible to determine whether or not a student has reached a goal unless the behavior which that goal calls for is observable. The evaluation of learning outcomes hinges upon the fact that those outcomes can be observed. It was just stated that a goal should contain a verb and an object of the verb. Now another requirement is being added: The verb must describe an observable action. Compare the verbs in Table 4.1 with those in 4.2. The verbs in both tables describe student behaviors. However, those in the Table 4.1 are vague and unobservable. How can one observe knowing, appreciating, or thinking? On the other hand, the verbs in Table 4.2 describe observable behaviors or at least behaviors which yield observable products.

There are innumerable processes and problem-solving skills which cannot be *directly* observed but which produce end products that *can* be observed. We may not be able to see, for example, what goes on in the mind of the student who is able to solve an algebraic equation. However, we can see the solution and decide whether or not it is correct. We may not be able to measure directly the creative processes which result in a completely unique poem, a creative piece of fine art, or a well-written prose paragraph, but we can observe the poem, the painting, and the written paragraph. These end-products can serve as "observables" which will help to indicate whether or not the expected behavior has occurred. It may sometimes be useful to keep this distinction in mind when we are writing goals.

TABLE 4.1

These verbs are open to a variety of interpretations and should be avoided when writing specific educational goals. These verbs do *not* describe observable behaviors.

to know	to understand
to grasp	to believe
to appreciate	to enjoy
to comprehend	to value
to think	to realize
to familiarize	to love

TABLE 4.2

These verbs should be used when writing educational goals because they are unambiguous and do describe observable behaviors (or behaviors which yield observable products).*

to list	to differentiate
to construct	to add
to divide	to write
to identify	to select
to analyze	to predict
to compute	to infer
to explain	to isolate
to locate	to draw

*For a more complete list of useful, unambiguous verbs that are categorized according to specific learning outcomes, see Appendix 3 in Gronlund, N. E., *Stating Behavioral Objectives,* London, Collier-Macmillan Limited, The Macmillan Company, 1970.

Both of these, the performance and the end product goals, can be useful instructional goals. The use of strong active verbs greatly aids the writing of these goals because they generally yield goals which are observable (or whose end products are observable). Although we cannot observe a student knowing, understanding, or appreciating, we can observe him *writing down* his spelling words, *reciting* the causes of the Civil War, *applying a grammatical rule* to his own writing, or *selecting Bach* over popular tunes.

Rewriting Poorly Defined Goals

What can be done to "save" an instructional goal which fails to meet any or all of the above criteria? A textbook, a course syllabus, a teachers' magazine, or a fellow teacher may suggest goals which seem to describe a worthwhile behavior but which for one reason or another are not well defined. There are two major faults which cause goals to fall short of the criteria just discussed. It is not difficult to recognize these faults, and once they are recognized, they are quite easily corrected.

Fault 1: Activities, not outcomes. A very common fault of instructional goals is that they are stated in terms of learning activities (either teacher or student activities) and not in terms of outcomes. Surely it is important to be able to specify what the teacher will do (lecture, demonstrate, encourage). What the student will do in the process of learning is also important (read, watch a film, write a paper, practice). But, these activities are designed to help the student reach the instructional goals. They should be designed with the goals in mind and should not serve as a substitute for them.

Examples of Activities versus Outcomes

WRONG (teacher-oriented learning activity): Discuss with the students the relationship between good writing and the use of active rather than passive verbs.

WRONG (student-oriented learning activities): Work in groups, finding the passive verbs in a passage supplied by the teacher. Change the passive verbs to active where possible.

RIGHT (student-oriented learning outcomes): When given a passage containing weak, passive verbs, the student should be able to improve the passage by changing those verbs to appropriate active verbs.

Notice that there is a great similarity between the learning activities and the learning outcome. That is because the activities are clearly designed to help the student reach the goal, the outcome. When rewriting goals which emphasize a learning activity rather than a learning outcome, you can take advantage of this close relationship between the two. By simply answering the question, "What will this activity help the student to be able to do?", you can arrive at a learning outcome, a usable instructional goal. A few more examples may help. Notice how the *activity* is translated to *outcome* by asking the quesion, "What will this activity help the student to be able to do?"

Examples of Activities versus Outcomes

WRONG: Activity—Study the life cycle of the butterfly.
RIGHT: Outcome—Draw and label the stages in the life cycle of the butterfly. Use no books or aids.

WRONG: Activity—Read pages 127–129, then work the problem at the end of the chapter.

RIGHT: Outcome—When given the total obligation, the amount of interest, and the number of monthly payments, the student should be able to compute the true annual interest rate.

Fault 2: Vague and unobservable.   This fault arises most commonly from a use of the wrong kinds of verbs. Verbs like those found in Table 4.1 should be replaced with verbs like those found in Table 4.2.

Examples of Vague versus Precise Use of Verbs

WRONG: To *know* the capitals of each of the fifty states.

RIGHT: To *write* down the capitals of each of the fifty states.

WRONG: To *comprehend* the meaning of the Monroe Doctrine.

RIGHT: To *describe* a situation where the Monroe Doctrine would apply.

The use of vague direct objects (or no object at all) in an instructional goal can also lead to poorly defined goals. Sometimes an objective can be greatly improved by clearly specifying the object of the verb.

Examples of Clearly Stated Objectives

POOR: To list the causes of inflation.

IMPROVED: To list those causes of inflation given in your textbook.

POOR: To be able to spell correctly.

IMPROVED: To be able to spell correctly 90 percent of the words in the back of the spelling book.

POOR: To calculate area.

IMPROVED: To calculate the area of any geometric plane which is defined entirely by straight lines.

EXERCISE 4.3

Indicate the major fault(s) of each of the following instructional goals. Use the following scheme:

   a. Teacher-oriented rather than student-oriented
   b. A learning activity rather than a learning outcome
   c. Vague (not explicit)
   d. No observable performance or product
1. To fill in the practice exercises.

2. To instill an interest in the students.
3. To review the multiplication tables.
4. To do page 34 in the math text.
5. To understand the life cycle of the moth.
6. To be intelligent.
7. To discuss the importance of listening carefully.
8. To listen to the lecture carefully.

Writing Your Own Instructional Goals

There are four simple steps to be followed when writing instructional goals. In general, these steps should be followed in chronological order. However, at each step you will make judgments about your progress, and you may need to go back and rework some aspects of a previous step. This means that you will not always follow from the first step to the last step in a neat, orderly sequence but may be working at a variety of these steps at any given time. Let me stress again the importance of realizing that you will not be able to write a complete set of goals for a full course in a short time. Therefore you may find it useful to concentrate on small units or parts of units, gradually building up a set of goals which will encompass the total course. Because it is important that even your small unit goals fit into the overall plan, the first two steps should usually be fairly well completed before you begin to break your general goals into specific areas which would serve as guides for a given unit.

Four Steps for Writing Instructional Goals

1. Identify the subject matter content or general area of development.
2. Specify general goals.
3. Break down these general goals into more specific, observable goals.
4. Check these goals for clarity and appropriateness.

Step 1: Identify subject matter content. Perhaps this step can best be completed by seeking answers to the following four questions:

1. In general, what is the course about?
2. How does this course relate to the total curriculum?
3. What could be included in a possible outline?
4. What value does this course have for the student?

The answer to the question "What is the course all about?" must be broad and very general. Just a short paragraph briefly discussing the kinds of things that the course will cover is all that is needed. It might help to imagine that you are to write a summary of the course to be sent home to the parents so that they could get a general idea of what the course is about. Or you might imagine that you need to write a short paragraph to be placed in a course description catalog. This summary will serve as a basis for a more detailed outline, which will follow. It will also serve as a basis for the selection of appropriate textbook materials and other major sources that you may want to make available to your students. Furthermore, it will begin to indicate the major kinds of cognitive and affective goals which this course will expect the students to be able to reach.

Now that you have identified the general content of the course under consideration, your next task is to write a short statement of how this course fits into the total curriculum. Writing this kind of statement forces you to find out what other things are being taught within the total school system. Note, for example, that the kinds of goals which are set for an introductory algebra course are different from those that might be set for a second or third course in some sequence. The difference is one of, on the one hand, specifying goals where no prerequisite knowledge need be assumed, and, on the other hand, specifying goals which will build upon prerequisite goals which have already been reached.

Answering the third question ("What could be included in a possible outline?") accomplishes several things. First, the kinds of topics to be covered are specified in more detail. Second, a logical and defensible sequence of these topics is established. Third, it allows you to develop goals for one part of the outline at a time.

So far, the cognitive aspects have been emphasized. However, there are probably a number of other goals which are either affective in nature or, if cognitive, not directly related to the concepts and principles in the course content itself. That is why the question "What value does this course have for the student?" is such an important question to ask. A useful way to arrive at a list of values is to imagine yourself having to defend your course to the students who must take it and to the administrative staff of your school.

Step 2: Specify general goals.   Once you have identified the subject matter content, the next step is to specify general goals which would be attained by the end of the year or semester (terminal goals) and also those which, although general in nature, would be met periodically throughout the semester (intermediate goals). These intermediate goals would be more closely aligned with the specific units that were designated in the course outline.

The goals which you expect the students to reach by the end of the course serve a real purpose in helping you to identify in a general way the kinds of behavior changes you expect in your students. They may initially be stated in unobservable terms and contain a certain amount of ambiguity, but at the same time they can serve a valuable purpose: they can set the stage for more specific, observable goals. It is sometimes helpful to categorize the goals according to one of the schemes presented earlier (e.g., cognitive goals, affective goals, or psycho-motor goals). Obviously the number of goals which you have in each classification depends upon the course, the grade level, and the kinds of students you have in your class.

If you were establishing goals for a course in physical education, they would be mostly psychomotor skill goals with a few cognitive and affective ones. Courses such as workshop, driver training, and typing contain a large number of psychomotor goals. On the other hand, courses such as math, science, social studies, and English contain mostly cognitive goals. Affective goals are more commonly found in music, art, and drama.

By the time you have reached this point in the development of goals, you *may not* need to write the goals in general terms first. After you become accustomed to thinking in terms of explicit, observable student behaviors, you will be able to take a terminal goal and directly produce well-specified intermediate goals. However, once general, intermediate goals *are* written, it is a rather simple task to construct specific, observable goals.

Step 3: Break down general goals into specific, observable goals. Having established the general goals for your course, you are then ready to take these general goals and make them more specific and more observable.

The first thing to do when breaking down a general goal into more specific ones is to identify the subject matter content which the student will be expected to act upon. Examine the two goals below. They are from an introductory psychology course.

Examples of Two Specific, Observable Goals for an Introductory Psychology Course

1. Students should be able to list in writing all the founders of psychological theory discussed in the textbook.
2. Students should be able to match each important theoretical concept to the theory with which it is associated. (This goal is limited to the theories found in Unit I in the text.)

In the first goal, the content is *"the founders of psychological theory."* The subject matter content of the second goal is *"important theoretical concepts and theories."*

Once you have identified the subject matter content, you then indicate the behavioral response the student is expected to make to that content. The behavioral response in the first objective is "to list in writing" and in the second, "to match." The "student behavior" part of any objective may be a behavior which can be directly observed, such as speaking, running, jumping, laughing, pushing, or gesturing, or it may be the kind of behavior which yields a product that can be examined, such as a written list, a matched list of words, an essay, a painting, a sculpture, or a set of answers from a true-false test.

Besides defining the content and the student behavior, it is sometimes valuable to specify the conditions under which we expect the behavior to occur. By indicating these conditions, we are also spelling out the conditions of the "test" situation. Look at the following objective:

> When given a description of a psychological research problem, the students should be able to select from among a number of alternatives the principles which would be most appropriate to the solution of that problem.

Notice that in this objective the student behavior is "to select" and the subject matter content is "the appropriate psychological principles." The conditions under which the student will be expected to select those principles is "when given a description of a psychological research problem and a number of alternative principles. . . ." Given these conditions, then, the student is expected to be able to select the correct principle. Phrases which describe the conditions or situations under which we expect the student to perform are often worded like the following:

> When given . . .
> In an open discussion, . . .
> After having been given directions, . . .
> Within a certain, limited amount of time, . . .
> During a free period. . . .

A second optional characteristic of well-written goals is the specification of a minimum level of performance. Sometimes it is desirable that we specify in advance what an acceptable minimum level of performance is, so that we can more readily make a judgment about whether or not an objective has been met. Typical statements of minimum performance levels might be worded something like the following:

> . . . 90 percent correct, . . .
> . . . within three minutes, . . .
> . . . with no more than two errors, . . .
> . . . 100 percent accuracy, . . .
> . . . recognizable by classmates, . . .

And so on. It should be recognized that minimum performance standards can be set for the individual or for the total class. For example, if we were to set a minimum level of performance for a third grade spelling objective, it might read something like the following:

> The student should be able upon the completion of the first six weeks to spell correctly eighty-five of the ninety spelling words in his spelling workbook.

Or in writing an objective for first grade reading, we might produce one which would have to be met before the students could go from the preprimer to the first primer. It would read something like this:

> Students should be able to read without error at least 90 percent of the sight vocabulary words introduced in the preprimer.

Besides the value that this specification of a minimum performance level has as an indication of whether or not a student can meet this goal, it also serves to indicate what level of performance must be reached before the student is allowed to progress to the next-higher level of learning. For example, a teacher may feel that a student should not go on to the primer until he has mastered at least 90 percent of the sight words that have been taught in the preprimer.

Sometimes these minimum levels of performance are set for the total group, thus giving the teacher a yardstick by which he can judge his teaching effectiveness. For example, in the spelling objective we might add a class minimum performance level to the objective and it would read like this:

> At least twenty-five of the thirty students should be able to spell correctly 85 percent of the spelling words in their book.

The teacher may feel in this case that if at least twenty-five students have not reached the minimum level of performance, he has not done an effective job of teaching. Perhaps this will help him decide to go back and reteach some of the things which were missed by the class as a whole. If, on the other hand, only a few students missed and the class as a whole was ready to move on, he might give extra help to those who had not been able to meet the minimum individual standards and try to bring them up to the class standards as he moves the class ahead.

By specifying minimal performance standards, we make it possible to make mastery judgments. Each student (or an entire class) can be judged against the criteria established as performance standards for each goal.

A teacher should always be willing to reconsider the level of performance expected. Evaluation may indicate that the students are not progressing as expected. Sometimes standards must be changed to be brought more in line with the actual abilities and accomplishments of the students.

It has just been suggested that there are two characteristics of specific, observable goals which are optional but nevertheless useful. These optional characteristics are given below.

Optional Characteristics of Observable Goals

1. A description of the conditions under which the students should be expected to perform,
2. A minimum level of performance for the individual and/or the class

Step 4: Check these goals: Are they well defined? Appropriate? Once goals have been written, they should be checked against the criteria specified earlier in this section. Those which fail to meet any of the criteria of a well-defined goal should be rewritten in accordance with the suggestions made earlier for rewriting goals.

EXERCISE 4.4

1. For each of the following three goals, identify the the subject matter content and the student's response to that content.
   a. A student will be able to repeat all the multiplication tables through 12×12.
   b. A student will be able to select from among a number of alternatives the statement which best describes the plot of a short story that has not been previously discussed in class.
   c. The student will be able to write the names of the notes in the treble clef.
2. For each of the next three goals, identify the conditions under which the student is expected to learn and the minimum level of performance expected.
   a. When given a description of five experiments involving the mixture of chemicals, the student should be able to select correctly from a number of alternatives the outcome of each experiment, making no errors.
   b. When given a completed business letter containing fifteen errors, the student should be able to identify at least twelve of the fifteen errors and make the appropriate corrections.
   c. When given the descriptions of six games which were taught during the last six weeks in Phys. Ed. class, the students should be able to correctly name five of the games.
3. Choose a subject matter of interest to you and write three or four goals for a given unit.
4. Indicate for each goal you have written whether it belongs primarily to the cognitive, affective, or psychomotor domain.
5. For each of the cognitive goals you have written, specify the level of learning. Use the taxonomy given in this chapter as a guide.
6. For each goal you have written, underline once the words which indicate the content referred to and underline twice the behavior called for.

PROCEDURE 3: CONSTRUCT A TABLE OF SPECIFICATIONS

One of the most popular ways to describe the information needed about student achievement is to construct a table of specifications. Typically, this table is a two-way chart indicating the subject matter content to be tested and the kinds of behaviors expected in connection with that content. An example of such a chart is found in Table 4.3. This chart describes the information taught in a unit of fourth grade English.

The approximate percentage of test items to be devoted to each kind of behavior for each content area is indicated by the numbers in the cells. For example, approximately 10 percent of a test over this unit would deal with the definitions or the parts of speech in context, etc.

To construct a table of specifications is essentially to describe the sample of knowledge or learned outcomes you wish to obtain information about. Consequently, the procedures for building a table of specifications are really nothing more than specific instances of the general rules for obtaining a representative sample (see Chapter 2).

A Preview of the Steps to Take When Constructing a Table of Specifications

1. Describe the major subject matter content and the kinds of responses expected of the students.
2. Place the content along one axis of a matrix and the kinds of responses expected along the other axis.
3. Indicate the proportion of items needed for each cell in your matrix.

Describe subject matter content and student response. The classroom teacher is in a better position than anyone else to know what subject matter was taught and what level of learning was expected from the students. A review of the instructional goals, the course outline, and the instructional materials should help the teacher to describe the population of knowledge the students

TABLE 4.3

Table of Specifications for a Unit in Fourth Grade English

Content	KIND OF BEHAVIOR			
	Define Terms	Identify in Context	Produce Examples	
Parts of speech	10	05	10	25
Phrases	05	05	10	20
Sentence patterns	15	10	20	45
Transformational rules	05	05	—	10
	35	25	40	100

were expected to learn. By specifying the important facts, concepts, and principles, the teacher will be in a good position to develop (or select) a test with
high content validity.

Produce a content-by-behavior matrix. The major facts, concepts, and
principles to be measured are usually listed along the vertical axis of a matrix.
Next, place the various levels of learning along the horizontal axis to complete
the matrix. Note that all the levels of learning may not apply to all the content
areas. There may be some content areas where the students may not be expected
to have reached as high a level of learning as in some other areas. This simply
means that there will be some empty cells in your matrix. Do *not* feel that *all*
the cells in a table of specifications should be applicable for a given test.

Indicate the proportion of items needed for each cell in the matrix. The
proportion of items in each cell in a table of specifications should represent the
importance of the information described by that cell. For example, in Table 4.3,
the most important information being measured is the ability of the students to
produce examples of various sentence patterns (that cell represents 20 percent of
the total table). Some cells have been designated as accounting for only 5 percent
of the information being measured (definition of transformational rules, identifying the parts of speech in context, etc.). Notice also that there is an "empty" cell:
producing examples of transformational rules. In this case, the teacher did not
consider that to be an expected outcome of the course and therefore did not in-
tend to write any test items over it.

A teacher should assign the proportions to each cell on the basis of
his ideas about what content areas are most important and/or on the basis
of the amount of time devoted in class to each content area.

EXERCISE 4.5

1. Describe in your own words the procedures for constructing a table of
specifications.
2. In constructing a table of specifications, one follows the rules for defining a
representative sample.
a. What is the population of interest?
b. In what way does a table of specification describe that population?

PROCEDURE 4: CONSTRUCT AN ACHIEVEMENT CONTINUUM

Criterion-referenced evaluation is a vital part of good teaching. When we are able
to judge with some degree of accuracy the *level* of achievement an individual has
reached, then we can decide how to help him move from there to a higher level.
When we can discover, for any given task, which operations a student can per-

form and which he cannot, then we can select appropriate learning activities for that student.

It is easier to make these kinds of judgments when an achievement continuum is first specified. You will recall from the brief discussion in Chapter 2 that an achievement continuum specifies the observable behaviors which represent various levels of achievement on a given task. In the next few pages you will be told how to construct such a continuum. Once you have done that, you can then use it as a guide for constructing criterion-referenced tests.

In order to construct an achievement continuum you must be able to:

1. Determine the major learning outcome(s) ultimately to be achieved.
2. List the behaviors associated with proficiency.
3. Phrase each behavior in observable terms.
4. Arrange the behaviors in a meaningful way.

Determine the Ultimate Outcome(s) of Learning

In this first step, you must describe what you *ultimately* expect your students to be able to do. This description may be very general (e.g., to be able to read with 80 percent comprehension books written at a fourth grade level) or more specific (e.g., to be able to sound out all English words which follow regular phonetic rules). However, whether general or specific, it must be *explicit*. It must describe exactly what it is you expect the student(s) to be able to do upon the conclusion of instruction and learning. There may be one ultimate goal or several related ones. Each major learning outcome will define the perfect performance end of an achievement continuum. A given course or unit of instruction may therefore be characterized by one or several achievement continuums.

Some of the "ultimate" goals we set for students are really intermediate goals when seen in relation to some larger continuum. The level of achievement we "ultimately" expect of high school algebra students represents a low level of achievement for college students taking algebra. The criterion for proficiency in organizing written reports is at a much lower level for fourth grade than it is for sixth, or for tenth, or for a newspaper journalist.

Once you have gone through the work of specifying your instructional goals in observable terms, you will have done a great deal of the work needed to construct an achievement continuum. Each terminal goal defines the "proficiency" end of an achievement continuum, and the intermediate goals (which are needed in order to eventually attain that proficiency) define the behaviors which lie along a given continuum.

List the Behaviors Associated with Proficiency

After you have defined the perfect performance end of the continuum by specifying the ultimate outcome of learning, the next step is to list the behaviors that lie along that continuum. Ask yourself the following question:

What are all the things a person can do who has achieved the ultimate goal defined as "perfect" achievement?

Two things are particularly important at this point: (1) *do not leave out any important behaviors* and (2) *do not add to the list* anything that can be done by someone who has no proficiency in the skill or ability being measured. Look over the examples in Figure 4.1. These examples may serve as an example when you try to construct an achievement continuum yourself.

EXERCISE 4.6

Select a fairly specific skill in a subject matter area you are familiar with.

1. Describe the terminal performance.
2. Describe some of the important intermediate behaviors leading up to it.

Phrase Each Behavior in Observable Terms

If you get into the habit of formulating your instructional goals in observable terms, then this step will be unnecessary. The behaviors listed in the above step will already be stated in observable terms. If that is the case, simply check to make certain each behavior meets the criteria for a well-written behavioral objective (see page 100) and then move on to the next step.

The importance of phrasing each behavior in observable terms should be obvious to you. Developing a way to measure each behavior (e.g., writing test items) is much easier if the behavior is stated so that it can be observed or so that an end product of that behavior can be observed.

Arrange the Behaviors in a Meaningful Way

Proficient achievement has been defined in terms of an ultimate learning outcome. All the behaviors which characterize someone who has reached that level of achievement have been specified in observable terms. Now these behaviors must be arranged in a meaningful way. There are three major ways in which behaviors can be ordered: (1) sequentially, (2) taxonomically, and (3) developmentally.

Ultimate learning outcome: *Be able to locate a book in the school library.*

Behaviors characteristic of one who has reached a level of perfect proficiency in the above skill:
> *Know the classification of the book.*
> *Know the book's author and call number.*
> *Be able to find a book in the card catalog, by title or author.*
> *Know which sections of the library contain which kind of books.*
> *Be able to "read" the classification numbers.*

Ultimate learning outcome: *To estimate the error in test scores.*

Behaviors characteristic of one who has reached a level of perfect perfection:
> *Know the sources of error.*
> *Recognize clues which suggest error has occurred.*
> *Compute reliability, validity, standard error of estimate.*
> *Select the most appropriate techniques for computing reliability and validity.*

Ultimate learning outcome: *Demonstrate "halves" of a set of objects as two equal subsets; thirds as three equal subsets.**

Behaviors characteristic of one who has reached a level of proficiency in the above skill:
> *Identify two apparently equal subsets as "halves" of total; three subsets as "thirds" of total.*
> *Identify the number of subsets of a group of objects as two or three.*
> *Construct subsets which are equal, by pairing objects, one to each subset.*
> *Deal out objects one to each subset.*
> *Apportion leftover objects, one to each subset.*
> *Identify one object of a set.*

* Adapted from Gagné, Robert M. *The Conditions of Learning* (2d ed.). New York: Holt, Rinehart & Winston, Inc., 1971, p. 252, fig. 17.

FIGURE 4.1. Examples of ultimate learning outcomes and their prerequisite behaviors.

The behaviors on an achievement continuum can be ordered in the following ways:

Sequentially—according to the order in which they would be executed by someone proficient at the task.

Taxonomically—according to the order in which they must be learned (i.e., each behavior serves as a prerequisite to those placed above it).

Developmentally—according to their order of occurrence as a person develops the skills (as he moves from no proficiency to "perfect proficiency").

Ordering behaviors sequentially. Some learning outcomes are defined by skills which are usually executed in a specified order. The behaviors which characterize these outcomes lend themselves well to sequential ordering. For example, in order to develop a roll of black-and-white film successfully, you must carry out certain steps *in a particular order.*

To be able to develop black-and-white film, you must be able to

1. Select the appropriate chemicals.
2. Put wetting agent in developing tank.
3. Load the film on the developing spool.
4. Place reel with film in tank-agitate.
5. Remove wetting agent from tank.
6. Fill tank with developer.
7. Set timer.
8. Agitate periodically.
9. When timer rings, remove developer.
10. Add stop bath.
11. Agitate.
12. Remove stop bath.
13. Pour fixer in developing tank.
14. Set timer.
15. Agitate periodically.
16. When timer rings, remove fixer.
17. Rinse in running water.
18. Set timer.
19. When timer rings, remove film.
20. Hang film to dry.

There are many of these kinds of learning outcomes among a teacher's instructional goals. A person who is proficient at the terminal task will carry out each subtask in proper sequence. For example, a student who has mastered the SQ3R study method will first skim (S) the material to be studied. Next, he will formulate questions (Q) for which he will seek the answers. Then he will read, reread, and review (3R). Notice that each subtask can be learned somewhat independently of the other tasks. Although skimming is the first step, it did not necessarily have to be learned first. In the photography example, this is also true. In order to develop film successfully, each step must be carried out in a certain order. However, a student might learn how to rinse the film properly before he learns how to load the film properly on the developing spool (someone could load the spool for him until he learns that skill).

EXERCISE 4.7

Below are some examples of terminal goals which require certain behaviors to be carried out in a particular order.

  a. To outline a chapter in a book
  b. To plan a woodwork project
  c. To write a library research paper
  d. To conduct a scientific experiment
1. Pick one or two and specify, in order, the specific behaviors which will lead to the finished goals described.
2. Try to think of some examples of other such terminal goals from your own experiences.

Ordering behaviors taxonomically. The taxonomic schemes for categorizing learning outcomes can be very helpful. Each level in a taxonomy is dependent upon the level below it and is, at the same time, a prerequisite to the level above it. This interdependence among the learning tasks is very common. Many terminal tasks can only be ultimately achieved if the prerequisite behaviors have been mastered. In an idealized taxonomy, a terminal task *cannot* be executed until each of the prerequisite tasks has been mastered. Mathematics includes many terminal tasks which can be represented quite well by a taxonomic scheme (e.g., Figure 4.2). Notice the interdependence among the subtasks.

You must realize that sequences as carefully worked out as those found in Figure 4.1 would normally require the knowledge and skill of curriculum specialists. Nevertheless, the classroom teacher *can* go a long way toward developing a good taxonomy for many of his instructional goals. It should be noted, however, that unless instructional goals are clearly stated in behavioral terms, it is virtually impossible to develop a valid taxonomy of behaviors.

Gagné (1965) has suggested a relatively simple procedure for developing a taxonomy of learning outcomes. You begin with a terminal objective and ask the following question:

> What would the learner have to know how to do in order to perform this task, after being given only instructions?

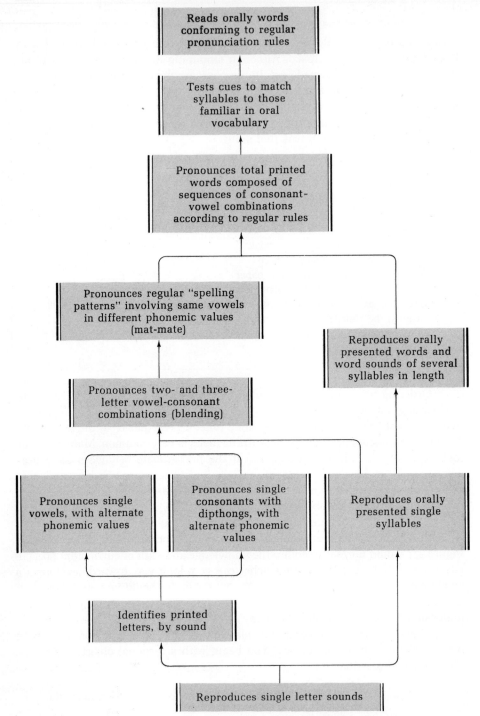

FIGURE 4.2 A learning hierarchy for a basic reading skill ("decoding"). From *The Conditions of Learning,* second edition, by Robert M. Gagné. Copyright © 1965, 1970 by Holt, Rinehart & Winston, Inc. Reprinted by permission of Holt, Rinehart & Winston.

To the behaviors found in your answer, you again ask this same question. You keep asking the question of each successive sets of behaviors you define, working backward from the terminal objective until you reach the point where it is safe to assume that the students have already acquired the capabilities needed. Occasionally, you may need to check the students' level of performance before you begin to teach a set of objectives. Students may *not* have previously acquired the capabilities that you think they should have.

If you design a criterion-referenced test based upon an achievement continuum which has been arranged taxonomically, you can pinpoint rather precisely which capabilities a student has acquired and which he still must acquire. When lower-level prerequisite goals have not been mastered, the students should not be expected to acquire the terminal objective. Sometimes it is possible for students to reach a minimum level of performance on a given task even though they have not successfully mastered all of the lower-level prerequiste tasks. This may keep students at a lower level of performance than they might have reached if they *had* acquired all of the prerequisite behaviors. Furthermore, it is possible for a student to advance quite far in a subject matter area before weaknesses caused by unlearned prerequisites will show up. For example, a child may read fairly well for the first few years of school even though some of the basic reading skills were not learned well. However, there may come a time (e.g., in later elementary or early junior high years) when the pressure of having to read large amounts of materials will cause reading problems which were previously unnoticed.

Ordering behaviors developmentally. Some skills are learned in "successive approximations" to perfection. For example, a child learning to walk the balance beam can do so in a limited way with very little instruction or practice. He is clumsy at first, falling often. Gradually he improves. His movements are smoother, he falls less often. He begins to approximate the performance of one who has attained "perfection." As the child develops motor skills, attitudes, and some cognitive abilities, his behavior can be characterized as developing gradually from no proficiency through stages of imperfect performance to "perfect" performance. If the behaviors of a person at various stages of development can be described, then a test situation can be devised which will estimate the level of achievement a person has reached.

Handwriting is one skill which can be so described. Handwriting product scales are sometimes used in standardized achievement tests. An example of such a scale can be found in Figure 4.3. Notice how the handwriting samples are successively closer approximations to the ideal or "perfect" model which serves as the ultimate goal. Product scales can be developed by the classroom teacher to help her evaluate skills in handwriting, art work, musical ability, etc. Chapter 10 describes the step-by-step procedures for developing these types of rating scales.

Table 4.4 compares and contrasts the three basic ways of ordering behav-

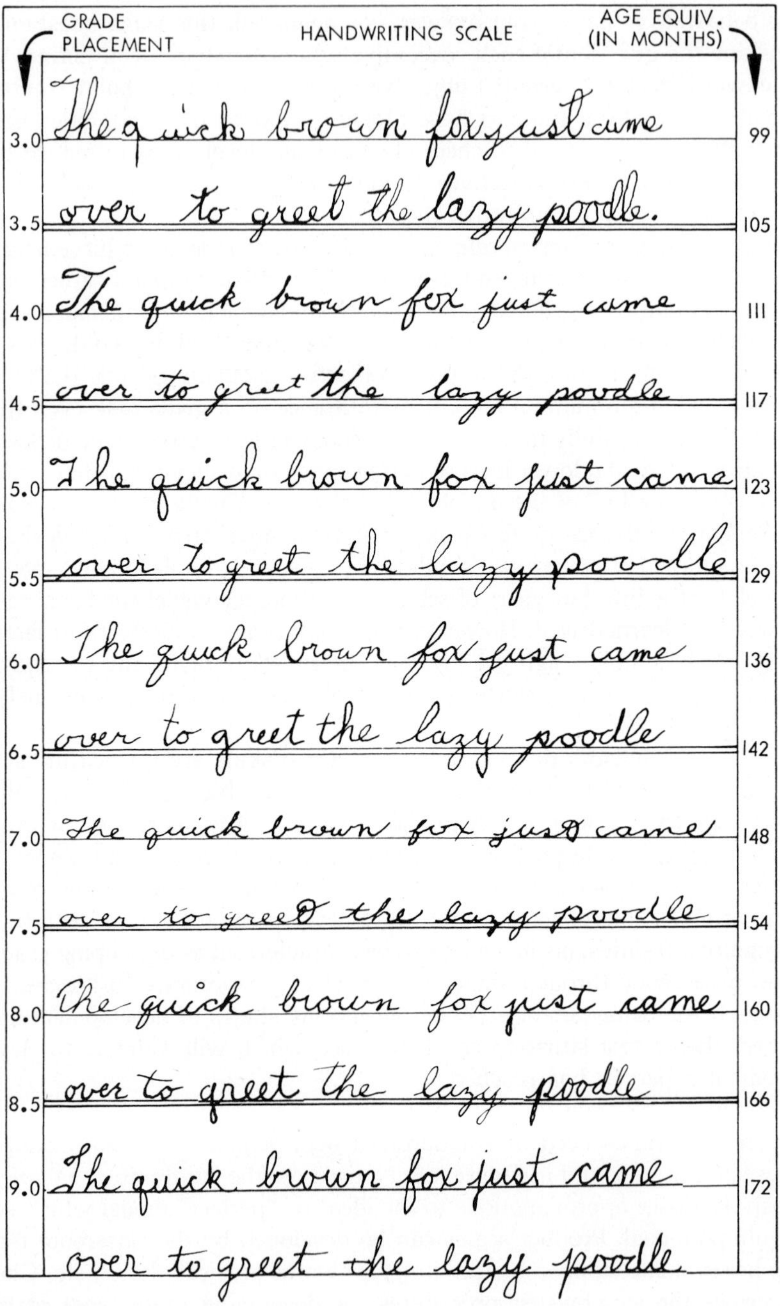

FIGURE 4.3 Handwriting scale used in *California Achievement Tests*. Used by permission: Ernest W. Tiegs and Willis W. Clark, *California Achievement Tests*. Copyright 1957 by McGraw-Hill, Inc., California Test Bureau, Monterey, California. All rights reserved.

iors along an achievement continuum. The learning outcomes which can most easily be ordered along each of these kinds of continuums differ in terms of how they are achieved as well as how they are executed once they have been achieved.

TABLE 4-4

Comparison of Three Ways of Ordering Behaviors along an Achievement Continuum

	Sequentially Ordered Outcomes	*Taxonomically* Ordered Outcomes	*Developmentally* Ordered Outcomes
During learning stage	Behaviors learned independently in any order.	Behaviors learned in a specified order. Each behavior is dependent upon prerequisite behavior.	Behavior learned as successive approximation to perfect performance.
Execution after learning	Different behaviors along the continuum to be executed in a sequential order.	Different behaviors along the continuum *not necessarily* to be executed in a sequential order.	One behavior which is executed at a given level of proficiency (or stage of development.)

SUMMARY

1. The more clearly you can describe information, the more easily you will be able to make appropriate preparations for obtaining it.
2. The information needed for evaluation can be described by answering four questions: (1) What is the information about? (2) What kind of behavior is to be observed? (3) How specific must the information be? (4) How accurate must the information be?
3. Teachers are usually concerned about the expected learning outcomes, but unexpected outcomes can also be important.
4. Instructional goals specify some subject matter content and the student's expected response to that content. The response should be stated in observable terms. A time element is either explicitly stated or is implied in every instructional goal.
5. Although behavioral objectives have some limitations, they can be very helpful in lesson planning as well as in evaluation procedures. Well-defined goals can also help the learner to decide what to study.
6. Useful classroom goals should (1) be student-oriented, (2) describe a learning outcome, (3) be explicit, (4) be observable.
7. Poorly defined goals should be rewritten to correct these two common faults: (1) that they are stated as activities rather than outcomes, (2) that they are vague and unobservable.

8. There are four simple steps to take when writing instructional goals: (1) identify the subject matter content; (2) specify general goals; (3) break down the general goals into more specific, observable goals; (4) check each goal for clarity and appropriateness.
9. A table of specifications describes the sample of learned behaviors you wish to obtain information about.
10. To develop a table of specifications you should (1) describe the major subject matter content and the kinds of responses exhibited by the students, (2) place the content along one axis of a matrix and the kinds of responses expected along the other axis, (3) indicate the proportion of items needed for each cell in the matrix.
11. Criterion-referenced judgments are often easier to make when an achievement continuum is first specified.
12. In order to construct an achievement continuum, you should (1) determine the major learning outcome(s) ultimately to be achieved, (2) list the behaviors associated with proficiency, (3) phrase each behavior in observable terms, (4) arrange the behaviors in a meaningful way.
13. Behaviors on an achievement continuum can be arranged sequentially, taxonomically, or developmentally.

References

Atkin, Myron J.: "Behavioral Objectives in Curriculum Design: A Cautionary Note," *The Science Teacher,* May 1968, pp. 27–30.

Bloom, Benjamin S. (ed.): Taxonomy of Educational Objectives, *Handbook I. The Cognitive Domain,* David McKay Company, Inc., New York, 1956.

Bloom, Benjamin S., J. Thomas Hastings, George F. Madaus: *Handbook on Formative and Summative Evaluation of Student Learning,* McGraw-Hill Book Company, New York, 1971.

Gagné, R. M. "The Analysis of Instructional Objectives for the Design of Instruction," in R. Glaser (ed.), *Teaching Machines and Programmed Learning, II: Data and Directions,* National Education Association, Washington, D.C., 1965.

Krathwohl, David R., Benjamin S. Bloom, and Bert Masia: *Taxonomy of Educational Objectives, Handbook II, The Affective Domain.* David McKay Company, Inc., New York, 1964.

McNeil, John D.: "Concomitants of Using Behavioral Objectives in the Assessment of Teacher Effectiveness," *The Journal of Experimental Education,* 1967, 36, pp. 69–74.

Popham, James W.: "The Instructional Objectives Exchange: New Support for Criterion-Referenced Instruction," *Phi Delta Kappan,* 1970, 52, 3, pp. 174–175.

Simpson, E. J.: "The Classification of Educational Objectives: Psychomotor Domain," *Illinois Teacher of Home Economics,* 1966, 10, 4, pp. 110–144.

Suggested Readings

A classic book on preparing instructional objectives (paperback):
Mager, Robert F.: *Preparing Instructional Objectives.* Palo Alto, Calif., 1962.

Answers to many of the objections about behaviorally stated objectives can be found in:

Popham, James W.: "Probing the Validity of Arguments against Behavioral Goals," in R. C. Anderson, G. W. Faust, M. C. Roderick, D. J. Cunningham, and Thomas Andre (eds.), *Current Research on Instruction,* Prentice-Hall, Inc., Englewood Cliffs, N.J., 1969.

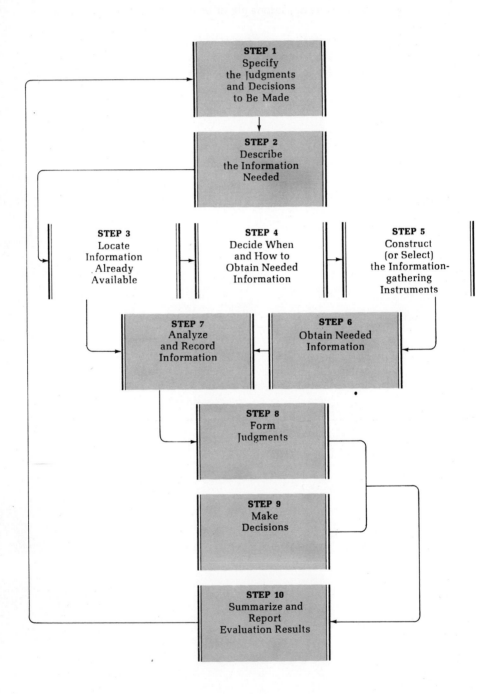

CHAPTER 5

Making Preparations for Obtaining Needed Information

The evaluation process begins with a question which calls for judgment to be formed or a decision to be made. By describing the judgments and decisions you plan on making (step 1), you can more easily determine the kind of information you will need in order to make those judgments and decisions (step 2). Given a good description of the judgments and decisions to be made and of the information needed, you can then make preparations for obtaining that information. There are three steps to take when making these preparations. The first involves locating any information that may already be available (step 3). Next, you must decide when and how the information still needed is to be obtained (step 4). Finally, any particular information-gathering instruments which will be needed must be constructed or selected (step 5).

LOCATE INFORMATION ALREADY AVAILABLE

A great deal of information is carefully gathered, recorded, and stored only to be misused or not used at all. The information in the records kept by the school as well as by individual teachers and others can be very useful. However, you must know where to look for this information, what you can expect to find, and how to use what you find. Consequently, this section has been written so that after you have finished studying it you will be able to meet the following objectives.

When given a description of the kind of information needed (and, where necessary, a statement of the judgments and decisions to be made) you should be able to

1. List the sources where the information is likely to be found.
2. Indicate the extent to which the information would be usable.

Where to Look for Available Information

There are five main sources of readily available information about students: the teacher's personal records, the school's records (the cumulative folder), the counselor's records, the records of auxiliary school personnel, and the records of a student's parents. Each of these sources provides a different kind of information.

The teacher's personal records. A good teacher will keep many kinds of information about his students. In Chapter 6 (step 7) a system is described which will help you to record many kinds of information which should be helpful to you and to other teachers who may work with the same student(s). You must realize, of course, that no teacher is likely to have all this information about all his students. Nevertheless, the following list illustrates the kind of information teachers could have about their students:

Information Which May Be Found in a Teacher's Records

Records of attendance

Anecdotes of Behavior

Observations of class participation

Record of assignments completed

Records of progress

Quiz and test scores

Performance on assignments

Sociometric data

Notes of private conferences

The information in a teacher's file varies not only in kind but also in quality. A teacher's records can contain information about the cognitive, affective, and psychomotor behaviors of students. It may be information about their typical as well as their maximum performance. There should be information available about performance before, during, and after instruction. Some of this information will be in the form of highly subjective observations. Some will have been gathered more systematically, with carefully constructed checklists or rating scales. Finally, some of the information will have been obtained with well-constructed teacher-made tests. Of course, even teacher-made tests can vary greatly in terms of objectivity, reliability, and validity. Consequently, it will be important not only to know what *kind* of information is available but also to know how reliable and valid that information is.

The school's records (the cumulative folder). In 1969, the Russell Sage Foundation sponsored a conference on the ethical and legal aspects of school record keeping. The results of this conference were published in 1970 by the Foundation. I would highly recommend this publication to anyone responsible for maintaining and using school records. The participants in this conference identified the kinds of information, outlined below, which might legitimately be kept in the school's records.

Information Which May Be Found in the School's Records

Category A—Minimum personal data necessary for operation of the educational system:

Identifying data

Birth date

Academic work completed

Level of achievement (grades and standardized test scores)

Attendance data

Category B—Verified information of clear importance but not absolutely necessary:

Standardized intelligence and aptitude test scores

Interest inventory results

Health data

Family background information

Systematically gathered teacher or counselor ratings and observations

Verified reports of serious or recurrent behavior problems

Category C—Potentially useful information but not yet verified or clearly needed beyond the immediate present:

Legal or clinical findings

Personality test results

Unevaluated reports of teachers, counselors, and others

Source: *Guidelines for the Collection, Maintenance, and Dissemination of Pupil Records,* Russell Sage Foundation, 1970.

The information contained in categories A and B (above) should be readily available to teachers who know how to use it in accord with the cautions discussed later in this section. Category C data should be available to teachers who can demonstrate that the information would help them to make significantly important judgments and decisions. The teacher should always make certain that the information in category C is clearly interpreted to them by professionals trained to do so. A teacher should *never* use any information from the school records unless he fully understands the implications of that information as well as the conditions under which the information has been obtained.

The counselor's records. The school counselor often has information about students which the teachers are not able to obtain. Much of this information is strictly confidential and a teacher should not expect a counselor to divulge it. Nevertheless, there are certain kinds of information which a counselor may be free to share with teachers who can demonstrate a need for it. The kinds of information a counselor is likely to have in his files are listed below.

Information Which May Be Found in a Counselor's Records

Expressed interests

Interest inventory results

Expressed concerns (and "dislikes")

Education and career goals

Records of behavior problems

Professional diagnosis of behavior problems

List of out of school activities

Statement of home conditions

Employment record

Teachers should feel free to discuss their students with the school counselor. However, they should respect the counselor's desire to keep certain infomation confidential. The teacher should also be willing to accept the counselor's interpretation of the information he has, for this is more likely to be of value than the actual information itself (e.g., an interpretation of interest inventory results is more valuable than the specific responses the student made).

The records of other school personnel. Besides the counselor and the other teachers, there are a few other school personnel who might have useful evaluative information. The *coach* and the *sponsors of clubs* and other extracurricular activities may be able to tell a teacher how a student acts in nonacademic situations. The *school librarian* can provide the teacher with information about the kinds of materials the student checks out. The *school psychologist* and the *social worker* which some school systems employ will have information much like that the counselor would have. These professionals should also be given the privilege of holding back any information they feel should be kept confidential. The teacher, in turn, should exercise care in using any information he might obtain from them.

The records of parents. Although information provided by parents is frequently inaccurate and biased, there are some kinds of information which a parent may have at home that is not available elsewhere. Some of these kinds of information are listed below.

Information Which May Be Available in the Parents' Records

Report cards from previous years (these may include assessment of typical behavior, attendance records, and teacher comments which would not be found in the cumulative folder)

Samples of the student's past schoolwork

Health records

Records of accomplishments and achievements from places other than school (e.g., Sunday school, scouts, special summer programs)

What to Look for in Available Information

When you obtain your own information, you at least have the opportunity to estimate the validity and reliability of that information. You can plan carefully to get the kind of information you need and you can select the techniques for getting it. You can watch for clues which would indicate that the information is inaccurate and you can take note of any possible sources of error. But when you get information which others have obtained you often do not know how reliable or valid that information is. It is important, therefore, to find out as much as possible about any information you plan on using. The following questions illustrate the important things to look for.

Whenever you plan on using information already on record, you should seek answers to the following questions:

1. Does it fit the description of the information needed?
2. How accurate is it?
3. Is it useful for making the anticipated judgments and/or decisions?

Does the information which is available fit the description of the information which is needed? Most of the useful information you will find in the school's records will be in the form of standardized test scores. It is not enough to know that a score was obtained from an aptitude test or an achievement test. You must also know the name of the test, who published it, when it was published, how valid and reliable it is, etc. As you will see when you read Chapter 14, each standardized test yields different information with differing degrees of accuracy. Although the published description of what the test is supposed to measure is one way to find out what a test does measure, it is best to examine a copy of the test yourself. If you have a need for highly specific information (as you would need for criterion-referenced judgments for example), then you should compare the test items with a table of specifications, a list of instructional goals, or an achievement continuum.

It is easy to ignore the important distinction between maximum performance and typical performance. We tend to think of observations as yielding typical performance information about the students and tests as yielding information about their maximum performance. Although this is generally true, it is not always the case. You should not assume, for example, that every test score is an accurate reflection of maximum performance. Many teachers give unannounced quizzes and tests. The results of these tests are more an indication of how well a student *does* do than an indication of how well he *can* do. Neither should you assume that all observations of behavior are indications of typical behavior. If the students are aware of the fact that they are being observed, they will be on their best behavior and you will be getting information about their maximum performance. As you can see, it is important to find out the *conditions* under which the information was obtained.

How accurate is the available information? What would you look for when trying to determine the accuracy of any information you anticipate using? The basic principles discussed in Chapter 2 would lead us to the following line of reasoning.

To Check the Accuracy of Available Information

1. Look for evidence of how well the sources of error have been controlled.

2. Obtain any available estimates of error (or freedom from it).

3. Make a judgment about how accurate the information is likely to be.

Look for evidence of how well the sources of error have been controlled. In Chapter 2, the following three rules for minimizing the sources of error were discussed:

Rules for Minimizing Error*

Rule 1. Relate everything you do to the reason you are evaluating.

Rule 2. At every step in the process of evaluation, be clear, concise, and consistent.

Rule 3. Always obtain an adequate sample of the information needed.

*These rules are discussed at length in Chapter 2.

Whenever you use information that has already been obtained, you need to find out as much as you can about *how* that information was obtained. This will help you to determine whether or not these three rules were consistently applied. Any evidence indicating that these rules were violated would be evidence that certain sources of error had not been controlled. Whenever possible, try to find out if an appropriate instrument was used to gather the information. Also, it is helpful to know whether or not it was properly administered and accurately scored and recorded.

Obtain any available estimates of error. Have any reliability or validity coefficients been reported? Are standard errors of measurements available? What kinds of reliability and validity coefficients are available? If there are none of these formal estimates of error available, then you need to rely on more subjective estimates. If, for example, a test is quite long, it will *tend* to be more reliable and valid than a short one. A standardized test will *tend* to be more reliable and valid than an observational technique. An unbiased observer's report will *tend* to be more accurate than the report of someone who is emotionally or financially involved.

Make a judgment about how accurate the information is likely to be.   Based upon the evidence you have obtained about control over error and the estimate(s) you have about the potential error, you can now make judgments about how accurate the information is likely to be. Although this kind of judgment is somewhat subjective, it is crucial to your decision to use or not to use the information. The rules of thumb given below should help you to decide if the available information is accurate enough.

Rules of Thumb: To Use or Not to Use Available Information

1. If the judgments and decisions are important and it is relatively easy to obtain more accurate information, then reject that which is available and obtain new information.
2. If any information you will obtain is likely to be no more accurate than what is available, then use what is available.
3. If it is relatively easy to obtain new information, do so.
4. If more accurate information is needed but there is neither time nor money available for obtaining it, then use what is available. But use it with caution, supplementing it with other information where possible. Constantly seek confirmation (or lack of it) that the information you had was essentially correct.

Is the information useful for making the anticipated judgments and decisions?   No matter how accurate available information is, it is of no value to you unless it can be used to make the particular kinds of judgments and decisions you need to make. There are four factors which you should take into account.

Appropriate referents.   Appropriate norms are needed if norm-referenced judgments are to be made. Without clearly specified criteria, criterion-referenced and mastery judgments will be difficult to make. Self-referenced judgments require referents based upon information about the same person(s) obtained at different times under similar conditions. Before using available information, make certain it will provide you with referents which are appropriate for the kind of judgment(s) you anticipate making.[1]

Evidence of estimative ability.   Is there evidence that the information does provide a good estimate of the ability being measured? Can you be reasonably certain that the information is descriptive of the particular ability or trait you are interested in? If it is a math score, did the test measure modern or traditional concepts? If a score from a history test, is it a measure of memorization or understanding? If it is information about achievement in science, does it provide evidence of familiarity with scientific terms or of ability to use the scientific method in problem-solving situations?

---

[1] You may wish to turn back to Chap. 3 and review the discussion on the selection of referents which are appropriate for particular types of judgments.

Before you use information to form estimative judgments, you should have evidence of content and/or concurrent validity. You can obtain evidence of content validity by examining the items in the test that was used. Evidence for concurrent validity can usually be found in the technical manual which accompanies a standardized test.

Evidence of predictive validity. There must be a relationship between the available information (past performance) and future performance if any predictive judgments are to be made. The strongest evidence is a high predictive-validity coefficient (see the manual of the standardized test that was used). Sometimes, a teacher will have evidence which he obtained over a period of years. For example, a math teacher keeps records of the scores his students make on the final exam in his course. Later, he compares these scores to how well they do in algebra. On the basis of this information, he can tell you approximately how well a student will do in algebra if he knows what that student's final exam score was in his math course. That is evidence of predictive validity.

Date that the information was obtained. Formative judgments should not be made on the basis of information obtained before instruction began. Grades (summative judgments) should not be made on the basis of information obtained in the early stages of learning a skill. Use information which has been obtained as close in time to the decision making as possible.

A final word of caution. It is very easy to pick up the wrong folder, to copy down the wrong score, or to get information which someone else had improperly recorded. Before you use a score in judgment and decision making, make certain that it is the score you wanted and that it is the one for the individual you are interested in.

Another common error is to record a raw score as a percentile or vice versa. Know what kind of score it is before you use it. Another common error is to read the scores from the wrong column.

EXERCISE 5.1

1. What are the advantages of using information which may already be available? The disadvantages?
2. What are the major considerations when deciding whether or not to use information that is already available?

DECIDE WHEN AND HOW TO OBTAIN NEEDED INFORMATION

Most of the time, the information you need will not be readily available. This means that you will have to obtain that information yourself. Careful planning will go a long way toward assuring you of valid and reliable information. You should plan as far ahead as possible, deciding when, where, and how to obtain the information you need.

The material in this section has been designed to help you to

1. Select an appropriate information gathering technique.
2. Select the type of instrument to be used.
3. Decide when the information should be obtained.
4. Specify the conditions under which the information should be obtained.

Select an Information-gathering Technique

There are four major techniques (or methods) for obtaining evaluative information: observation, inquiry, analysis, and testing. The kind of information needed, the amount of time available, and the amount of accuracy needed all are important in deciding which technique to use. Once a general technique has been decided upon, then the particular instrument to be used can be chosen. Notice that I have made a distinction between an information-gathering technique and an information-gathering instrument. This is an important distinction. An information-gathering technique is a method of obtaining information whereas an information-gathering instrument (or tool) is the particular device that is to be used. Some kinds of instruments can be used with more than one technique. For example, one checklist could be used to *analyze* a written assignment and another to *observe* a person making a speech. When deciding how to obtain information, you must first choose the technique you plan to use and *then* the type of instrument that would be appropriate.

Observation.   Observation is the process of looking and listening, noticing the important elements of a performance or a product. Observation allows teachers to gain information about a student's congnitive as well as his affective and psychomotor skills. However, observation is best suited for the gathering of information about a person's psychomotor and affective behavior. Any skills which are themselves observable (singing, dancing, gymnastics, speech) or which yield observable end products (writing, drawing, painting) can be assessed through the use of observation.

Skills such as oral reading, speaking, listening, carrying out experiments, dancing, playing musical instruments, and singing are the kinds of skills which cannot be measured well with paper-and-pencil tests but can be measured quite accurately through the use of observation. Study habits, attitudes, interests, social adjustment, and leadership qualities are other examples of the kinds of things that can be assessed through the use of this technique.

When assessing a student's capabilities as a learner, it is often more important to know what he is *likely* to do in a given situation than how well he *might* do under ideal conditions. Observation is an excellent method for obtaining information about the typical behavior of students as they study, as they take tests, as they take part in class discussion, and as they engage in any number of classroom activities.

Inquiry. To inquire is to ask. There is a great deal of information which we can obtain best by simply asking. Whenever you wish to know what opinions an individual has about something, ask him. Whenever you wish to know what an individual's interests are, ask him. Whenever you wish to know whom a person admires, ask him. Information about attitudes, interests, and interpersonal relationships can usually be obtained most efficiently through the use of interviews, questionnaires, and sociometric devices — the basic instruments of inquiry.

A great deal of information about the affective domain can be obtained in a relatively short time through systematic inquiry. You should realize, however, that this information is highly subject to individual error. The individual being questioned will usually select his answers so that they will reflect favorably upon himself. He will tend to select answers which are socially acceptable, currently popular, and personally flattering. It is sometimes desirable (if there is enough time) to supplement the information obtained in this manner with information obtained through careful observation.

You can obtain information about a person by aking him questions about his perceptions of himself and his environment. You can also obtain information about a person by asking someone else about him. This latter kind of inquiry yields highly subjective judgments and, because we normally do not know the basis for those judgments, we should be very cautious when using them in decision making.

Analysis. Analysis is essentially a process of separating something into its component parts — breaking it down "to find out" what it is made of. The content of student papers, assignments, tests, and projects can be analyzed for a variety of factors. For example, a student's math assignment might be separated into types of errors or kinds of solutions proposed. A student's theme might be analyzed for sentence structure, topics covered, facts used, or opinions expressed.

By carefully analyzing a student's work *as he learns,* the teacher can obtain a great deal of useful information. He can find out how quickly a student learns, how well he retains what he learns over various time periods, and how well he can use what he has learned when facing a similar learning task. Probably the biggest source of information about a student is the work he does during learning. The projects, daily assignments, workbook pages, and ditto work sheets provide the student with an opportunity to learn and the teacher with an opportunity to watch him learn.

Howard was reading in the top reading group when he finished first grade. By the middle of second grade he was beginning to drop back. The other pupils in his group were outperforming him and he was moved to a lower group. When Howard began third grade he was placed in the lowest reading group. What had happened? Some said, "Howard is immature, he'll come out of it as he gets older." His reading teacher said, "He is just slow at completing his work. If he would work faster and get done on time, he would improve."

Because the parents were concerned, a team of specialists were called in and many suggestions were offered:

Howard has a perceptual problem.

Howard's auditory closure is weak.

Howard could have an auditory discrimination problem.

Have you had his eyes checked?

When was the last time Howard had a physical examination?

Is Howard given the love he needs at home?

Howard doesn't assume responsibility. Give him some jobs to do around the house. *Make him responsible.*

After much investigation of Howard's personality, physical health, intelligence and perceptual skills, Howard was found to be withdrawn and unhappy in school but physically healthy, above average in intelligence, and suffering from no perceptual disabilities. It was finally decided that he *should* be able to learn to read, and so he was placed in a special reading class.

The reading teacher gave several diagnostic tests and discovered that Howard had a good sight vocabulary but was unable to sound out any unfamiliar words. His word attack skills were very weak. There were, for example, many phonetic rules he had failed to learn. A carefully tailored teaching program was developed and Howard began again to learn to read. Before he finished fourth grade, he was reading on grade level, was back in the regular class, and was rapidly gaining on the pupils in the top reading group who had left him behind more than two years before.

Howard's story is a true one. And it has a happy ending. Howard made it back!

But it has a sad ending also. Howard could have been saved all this trouble and frustration. The regular classroom teacher could have discovered his problem.

Back in the pages of Howard's second grade reading workbook the evidence was hidden. If you looked back at his second grade work, you would soon locate the time that the trouble began. His work had been virtually without error. But his assignments were beginning to be less accurate. He began making more and more errors. Soon there were pages not completed and some not even begun. The teacher had noticed this. However he did *not* notice the kinds of errors Howard was making. A careful analysis of Howard's work would have helped the teacher to discover, very early, the phonetic skills he was having trouble learning. Further assignments, carefully designed to teach those skills, could have been given. Continuous checking of these assignments would have given the teacher information about which skills Howard was learning and which he still did not know.

Testing.   In general, testing yields more accurate information more efficiently than any other method. Although there is not complete agreement about what a test is, most experts would agree that a test has the characteristics outlined below.

Tests are characterized by

1. A common situation to which all students respond.
2. A common set of instructions governing the students' responses.
3. A common set of rules for scoring the students' responses.
4. A numerical description of each student's performance.

The first three characteristics assure standardization of procedures and objectivity in scoring. If these three characteristics are all present, then two persons independently giving the same test should obtain the same results. This standardization of the situation, the instructions, and the scoring is what makes testing more accurate than the other information-gathering techniques.

The fourth characteristic provides for precision of the information obtained and allows the test user to perform mathematical manipulations of the results. A numerical description of a person's performance can be far more precise than a verbal description. How many adjectives and qualifying phrases could you come up with to describe varying degrees of intelligence? (Extremely unintelligent, very unintelligent, somewhat unintelligent, very slightly intelligent, slightly intelligent, intelligent, very intelligent, etc.) By contrast, our numerical system allows us an infinite number of possibilities from zero to infinity. This allows us to differentiate between two students who are both very intelligent (Sam's IQ = 138, George's IQ = 132; Sam and George are both very intelligent). Of course, our numerical descriptions cannot be more precise than the accuracy of our tests.

Tests can be oral or written, formal or informal, designed to measure knowledge or performance. Nevertheless, the four characteristics should be present to some degree in any test.

Many kinds of information can be obtained through the use of tests. Cognitive, affective, and psychomotor skills can all be tested. Testing is usually considered to be the major information-gathering technique for obtaining information about the cognitive aspects of a person's behavior. Therefore, testing is often associated with paper-and-pencil measures of subject matter knowledge and ability to think. However, testing can also be used to obtain a measure of a person's skill in such areas as writing, speaking, sports, and physical education.

Table 5.1 presents a summary of the major characteristics of the various information-gathering techniques.

Notice that the four major information-gathering techniques vary in many ways. It is not simply a matter of saying, "Which technique is most accurate?" because testing would win out every time. When selecting a technique, you must decide which technique will give you the kind of information you need and allow you to get it as efficiently as possible.

TABLE 5.1

A Summary of the Major Characteristics of Each of the Four Information-gathering Techniques

	Inquiry	Observation	Analysis	Testing
Kind of information obtainable	Opinions Self-perceptions Subjective judgments Affective (especially attitudes) Social perceptions	Performance or the end products of some performance Affective (especially emotional reactions) Social interaction psychomotor skills Typical behavior	Learning outcomes during the learning process (intermediate goals) Cognitive and psychomotor skills Some affective outcomes	Attitude and achievement Terminal goals Cognitive outcomes Maximum performance
Objectivity	Least objective Highly subject to bias and error	Subjective but can be objective if care is taken in the construction and use of the instruments	Objective but not stable over time	Most objective and reliable
Cost	Inexpensive but can be time-consuming	Inexpensive but very time-consuming	Fairly inexpensive Preparation time is somewhat lengthy but crucial	Most expensive but most information gained per unit of time

---

EXERCISE 5.2

Match the descriptions of needed information (numbered items) with the "best" technique for getting that information (lettered items). You may use the terms among the lettered items more than once.

    a. Observation
    b. Inquiry
    c. Analysis
    d. Testing
1. How well a tennis player executes the backhand stroke.
2. Aptitude for algebra.

3. Memory for historical events.
4. What misunderstandings have led the fifth graders to develop faulty problem-solving strategies.
5. Who is the most popular child?
6. What social cliques exist in the class?
7. Which student knows most about the process of osmosis?
8. Are my students learning rapidly enough?

Select the Type of Instrument

Once you have decided which of the four basic information-gathering techniques to use, you then need to decide what instrument(s) would be most helpful. Suppose, for example, you plan on using systematic observation. Would a checklist be most helpful, or a rating scale? Maybe a set of anecdotes would be more appropriate. And, if you are going to test, should you use a standardized instrument or a teacher-made one? If teacher-made, would essay questions be more appropriate than multiple-choice or true-false? In the next few pages, the major characteristics of the various information-gathering instruments will be discussed. In Chapters 10 through 13 you will learn how to construct each type of instrument. In Chapter 14, you will learn how to select a standardized instrument.[2]

Instruments of observation. The major instruments of observation are: anecdotal records, checklists, rating scales, and rankings.

Anecdotal records. Anecdotal records are written descriptions of the observations the teachers have made of their students. These descriptions are factual records rather than interpretations of what happened. The anecdotal record, like the single-frame movie camera, is a kind of "time-lapse" recording technique which is extremely useful to the classroom teacher. These brief pictures of behavior will allow the teacher to see a pattern of behavior over a period of time in much the same way that a photographer, through time-lapse photography, watches a plant grow.

Anecdotal records are most appropriate for gathering information about the social adjustment of students. However, they *can* be used to record a wide variety of student behaviors. Whenever a record of a student's *typical* behavior is called for, the anecdotal record may be an appropriate information-gathering instrument to use. An important advantage of this instrument is that it does not depend upon the student's capacity to communicate with the teacher. Thus, teachers of small children, retarded children, or children who are somehow inhibited in their ability to communicate can obtain important information by using

[2] After reading this section you should be able to make a preliminary selection of the type of instrument you wish to use. You should then turn to the chapter which deals specifically with that instrument. As you read about how to construct each type of instrument, you will also become more aware of its strengths and weaknesses.

this technique. A disadvantage of anecdotal records is that they take a great deal of time to use. The problem of finding the time to write down the verbal descriptions of student behaviors can be solved, however, and various solutions will be discussed in Chapter 6. Another disadvantage of the anecdotal record is that, since it is not highly objective, it is very difficult to establish the reliability of the results obtained through this kind of approach. However, this disadvantage is partially offset by the fact that the information gained is a valid measure of the person's typical behavior in a natural setting.

Checklists.   A floodlight is to a spotlight as an anecdote is to a checklist.

Although the above analogy is rather crude, it does point out a very important difference between the anecdote and the checklist. The anecdote is used to investigate large areas of behavior, *to see what can be seen.* The checklist, on the other hand, is used to search out very specific behaviors, *to see if what you are looking for is there.* When using a checklist, you decide that certain behaviors or certain characteristics are important. You put these down in a *list* and then *check off* each one that is present.

The checklist provides information as to *whether or not* a given characteristic is present. The major value of the checklist is that it is an easy, objective technique to use in evaluating performance skills which can be clearly divided into specific steps. A modification of the checklist can be made by indicating on the checklist the *order* in which the steps were taken. This modification allows an assessment to be made of the sequencing of behaviors or operations.

Rating scales.   The rating scale is simply a set of characteristics to be judged accompanied by some kind of a scale. The observer uses the scale to indicate which of several descriptions best characterizes the individual being judged. The rating scale specifies ahead of time which characteristics are to be judged *and* which descriptive statements are to be used in judging those characteristics. The specific, most important aspects of the characteristic being judged are selected and the observer's attention is directed specifically to those aspects. This process causes the observer to be somewhat more objective, and probably more accurate, in his judgments.

The rating scale, like the checklist, can be used to judge objects or end products as well as behavior. This makes the rating scale an extremely versatile observational tool because it can be used for obtaining information about a student's performance as judged by observing his behavior or as judged by observing the end product of his behavior. Furthermore, the rating scale is useful in judging products themselves (for example, textbooks or other classroom materials).

Ranking.   Ranking is a relatively crude observational tool and is somewhat subjective, for it simply calls for the observer to rank the persons or objects being judged on the basis of the degree to which they possess the characteristic being measured. There are a number of useful modifications of the strict rank-order method. For example, it is possible to rank by dividing a group of persons or products into some preestablished number of groups. This is the procedure followed when themes or art objects are divided into average, above-average, and below-average groups. Another modification of the ranking method is called *the paired-comparison method.* In this approach each student is compared to every other student and in each case the rater indicates which of the two is judged to be better.

Besides the fact that ranking is a fairly easy procedure and does not require too much previous preparation, it has the advantage that it forces the rater to differentiate among all of the persons or objects being rated. It also has the advantage that it can be used to rank objects as well as individuals. Perhaps one of the biggest drawbacks to ranking is that the meaning of a particular rank is dependent on the size and the nature of the group being ranked. To rank fifth out of six students is far different than to be fifth out of twenty students. Also, to be fifth in a group of twenty *gifted* students is something quite different from being fifth in a group of twenty *below-average* students. Ranking has a very limited use and should be used only when a rough estimate is needed for a relatively small group of individuals or objects.

Instruments of inquiry. The following instruments can help the teacher to obtain, more systematically and more objectively, information about an individual's perceptions of himself or others: the questionnaire, the interview, sociometric instruments, and projective techniques.

The questionnaire. A questionnaire is simply a list of questions written down so that they can be read and responded to by the student (or other respondent). The questionnaire is usually duplicated so that copies can be given to each person being questioned. Consequently, large groups of individuals can be questioned at the same time. The questionnaire can be filled out at the individual's own convenience. In fact, questionnaires are often mailed out to individuals to be filled out and returned.

The questionnaire is designed primarily to get information about the opinions and attitudes of individuals. Another use of the questionnaire, however, is to obtain reports of what individuals did (or might do) in a given situation. For example, questionnaires can be used to obtain information about reported study habits, perceived use of the library, or amount of time spent on practicing for a performance.

Perhaps the biggest disadvantage of questionnaires is that they yield *perceptions* of what is rather than evidence of what actually is. It must be remembered, however, that it is our perceptions about what is that guide our behavior. If my students *perceive* the content of my course to be irrelevant, that is important for me to know. I may know that the content is indeed relevant, but if my students do not think it is, I may wish to try to change their perceptions by changing the way I present that content. I may know that my students are not utilizing good study habits, but I will probably not get them to change if they perceive their study habits as "good." This often cited disadvantage can become an advantage if we use the questionnaire specifically to obtain information about the discrepancy between what is and what is perceived to be.

One disadvantage of questionnaires which is difficult to deal with is the fact that individuals often treat them lightly and do not respond carefully and honestly to them. A final disadvantage lies in the fact that individuals will usually respond so as to make themselves look good. This is a problem which is common to all the instruments of inquiry and we will deal with it at length in Chapter 6.

The inventory is a special kind of questionnaire designed to get self-reports. It is highly structured and is usually used to obtain information about an individual's interests. The inventory can provide the teacher with checklists of likes and dislikes, attitudes, habits, opinions, and typical behaviors. Most personality tests are really not tests at all but inventories — checklists of a person's perceptions about his own behavior.

Another special kind of questionnaire is the attitude scale. This instrument combines the features of a self-report questionnaire and the rating scale. The respondent is asked to report his attitudes toward various "things" by matching his feelings to those described on some scale. A common scale, for example, asks the respondent to read a statement and then to indicate if he strongly agrees, agrees, is undecided, disagrees, or strongly disagrees.

The interview. The interview is a very familiar information-gathering tool. The man-on-the-street interviews of radio and television have been popular for years. Interviews are conducted daily to obtain public opinion about political issues, commercial products, news events, and new TV programs. The typical classroom teacher does a great deal of interviewing. He talks with students about their problems, has conferences with parents from time to time, and discusses issues and problems with fellow teachers. Most of the time, teachers use the interview in very informal settings conducted in a fairly unstructured manner. These informal, unstructured interviews are valuable, for they often uncover information which is unexpected but important. For example, a third grade teacher found out in an informal discussion with one of his students that he had developed a real interest in dinosaurs and had been reading a number of library books about them. On another occasion, a high school teacher was unable to find out why one of his better students began to do work of a much lower quality than usual. The student seemed to be spending as much time on his studies, he claimed still to enjoy them, and he said that he was trying just as hard. One day, when talking informally with the student, the teacher discovered that the boy's best friend had begun to experiment with drugs. He thought about this a great deal, and the concern he had for his friend made it difficult to concentrate on his studies.

Interviews, whether informal and unstructured or formal and highly structured, can provide the teacher with information about opinions, interests, self-perceptions, typical behavior patterns, etc. Interviews can be conducted often, as a normal part of the continual communication between teacher and student. Consequently, they are particularly valuable for keeping track of traits and characteristics which change rapidly (e.g., interests, opinions, attitudes, and interpersonal relationships).

The major advantage of the interview is that it allows you to obtain affective information of a highly personal nature. Of course, the major disadvantage is that the information is highly subjective and likely to contain a great deal of error. Another important disadvantage is that it takes a great deal of time. If the same information is needed about all your students, then a questionnaire or inventory would be more appropriate.

Sociometric instruments. Sociometric instruments are designed to obtain evidence about the social acceptance of individuals within a group and about the perceived relationships that exist within that group. The social acceptance of individuals within a group is best determined by nominating devices. These instruments establish the need for various persons to be selected for some position or some activity.

A *typical nominating device* asks elementary pupils to choose three classmates (or some other predetermined number of them) that he would most like to have attend a party with him. The interpretation of data from nominating devices is difficult. For example, one must consider the nature of the position or activity for which individuals are being nominated. The person most often nominated to be a partner in a science project may not be the same person nominated most often as a dance partner. Another problem with information from nominating devices is that it is not stable over time. Especially among elementary school children, friendships shift very often.

There are two other types of instruments used for getting information about the perceived social relations within a group. The first is often referred to as the *guess who technique.* A "guess who" instrument describes a number of individuals, and the respondents are to guess who is being described. If we wish to know who is perceived of as a loner, for example, we would describe someone who usually plays alone and does not interact much with the others. A "guess who" instrument might describe the class leader, the class clown, the class brain, the class peacemaker, etc. Each time the description would be followed by the question, "guess who?"

The second type of instrument for discovering perceived relations might be called a *placement device.* With this type of instrument a situation is described (verbally or pictorially) and the respondents are asked to place the members of the group in the various positions which have been described. For example, a map of the playground might be presented to fifth graders with the instructions to put the names or initials of their classmates in the place on the playground where they would most likely to be found during recess.

Despite the problems of interpretations, sociometric instruments are gaining in popularity because they offer a systematic way of determining the social interactions of a group. When used cautiously, the information thus obtained can be very helpful in making decisions about how to group students for various activities. Self-referenced judgments about a person's social development are also greatly aided by information obtained at different times with the same sociometric instrument.

Projective techniques.   Projective techniques are designed to find out about personality and social adjustment characteristics of individuals. These instruments generally present highly ambiguous stimulus materials (e.g., pictures or inkblots) to an individual. The individual is told to describe what he sees, and his responses are analyzed. The assumption is that a person will project his feelings, biases, and idiosyncrasies into the ambiguous stimuli. These instruments are highly unreliable, and we introduce them here only so that you will know what they are and how to react to their use. I would offer two pieces of advice to classroom teachers concerning projective techniques:

1. Do *not* attempt to use them yourself.
2. If you have information about the results of a projective technique, treat the information with great caution. Do *not* accept projective evidence as "true" unless you have confirmation from other, more reliable sources of information.

It is especially tempting for teachers to "read between the lines" of the themes and other creative products which their students have produced. Resist this temptation. Do not try to be a clinical psychologist.

Instruments of analysis.   Teachers can use observational tools *and* content analysis procedures to analyze the work the student does *as he learns.* Observation is to be used when the work being analyzed is some performance (e.g., a speech, a dance routine, brushstrokes during the production of an oil painting) or some nonverbal product (e.g., a map, a piece of sculpture, an oil painting). Content analysis should be used when analyzing some verbal or written communication (a speech, a theme, a math problem, an outline).

Content analysis is essentially a counting procedure. Written or spoken communications are analyzed for the presence or absence of certain characteristics. Once the important characteristics have been identified (e.g., properly spelled words, creatively used verbs), they are counted. The number attained is compared to some standard, and judgments are then made about the quality of the communication. For example, we might decide that an eighth grade theme is of high quality if it has a topic sentence for every paragraph, no more than 1 percent misspelled words, a single unifying theme, etc.

Note that to analyze, whether by observation or by content analysis, you must know what it is you are looking for. Consequently, the most important instruments for the analysis of learning are well-designed projects and assignments which specify *in advance* the characteristics of importance. Three kinds of projects and assignments are particularly important instruments of analysis: acquisition assignments, review assignments, and transfer assignments. You will notice that these correspond to the three stages of learning: acquiring information, putting it in memory, and using it to acquire new information.

Acquisition assignments. The assignment designed to help the student acquire new skills or new information is usually not very well conceived. Typical of this kind of assignment is the following:

Study the spelling words for Unit V; there will be a test Wednesday.

Read chapter 6 in your history book. Know what each explorer discovered.

Memorize your "fives" multiplication tables through 5×10.

The problem with the above assignments is that no instructions are given as to how to study, when to study, how long to study, etc. There is no effective way for the teacher to find out how a student acquired the information, how long it took him to acquire it, or why he did not acquire it. Yet these are all important things for the teacher to know, and well-designed acquisition assignments can help him to find out these things. The most difficult task in all assignments designed to yield evaluative information is that of controlling the many variables which can affect learning. Whenever variables are left uncontrolled, it is difficult if not impossible to determine why or how learning occurred. This problem of control will be discussed more thoroughly in Chapters 6 and 12.

Review assignments. If newly learned information and skills are to be retained, a certain amount of review is necessary. Assignments and projects which give the student the opportunities for review are plentiful. Pages of math problems "like the ones we just learned to do" are a good example of this kind of assignment. The stories in the elementary readers are designed (among other things) to give the students practice in using newly learned words and recently learned reading skills. Many workbook pages are really review assignments designed to give the student practice at a newly learned skill. When review assignments are properly designed and given at the appropriate time, a great deal of information can be obtained about the *process* a student uses for review as well as about the level of the original acquisition.

Transfer assignments. Periodically, educators reconfirm the fact that a primary goal of education is to get the student to the point where the things he learned in school will help him to learn more on his own. We hope that the knowledge and skills he gains in school will transfer to situations in real life. Transfer assignments can help us find out how well we are attaining that goal. Can our student transfer newly learned information to a new learning situation? What are the conditions under which that transfer will or will not occur? How well must students "know" before that knowledge will transfer? These and other similar questions can begin to be answered with information gained from properly constructed transfer assignments which have been carefully analyzed. Chapter 12 tells you how to construct them and Chapter 6 how to analyze the responses the students make to them.

Tests

Teacher-made tests. The teacher-made test is best suited for obtaining measures of cognitive achievement of students covering the learning outcomes specified by the teacher's own instructional goals. The teacher-made test can be used to measure all the levels of the cognitive domain which were discussed in Chapter 4. Unfortunately the vast majority of teacher-made tests measure only at the factual or knowledge level, and therefore teachers are getting incomplete information on how much their students have achieved. Teacher-made tests are extremely versatile. They can be constructed from any number of a wide variety of test items. Each of these kinds of items has certain advantages and disadvantages. These will·be discussed in Chapter 13, where item-writing and test-construction procedures are presented.

All kinds of decisions must be made during the instructional process. Decisions about how to group the students, what assignments to make, how much time should be allowed for the students to learn a certain amount of material, whether or not to move on to the next unit in a workbook, etc. These numerous instructional decisions rest upon the question "How much has the student achieved?" This judgment calls for a careful measure of what the student was expected to achieve. This information, in turn, can often be most efficiently obtained with teacher-made tests. Standardized tests are usually too general and do not explicitly measure the instructional goals of a given classroom.

Another important advantage of teacher-made tests is that they can be given at any point in the instructional sequence. Consequently judgments can be made about achievement over very small units of instruction as well as very large ones. It is desirable, for example, to discover, as early in the learning process as possible, any mistakes students are making in the development of a new skill, so that these errors can be quickly corrected. Consequently, judgments of achievement must be made *while the student is learning.* Teacher-made tests, along with the instruments of observation, inquiry, and analysis, can help the teacher make accurate judgments of this type.

Standardized tests. A standardized test is an instrument designed to obtain many kinds of information under standardized conditions. Usually a table of norms accompanies the test. The information obtained from a standardized test is distinguished from that obtained from other instruments because it is clearly defined, has known parameters (e.g., estimates of reliability and validity) and has been obtained under "ideal conditions." Because of these features, the information from standardized tests is particularly valuable when important decisions must be made.

Standardized instruments are available which will measure various kinds of general and specific aptitudes and achievement in a wide variety of subject matters. Furthermore, there are instruments available to measure personality traits, opinions, attitudes, interests, and other noncognitive characteristics.

Standardized tests are useful for making selection and placement decisions and can be valuable in diagnosing problems as well as in predicting success. A more thorough discussion of the kinds of standardized tests can be found in Chapter 14. Also, in that chapter is a discussion of the procedures for selecting the standardized test(s) which best fit your needs.

Decide When the Information Should Be Obtained

Once you have decided what information you need and what instrument(s) you will use to obtain it, you then need to decide when to obtain it. The decision about when to obtain information should be made primarily on the basis of the kind of information needed and the types of judgments and decisions that are to be made. For example, if information about a student's maximum performance is needed, then the student must have had an opportunity to reach his maximum and he must know far enough in advance so that he can get prepared to do his best. On the other hand, if information about typical performance is needed, then the information should be obtained without warning, with no advance notice. If we are trying to make formative judgments, we need to get information *during* the learning, not after it is completed. On the other hand, if we want a measure of the achievement of terminal goals, then we need to wait until each student has had an opportunity to reach those goals.

It is important to anticipate, as far in advance as practical, when instruction will begin and end, so that you will have plenty of time to select or construct the instruments you will need for your information gathering. Standardized instruments take several weeks to arrive once they have been ordered. Teacher-made tests take a great deal of time to construct if they are to be prepared well.

One final consideration: Do not try to obtain information when circumstances may make it difficult for the students to respond well. For example, some teachers assign tests on days for which other important but distracting events have been planned. Tests should not be scheduled for the day after homecoming or the day of the school picnic. Check your calendar of events before deciding on a day for testing.

Specify the Testing Conditions

Although this is a relatively easy task, it is nevertheless an important one. The conditions under which information is to be gathered do need to be decided in advance. The first and perhaps most obvious determination to be made is how formal the situation will be. Most standardized tests, for example, are to be administered under very formal, "ideal" conditions. There must be proper lighting, proper ventilation, spaced seating, etc. Most teacher-made tests are usually administered more informally. If test anxiety is a concern, less formal conditions might be in order.

Another consideration is whether maximum or typical performance measures are needed. Should the setting be quiet and without interruptions or should it be more natural and realistic? It depends on the kind of information you need. Should the students know they are being measured or observed? Again, it depends on the kind of information needed.

Is the information to be gathered individually, one student at a time, or in a group (all the students at once)? Individually administered tests are sometimes necessary, but they require a tremendous amount of time. Rarely should individually administered instruments be used when the same information is needed about everyone.

It is important to specify these conditions in advance so that you can plan for the facilities and the time needed to obtain the information under the conditions desired.

EXERCISE 5.3

1. Briefly, *in your own words,* describe the major characteristics of each of the following:
   a. Observation
   b. Inquiry
   c. Analysis
   d. Testing
2. What is the difference between an information-gathering *technique* and an information-gathering *instrument?*
3. What are the major considerations when deciding *when* and *how* information is to be gathered?

CONSTRUCT (OR SELECT) THE INFORMATION-GATHERING INSTRUMENT

Once you have decided what information you need and how and when you plan on obtaining it, you then need to *construct* the particular instrument you plan on using. Or, if you decided to use a standardized instrument, you will need to select one. This fifth step in the evaluation process is an extremely important one. The information you obtain can be no better than the instrument you use to obtain it. In this chapter, you will learn some basic principles for constructing teacher-made instruments. In Chapters 10 through 13, you will find the application of these principles to the construction of particular types of instruments. In Chapter 14, guidelines are set down for the selection of standardized instruments. This section has been written to introduce you to the basic process involved in the construction of teacher-made instruments.

This section should help you to be able to

1. Explain why the same basic procedures apply to the construction and evaluation of all types of information-gathering instruments.
2. Apply the general suggestions for constructing information gathering instruments to the construction and evaluation of specific types of instruments. (You will start toward this goal in this chapter and complete it when you have finished Chapters 10–13.)

GENERAL GUIDELINES FOR THE CONSTRUCTION OF TEACHER-MADE INFORMATION-GATHERING INSTRUMENTS

When producing an information-gathering instrument, your primary concern is to produce one which is valid and reliable; that is, you will be concentrating on minimizing the possibility of error when the instrument is used. Consequently, the procedures for producing such an instrument should be based upon the principles for minimizing error which were discussed in Chapter 2.

Principles for Minimizing Error

1. Relate everything you do to the reason you are evaluating.
2. Be clear, concise, consistent.
3. Obtain a representative sample.

You should be able to construct a good information-gathering instrument if you keep these principles in mind and if you follow these suggestions.

General Suggestions for Constructing Any Information-gathering Instrument

1. Review what you learned from the first four steps in the evaluation process.
2. Define the format.
3. Write the items.
4. Write the instructions.
5. Assemble and reproduce the instrument.

Review what you learned from the first four steps in the evaluation process. Before you begin construction of any information-gathering instrument, review what you found out up to this point. What judgments and decisions do you anticipate making? What information are you trying to get? What technique and which type of instrument do you plan on using? When are you going to obtain that information? How much time do you have to construct the instrument? Will you obtain the information individually, about one person at a time, or will you obtain the information from a large group of persons at one time? Obviously, the answers to these and related questions will affect decisions about the format, content, and instructions of your instrument.

Define the format. The possible formats which various instruments can take are myriad. However, the basic dimensions are the same across all the various instruments: (1) presentation mode and (2) response mode.

Typically an information-gathering instrument presents some material to which the student is expected to respond. How will that material be presented? Orally or in writing? On paper, on the blackboard, on a movie screen, or on a tape recorder? If the instrument is to be administered orally in a one-to-one situation, a different format would be selected than if it were to be administered to a large group. A different format would be used for handicapped students than for those who are normal.

Not only the presentation mode but also the response mode needs to be determined. How will the students respond? Orally or in writing? With complete freedom or with restrictions (e.g., topic, time, number of words)? The more restricted responses will *tend* to yield more reliable results. The responses which give the student more freedom are better suited for obtaining creative, individual responses. With a greal deal of freedom to respond, norm-referenced judgments of achievement become difficult to make.

Write the items. The item is the individual unit the person is asked to respond to. In tests, questionnaires, and interviews, it is the question being asked. In checklists and rating scales, it is each trait or behavior to be checked or rated. Item writing is an art. It requires knowledge, skill, and practice to become a good item writer. The specific suggestions for writing each of the many kinds of items can be found in Chapters 10 through 13. Good item writers seem to have particular identifiable abilities and characteristics. According to Wesman (1971), good item writers have the following characteristics:

A Good Item Writer

1. Knows his subject matter well.
2. Possesses a rational set of educational values.
3. Understands the individuals who will take his tests.
4. Has good verbal communication skills.
5. Skillfully uses the techniques for writing each type of item.

Because so many of the information-gathering instruments rely on well-formed questions, it might be useful to explore the art of writing good questions a little further.

What should be asked? What *can* be asked? What kinds of things can we get someone to tell us about? We can ask someone to tell us what he "knows" about some topic or about some person. Or we can ask him how he "feels" about that topic or person. So first of all we should decide if we want to find out what a person knows or what he feels. Are we interested in a person's knowledge or in a person's opinions and attitudes? The description of the information you need should tell you this.

If it is knowledge you are interested in, then you should ask: "Knowledge about what (or whom) and knowledge at what level?" At this point you should specify the subject matter content or the name of the object or individual that you expect the person to be knowledgeable about (e.g., World War II, the moon, the new boy in class). Next, you should decide what level of "knowing" you are trying to get information about. Do you want information about how well *facts* have been *memorized* or how well *concepts* have been *understood?* Do you want to find out if the knowledge someone has can be *applied* to a new situation or if it can be *synthesized* with other knowledge to form a new concept?

If it is opinions or attitudes you are interested in, then you should ask: "Opinions about what or whom (or attitudes toward what or whom)?" The answer to this question is easy. But be certain that you are getting opinions about the right thing. If you want opinions about an educational program as a whole, do not ask only for opinions about some limited aspects of it. If you wish to know how a person feels about the content of a speech, do not ask about the delivery or about the dynamics of the speaker.

How should I ask it? By answering the question "What should I ask?" you are helping to make your questions valid. Your answer to the question "How should I ask it?" may have a lot to do with the reliability as well as the validity of a question. the *most important thing you can do to reduce measurement error is to be clear, concise, and consistent.* So be consistent in the way you ask questions, be concise in your statement of each question, and avoid ambiguity by making certain each question can be interpreted in only one way.

What kind of response should I ask for? What choices in response format can you give those you are questioning? An obvious choice is between oral or written response. Oral response allows you to obtain a great deal of information in a short time, but it is more difficult to analyze. Using a tape recorder to record oral responses makes analysis easier but does not eliminate the major problem associated with the analysis of oral responses. That problem is the fact that respondents usually do not organize their oral responses as carefully as their written ones. They tend to include much more irrelevant material and are often highly repetitive.

Written responses can be classified into three broad categories: scaled responses, open-ended responses, and choice responses. Scaled responses are those in which the respondent indicates his response on a checklist or rating scale (see Chapter 10 for further details). Open-ended responses would include fill-the-blank and short-answer items, but they often allow the respondent to respond in almost any way he chooses (i.e., the answers are not formed in advance and merely given to him to select). The amount of freedom one might allow in an open-ended question may vary considerably (see the discussion of essay questions in Chapter 13). Choice responses call for the respondent to select from among a number of alternative answers the one he likes best (see Chapter 13).

Oral responses are usually open-ended, but scaled responses and alternative-choice responses can be made orally. In this case the responses are written down by the interviewer.

Write the instructions. Instructions must be clear. If the student does not know what he is supposed to do, his responses will not provide you with the information you were trying to get. If an observer is not clear about how to use a rating scale, his observations will probably be in error. If an interviewer is not sure about what he is to ask at what point in time, the interview will probably not yield valid, reliable information.

In general, instructions should include the information listed below.

Good Instructions Include

1. A statement about the content and format of the instrument (e.g., questions about World War II).
2. An indication of what is to be done with that content (e.g., read each question and formulate an answer).
3. A statement describing the response to be made (e.g., Write each answer in less than twenty-five words).
4. An explanation of how the results will be used (e.g., You will be graded on your responses. Each question is worth 15 points).
5. A statement of any possible restrictions (e.g., You will have only twenty-five minutes to complete the test).

In actual practice there are many test formats which are so common that such elaborate instructions are not needed. Nevertheless, it is important that all the elements are clearly understood by anyone using an information-gathering instrument.

Assemble and reproduce the instrument. At this stage you must make a number of important decisions about what the final copy of the instrument will be like. Here is where you get your last chance to make sure that (1) all the items work together to provide you with the information you need; (2) all items and instructions are clear, concise, and free of inconsistencies; and (3) the items represent a representative sample of the items which might properly have been included.

EXERCISE 5.4

1. Why do the same basic principles apply to the construction of all types of information-gathering instruments?
2. In this section you reviewed the three rules for minimizing error. You were also introduced to the characteristics of a good item writer. How does each characteristic help the good item writer to carry out the three rules? Are there any characteristics that seem to be particularly important for carrying out any one of the three rules?
3. How many of the characteristics of a good item writer can be learned? How many are innate talents?

Evaluating Teacher-made Instruments

The step-by-step procedures for evaluating each teacher-made instrument will be presented in Chapters 10 through 13. However, there are variations of these instruments which have not been discussed in this book. Furthermore, in the future, you may find occasion to use an information-gathering instrument that you had never heard of before. Consequently, it would be valuable for you to understand the basic procedures for evaluating any information-gathering instrument. Very simply, there are three criteria against which we judge any instrument and two methods for obtaining information about the instruments that will allow us to make these judgments. The three criteria are validity, reliability, and ease of use. The two basic procedures for checking on these criteria are to check for obvious flaws and to try the instrument out.

You will notice that this process parallels the procedures for estimating error which were discussed in Chapter 2. That is because the basic principles of evaluation are again being used to help us solve an evaluation problem: "How do we know if our instrument is any good?"

When you look for obvious flaws in an information-gathering instrument, look for the major sources of instrument error: ambiguity, lack of conciseness, inappropriate content.

When trying an instrument out, you ask yourself "What is this instrument designed to do?" "Did it do it well?" "What judgments were made from the information obtained?" "Do they hold true?" "Can they be verified?"[3]

Also, try the instrument out and look for consistency across alternate forms, across time, across items, etc. If you keep getting consistent results, it is likely that your test is reliable.

Finally, as you use your instrument, note any problems that arise which indicate that it is difficult to use. Is it too long? Hard to read? Difficult to keep your place as you work? These kinds of questions, asked of yourself and your students,

---

[3] The procedures for verifying judgments are explained in detail in Chap. 8.

should help you to discover any problems which make the instrument difficult to use.

SUMMARY

1. There are three steps to take when preparing to gather information: *(a)* locate information already available, *(b)* decide when and how the information still needed is to be obtained, and *(c)* construct (or select) the information-gathering instruments you plan on using.
2. There are five main sources of readily available information about students: *(a)* The teacher's personal records, *(b)* the school's records, *(c)* the counselor's records, *(d)* the records of auxiliary school personnel, and *(e)* the records of the student's parents.
3. Before using any available information, ask yourself these three questions: *(a)* Does it fit the description of the information needed? *(b)* How accurate is it? *(c)* Is it useful for making the anticipated judgments and decisions?
4. It is very easy to copy available information incorrectly. Make certain that information you obtain from someone else's records is transferred carefully to your records.
5. An information-gathering technique is a method of obtaining information. An information-gathering instrument is the particular device that is to be used.
6. The major information-gathering techniques are observation, inquiry, analysis, and testing.
7. The major information-gathering instruments are anecdotal records, checklists, rating scales, rank order, questionnaires, interviews, sociometric instruments, projects and assignments, and tests.
8. Information should be obtained as close to possible to the time that the judgments and decisions must be made. Do not try to obtain information when circumstances make it difficult for the student to respond.
9. The procedures for constructing all information-gathering instruments follow from the principles for minimizing error. The following suggestions are offered: *(a)* Review what you learned from the first four steps of the evaluation process. *(b)* Define the format of your instrument. *(c)* Write the items. *(d)* Write the instructions. *(e)* Assemble and reproduce the instrument.
10. Teacher-made instruments can be evaluated by looking for obvious flaws and by trying the instrument out. You should look for validity, reliability, and ease of use.

References

Russell Sage Foundation, *Guidelines for the Collection, Maintenance and Dissemination of Pupil Records,* 1970.

Wesman, Alexander G.: "Writing the Test Item" in Robert L. Thorndike *Educational Measurement,* 2d ed., American Council on Education, Washington, D.C., 1971.

Suggested Readings

For a number of good articles on test design and construction, read:

Thorndike, Robert L. (ed.): *Educational Measurement,* 2d ed., Washington, D.C.: *Educational Measurement,* part one, American Council on Education, 1971.

A valuable set of pamphlets discussing several aspects of selecting and constructing tests can be obtained from the Educational Testing Service. Write to ETS in Princeton, New Jersey, and ask for its *Tests and Measurement Kit.*

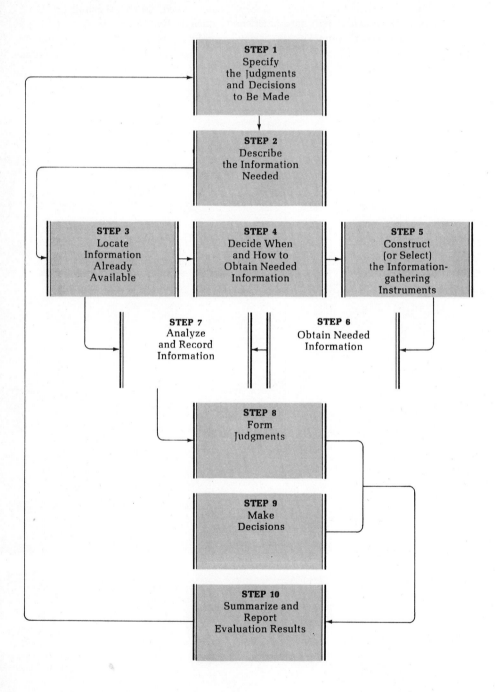

CHAPTER 6

Obtaining, Analyzing, and Recording Information

No matter how well you plan your evaluation activities, the information you obtain will be grossly in error unless you use the various information-gathering techniques carefully (step 6). Then, once the information has been obtained, you need to carefully analyze and record it (step 7). This chapter has been written to help you learn to carry out these two steps (6 and 7) of the evaluation process. The first part of the chapter includes a discussion of step 6 and the second part of step 7. The specific objectives are listed at the beginning of each part.

OBTAINING INFORMATION

You have now reached step 6 and are ready to obtain information. However, just having the right tool for the job does not guarantee that the job will be done. So you need to know how to use the information-gathering tools described in the last chapter. Consequently, the first part of this chapter has been designed to help you learn how to observe, inquire, analyze, and test.

> When given a need for specific information, you should be able to successfully use the appropriate information-gathering techniques to obtain it.

The first part of this chapter has been written to help you attain the general goal stated above.

> When you have finished the first part of this chapter, you should be able to
>
> 1. Apply the basic overall suggestions for obtaining information to the specific problems of any information gathering session
> 2. Make valid and reliable observations
> 3. Make valid and reliable inquiries
> 4. Make valid and reliable analyses of projects, assignments, and other student communications
> 5. Successfully administer and score both teacher-made and standardized tests.

General Suggestions for Obtaining Information

Obtaining useful information depends to a great extent upon good timing. Before you set about the task of obtaining evaluative information, you should ask yourself the following two questions: Am I ready? Are my students ready?

Make sure you are ready. We have already given considerable attention to the problem of preparation in information gathering. You know, therefore, that it is important for you to think carefully about what judgments and decisions you must make and what kind of information you need before you begin to obtain that information. However, even if you have done all these things and have also selected the instruments best designed to get the information you need, you still may not be ready. A very common mistake is to try to use an instrument before you are familiar with it. It is not uncommon, for example, for teachers to set out to give a standardized test only to find that they have forgotten some needed materials. Or a teacher may begin to read instructions to students only to find out that these were instructions for the teacher only (those to be read to the students were further down in the manual). Another common mistake is to misread the amount of time students are supposed to have for a given subtest. When standardized tests are not carefully timed, proper interpretation of the score is virtually impossible. It is important, then, that you become very familiar with the instrument that you are to use before you begin to gather information. Roleplay the administration of a test, try using the rating scale on friends or student volunteers, and make certain that you know exactly how the instrument is supposed to be used. Finally, it is important for you to have all the materials that are needed ready and at hand. When a test is going to be given, for example, make certain that there are extra pencils available for the students, that you have enough copies of the test and any answer sheets that might be used, etc.

Make sure your students are ready. If you are trying to obtain maximum-performance information, then it is absolutely necessary that you give the students ample opportunity to learn (i.e., to reach maximum performance). Pop quizzes may have their value, but they do not give you information about how well your students *could* do. They only tell you how well they have done at that moment in time. Information from pop quizzes is very difficult to interpret. This is especially true when making norm-referenced judgments, because you do not know whether the differences in the scores are due to how well students *can* understand the material or to how much time the students spend studying.

It is important not only to give the students an opportunity to learn but also to tell them what it is they are expected to learn (i.e., give them carefully written instructional goals). What are you measuring if you give a test on material students have not yet had an opportunity to learn or on material students did not expect to be held accountable for?

Students must be prepared cognitively, but they must also be prepared emotionally. Students must feel that the information you gather about them is for their own good and in their best interest. Students come to fear tests because they see them as potentially harmful, as a way for the teacher to label them and as a means for the teacher to uncover the students' weaknesses. The students' attitudes toward the test and other information gathering can be positive. If you use the information you get wisely, the students' attitude will be positive.

Suggestions for Using the Instruments of Observation

Observation is a very important information-gathering technique. However, it requires a great deal of concentration and skill to obtain valid and reliable information through the process of observation. If you are to successfully use observation as a legitimate information-gathering technique, you should use the best instruments of observation available and be very familiar with their use; observe constantly, verifying the information you obtain by comparing it with other information you have; and carefully adhere to the specific suggestions discussed in the paragraphs which follow.

Suggestion 1: be objective.   Perhaps the biggest source of error in information obtained from observation is the personal bias and prejudice of the observer. We are easily influenced by our own attitudes toward particular people, toward particular ways of doing things, and toward particular ideas. A good observer is constantly striving to be aware of these biases and prejudices in an attempt to keep them from influencing his observations. Among the many things you can do to maintain objectivity while making observations perhaps the most important one is to concentrate on the behavior under observation or the specific characteristics of the product being observed. By concentrating on those things we sense (see, hear, touch) rather than on those things we feel (attitudes and opinions), we can more readily maintain objectivity.

There are three kinds of errors which are so common among observers that you should be aware of them and learn to watch for them in your own observations. The first is frequently referred to as the *halo effect*. The halo effect occurs when an observer is influenced in his observations by his general impression of the person or product he is rating. If the first general impression is good, he will tend to rate the person or product high on all characteristics being rated. On the other hand, if he tends to have an unfavorable impression of the person or product he is rating, he will tend to rate him low on all the characteristics being rated.

The second common error made by observers is due to *personal response tendency*. Some observers have a tendency to rate everyone high (this is called *generosity error*). Other observers have a tendency to rate everything and everyone very low (this is called *severity error*). Some observers have a tendency to rate everyone or everything somewhere in the middle, perceiving everyone as "average" (this is called the *central tendency error*). You can usually discover your own response tendencies by going back and looking over several ratings you have done. When you find yourself using either one end or the other of a rating scale (or tending to rate in the center), then you should make a conscious effort to spread out ratings utilizing the full width of the rating scale. This same kind of response tendency also shows up in the use of anecdotal records. Some observers tend to write down only those anecdotes which reflect positively on those being observed and others tend to write down only those anecdotes which reflect negatively on those being observed.

A third kind of error which is very common among observers is sometimes called *logical error*. This is the kind of error which occurs because the observer does not fully understand the relationship among the many variables which interact in a given situation. Consequently, he may let his observations be influenced by what he *thinks* are important relationships among characteristics he is rating. For example, in rating intelligence, teachers often overrate the high achievers and underrate the low achievers because they assume a stronger relationship between intelligence and school achievement than really exists. Many teachers assume that quiet children are good children and good students. They also frequently assume that the student who talks a lot in discussion sessions knows a great deal about the material. These assumptions are frequently not warranted and yet they do influence the way teachers rate their students.

One final suggestion for maintaining objectivity is to keep the identity of the author of any product you are observing hidden. In other words, whenever you are rating or ranking students' products (e.g., themes or art projects), it is best to have the student's name out of sight when you are making your observations. Whenever possible, it is easier to maintain objectivity if you do not know whose product you are rating.

Suggestion 2: focus on relevant behaviors.   When making observations it is very easy to get sidetracked, distracted, and "thrown out of focus." We begin to see things other than those we were planning on observing and soon stray from the characteristics which we had decided were important to the performance or product being rated. When you try to see everything at once, it is like holding a magnifying glass too far from the print. Everything is thrown out of focus. Therefore good observers keep focused on the characteristics of interest.

When using checklists and rating scales, for example, it is important to note *only* the characteristics which are specified by the instrument being used. For example, if you are rating a speaker and you are primarily interested in the mechanics of eye contact, gesturing, and voice control, then you should not pay much attention to the content of the speech (except where the content is important to the mechanical features).

Suggestion 3: be unobtrusive.   A good observer blends in with the scenery. He is unnoticed, unobtrusive, and unoffensive. Even if you are obtaining maximum-performance information, you should not call attention to yourself by making obvious signs of approval or disapproval or by making your note-taking obvious. Of course, if you are obtaining typical-performance information, it is even more important for the students to be unaware of the fact that they are being observed. Sometimes the only way you can remain unobtrusive is by waiting until later to write down your observations. When this is the case, try not to be involved in numerous activities between the time you make your observations and the time that you write them down. After observing, move quickly to some other place in the room (or even into the hall or another room) and jot down your observations while they are still fresh in your mind.

One very useful way to remain unobtrusive is to make your observations about the behaviors of your students after the fact. In other words, do not observe the behavior directly but observe the effects of those behaviors. For example, if you wish information about what your students are reading, go to the library and find out what books they are checking out. If you wish to know how your students are working out problems, collect the scratch paper they use in solving the problems. If you want to know what the students are doing at recess, find out what equipment was checked out. Obviously this technique has limited value, but it can yield information which is valuable if used appropriately.

Suggestion 4: observe often.   By making systematic observation a natural part of your everyday activities, you will accomplish two things. First of all, it is only through constant use of systematic observation that you will become a good and accurate observer. Therefore by observing daily you will increase your ability to make observations. Secondly, by making many observations you will stand a better chance of getting an accurate indication of what your students are like and what they are capable of doing. The more observations you have, the better will be your chances of having a good sample of the students' behavior and the better will be your chances of making accurate judgments and correct decisions.

Suggestions for Observing without Any Instruments

There are two observational techniques which require no formal information-gathering instrument: (1) the recording of anecdotes and (2) the use of ranking procedures. Each technique will be discussed briefly.

Anecdotal records. Teachers are often called upon to make judgments about the typical behavior of their students. All too frequently, they must rely on their memory, trying desperately to recall enough evidence to support an opinion they have formed. It is exactly at this point that the anecdotal record is useful. An anecdote is simply a statement describing an observation. The basic idea is simple: write down your observations in behavioral terms. Put down only what you see or hear, do *not* make any interpretive statements about what you *think* is happening or about what you *feel* the reasons for the behaviors are. Collect a number of these recorded behaviors over a period of time. Later, go over them, looking for patterns of behavior, and at that time make your interpretations and judgments.

Example of an Anecdote

John Smith — observer
Mary Y. — student

                                                    10/27/69
                                                    just as reading began

Mary came to reading class without her book. She talked to Sue, John, and Amy on her way to get her book. When we began to read, Mary had her book open to the wrong page. Reading Group II — Mary was transferred to this group yesterday.

Although anecdotal records have been used primarily in the past for obtaining evidence and recording information about unusual behavior, they can also be used successfully for obtaining information about typical, ordinary behavior. They can be helpful in obtaining general behavior patterns of a class as a whole as well as of the individuals within that class.

One does not construct an anecdote in the same way that one constructs a test, a rating scale, or a checklist. An anecdote is simply a written description of something which occurs and is observed. A single anecdote is of little value. Anecdotes are used for discovering *patterns* of behavior which may have explanatory or diagnostic value. In order to get evidence of a behavior pattern, several anecdotes must be obtained. When enough anecdotes have been recorded that a good picture of *typical* behavior has been obtained, then it is appropriate to examine the full array of anecdotes and try to interpret them.

Scheduling the recording of anecdotes. Many anecdotes get recorded because some unexpected behavior occurs (it is the unusual, "loud" classroom occurrences which attract our attention). One does not plan ahead to record these. They happen. They are recorded. However, the really unusual incidents are fairly easily remembered anyway and *just because they are unusual* rather than typical, *they may not really be important.* More important are the typical everyday occurrences and behaviors which can give us insights into how a student responds to his environment. To get this kind of information, you must plan your observations and set a schedule for obtaining anecdotes. The rules for setting up a schedule should fit your own style of teaching. If you are highly organized and tend to stick closely to plans, then your schedule should probably be fairly rigid. Establish a goal of so many anecdotes per day and stick to it (be realistic, do not try to collect more than just a few anecdotes per day). If you tend to be less highly organized and flexible, do not set yourself a rigid schedule. You probably will not follow it anyway and you will end up feeling guilty about not sticking to plans. Set yourself a long-range goal (e.g., approximately so many anecdotes this week) and work toward that, scheduling only for the day. Do not plan too far in advance.

A basic format for recording and filing anecdotes. Some teachers find it very convenient to use index cards (5 × 7 is a good size) and a small file box in which they arrange the anecdotes according to time and date under the name of the principle individual involved. The information is always placed on the card in the same location (some even "ditto" the major headings onto blank cards, thus producing a standard form).

Another method for keeping anecdotes utilizes file folders. One folder is made for each child and may contain other evaluative information also (e.g., sample workbook pages, samples of handwriting, grades on papers, and scores on tests and exams). Rather than an index card, anything that is handy is used. It is better to write the anecdote on a napkin than not to write it at all (because you could not find the proper form). Write on whatever you wish. File it any way that makes it easy for you to retrieve. But *always* include, somewhere on anecdote, the following information:

Information to Be Included on Every Anecdote

1. The name of the person(s) being observed
2. The name of the observer
3. The date *and* time of the observation
4. The class and/or location of the event observed
5. The anecdote itself
6. The context
7. Any *necessary* interpretation

The first two items on the above list are self-explanatory. Items 3 and 4 may need a brief explanation. When you write down the date and the time, put it in meaningful terms. The day is usually just as important as the actual date. Furthermore, activity-oriented time is as valuable as clock time (so you might write: 10:15, just as the class began working on the history assignment). Item 4 should specify what subject matter (if any) was being worked on and where the activity occurred (e.g., in the back of the room, in the hall, on the baseball diamond, in the photo lab).

Item 5, the anecdote itself, is the vital information (the other data are only to help you better interpret the anecdote later on). It is vital that you obtain a clear, objective statement of what happened, what behavior occurred, and what was said. However, you cannot possibly write down all details. The following suggestions may help you to obtain the crucial information.

Suggestions for Writing Down Anecdotes of Behavior

1. Limit each anecdote to a single specific incident.
2. Be brief, but include enough detail so that it will be meaningful later.
3. Use behavioral terminology (like that used when writing objectives). Watch those verbs!
4. Use phrases. Sentences need not be complete as long as they are understandable.
5. Preserve the sequence. Try to jot things down in the order in which they occurred.
6. Think visual. Capture a "mental snap-shot" and then describe it so someone else can see it.
7. Quote significant statements (those preceding and following significant action). Indentify direct quotes with quotation marks.
8. Record both positive and negative incidents.

There is a certain amount of supplementary information you will need to make sense out of the anecdote later, when you try to interpret it. The "context" of an incident is any related event which might help interpret the anecdote (e.g., activities of other students nearby, events leading up to the anecdote, or an indication of some more general activity that the anecdote might be a part of). Usually, no interpretation should be made until several anecdotes have been made. Occasionally, some interpretation may be necessary in order for the incident to be meaningful. If you do find it helpful to suggest a possible interpretation at the time you recorded an incident, make certain that you keep your interpretation *separate* from your objective description.

Ranking. There is an observational technique which requires no scale. In fact most often no instrument of observation is used at all. The technique is called *ranking* and the most common variation is called the *rank-order method.* The observer/rater simply ranks or "orders" the individuals from "worst" to "best." The individuals are judged against each other (a norm-referenced judgment) and ranked according to the relative amounts of the good characteristic(s) being evaluated. The most efficient way to do this seems to be to first identify the best and the worst and then put the rest in place in between, working toward the middle.

Another useful ranking method is called the *sorting method.* In this procedure, the observer sorts the individuals into a predetermined number of piles. For example, a coach sorts his boys temporarily into first-, second-, third-, and fourth-string teams. The sorting of English themes, art projects, or term papers into five piles representing the grades A to E is another example of this method.

A third ranking method is called the *paired-comparison method.* This is very time-consuming because each individual is compared with each other individual. For each comparison, one point is awarded to the better of the two being compared. After all possible combinations of two individuals have been compared, the number of points earned by each individual is tallied and serves as the basis for the rank ordering. This method forces the rater to differentiate among the pupils being rated but is only worth the effort when it is extremely important that norm-referenced judgments be made.

All the above ranking techniques have some value (though limited use should be made of them). The objectivity and the accuracy of rankings can be improved by carefully establishing the criteria for making the multitude of norm-referenced judgments which enter into the completion of a rank order. If the rater has some criteria clearly in mind when he makes his comparisons, he is more likely to be accurate in his judgments.

The rules for establishing good criteria are simple. The first rule is this: Decide on the important characteristics you will be looking for when comparing any two individuals. One way to do this is to take a large index card or a piece of paper and complete the following statement: "I am going to compare these individuals of the basis of their. . . ." or "I am going to compare the _____ of these individuals."

Examples of Criteria for Comparisons

I am going to compare these individuals on the basis of their class participation and their achievement in social studies.

I am going to compare the quantity and the quality of the class participation of these individuals.

You can see how a brief statement like one of the above examples could help the teacher become more aware of just what he is comparing people on. This may be enough of a description of the criteria to be used. However, occasionally you may wish an even sharper focus. In that case, you should describe in observable terms the important aspects of each characteristic.

Example of Criterion Stated in Detail

I am going to compare individuals on the basis of their class participation by noting the differences in how often they raise their hand, how well they express their views, and how graciously they admit they may be wrong.

Ranking *can* be used and occasionally should be used (especially where norm-referenced judgments are needed about "nontestable" kinds of things). However, the objectivity and accuracy of those rankings can usually be improved by establishing, ahead of time, the criteria to be used when making the comparisons among individuals.

EXERCISE 6.1

Answer each of the following questions briefly. These questions should help you to review the highlights of the last few pages.

1. What is the biggest source of error in information obtained from observation?
2. What are some of the things an observer can do to remain objective?
3. List the three kinds of errors commonly made by observers and briefly describe each one.
4. Why is it important to remain unobtrusive?
5. Explain the value of collecting anecdotes of typical as well as of unusual behavior.
6. What are the advantages and disadvantages of ranking?

Suggestions for Using Instruments of Inquiry

To ask is not always to find out what you wish to know. Interviewing is an art which takes much practice to master. To obtain unbiased responses from a questionnaire—indeed, to obtain any answers at all—is difficult at best. Sociometric techniques, useful as they *can* be, must be administered with care. Therefore do not be discouraged with your first attempts to use inquiry as an information-gathering technique. Rather, follow the specific suggestions discussed below for each of the tools of inquiry.

Questionnaires. Most of the questionnaires which the teacher will use in the classroom are not difficult to administer. They can usually be given to a group. This means that the teacher need only hand the questionnaires out, make sure the students understand the questions, and have them fill in their responses. However, in administering questionnaires you should be aware that everything may *seem* to go smoothly and yet you may be getting useless information. There are three major reasons why the information in questionnaires may turn out to be useless:

1. The respondents do not know why they are filling out the questionnaire and therefore they do not care.
2. The respondents do not understand how they are to fill out the questionnaire and therefore do it incorrectly.
3. The respondents feel threatened by the questionnaire and therefore are afraid of being honest.

Let us briefly discuss each of these problems. We will suggest some specific things which you can do when administering a questionnaire that will help you to overcome these problems.

Convince the respondent that the questionnaire is worthwhile. If you can convince the students that the information you gain from the questionnaire they are about to fill out will be used to help them (and/or to help you to help them), they will be more willing to fill out the questionnaire carefully. There are two things you can do to accomplish this. First of all, explain carefully how you will use the information. For example, if you are asking the students to fill out a questionnaire about their interest, you might describe to them how this information will help you to make assignments which they will enjoy. Unless there is a clear-cut and obvious relationship between the kinds of responses the students are making and the anticipated use of the responses, the students will not believe you when you describe to them the intended use of the results.

The second important thing you can do to convince students that questionnaires are worthwhile is to follow through. In other words, when you do use a questionnaire, make sure that you use the information you obtain. Furthermore, make certain that your students are aware that you have used the information.

Finally, wherever possible, show the students how the results were used in a positive fashion and how they were used to help the students.

Make certain the respondents understand the instructions. Read the instructions very carefully with the students. Ask for any questions as a double check on whether the students do understand.

Put the students at ease. Whenever possible, questionnaires would be given anonymously. Unless it is absolutely necessary to know which students filled out the responses to a questionnaire, you should ask them to leave their names off the questionnaire and assure them that there is no way that anyone will know who filled out each questionnaire. Of course, it is sometimes necessary to know who filled out a questionnaire so that the answers provided by a given individual can be used to help that individual. It is then important for you to assure the students (and make them believe it) that this information will be held confidential and that it will be used only to help you do a better job of teaching them. Furthermore, assure them that any information will not affect their grade or your feelings toward them.

Conducting an Interview. Interviewing is a valuable information-gathering technique because it allows you to get information which would be difficult to obtain in any other way. It is a highly flexible technique. The interviewer can reword questions, add new questions, seek for clarification of information not understood, pursue interesting topics as they arise, or change the line of questioning altogether. However, this same flexibility, which is such as asset, can turn out to be a hindrance. If extreme care is not taken, the interviewer can ask the wrong questions, confuse the interviewee with poorly worded explanations, frustrate the interviewee by skipping from topic to topic, threaten the interviewee by getting too personal, and finally cause the interviewee to "clam up" entirely. Furthermore, without realizing it, the interviewer can easily bias the interviewee, obtaining only those responses that he "wants" to hear. The following suggestions are made to help you take advantage of the flexibility of interviewing rather than to have the flexibility lead to chaos and useless information.

Be prepared. The interviews which teachers have with their students are frequently informal and "on the spur of the moment." Obviously these interviews cannot be prepared in advance. However, if you get in the habit of preparing as carefully as possible those interviews which you *can* anticipate in advance, those interviews will go more smoothly and so will your informal interviews—which will tend to take on more structure. Follow the suggestions in Chapter 11 for deciding upon an overall structure for the interview and for preparing key questions in advance.

Establish rapport (and maintain it). A successful interviewer establishes rapport by beginning with a noncontroversial and nonthreatening topic. Then, throughout the interview, he is friendly, relaxed, and patient. Whenever possible, he is positive, showing approval of the fact that the respondent is talking. Notice that it is not always possible to approve or agree with what the respondent says, but you can approve of the fact that he is saying something. Constant reinforcement by nods of the head and verbal encouragement to continue can go a long way toward establishing and maintaining rapport with the respondent.

Guide the respondent. Through a series of carefully planned questions, an interviewer can usually keep his respondent on the right track. However, occasionally a respondent may balk at a given question because he feels threatened by it or because he does not feel qualified to answer. When this occurs, it is legitimate to probe for related information, but do not push the respondent to the point that he becomes irritated. If the respondent is continually reluctant to talk about a given topic, then you should raise questions about topics vaguely related and gradually work the respondent back to that topic again. After two or three times of this, if you are still unsuccessful, it is best to drop that topic and move on or to terminate the interview.

Usually, all it takes to keep the respondent talking and giving you information is to be supportive and occasionally ask for more details or more explanation. Small comments such as "Yes, go on," or "And then what happened?" or "Was anything else said?" can go a long way toward helping the respondent to remember important information.

Obtain accurate information. Of course, the information you obtain from a respondent will be only as accurate as that which he gives you. However, unless it is carefully recorded, it will be even less accurate. Consequently, it is important for you to record what has been said. Furthermore, a very useful technique is to repeat the key information supplied by the respondent and see if the respondent agrees that that is indeed what he has said. This will help you to determine whether or not you have recorded accurately.

Sometimes you will get inaccurate information in an interview not because the respondent purposely distorts the information but simply because he is not qualified to answer. Do everything you can during the interview to find out if the respondent is qualified to give the information you are asking for. Teachers have on more than one occasion obtained "eyewitness accounts" of quarrels on the playground only to find out later that the students being asked were not even there but had heard second-hand.

A final way to ensure the accuracy of the information from an interview is to check the respondent's information for consistency. Once you have identified the key information given by a respondent in an interview, ask for that same information again. Rephrase your original questions and ask for elaboration of the information given. By doing this you will get more than one opportunity to get the same information from the respondent. If there is no agreement, then either the respondent is not being consistent in his story or you are not recording it accurately. In either case the inconsistency should be cleared up through further discussion or the information should be treated as highly inaccurate and you should seek other ways to obtain it.

Know when to quit. A good interviewer recognizes that point when the questioning is no longer yielding valuable information and he knows when to quit. Sometimes this means simply quitting a line of questioning and moving to another topic and sometimes it means quitting the interview altogether. There are a number of signals which should indicate to the interviewer that it is no longer profitable to continue an interview. Among the more common ones are the following: the interviewer has run out of questions and can think of nothing more to say and the interviewee is silent; the interviewee is constantly changing the topic or refuses to answer except with brief yesses and nos or grunts and groans; the interviewee becomes hostile and angry and begins to turn the interview around, asking the questions and refusing to answer.

Administering sociometric instruments.   Nominating devices, guess-who techniques, and placement devices are relatively easy to use. The suggestions that we made for using questionnaires are also appropriate for the use of sociometric techniques. Make certain that you give clear instructions and that the student understands the basis of the nomination, selection, or placement. Furthermore, be sure that he understands who he is allowed to nominate, select, or place. Whenever possible, it is also helpful to provide a reminder to the students of those that they are allowed to choose from.

EXERCISE 6.2

1. List the problems leading to useless questionnaire information. What can be done to overcome each of these problems?
2. Briefly summarize, in your own words, the suggestions for conducting interviews.

Suggestions for Analyzing Daily Work

The biggest source of information available to teachers is the student's daily work. However, that source usually remains virtually untapped. There are undoubtedly a number of reasons for this but the three given below are probably the most important.

Three Reasons Why Teachers Rarely Analyze the Daily Work of Their Students

1. Assignments are not made carefully enough to yield useful information when they are analyzed.

2. The teacher does not know what to look for when analyzing assignments.
3. The teacher does not have enough time to analyze the students' daily work.

In Chapter 12, the procedures for selecting and constructing worthwhile assignments will be discussed. Now, we will deal with the problem of finding enough time to analyze daily work. If there is one thing the teacher never has enough of, it is time. However, a second thing which teachers rarely have enough of is information. The secret is to get as much valuable information in as little time as possible. Some of the teacher's most valuable information can come from analysis of daily work. Analyzing daily work does not have to require a great deal of time. The following suggestions should help you get the most information from your students' daily work in the smallest amount of time.

Analyze continuously. If you are continuously analyzing, day by day, making notes of the kinds of errors particular students make and jotting down patterns of responses over a period of time, you will obtain a good sampling of the kind of work your students do. Furthermore, you will be able to get a great deal of information about the students' study habits, the way they organize their material, and the particular, recurring topics which seem to interest them most. Much of the analysis you do will simply take the form of the skimming through the assignments as they come in, looking for anything unusual, and then writing that down.

Save samples of student work. Sometimes you will not want to take the time to make a thorough report on a student's paper. Samples of a student's work can then be placed in a file folder and saved for a short time. After you have a number of work samples dealing with the same subject matter, you can go over those assignments and look for recurring topics, consistent errors, and other patterns of student responses. Many times you will be able to discover information about student's communication skills and problem-solving skills that you would not notice on a single assignment.

Analyze on the spot. Another way to keep down the number of analyses you have to do is to analyze while the students are doing their work. You can do this by walking around the room as the students are working on assignments or workbook pages and spotting those students who are doing the work incorrectly. If the mistakes are corrected as soon as the student begins making them, it is much less work for the students to overcome them. Many teachers still use the technique of having students work problems on the blackboard. When this is done, an analysis of the types of errors can also be readily made on the spot.

Another technique which can be used is to ask the students as a group questions while they are working on a common assignment. From time to time ask how far the students have gone in working out the assignment and take a quick note of which students are working most slowly and which have progressed most rapidly. Then pick out a point in the assignment that everyone has reached and check to see what responses the students made. If there are a large number of students who missed that part of the assignment, then it is time to stop and find out what the trouble is. If only a few students have missed that part, you may go quietly to their seats and try to help them with their problems. This kind of analysis-diagnosis-remediation procedure is very useful because it helps the students to correct errors very early in the learning process.

EXERCISE 6.3

How can a teacher analyze continuously? Teaching already takes a great deal of time! List some of the ways (at least three) that continuous analyzing of assignments can be done without taking up all the teacher's time.

Administering Tests

Tests should be given carefully or the information obtained will be far less accurate than it could be. It is not difficult to administer a test properly, especially if you are aware of the things you must do at each of the three stages in test administration: the preparation stage, the administration stage, and the scoring stage.

The preparation stage. The first stage in the administration of a test is to prepare the room and the students for taking the test. The conditions under which the test is taken can greatly affect the scores which the students receive. You should do everything you can to make the room where the test will be taken as comfortable as possible. Try to maintain a comfortable temperature, make certain there is good lighting, and if possible have the desks spaced well enough apart so that the students do not feel cramped. Also, be certain that the desks are large enough so that the students can comfortably handle the test materials and write on them.

Although if is important to have a quiet, comfortable place to take the test, it is even more important that you prepare the students for the test. You should be friendly and cheerful when the students enter the room on test day and you should give them encouragement (do not try to frighten them with tales of how hard the test is). Make certain that the students understand *why* the test is going to be given and what the results will be used for. Furthermore, help them to feel a need to do their best without making them worry unnecessarily about mistakes they may make.

Just before the test begins it is helpful to remind the students of those techniques used by the test-wise student. Unless there is a correction for guessing,[1] you should encourage the students to work all problems and make an intelligent

---

[1] Correction for guessing is a technique sometimes used when scoring alternative-choice items. It will be discussed later in this chapter.

guess on those they cannot do. Furthermore, remind them to budget their time carefully, not spending an inordinate amount of time on any single problem. It is also usually best for students to work quickly through a test, answering those questions which they know very well and then returning to work out those they have some trouble with. Finally, encourage students to ask questions about anything they do not understand in the instructions you give them and encourage them to ask you privately about any questions that they are having trouble interpreting. Remind them that you cannot give them the answers to questions they do not know but that you are there to help them understand what the question is asking.

Administering the test. The first step after you have prepared the room and students is to hand out the materials. If the test is timed at all (and most classroom tests are), it is important that you hand out the materials as quickly as possible. Furthermore, you should tell the students to keep their tests face down on their desks and not to turn them over until they are told to do so. Thus, you can wait until all students have copies of the test before you tell them to begin. Before you start the test, be sure each student has a copy of the complete test booklet. Also, be certain that each has any answer sheets he may need, and, where necessary, scratch paper and pencil. It is also valuable to have extra materials handy so that if a problem arises during the test, any faulty test booklets or pencils can be replaced.

After all the materials are handed out, get the attention of the students and carefully go over the instructions with them. If the test is the kind that the students are very familiar with, the instructions may be brief. If not, you must make certain that the student understands what he is to do. After you have given the instructions, ask if there are any questions, and then instruct the students to begin.

Many teachers feel that once students are busy working, their job is done and they can sit back and read a book, grade papers, or make some better use of their time. However, it is important for teachers to monitor tests. They should watch for students who are having trouble or who do not understand the test, as well as for students who are cheating or just randomly filling in answers to get finished. These, and other clues that the test information will be in error, should be carefully watched for. We discussed these clues at length in Chapter 2, and it might be worth your time to quickly go back and review these. While you are monitoring a test it is sometimes useful to walk around the room and give encouragement to those who seem to be having concerns. Also at that time you can help them to move faster, slow down, or move on to problems they may not have as much trouble with.

The collection of the completed tests is also very important because it can be a source of test error. Collect the students' tests in a very orderly fashion—because when there is a lot of chaos it provides those who want to cheat with an opportunity to do so. Furthermore, if you call a time limit and then collect the tests from the front of the room and gradually move to the back, those in the rear of the room may take advantage of those few extra minutes and could gain some points over the people in the front row simply because they had more time to work. Some of these problems can be overcome if you call the time and then ask all the students to close their test booklets, turn over their papers, and stop working on the test. Then go around and collect the tests in an orderly fashion.

Scoring the tests. Three simple rules can help you to reduce the amount of error you could make scoring tests:

1. Be consistent
2. Avoid bias
3. Double check

The first rule for test scoring is to be consistent. Do not give credit for some information to one child and no credit to another for the same information. If you have a well-designed answer key and you stick to it, there can be very little trouble. If you are scoring objective tests, it helps to go consistently through the items in the same order. This will help you to avoid missing items and simply not scoring them. In scoring essay tests, there is more leeway for interpretation of the students' responses, and you must be particularly careful to be consistent in what you call right and what you call wrong as well as in the number of points that you give for a particular answer.

When scoring any subjective test, it is easy to let your biases affect how you score an answer. However, if you avoid looking at the names (some teachers have the names put on the back of the papers so they cannot be seen when scoring) and if you check one question at a time rather than all the questions on a given paper, you can avoid some of this bias. If you have a series of essay questions to score, the best procedure is to score all the first questions first, then scramble the papers and score all the second questions, again scramble the papers and score all the third questions. Follow this procedure until you have all the questions scored.

Whenever you have tests to score, use as efficient a method as possible. In an objective test, for example, it is helpful to use separate answer sheets. This way you do not have to thumb through the test booklet to score each person's paper. Furthermore, by using a separate answer sheet you can make an overlay that you can put over the student's answer sheet. This overlay should be designed to let the right answers show. You simply need to mark on the student's answer sheet those items where his answers do not show through and you will have a tally of the number of incorrect responses he has made.

Some standardized tests include a correction-for-guessing, and some authors recommend it as a way to increase the reliability of a test. A correction-for-guessing is a process by which you alter the person's score according to some predetermined formula. The notion is that students should not be given credit for answers they got correct by guessing. Guessing also introduces error (See Chapter 2) because some students are better guessers than others.

It is my opinion that the added reliability gained from applying correction-for-guessing formulas is not worth the effort they take. Classroom tests will probably gain as much in reliability if everyone is told to guess and then is taught how to guess intelligently.[2]

EXERCISE 6.4

1. "To give a test is easy enough, all you need to do is hand them out and let the students have at it." What would you say to the teacher who said this if you were going to try to convince him that test administration is not that simple?
2. Why is careful test administration important? What kinds of errors can occur because a test is poorly administered?

ANALYZING AND RECORDING INFORMATION

After information has been obtained (step 6) or located from available records (step 3), it must then be analyzed and recorded. To analyze the information simply means to find out everything you can about it which will be important when using that information in making judgments. This supplementary information should be recorded along with the evaluative information (i.e., along with test scores, observations, etc.). First, we will discuss the analysis of information, noting the kind of supplementary information we should find out. Then we will discuss ways to record the evaluative data we have obtained along with the supplementary information our analysis has provided us.

These two parts of this chapter should help you learn how to analyze and record information so that it can be easily retrieved and readily used in making judgments and decisions.

Analyzing Information

The suggestion was made in Chapter 5 that information which is already available should meet certain standards before it is to be used. To be useful, information should be valid, reliable, and up-to-date. These same things should be true of information you obtained. Any information you plan on using should be analyzed for these three factors.

---

[2] For a fuller explanation of correction-for-guessing formulas and a discussion of their value, read the appropriate sources listed in the annotated bibliography at the end of this chapter.

Information alone is useless. Raw scores, observations, anecdotes, interview notes, etc., are meaningless if you do not know who (or what) the information is about or how it was obtained. There are a number of details about the information you have obtained that are easily forgotten and therefore should be recorded along with the information. If you can answer the following questions, the information you have obtained will be useful to you in making judgments and decisions.

Questions you must be able to answer in order to be able to use information in making appropriate judgments and decisions:

1. Who or what is the information about?
2. Who obtained the information?
3. What instruments (if any) were used to obtain the information?
4. When was the information obtained (day, date, time)?
5. Under what conditions was the information obtained?
6. Is this same information available on anyone else?
7. Is the information related to any instructional objectives or learning outcomes?
8. If the information is a score, what type of score is it (raw score, derived score)?
9. Is there any evidence of reliability or validity?

Recording Information

It is so easy to get into the habit of recording only the important test scores and the grades from a few assignments. The typical teacher's record book encourages that kind of recording. Small spaces, barely big enough for a letter grade or numerical score, make it difficult to record anything but numbers or letter grades. However, if you do not limit your recording to the confines of a "little black book," you can easily record all types of information. When evaluative information is seen as a data base for a multitude of instructional judgments and decisions, it becomes apparent that a wide variety of information should be recorded. Some of the more important kinds of evaluative information are listed below.

Examples of the types of information which could be recorded because of its usefulness in making judgments and decisions:

Quiz and text scores

Records of attendance

Observations of class participation

Observations of performance(s)

List of assignments completed

Anecdotes of behavior

Performance on assignments

Sociometric data

Notes from conferences

Questionnaire data

Besides the above types of information, records should be kept of the major judgments and decisions which have been made. Past judgments and decisions can be used as information when making new judgments and decisions (e.g., self-referenced judgments are frequently made on the basis of a comparison between judgments about the same individual made at different times).

Recording test data. There is nothing more frustrating than trying to make judgments with a set of test scores from your record book and not being able to do so because you do not know where the scores came from. Simply to know that the scores represent performance on tests and/or quizzes is not enough. But the typical record book has little or no room for the supplementary information that is required to answer the questions discussed above. There is a simple way to overcome this problem. First of all, assign a number to each test as it is given. Secondly, write down the supplementary information needed about that test on a separate sheet. Third, number that sheet with the same number assigned the test and file it for future reference. Figure 6.1 illustrates one format that could be used for recording supplementary information about tests. This form (or some modification of it) could be mimeographed and used each time a test was given.

Notice that the form in Figure 6.1 provides you with spaces to record all the kinds of information you will need in order to use the test scores in judgment and decision making. On any given test, there may be information which you feel you will not need (e.g., the reliability of the test), and that information could be omitted. By using a separate sheet, such as the one described in Figure 6.1, you can record all the supplementary information needed about a given test and later find that information readily. When the scores are recorded in the teacher's record book, a number is placed above the column that the scores are recorded in. This number refers to the number of the test and is the same as the number found on the supplementary information sheet.

Recording observational data. The data from checklists or rating scales can easily be summarized. If you have checklist data, you can tally all the checks

Test number:_____5_____ Date given:__3/13/72__

Grade and/or section number:___Section 7____

Subject matter:_English___ Description of

test:__Multiple-choice; measuring ability to__

identify styles of authors we studied.

Location of copy:__On file in brown cabinet.__

Testing conditions:_____Normal; no unusual

occurrence.

Summary statistics:_$\overline{X}$-12_; S.D.__2.6__; r___.51_

Total possible:__18__; __low score:__3_____;

high score:__17;__

Comments:__r (split half); item analysis on

file.__

a student received on similar characteristics or behaviors. For example, Mary got 5 checks for behaviors which exhibited friendliness, 2 for unfriendly behaviors, and 9 for cooperation in working on the group project. If you have rating-scale data, you can average the ratings on similar traits. For example, Sarah's average rating for maintaining rapport with the audience was 6 on a 7-point scale. She used good eye contact, paused effectively, used appropriate anecdotes, etc. On the other hand, her average rating for her speech *content* was 2.5 on a 7-point scale. She had only a fair introduction, used poor examples, and her outline was not logically organized. However, the easiest way to store information from checklists and rating scales is to file them simply in a folder along with assignments, anecdotes, and other information you may have about a student. Maintaining a file folder on each student is probably one of the most important things a teacher can do to provide himself with information for making judgments and decisions. Whenever you observe a child, you simply place the record of your observations in his file. Later, when you wish to use that information, it is all there.

However, there is one hitch. If you simply toss a completed rating scale or checklist in a student's file, you will not be able to interpret that information *unless* you also have the kind of supplementary information we have been referring to throughout this section. If you have observed only one or two students, this supplemental information could be jotted down on the back of the instrument (checklist or rating scale) which is being filed. If many students were observed under basically the same conditions, then a single sheet containing this supplementary information is all that is needed.

Procedures for collecting anecdotes were discussed in the last chapter. At this point, we would simply remind you that anecdotes should be written down in a form which is convenient for you to file and easy for you to retrieve. There is usually no problem figuring out a storage space (a file box, a file folder, or an old shoe box will do as well). The main problem arises when one wishes to retrieve the information. Many anecdotes contain descriptions of the behavior of more than one individual. At the time that the anecdote is recorded, there may seem to be one individual whose behavior is most important. However, later on it may be clear that the behaviors of the other individuals were also revealing. But you may not ever discover this if you only file anecdotes under the name of the "principal character." Suppose, for example, that Verda was sly enough to get trouble started and then fade to the periphery of the action by the time the teacher looked to see what is going on. Verda's part in the troublemaking might not be noticed unless one realizes that Verda (unlike many others) is *always* near by when trouble breaks out.

A useful way to make certain that an anecdote can be retraced to everyone involved is to file the full anecdote under the name of the principal person involved (if you are uncertain as to whom that is, just pick any one of the individuals involved). Next, make an index card for each of the other individuals involved in the anecdote. On each card put the individual's name and a note saying "see *(name of person the anecdote is filed under)* for anecdote on *(date anecdote was collected)*." Now file each card according to the name on that card. When looking in that person's file, you will find the card referring you to someone else's file for anecdotal information.

Recording data from inquiry

Questionnaire and interview data. The data from questionnaires and interviews can usually be summarized in a few statements. Frequently it is just as easy to file the questionnaire or the notes you have taken. Simply put them in the file folder of the person who filled out the questions *or* of the person that the questionnaire or interview was about.

Sociometric data. The information you obtain from nominating devices, placement devices, and guess-who techniques is always difficult to interpret. What you are usually looking for in these cases is the interrelationships among the individuals in the class. These relationships are derived from the choice patterns of all the individuals and are supposed to reflect the social structure of the class. A first step toward interpreting sociometric data is tabulating that data and if possible diagraming (i.e., drawing a picture of) the interrelationships found in the data.

Trying to make sense out of the information from nominating devices

TABLE 6.1

A matrix showing "who chose whom" when asked to choose the person they would most like to work with. First choices are indicated by a 1 and second choices by a 2.

CHOSEN

Choosers	Allen	Gary	George	Peter	Tim	Ann	Eloise	Jill	Joy	Mary	Sarah	Sue
Allen		1					2					
Gary			2	1								
George				2		1						
Peter		1			2							
Tim	2					1						
Ann		1								2		
Eloise						2				1		
Jill									2			1
Joy								1				2
Mary						1					2	
Sarah		2					1					
Sue								2	1			
First Choice	0	1	2	0	1	3	1	1	1	1	0	1
Second Choice	0	2	0	2	1	1	1	1	1	1	1	1
Times Chosen	0	3	2	2	2	4	2	2	2	2	1	2
Score	0	4	4	2	3	7	3	3	3	3	1	3

essentially comes down to answering the question "Who chose whom?" The answer to this question leads to several others: Were there some individuals who were chosen by many others? Were there some mutual choices? Were there any individuals chosen by no one?

There are several ways in which the information from nominating devices can be recorded. We will discuss three of the most popular techniques. First of all, a simple matrix can be devised. The names of all the students are listed along the side of the page *and* along the top of the page (if you wish to maintain anonymity, you could assign letters or numbers to each student). Now you simply transfer the information from the sheets upon which the nominations were made, indicating on the matrix who chose whom. Look at the example found in Table 6.1. These data are from a hypothetical class of only twelve students.

The students were given these questions:

> If you could select just one person to work with you on a project, whom would you select?
>
> Now, suppose that person was already working with someone else. Then whom would you choose?

You can see that these two questions yield a first and second choice for everyone in the class. In the matrix we labeled the vertical axis "choosers" and the horizontal axis "chosen." Taking one student's response at a time, we entered the data. For example, Allen's responses were placed in the first row. He chose Gary as his first choice and Eloise as his second. Notice that Allen was chosen by no one. If you look at the column which has been designated for Allen, you will see that he did not get chosen by anyone.

The totals for each column are indicated at the bottom of the matrix. First, the number of times a student was chosen as a first choice is recorded. Next, you record the number of times he received a second-choice nomination. You then add these together to get the total number of times each individual was chosen. Finally, a score is assigned which weighs being chosen first more heavily than being chosen second. This is a common procedure, but one should be careful not to overinterpret these scores. You are really interested in some picture of the way the group interacts and not so much in individual scores except to locate the "isolates" (those chosen by no one) and the "stars" (those who were most popular). In this case, a first choice was worth 2 points and a second choice 1 point. Gary, for example, got one first choice (1×2 points $= 2$ points) and two second choices (2×1 point $= 2$ points) for a total of 4 points.

Because we are more interested in the interrelationships among the students, we want not only to identify the isolates and the stars but also to identify clusters of students and any cliques (small groups that are isolated from the rest). To get a better picture of these interrelationships, a sociogram is used. A socio-

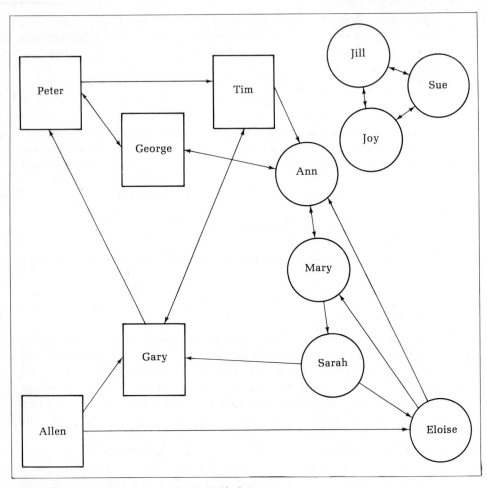

FIGURE 6.2 A sociogram for the data in Table 6.1.

gram is a diagram which you draw from the data you have. The sociogram in Figure 6.2 was drawn from the data summarized in Table 6.1. The squares represent the boys and circles represent the girls. There is nothing sacred about this particular diagram. If someone else were to arrange the same data, the placement of the individuals would probably be different. However, because there are certain rules to follow, the same clusters would show up, the clique of Jill, Sue, and Joy would be there, and Allen would clearly be an isolate.

If you have a fairly large group of students (twenty-five or more) you may find it very difficult to get the squares and circles arranged so that it is convenient to draw the arrows between them. One way to make this task easier is to cut out little squares and circles, write the students' names on them, and lay them out on a large sheet of paper. Move them around until you have an arrangement which you feel is workable and best represents the data. Then paste or tape them down and draw in your arrows.

Without getting involved in a lot of elaborate rules, you can produce useful sociograms if you take the following steps.

Steps to Take When Producing a Sociogram

1. Identify the isolates and place them on the outer edges of the page.
2. Identify the stars and place them in the center of the page.
3. Fill in the space between the stars and the isolates with the names of the other students.
4. Keep rearranging until you get the arrangement in which it is easiest for you to draw in arrows representing who chose whom (try to keep mutual choices near each other).
5. Draw arrows from the chooser to the chosen. Draw double-pointed arrows ($\leftrightarrow$) between mutual choices.
6. (Optional) Indicate whether the choices were first, second, or third choices. You can put a little number on the arrow ($\overset{2}{\rightarrow}$), or you can use different-colored arrows to represent different choice levels.

The data from a guess-who technique should simply be recorded on a graph. Place the students' names along the left-hand side of the paper and the characteristics used to elicit the responses along the top of the page. Each time a student is identified with a characteristic, place a tally mark. When you have completed such a graph, you will have a frequency count for each student (indicating how many of his classmates felt he fit each of the described characteristics). Table 6.2 presents some typical guees-who results.

Recording data from the analysis of assignments. In Figure 6.1 we presented one possible format for recording the supplemental information needed in order to make adequate interpretation of test scores. This same basic format can be used to record the supplemental information about grades on assignments. Figure 6.3 presents a modification of the form found in Figure 6.1. The modifications make the form useful for recording the supplemental information needed in order to interpret and use the grades given on assignments. You can see that what is critical in any case is a clear description of what was being measured (what was expected of the students) and what rule(s) were being used to assign values (grades) to the work. Another important bit of information is some indication of the constraints which have been placed on the students. These same kinds of descriptions of what was being measured, and how, are important when using information from rating scales, checklists, and other observational techniques.

A final word of caution is in order. Do not become a slave to your recording system. Many times you will wish to analyze the papers of only one or two students, and you may not even be certain exactly what you are looking for (e.g., you simply know that these students are having trouble and you would like to find out why). In this case, you will not want to draw up elaborate graphs or write up full reports like those pictured in Figure 6.3. Instead, you will probably find it more convenient to put the assignments of these few students in a file folder as they come in. After you have a number of them, you may want to make

TABLE 6.2

"Guess-Who" Results of a Typical "Guess-Who" Sociometric Technique with a Sixth-Grade Class*

Positive Characteristics (10): Quiet through Best Friend. Negative Characteristics (11): Restless through Does Not Work Well with Others.

Pupil No.	Quiet	Most Active in Games	Best Liked	Not Bossy	Polite	Happy	Tidy	Takes Care of Things	Best Friend	Restless	Talkative	Silent	Not Liked	Bossy	Not Polite	Does Not Take Care of Things	Unhappy	Untidy	Wastes Time	Does Not Work Well with Others	Sum of Positive Traits	Sum of Negative Traits
1 A.B.		14	2	1		2	2	1	2						1			1			22	2
2 B.L.							1	1	1					1							3	1
3 B.C.				2	4		1	2	3								1				12	1
4 C.R.						1	1	1	1	1					1	1		1		1	2	5
5 E.R.										1	4				6	2	1	2	3	2	0	21
6 B.B.				4	1	1	1											3		1	7	4
7 C.J.						1			1	1	1				3		1		2	1	1	9
8 E.J.	1			2		1	1	2	2							1	1				9	6
9 E.T.		1		1						1							1	2		2	1	6
10 G.P.		2	5	2	2	7	3	2	3	2				9						2	28	13
11 H.C.										14	2		34	5	6	22	17	9	15	9	5	133
12 H.S.				1					1	23					5	2	2	2	7	4	2	45
13 H.C.								1	1								1	1		1	2	3
14 J.J.						2															2	0
15 L.L.	13			7			3	3	2			17					2				33	19
16 M.E.					1	1			1					1		1	2	3			4	6
17 M.S.			1		3	1		1	2					2	2			1			8	6
18 M.C.	6				3	1	1	1				3					2				13	5
19 M.M.							1	1											1	1	2	2
20 N.R.				1				1	1					1				5		3	3	10
21 O.R.						1				1					1						1	2

Student	Recorded frequencies
22 O.S.	6 · · 1 3 6 · 1 9 2 · 1 1 · 2 · 1 · · 2 1 · 28 4
23 R.D.	· 2 5 1 · 1 8 · 1 1 · 6 1 1 · 1 1 · 1 1 10 4
24 R.P.	2 5 · 4 · 1 2 7 · 1 1 · 1 1 2 · 2 3 · 22 8
25 S.M.	· · · · 1 1 · 2 2 · 3 1 · · · 3 · 1 9
26 S.D.	· · 5 · · 2 2 · 3 2 · 3 · · 4 3
27 S.V.	5 · 1 3 2 1 3 1 1 1 · 2 · 15 6
28 F.J.	1 · · · · · 1 1 1 1 1 · 1 4
29 T.R.	16 15 2 7 4 3 1 1 4 1 · 52 1
30 T.K.	· · 1 · 1 2 · 1 1 2 1 5 2
31 T.B.	· · 1 1 3 3 · 1 1 · 8 1
32 W.B.	· · · 2 2 1 1 · 1 1 3 2
33 M.E.	· 3 1 1 1 2 1 · 1 1 1 11 3
34 D.C.	9 · 3 4 1 2 10 · 3 1 3 17 14
35 A.E.	· · · · · · · 3 · 3 1 8
36 B.S.	· 2 4 1 2 4 1 1 1 1 · 3 14 3

SOURCE: Courtesy of Frank Thompson, principal of Hillgrove School, La Puenta, California. From Stanley and Hopkins, *Educational and Psychological Measurement and Evaluation*, Prentice-Hall, Inc., Englewood Cliffs, N.J., 1972.

* Numbers indicate the frequency with which each student was associated with the "guess-who" description by his classmates.

Assignment number: _____ Date assigned _____ Date due _____

Grade and/or section number: _____ Subject matter _____

Objective of the assignment: _____

_____

_____

Instructions to the students: _____

_____

_____

Type of analysis: _____

_____

_____

_____

_____

Summary statistics (if appropriate): _____

_____

_____

Comments _____

_____

_____

_____

_____

FIGURE 6.3. Sample summary sheet for recording supplementary information about assignments and projects.

comparisons among them. You will be looking for some pattern of responses that may help you formulate hypotheses about where the students are having difficulty. These hypotheses can then be checked out through a series of carefully designed tests and/or further assignments. In these tests and assignments you will simply present variations of problems which require the specific skill you think the students have not mastered. If your hypothesis is correct, the students will not be successful and you will have discovered their problem (or some part of it).

Recording judgments and decisions. If evaluation is really a process of forming judgments and using them in decision making, then it makes sense to keep track of the important judgments and decisions one makes. It is often valuable to be able to look back over a series of decisions which have been made. It may tell you something about the wisdom of the individual decisions. It may also help you to defend decisions you have made (particularly if you indicate, for each decision, the judgments which led you to the decision). Furthermore, from time to

---

Dartmoth M.   7/13/72

Decision: Move Dartmoth to lower reading
group (group C)

Judgments: (1) Dartmoth cannot keep up
with his group during oral reading (see
checklists 6/19, 6/23, 6/30, 7/4).

               (2) Dartmoth's reading
comprehension is below those in his group
(see reading test scores 7/10).
                  (Over)

FIGURE 6.4 Index card illustrating how to record major decisions which have been made.

time you may be asked to report the judgments and decisions you have made. If you have recorded the major ones, it will be easier to report them more accurately (the reporting of evaluation results is treated in Chapter 9).

The easiest way to record major decisions is to jot them down on an index card or piece of paper. Put the decision at the top. Any judgments which helped you to make that decision can then be placed below it. Make certain you also put down the date you made the decision. Finally, if there is good information to support those judgments, make a brief note of that. Now file this record under the name of the person about whom the decision was made. Figure 6.4 presents an example of how this procedure works. The decision was made to move Dartmoth to a lower reading group. The reasons for the decision appear as judgments. Under each judgment, the teacher has referenced the major information supporting it.

Developing Norms from Your Records

Whenever you need to make norm-referenced judgments, it is important to identify an appropriate reference group. One of the most valuable reference groups is the local classroom (and local school). Suppose that you wish to make interpretive judgments by comparing each student's performance on a given task to that of his classmates on the same task. That is easy enough. For example, you could compute his rank in class. However, you know that differences from class to class (in a given year or across three or four years) are quite noticeable. If you are giving the same test every year (e.g., an end-of-the-year exam or a standardized achievement test), you might wish to combine the scores of the students over a three- or four-year period. This would give you a greater number of students in your reference group, and your interpretations could be made by comparing an individual to this broader (more stable) norm group. This is called developing "local" norms, and the procedure for doing so is discussed below.

Local norms can be developed for a single classroom, a given grade, an entire school, or a whole school system. The procedure is the same. You simply develop a frequency distribution by keeping track of the number of students scoring at each score (or range of scores). On the basis of this frequency distribution, you compute percentiles. Now when you wish to compare a student's performance to the group, you simply find out what raw score he got and look on your chart to see what percentile rank was associated with that raw score (or with the range of raw scores in which that raw score was included). Look at Table 6.3. Suppose that this is a distribution of scores for a fourth grade class on an "end of the book" test in reading. The test has been provided by the publishers of the reading text. The data were collected on a specific fourth grade class. Each year, for three years, the teacher added the scores of the new class to the distribution. Next year she plans on dropping out the scores from the first group (those will then be four years old) and adding in the new group's scores. This way she will keep the data updated. Furthermore, by having data over a three-year span, her frequencies are larger and the norms more reliable.

The procedures for computing frequency distributions and percentiles are discussed in Appendix A. You simply follow those instructions step-by-step. Use any test you wish. The results will be a norm table based on the performance of students who are "most like" those whose scores you are interpreting (i.e., a student's score is compared to the scores of students from the same school).

EXERCISE 6.5

1. Why should data be analyzed before being recorded?
2. What is the difference between the information upon which judgments are based and information which is supplementary to that?
3. What are some of the reasons a teacher might want to develop a set of "local norms" on one of his exams?

Some Final Considerations for Recording Data

Maintain security.   When the teacher maintains a file of information about each student which is as comprehensive as that which we have been suggesting, he has an obligation to keep that information very secure. There is no excuse for not keeping test scores and other evaluative information under lock and key. It is especially important to keep notes from interviews, observations of behavior, and other subjective information in a place where others cannot get hold of it.

TABLE 6.3

Development of Local Norms— Distribution of Scores over a Three-Year Period ("End-of-the-Book" Reading Test)

Number correct	Frequency
15–16	卌 1
13–14	卌 1111
11–12	卌 卌 111
9–10	卌 卌 卌 卌 11
7–8	卌 卌
5–6	卌 1
3–4	111
0–2	11

Periodically update your files.   From time to time it will be important for you to summarize the information you have about your students, throwing out that information which is no longer valid because it is outdated or no longer needed. Some of the information you have in your own personal files will need to be transferred to the school records. Some of the information you have in your files will need to be destroyed. Some of the information you have in your files

TABLE 6.4

Guidelines for Updating Classroom Records

Action	Typical Reason for the Action
Summarize the information	You need to make summative judgments. You need to make judgments about a group of students (or about the effect of some instructional event on the group) You have related bits of information but do not represent cumulative learning
Transfer information to the school records (i.e., put in the cumulative folders)	It can be meaningfully interpreted by those who have access to the school files *and* It is needed by them for making judgments and decisions
Destroy the information	It has been demonstrated to be completely in error You do not have enough supplemental information to make accurate interpretations It has served its purpose and/or has been summarized for use in a different set of judgments and decisions

will need to be summarized in a meaningful way. Table 6.4 presents a set of guidelines for updating information you have on record.

SUMMARY

1. Before beginning to obtain information, make sure that both you and your students are ready.
2. When making observations, it is important to be as objective as possible, reducing the chances of bias affecting your observations.
3. There are three kinds of errors which are common among observers: (1) the "halo" effect, (2) personal response tendency, and (3) logical error.
4. Questionnaires are fairly easy to administer, but you should be certain to convince the respondent that the questionnaire is worthwhile. Also, make sure that he understands the instructions and put him at ease.
5. When interviewing, it is important to (1) be prepared, (2) establish and maintain rapport, (3) guide the respondent so as to keep him on the right topic, (4) obtain accurate information, and (5) know when to quit.
6. When administering sociometric instruments, follow the suggesions for administering questionnaires. Be certain that the student understands whom he may choose and what the basis for his choice should be.
7. When analyzing assignments, get in the habit of continuously analyzing, saving samples of student work, and analyzing "on the spot."
8. Test administration should not be treated lightly. Prepare yourself, your students, and the physical environment in which the test will be taken. Next, hand out the materials, give instructions to the students, and monitor the test session. Finally, collect the tests in an orderly fashion and score carefully, avoiding bias and common error.
9. Before recording information you should analyze it to make certain that it is valid, reliable, and up to date. There are a number of important questions which should be answered, and the answers should be recorded as information which supplements (is helpful when interpreting) the evaluative data.
10. A wide variety of evaluative information can be conveniently recorded if you do not limit your recording to the confines of the typical teacher's record book.
11. Sociometric data can be recorded in tabular form or in the form of a sociogram which is designed to show the social interrelations of a group.
12. Local norms can be developed easily by accumulating information on the same instrument over a period of time and recording this information in a frequency distribution.
13. When appropriate, keep samples of your students' work.
14. Maintain security of your records and periodically update your files.

Reference

Stanley, Julian C., and Kenneth D. Hopkins: *Educational and Psychological Measurement and Evaluation,* 5th ed. Prentice-Hall, Inc., Englewood Cliffs, N.J., 1972.

Suggested Readings

Test administration is explained especially well in

Ebel, Robert L.: *Essentials of Educational Measurement,* Prentice-Hall, Inc., Englewood Cliffs, N.J., 1972, chap. 9.

For problems associated with the administration of observational techniques and tools of inquiry, see

Brandt, Richard M.: *Studying Behavior in Natural Settings,* Holt, Rinehart, and Winston, Inc., New York, 1972.

Gronlund, N. E.: *Sociometry in the Classroom,* Harper and Row, Publishers, Inc., New York, 1959.

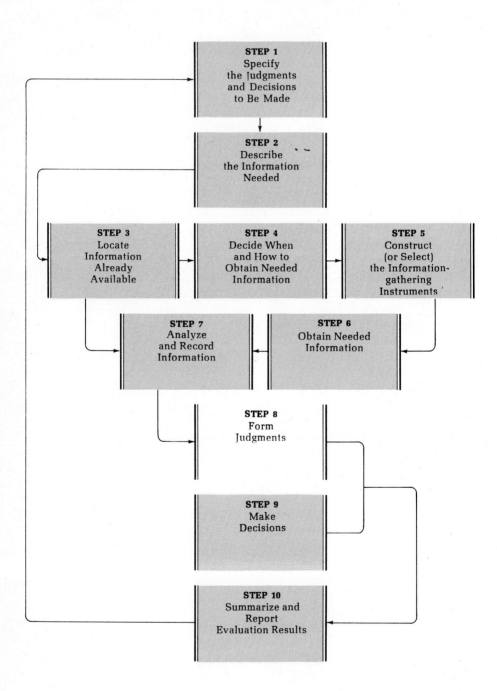

CHAPTER 7

Forming Judgments

Evaluation is the process of obtaining information and using it to form judgments which, in turn, are to be used in decision making.

This quotation from Chapter 1 highlights the fact that to evaluate is to judge. Everything you do in the first seven steps of the evaluation process helps you to achieve this eighth step. The importance of learning how to form accurate judgments cannot be overemphasized. The many instructional decisions which teachers make rely on judgments. Diagnosing problems, grading papers, predicting success, and assigning semester grades are all examples of the kinds of important judgments which teachers make.

In previous chapters you learned how to decide what kind of judgment to make, what type of referent to use, and what kind of comparison would make your jukgment most useful to you. In this chapter you will learn how to make various kinds of judgments.

Reading this chapter should help you to be able to

1. Interpret standardized test scores
2. Assign grades
3. Make judgments on the basis of observations and inquiry
4. Make predictions from classroom data

As you read about the procedures for making various judgments in the classroom, keep in mind the three factors which determine how a judgment is made: (1) whether it is an estimate or a prediction, (2) what type of referent is used, and (3) whether it is a mastery or a deviation judgment.[1] Notice how each of these factors influences the way in which a judgment is made and determines to some extent what type of decision the judgment can be used for.

INTERPRETING SCORES FROM STANDARDIZED TESTS

Test interpretation is frequently explained as the process of converting raw scores into a form which can be understood by those who are to use the test results. Raw scores are the direct results of tests. In most cases the raw score is equal to the number of correct responses an individual makes. It is difficult, if not impossible, to make interpretations on the basis of those raw scores alone.

Making Estimates

Before raw scores can be useful, they must be compared to some referent. The process of making this comparison is essential to the interpretation of standardized test scores. The result of such an interpretation is an estimative judgment. However, it is important to keep in mind that an underlying assumption is being made every time we use a test score as an estimate of some achievement or ability. It is assumed that the test score is a valid and accurate estimate of the person's ability in that subject matter. This assumption is not always met. You should always look for evidence of a relationship between test performance and the achievement or ability it is supposed to measure.

Predictions are usually made on the basis of estimates (i.e., interpreted scores), and an explanation of how that is done will be made later. First, let us

---

[1] You may wish to review these concepts. They were introduced and explained in Chapter 3.

discuss briefly the various kinds of interpretations commonly made from standardized test results. Many different kinds of comparisons can be made, and each one yields a different kind of score. Collectively, the scores which result in the comparison of a raw score to some referent are called *derived* scores.[2]

Norm-referenced estimates. Many of the kinds of decisions made with standardized test results call for norm-referenced judgments. Consequently, derived scores which result from the comparison an individual's score with the average score of some reference group are very popular. Almost all standardized tests provide one or more of these kinds of derived scores. These scores are particularly valuable because they allow you to make comparisons among individuals with a wide range of abilities.

Rank. One of the easiest ways to compare an individual's score to that of some reference group is to indicate the individual's rank within the group. The problem with this type of derived score is that rank within a group takes on a different meaning as the size of the group changes. To be fifth in a group of six individuals means something far different than to be fifth in a group of six hundred. One way to overcome this problem is to use percentile rank rather than absolute rank. The *percentile rank* indicates a person's rank in the group in terms of the *percentage of individuals who score lower than he does.*

The referent being used in computing rank and percentile rank is the lowest score in the class. The derived score, then, is an indication of how far an individual's score deviates from the bottom of the class.[3] Suppose, for example, Alfred obtains a raw score of 72 on some standardized test. Turning to the manual accompanying the test, we find that this raw score is equivalent to a percentile rank of 85. This means that 85 percent of persons in the reference group (norm group) scored *at the same level or lower* than Alfred. On the other hand, Joanne received a score of 63, which was equivalent to a percentile rank of 75 percent. This means that 75 percent of the individuals in the reference group obtained a score equal to or lower than Joanne's. This derived score represents a deviation judgment.

There are a number of cautions to be exercised when using percentile ranks. First of all, it should be remembered that percentile ranks are not the same as percentage correct scores. Percentage correct scores indicate what percentage of items a student responded to correctly, and this is heavily influenced by the difficulty level of the test. A person getting 90 percent of the items correct on an easy test may fall at the 50th percentile. On the other hand, a 90 percent correct on a difficult test may place him at the 98th percentile.

---

[2] In this chapter the meaning of each of these scores will be explained briefly. Appendix A also includes information on how some of them are computed. For a detailed explanation, read H. B. Lyman, *Test Scores and What They Mean,* 2d ed., Prentice-Hall, Inc., Englewood Cliffs, N.J., 1971.

[3] It should be noted that sometimes, when indicating absolute rank, the referent is the top of the class. In other words, the person scoring highest is assigned number one. The next highest is then given number two, etc., until all students have been assigned a rank.

Another disadvantage of percentile ranks is that they cannot be averaged. You cannot average a group of percentile ranks across several individuals nor can you average the percentile ranks for a single individual across several tests. This disadvantage can be fairly easily overcome by averaging the raw scores and then converting this average raw score to a percentile rank.

Despite disadvantages, a percentile rank is an extremely useful score because it is easily understood even by those not having a background in measurement and evaluation.

Standard scores. The standard score is another very popular and useful derived score. Basically, it is the result of comparing an individual's raw score with the average score of some group. Notice that the referent in this case is the average score of some norm group. The extent to which a person's score deviates above or below that group average determines his standard score. Notice that this is also an example of a norm-referenced deviation judgment.

A basic standard score called the z is a ratio of an individual's deviation from the mean compared to the standard deviation (see Appendix A). A z score tells us how many standard deviation units a person's score is above or below the mean. You can see that if a person scored right at the mean, his z score would be zero because his score did not deviate at all from the mean. A z score of $+1$ would mean the person deviated one standard deviation from the mean. The plus sign tells you he scored above the mean. A z score of -1 means the person scored one standard deviation unit below the mean. Rarely do people deviate more than 3 standard deviation points (plus or minus) from the mean of their group.

Constructors of standardized tests have used a number of scores which are derived from the z score. Some test constructors have decided to set the means of their distributions at 500 and the standard deviations at 100 (e.g., the Graduate Records Examination and the test of the College Entrance Examination Board). In these situations, a person who has a raw score which deviates one standard deviation below the mean will have a standard score of 400 (100 standard score points below the mean of 500). One other deviation score which could be a type of standard score is the deviation IQ. Many intelligence tests report scores in deviation units. Often the mean IQ is set at 100, with a standard deviation of 16. Therefore, a person who obtained a raw score equivalent to the average raw score of the norm group would be assigned an IQ of 100. A deviation IQ score of 116 would mean that the person is one standard deviation above the mean. Anyone who scored two standard deviations above the mean would have an IQ of 132.

There is an important difference between deviation IQs and most other standard scores. The deviation IQ is usually computed on the basis of the person's deviation from the average score of persons his age. This means that instead of a single referent, many referents are used (one for each of several age groups). The person's deviation IQ is computed, then, on the basis of how far he deviates from his own age group.

One final standard score is the stanine. Stanines divide a distribution of scores into nine parts (*stan*dard *nines*). Stanine 5 is in the middle of the distribution. All the scores within one-fourth of a standard deviation on either side of the mean are included in this stanine. The rest of the scores are distributed evenly above and below stanine 5.

Grade-equivalent scores.   The grade equivalent score or grade placement score has been very popular in the past because it is thought to be easily understood. However, it is finally losing in popularity, and rightly so. The grade equivalent score is probably the most confusing and the most misleading of all derived scores. Lyman (1971) describes the dilemma very well:

> Grade-placement scores are so confusing that a lower score on one test indicates relatively higher performance than does a higher score on another test. Because of the difference in size of standard deviations, this might easily happen: a grade-placement score of 8.5 on reading may be equal to a percentile rank of 60, but a grade-placement score of 8.2 on arithmetic fundamentals may be equal to a percentile rank of 98. Especially for higher elementary grades and beyond, grade-placement scores cannot meaningfully be compared from test to test—even with the same battery!
>
> The difficulties noted above are accentuated when we consider subtests based on very few items. Here the chance passing or chance of failing a single test item may make the difference of one full grade equivalent. Who can get any meaning out of such a state of affairs?[4]

In defense of grade-equivalent scores, it might be stated that if an individual scores fairly close to the average performance of students who are placed in the same grade, his grade-equivalent score will be fairly accurate.

Age-equivalent scores.   Age-equivalent scores are very similar to grade-equivalent scores. Instead of the average scores obtained by individuals at various grade levels, the referents in this case are the average scores obtained by individuals of various ages. Mental age, educational age, social age, etc., are all variations of the same basic interpretation rule: Assign a value to an individual based upon how close his score comes to the average score for individuals at a given age. Again, these scores are fairly easily interpreted if the individual is in fact "average" and scores at about the same level as his peers do. For interpretation of extreme deviations from the average, these scores can be very misleading.

Criterion-referenced estimates.   Criterion-referenced estimates are a bit more difficult to make and are not as clearly understood by psychometricians as are interpretations made on the basis of norm-referenced judgments. This is due to the fact that the referent is more difficult to determine in criterion-referenced

---

[4] Quoted from Howard B. Lyman, *Test Scores and What They Mean,* 2d ed., p. 117. Copyright © 1971; by permission of Prentice-Hall, Inc., Englewood Cliffs, N.J.

interpretation. Nevertheless, some constructors of standardized tests are beginning to devise criterion-referenced interpretation schemes and are placing them in their teachers' manuals (e.g., the Tests of Achievement in Basic Skills).[5]

I would urge you to be cautious in the use of standardized tests which are criterion-referenced. Whenever there are only a few items measuring a given objective, it is difficult to estimate a student's ability to meet that objective on the basis of the evidence supplied by the test. Nevertheless, these tests do have the advantage of helping you to analyze systematically the strengths and weaknesses a student has in a given subject matter.

It should be pointed out that TABS has provided the test user with norm-referenced data so that, if decisions must be made on the basis of norm-referenced judgments about general mathematics achievement, the test scores can be used for this purpose. It is anticipated that other standardized criterion-referenced tests will also provide the user with normative data.

EXERCISE 7.1

In your own words, describe each of the following derived scores:

1. Rank
2. Percentile rank
3. Standard score
4. Deviation IQ
5. Grade-equivalent scores
6. Criterion-referenced interpretation. (This is not a score but a description of the level of performance achieved.)

Predicting from Standardized Test Results

Producers of standardized tests provide the counselor and the administrator with formulas for predicting rather precisely how well a student will perform on a given task or in a given academic setting. Rarely, however, does a teacher have to make these kinds of accurate predictions from standardized tests. Nevertheless, teachers are constantly making predictions as they teach. The predictions which teachers make are more often informal in nature and are frequently made "on the spot."

Standardized test scores are used to make two major types of predictions: (1) predictions of general achievement and (2) predictions of success in a specific area.

General achievement is usually predicted through the use of an IQ test or some general aptitude test. Both these kinds of tests rely heavily upon measures

[5] The Tests of Achievement in Basic Skills (TABS), Educational and Industrial Testing Service, San Diego, Calif., 1971.

of past achievement (e.g., you will find questions requiring reading and math ability on almost all general aptitude tests).

When predicting success in a specific area (e.g., algebra or a foreign language) it is not as easy to rely on past achievement as a predictor, because the individuals whose success you are predicting may have had no past achievement in the specific area being predicted.

In this kind of situation, the authors of standardized tests frequently take a different approach. A common approach is to build a learning task which calls for the use of skills like those that are needed to learn in the predicted situation. When building a test to predict success in learning French, for example, they might design a test which measures auditory perception, ability to pronounce sounds commonly found in French, ability to learn a list of French vocabulary words, or ability to discover a grammatical rule by trying to decode a message in a pseudolanguage.

TABLE 7.1

Expectancy Table from MLAT: "TABLE 10" — Expectancy Tables for Adults in Intensive Language Courses for Total Score and for Short-Form Score (Probabilities of being in the Top Two-Thirds and Top Third of the Group with Respect to Criterion Score)

| MLAT TOTAL SCORE | N | PROBABILITIES | | SHORT-FORM SCORE | N | PROBABILITIES | |
		Top 2/3	Top 1/3			Top 2/3	Top 1/3
180–189	1	0.989*	0.902*	110–119	3	0.990*	0.840*
170–179	13	0.980*	0.860*	100–109	13	0.977*	0.760*
160–169	21	0.966*	0.800*	97–99	29	0.958*	0.680*
150–159	34	0.970	0.765	80–89	71	0.958	0.746
140–149	58	0.983	0.707	70–79	113	0.894	0.487
130–139	68	0.794	0.515	60–69	173	0.694	0.364
120–129	111	0.811	0.432	50–59	147	0.707	0.292
110–119	101	0.762	0.366	40–49	184	0.549	0.190
100–109	126	0.683	0.270	30–39	145	0.524	0.179
90–99	131	0.626	0.237	20–29	57	0.421	0.105
80–89	115	0.478	0.209	10–19	22	0.273*	0.070*
70–79	83	0.446	0.096				
60–69	50	0.500	0.100				
50–59	26	0.240*	0.055*				
40–49	14	0.180*	0.035*				
30–39	4	0.125*	0.020*				
20–29	1	0.082*	0.011*				
All	957	0.672	0.333	All	957	0.672	0.333

* Estimated from ogive curve on normal probability paper, since there were fewer than 30 cases in this class interval.

Frequently, producers of standardized tests utilize expectancy tables to provide an estimate of the probability that a student's performance will fall at a given level. If one wishes to predict future performance on the basis of some standardized test scores, he can usually do so by locating the appropriate expectancy table in the teacher's manual. In Table 7.1 we have an example of an expectancy table taken from a standardized test. This expectancy table has been taken from The Modern Language Aptitude Test (MLAT). You can see from this table that anyone scoring very high on the MLAT has a high probability of scoring in the top third of his class (intensive language course). For example, with an MLAT score of 180 to 189, the chance of being in the top third of the class is 0.902.

Expectancy tables are very commonly used by constructors of standardized tests to demonstrate the validity of their instruments as well as to provide the teacher and counselor with a way of predicting future performance.

Notice that when expectancy tables are being devised, persons are first grouped on the basis of their performance on some predictor variable. Next, the proportion of the students in each grouping that falls at each of the various levels on the predicted variable is computed. Finally, that proportion is used as an estimate of the probability that someone at a given level on the predictor variable will fall at some specified level on the predicted variable.[6]

Using the standardized test manual to locate derived scores and predictions. The first thing you should do when you wish to make an interpretation of standardized test results is to obtain the teacher's manual which accompanies the test which was used. Find the section which deals with interpretation and read through it very carefully.

When you are going to interpret scores from a standardized test, search the examiner's manual for the following:

1. The types of scores which are available.
2. The types of norm groups which are available.
3. The kinds of information which are measured by the test (this will be a list of behavioral objectives if the test is criterion-referenced).
4. The location of charts which are to be used for converting raw scores to derived scores.
5. Any formulas that are given for converting raw scores to derived scores.

Once you have familiarized yourself with the manual and have located the information indicated above, you must decide on the kind of judgments you plan on making. If you plan on making norm-referenced judgments, you must decide

---

[6] Procedures for producing expectancy tables will be discussed later. They provide an easy method whereby classroom teachers can make sound predictions.

which of several possible norm groups you will wish to use as a reference group. Sometimes a standardized test will have only one norm group (frequently referred to as *national norms*). This norm group is supposedly a group of students representative of all the students in the United States at the particular grade level(s) being measured.

In actual practice, this norm group does not provide you with very meaningful interpretations. It may be interesting for you to know how well a given student compares with "the students of the nation as a whole," but it is of very little practical value. What you really wish to know is how your student compares with other students like him and with students against whom he must compete. Some test publishers are now providing geographical norms and/or socioeconomic norms (that is norms based on different geographical locations in the United States or norms based on the socioeconomic class of the average student in the school). You may wish to look for those norms which most closely resemble the individuals for whom you are making an interpretation.

Another thing which must be considered when trying to find the right norm table (or the right reference group) is the time of year at which the test was given. Many achievement tests, for example, have norms developed for different times of the year. This makes very good sense, because students may have achieved much more by the time they have completed most of a year's work than when they have just begun that grade. If achievement tests are given in the spring, you should use norm tables based upon results also obtained in the spring.

Finally, make certain that you are using a chart which is based upon individuals of approximately the same age or grade placement as those for whom you are making judgments.

If you are making criterion-referenced judgments, make certain that the judgments are based on a comparison of objectives which are in fact important to you. The TABS program, for example, specifies very clearly in the manual that the teacher should select to measure those objectives which he feels are most important.

Once you have located the charts for making interpretations, you simply take the raw score for each individual student and locate the derived score which is associated with that raw score on the appropriate chart. Sometimes you may wish to obtain several derived scores for each individual. A percentile rank is usually easily understood by the parents and is a good score to report to them. However, you may wish some other standard score to be recorded in the cumulative folders.

One final word of caution is in order at this point. The interpretations which you make will be only as good as the data which you have collected and only as good as the reliability and validity of the tests used. Before you place too much confidence in any interpretations made on the basis of a standardized test scores, you should make some judgments about the quality of that test and the quality of the norms which it reports. Various suggestions for judging the standardized tests and their norms are found in Chapter 14.

MAKING ESTIMATES FROM TEACHER-MADE TESTS AND ASSIGNMENTS

Placing a grade on a paper or assignment is really nothing more than making an estimative judgment. The grade is a value assigned to the work done—a judgment if you will. However, grades are only one form of judgment and this section will deal not only with grades per se but also with other *equally* important kinds of judgments. Teachers may make many judgments about their students' work without placing a traditional grade upon that work. That is particularly true when teachers make criterion-referenced judgments. In the next few pages some of the typical grading practices will be examined. In each case we will discuss what kind of judgment is being made, the rationale for the procedure, and the actual steps involved.

Grading on the Curve (Norm-referenced Deviation Judgments)

Strictly speaking, grading on the curve involves dividing the distribution of scores from a given test in such a way that the final grades are distributed in the approximate shape of a normal distribution.[7] In actual practice, grading on the curve means dividing a distribution of scores into groups of different sizes. The smallest groups occur on either end of the distribution (those assigned A's and F's). The largest group is usually the middle group, and these persons are assigned C's. The next-largest groups are two groups just below and just above the middle group (these are assigned D's and B's). If you adhere rigidly to a curve on any given test, *some* students are doomed to failure, no matter how well they do. Even if a student does quite well on a given test, if his peers do better, he may still end up with an F.

Grading on the curve is done on the assumption that students in a typical classroom should fall into a normal distribution on achievement because they are normally distributed on aptitude. This assumption is invalid for many classrooms. In such a small group of individuals composing the typical classroom, it is very rare to find a normal distribution of aptitude; and hence it is unreasonable to expect a normal distribution of achievement. Also, as the proponents of mastery learning advocate, even if the aptitude is normally distributed, this is no reason to expect that the achievement will be so distributed. If the teacher is doing a good job of helping all the students to attain the objectives set for the course, then the level of achievement reached by the students should dictate their grade. That grade should not be a reflection of their position relative to their peers.

As long as you realize that the referent being used is the large group of students that falls in the middle of the distribution and that the rule for assigning grades is somewhat arbitrary (i.e., those that deviate a great deal from the large middle group get A's and F's and those that deviate only slightly get B's and D's), this kind of grading can be used with some success. However, remember that

---

[7] See Appendix A for an explanation of the normal distribution.

arbitrarily filling quotas on a "magical" curve does little to help evaluation improve the decision-making process.

Grades as Percentage-Correct Scores (Criterion-referenced Deviation Judgments)

One way of interpreting how well a student has done on a given assignment is to indicate the percentage of the total number of items the student got correct. This way of interpreting test scores and other evaluative information is very popular. If you know something about the kinds of items which were included on the test and you are aware of the particular concepts being measured by these items, then a percentage correct can be somewhat meaningful. However, the biggest problem with percentage-correct scores is that their meaning varies depending upon the difficulty level of the test. A student obtaining a high percentage of items correct on a very easy test may be performing close to the majority of his peers. However, a high percentage-correct score on a difficult test may place a student far above the level of performance of most of his peers.

It may help you to better understand and interpret percentage-correct scores if you stop to think about what referent is being used in this type of judgment. The referent in this case is the total number of items in the test (or the total number of possible points on the test). The scores assigned to each individual are based upon how far the student deviates from that 100 percent. The deviation is recorded in terms of percentage. Now you can see why it is so important that we see what is being measured when percentage-correct scores are reported: *A full description of the test content is the only valid description of the referent for interpretative judgments of this type.* Then, this becomes a kind of criterion-referenced deviation judgment.

Grades as Percentiles (Norm-referenced Judgments)

You will recall from our discussion of standardized test interpretation that the percentile rank is considered to be one of the best derived scores for making norm-referenced interpretations. The computation of the percentile rank is explained in Appendix A. Whenever it is important to know how a student's performance compares to the performance of the rest of the class, the percentile rank can be used. The student can tell at a glance approximately where he stands in relationship to the performance of the class as a whole.

Grading on an Achievement Continuum (Criterion-referenced Judgments)

As you know, the basic idea behind criterion-referenced interpretation is that of making judgments about the *level of achievement* that a student has reached. Underlying this idea is the assumption that there is a continuum of knowledge acquisition ranging from no proficiency at all to perfect proficiency.

An example of criterion-referenced evaluation. The specific learning outcome being evaluated is: "When given a set of raw scores from some test,
the student should be able to convert them to z scores with 90 percent
accuracy."

Theoretical Achievement Continuum

				Perfect
No proficiency				proficiency
0	1	2	3	4

Cannot compute the $\bar{x}$	Can compute the $\bar{x}$	Can compute the $\bar{x}$ and deviations from the $\bar{x}$	Can compute the standard deviation	Can compute z scores

Continuum of Test Behaviors

0	10	20	30	40

Cannot compute the $\bar{x}$ from raw sources	↑ Correctly computes the $\bar{x}$ from raw sources	↑ Correctly computes the squared deviation from the $\bar{x}$ when given raw sources	↑ Correctly computes the standard deviation from the raw scores	↑ Correctly computes z scores from the raw data
	When given raw score total and "N," correctly computes the $\bar{x}$	When given the deviations from the $\bar{x}$, correctly computes the squared deviations	Correctly computes the average squared deviation from the mean	When given the $\bar{x}$ and standard deviation correctly computes z scores

Test: Part One

Using the raw data given below, work out the z scores for Harry, George,
Glen, Stan, and Betty. Use the formulas given below. When you have
finished, bring your paper to the instructor to be checked. If you get at
least four of the five correct, you may leave. If you get more than one
wrong, you will be asked to do part two of this test. When completing
that, you may leave. If you have any questions, ask them now; if not,
begin to work.

FIGURE 7.1. From theoretical achievement continuum to test items.

Formulas: $\overline{X} = \dfrac{\Sigma X}{N}$

$S.D. = \sqrt{\dfrac{\Sigma(X - \overline{X})^2}{N}}$ $\quad z = \dfrac{X - \overline{X}}{S.D.}$

Data

Fred	15	George	21
Harry	17	Stan	12
Sue	22	Jill	18
Betty	16	Elmer	10
Pete	23	Glen	15

Test: Part Two

1. A class of twenty students had a combined score of 200. What was the class mean?
2. What is the mean of the following scores: 7, 8, 3, 2, 1, 3?
3. Compute the squared deviation from the mean for each of the following deviations from the mean:

$X - \overline{X}$	$(X - \overline{X})^2$
5	?
2	?
0	?
3	?

etc.

FIGURE 7.1 (*continued*)

Before you can make judgments about the level of achievement attained by a given student, you must first have a clearly defined achievement continuum (procedures for defining such a continuum were discussed in Chapter 4). An achievement continuum describes the behaviors of persons who have reached various *levels* of proficiency. A good criterion-referenced test provides a measure of the objectives at each point along such a continuum.

Once you have obtained information about how well a student has performed in certain tests or testlike situations which were designed to measure the objectives along an achievement continuum, several different kinds of judgments can be made. An illustration may help. Suppose, for example, we have defined a theoretical continuum describing the various levels of achievement on a given school task. Suppose, further, that we have defined a continuum of behaviors during testing. Our continuum of behaviors during testing is supposed to reflect the behaviors defined by our theoretical achievement continuum. In other words, we have defined what it is we are trying to measure in specific behavioral terms, and we have arranged these in some hierarchical order from no proficiency to perfect proficiency. Next, we constructed a number of test items which were designed to measure the particular behaviors as described by the points along our theoretical continuum. Finally, we described the various kinds of responses the students could make to that test, and this description of student responses was also placed on a continuum. Figure 7.1 illustrates such a situation.

There are various kinds of continuums, i.e., ways in which continuums can be arranged. The continuum shown in Figure 7.1 is arranged in hierarchical fashion. This allows us to make a mastery judgment on the basis of part one of the test. If a student gets part one correct, then it can be assumed that he can also do part two. This assumption seems quite valid when we realize that the various computations being called for in part two are all computations which are necessary in order for the student to complete the work asked for in part one.

Why then have we included a second part to this test? If a student cannot correctly work out the problems presented in part one, then part two will reveal those particular operations which the student cannot do and will tell both student and teacher what needs to be worked on next. Here again, we have an example of how criterion-referenced evaluation can be used to help the teacher and student make instructional decisions. Notice that there are many kinds of judgments which can be made, given the situation described in Figure 7.1. First of all, we might ask "How well has the student performed on the test?" The answer to this question could be a norm-referenced deviation judgment (he scored better than 80 percent of his peers); a criterion-referenced deviation judgment (he got sixteen out of twenty-four concepts correct); or a criterion-referenced mastery judgment (he only missed two items, he has mastered the material).

If a student has not mastered the terminal performance, it must be decided which tasks along the continuum he has mastered. Whenever a student can succeed on a given task *and* all the prerequisite tasks (i.e., those preceding it on the continuum), then that given task defines the student's level of achievement. This seems reasonable enough and simple enough. However, answer this question: "How does one determine whether or not a student has mastered a given task (or set of tasks)?"

Does the student have to get *all* the test items correct which have been designed to measure skill on that particular task? (Remember measurement error!) Can we consider 80 percent of the items on a given task to represent mastery? Or is 50 percent enough?

The procedures to follow when making mastery judgments and thus answering the above questions will be discussed under the topic of grading on a standard. In the meantime you must realize that for each point or value along a continuum of test behaviors, a minimum level of performance must be established (i.e., a mastery judgment must be made). In the example in Figure 7.1, the minimum level of performance for mastery of the ultimate learning outcome is specified by the behavioral objective which describes that outcome: ". . . with 90 percent accuracy." Many times the objectives we specify will include minimum level of performance statements. When they do, the task of making mastery judgments becomes easier.

Although we have not included all the items from part two of the test, it has been designed to measure the specific tasks as defined by the theoretical continuum. A student has to be able to do *all* the tasks before he reaches "perfect" proficiency. The test could therefore include items designed to measure the objectives as described at points 10, 20, 30, and 40 on the continuum of test behaviors. If we wish to be even more diagnostic, looking for precisely the kinds of errors students might make, we could also include items measuring the descriptions which would fall at points 5, 15, 25, and 35 along this same continuum. Another possible way to proceed would be to include the items measuring points 10, 20, 30 and 40 in part two and then devise a part three for those students who were not able to master part two. This third part then would include a still further breakdown of the objectives on the continuum of test behaviors and would measure the specific skills described at points 5, 15, 25, and 35.

If several forms of this test were used, students who do not master the test the first time will know from the feedback why they did not. They will know which tasks they still have not mastered and can study these prior to taking an alternate form of the same test at a later time. If the tests are indeed alternate forms, then self-referenced judgments can be made in answer to the questions: "How far have I come?" "How much further do I have to go?" This procedure of taking a test, finding out what you have not yet mastered, studying that material, and taking an alternate test can be continued until mastery occurs. When the test covers a relatively small amount of material, as does the one in Figure 7.1, only a couple of alternative forms would probably be necessary. If the test covers an entire unit of descriptive statistics (e.g., all the material contained in Appendix A), then some students might need several "testings" before they mastered the material.

Grading on a Standard (Mastery Judgments)

The idea of judging a student's performance against some standard rather than against his peers has a great deal of appeal. Highly motivated students working under a good teacher can often accomplish a great deal, and a large number of high grades can be legitimately given. Bloom (1968) has estimated that 90 percent of the students in our schools today can master the materials we have to teach them if they are given good instruction and enough time.

Setting a standard of performance allows you to judge your students in terms of mastery of the material. However, appropriate standards are not easy to specify and they frequently are not really related to mastery at all. Although there is no magical formula for setting appropriate standards, the following suggestions should help.

Setting Standards

Suggestions for determining a minimum level of achievement:

1. Know your subject matter well.
2. Obtain the opinions of others.
3. Keep records of past performance.
4. Obtain empirical evidence.

Know your subject matter well. The major value in setting a minimum level of performance as the standard against which you can judge your students lies in the fact that you can make decisions about whether or not they are ready to move on to a further unit. If you know your subject matter well, you are more likely to be able to indicate which skills are prerequisite to which others.

Knowing your subject matter well implies more than knowing just the facts, the concepts, and the principles that are important to the particular subject matter you are teaching. It also means understanding the structure of that subject matter. If you *do* understand how the various concepts and principles are interrelated and which are more likely to give students difficulty, then it will be easier for you to establish minimum standards of performance.

Obtain the opinions of others. After you have decided what the minimum level of performance for a given objective ought to be, ask the opinions of some of your fellow teachers. Make certain that you provide them with a basis for making a judgment about whether the standard is set too high or too low. This means that you should indicate to them what decisions will be made. Tell them what you are likely to do if a student passes (or fails to pass) a given standard. For example, you could be using the standard as a basis for judging whether or not the student is capable of moving to a faster or more advanced group. So ask for the opinions of your fellow teachers and other experts, but make certain they understand what decisions will be made once the standard of achievement has been set.

If you want to know whether you set the minimum level of performance high enough, ask the teacher to whom the students will go next. He will probably have a good idea about the expected level of performance needed for the students to work successfully at the level he is teaching.

Keep records of past performances. The experienced teacher has an advantage over one with inexperience because he is more likely to know what to expect of the students. But experience becomes more valuable when you keep a record of past experiences. Whenever you use the same (or similar) tests, assignments, or projects, keep track of the performance of the students. Write down not only the students' scores but also something about their past performance. Keep track of the kind of instruction they get prior to the time the information was obtained.

Make note of the conditions under which the information was obtained. These notes will serve as a valuable indicator of what you might expect from a new group of students.

Besides setting general standards for the class as a whole, standards can also be set for individual students. It is helpful, therefore, to keep track of student performance over a period of time within a given subject matter. Soon you will begin to learn what you can expect from any given student in terms of the level of performance achieved as well as in terms of how fast he might be expected to reach that level.

Obtain empirical evidence.   All the suggestions so far should be helpful for determining a minimum level of achievement. However, despite these suggestions, any standard you set is still nothing more than an educated guess. With a little effort, you can do better than that. For the kinds of judgments that will lead to important decisions, it is frequently worth the time and effort to obtain empirical evidence about how well a student might be expected to perform once he has reached a given level of performance. When you want to know what the chances of success on a future task might be (given the student has reached a particular level on some present or prerequisite task), the best way is to obtain empirical evidence.

First of all, you test a number of students on a task and determine their levels of performance. Now expose these students to the next level of learning, the next concept to be studied, or the next series of assignments in the sequence of instruction. Some students may be ready and some may not. Therefore it is important for you to expose them to this new work without the threat of penalty if they do not succeed. Tell the students that you simply want to find out how well they can do on a new task and then expose them to the task you want them to learn. Next, keep track of how well they succeed. Success might be measured in terms of how much time the students have to spend before they can learn a new concept or succeed at the new task.

Another way to obtain evidence of success (or lack of it) would be to give all the students a certain amount of time to learn the new task and then test them on their knowledge of the skill. Now you have information of how well they have performed on this new task. The next step is to construct an expectancy table which would tell you how well a student might be expected to perform on some task, given his level of performance on the prerequisite task.[8]

Grading on a Standard Scale (Deviation-from-Mastery Judgments)

In the above discussion we have mainly talked about setting a standard above which is mastery and below which is failing. Sometimes it is useful to set a standard scale. In other words, rather than have a single point which serves

[8] Procedures for developing an expectancy table are explained in Appendix A.

as a pass/fail standard, one might have several points which serve as standards for judging performance in terms of some rating scale (e.g., A, B, C, D, and F). This would provide you with a tool for making deviation-from-mastery judgments. There are two basic techniques for establishing a standard scale. The first is to derive an achievement continuum and then to place values on the various points along that continuum. These values can be numerical in nature or they can be letter grades.

A second technique would be to set a minimum level of performance that you would consider passing and assign a letter value to it. For example, you might assign a D to the lowest level possible that is still passing. Or you might assign a C to the mastery level. This would allow for one grade below the minimum level of performance needed to go on but would not be considered failing. Next, you would find the level of performance which is considered the maximum that one might reasonably expect from students at this grade level and assign that a letter grade of A. Now one could merely fill in the rest of the scale at equal intervals between the minimum level performance and the maximum performance.

EXERCISE 7.2

For each of the following kinds of grading, indicate
  a. The type of judgment involved
  b. The basic procedures
  c. Any problems which may arise
1. Grading on the curve
2. Grades as percentage-correct scores
3. Grades as percentiles
4. Grading on an achievement continuum
5. Grading on a standard
6. Grading on a standard scale

Grading for Report Cards (Summative Judgments)

There are a large number of involved schemes for arriving at final grades. Some of these schemes entail a great deal of statistical manipulation of the scores from tests and other information-gathering techniques. Most of these schemes are not really worth the effort they take. It does not need to take a lot of effort to produce report card grades. If, in fact, grades are judgments of achievement (and I would argue that they should be), then you simply need to determine what kind of judgment you anticipate making and follow the rules for making judgments which were discussed earlier. There is one slight problem which does arise, however: report card grades are based upon information which has been collected from a wide variety of situations over a long period of time. This frequently means that we try to combine information which ought not be combined. Furthermore, it means that we sometimes take into account information which has become outdated (or updated), and our grades are not accurate. The following suggestions are made to help you overcome these problems.

Suggestions for Assigning Report Card Grades

1. *Use grades as judgments of achievement only.* (Use some other way to report effort, attitudes, etc.)
2. *Use an appropriate method for combining data.* (Convert to some common unit of measurement such as standardized scores.)
3. *Do not always combine all data.* (Sometimes level of achievement attained is more important that "average amount" of achievement.)

If grades are to be accurate indications of information not reported in other ways, they probably ought to be limited to achievement. More particularly, they ought to be based upon maximum performance measures such as assignments, quizzes, and tests. They should *not* be a reflection of other aspects of student behavior, such as the amount of effort put forth or his achievement relative to his aptitude. These other aspects of student behavior should be reported in some other way and should not be combined with the information that goes into making up the grade. Thus any judgments or decisions that might be made on the basis of students' grades can be made with the realization that the grades are an indication of what the student has achieved, *what he is capable of doing at his best.*

When you do combine data, realize what it is you are combining. Are you combining scores (raw data) or judgments? If judgments, were the same referents used for all judgments combined? If you wish to make norm-referenced grades, you should either add up all the scores (this is possible, for example, if you have all scores on objective tests which have approximately the same standard deviation), or you should convert all achievement information to norm-referenced grades and use some system for averaging them. You can compute a straight average *or* you can weigh some grades more than others. Suppose, for example, that a teacher had three essay tests, a final essay exam, and four assignments. A given student received a letter grade of B on each of the tests, a letter grade of A on the final exam, and two B's and two C's on each of the written assignments. Now perhaps the assignments were quite important and we felt they were equal in weight to the tests that were given, but we decided that the final exam should count twice as much as these. These grades can be averaged by first converting the letter grades to a 5-point scale (the A getting a 5, the B getting a 4, and the C

TABLE 7.2

Grades Averaged (Exam Weighted Twice as Much as the Other Grades) for Three Students

Source of Grade	Tom	Dick	Harry
Test 1	A = 5	C = 3	D = 2
Test 2	B = 4	C = 3	D = 2
Test 3	B = 4	E = 1	E = 1
Assignment 1	C = 3	D = 2	C = 3
Assignment 2	D = 1	C = 3	D = 2
Assignment 3	B = 4	C = 3	E = 1
Assignment 4	A = 5	D = 2	E = 1
	B = 5	B = 5	D = 2
Final exam*	B = 5	B = 5	D = 2
	9 $\lfloor 36$	9 $\lfloor 27$	9 $\lfloor 16$
	4 = B	3 = C	1.8 = D

* Final exam weighted twice as much as other scores.

getting a 3). Next, in order to give the exam twice the weight, we add it in twice. Now we add up the total and divide to obtain an average of 3.8, which would be a B. The grades of three other students have also been worked out and are recorded in Table 7.2.

Another way that a wide variety of tests and assignment scores can be accurately combined to arrive at a final grade is to convert all of the scores to z scores, Z scores, or some other standard scores (see Appendix A) and then simply to average these standard scores. This would give us a final standard score, which could be reported directly or could be converted to a letter grade.

Most systems devised for arriving at final grades utilize some way of averaging all the grades assigned earlier (e.g., test scores and grades on assignments). If we are really interested in reporting what a student is capable of doing, what his maximum performance is, then a system which combines all the scores obtained throughout the whole marking period can be invalid and unfair. Many subject matter areas are highly cumulative in nature. Furthermore, a great number of the goals we set for our students are transitional in nature. In these cases, our real concern should be what the student has achieved at the time of the reporting (and not what has he achieved at each of the small, relatively unimportant steps along the way).

If two students have reached the final goal that you have set in some course but one got there with less trouble, with less work, and in less time, does that mean that he should have a higher grade? If so, then the grade is a reflection of more than achievement alone. It is also a reflection of how fast and how easily a person reached the goal. If two students reach a given goal by the time the report card is due *and* the goals have been achieved at the same level of proficiency, then the students should get the same grade.

Take, for example, students in a course in creative writing. Suppose the instructor has the following instructional goals: "The student should be able to write well-organized compositions of an explanatory nature." Now suppose that on the first assignment some of the students do very well, writing excellent compositions (these students get A's for their effort). Some other students do not do quite so well (getting perhaps C's or B's.) Finally, some students may have had very little experience in writing and turn in compositions deserving of F's. Let us further suppose that the teacher is a good teacher who does all he can to help the students learn. He writes comments to those who scored poorly in the first composition, pointing out their errors. Furthermore, he helps them to correct these mistakes on future compositions.

Now, as the term progresses, the students who started out writing good compositions continue to do so, getting A's throughout the term. On the other hand, some of the students who scored poorly on the first composition are learning from their mistakes and are improving their scores. There may be a student, for example, who gets an F on his first composition but, by the time he has written two or three, he is getting C's. Finally, as the term draws to a close, this student is writing compositions that are receiving a grade of A. (Compositions which are, in fact, equivalent to those written by the student who has written A compositions throughout the semester.) This student's last two or three compositions have satisfied all the criteria for a good composition and he has now reached the same goal as the students who were practically there when the term began.

Now if we take the traditional approach to assigning a final grade for report card time to these two students, the student who had gotten A's from the beginning will have the highest total composition score and the highest average grade (he should be given an A). The student who received an F in the beginning and worked his way slowly up until he got A's on the last few assignments will receive an average grade probably near C. So there are two students who have both reached the same goal, who have both achieved the same amount. The one student, who had very little distance to go and who achieved his goal with ease, gets an A. The other student, who started out far behind but was capable of catching up despite his problems at the beginning, gets a C.

If a student can read well, can make an excellent speech, can write a good report, can answer the vast majority of questions on a cumulative exam in history —in short, can accomplish the goals that we have set for a given term, that student deserves a good grade (no matter how poorly he may have done at the beginning). It is not difficult to see the resolution to the problem we have just defined. It is in *criterion-referenced grading*. You should be able to figure out for yourself how criterion-referenced report card grading would work. Here are the major steps to take. You will be able to work out the details by using the skills you have already developed.

Steps to Take in Criterion-referenced Summative Evaluation

1. *Develop an achievement continuum for the course you are teaching.* Place the ultimate terminal performance on one end and call the other end "the no-performance end." Describe the levels of behaviors between these ends.
2. *Decide on ways to obtain information about the student's performance* at each level along the continuum. In other words, develop a continuum of test behaviors which match the achievement continuum.
3. *Establish a standard scale* by placing a grade to each level of performance along the continuum of test behaviors.
4. *Assign each student a grade* based upon the level of achievement he has attained at the time of the report.

EXERCISE 7.3

1. What is the advantage of keeping report card grades a measure of achievement only?
2. When should grades from tests and assignments *not* be averaged?
3. How do formative and summative criterion-referenced judgments differ? How are they alike?

ESTIMATES OF TYPICAL BEHAVIOR

Judging a person on the basis of typical behavior presents some special problems. There are no "right" answers to interest inventories or sociometric devices. Anecdotes may uncover undesired behavior patterns, but there is frequently no clearly right or clearly wrong pattern of behavior.

If you have selected an appropriate referent (step 1 of the evaluation process), the task of making these kinds of judgments is easier. It should be noted, however, that sometimes an appropriate referent cannot be made until after the data have been obtained. When you are not really sure what the data will look like (as is certainly the case with anecdotes), it is difficult to select a specific referent. Let us explore this problem a little further, examining some of the various kinds of judgments you might make from typical performance data.

Norm-referenced versus Criterion-referenced Judgments of Typical Behavior

Norm-referenced judgments are probably used most often when evaluating typical performance. The following kinds of questions about typical behavior exemplify those for which norm-referenced judgments would be appropriate:

"Who is the friendliest? Politest? Most outgoing?" "Does Jaleen leave her seat more often than the other students?" "Could Marvin be trusted to monitor the room more than Dale could?"

But, how do you determine mastery of typical performance? One useful way is according to the effect that typical performance has on the individual himself and his surroundings (including others). One might conclude for example, that a student has mastered the art of friendliness when others respond to him in a friendly manner. You *could* conclude that good study habits were mastered if good grades resulted. The task of keeping your desk in order is "mastered" when things can be located in it easily.

Self-referenced Judgments

Are the behavior patterns of your students changing? Are they improving? Getting worse? Are the interests of your students shifting? These kinds of questions require self-referenced judgments. Make certain that any self-referenced judgments of typical behavior which you make meet the criteria for self-referenced, judgments (see Chapter 2).

> Whenever you make judgments about typical performance, be especially aware of the type of judgment you are making (norm-referenced, criterion-referenced, self-referenced) and the kind of comparison you make to that referent (deviation, mastery).

Criterion-referenced judgments *can* be used in situations where a scaling of desired behavior is possible. For example, it may be possible to develop a scale of good-to-bad study habits or a scale of good-to-bad sportsmanship. When these kinds of scales can be developed, typical behaviors can be judged against the criterion established by the points on the scale.

However, whether norm-referenced or criterion-referenced judgments are made, the problem of placing a valve on typical behavior (i.e., good to bad, fast to slow, mastered to not-mastered) still remains. This brings us back to the problem of setting standards: what is "good" typical behavior? What is "bad"? (See the earlier discussion in this chapter entitled "Grading on a Standard.")

Deviation versus Mastery Judgments of Typical Behavior

To make deviation judgments, you simply determine how far a student's behavior (or response to inquiry) deviates from the behaviors or responses of other students. If you have the same data on all of your students, this is a simple procedure. Often, you will *not* have the same information on all the students. Then mastery judgments might be appropriate.

MAKING CLASSROOM PREDICTIONS

There are a few occasions when the teacher will want to make formal predictive studies, determining rather precisely how a predictor variable is related to a predicted one. If you understand the procedures for doing this, you will be more likely to be aware of the thinking process you go through when you make informal predictions.

In the first stages of the evaluation process, you decide what predictive judgments you need to make and what it is you are trying to predict. Now, in order to make that prediction, you will need to carry out the steps outlined below.

Steps to Take When Making Predictive Judgments

Step 1: Choose a predictor and obtain information about the students' performance on that variable.

Step 2: Obtain information on the predicted variable.

Step 3: Estimate the relationship between the two sets of data obtained in steps 1 and 2 and use this estimate to make predictions.

Step 1 : Choose a Predictor and Measure Student Performance on It

The predictor you choose should be a measure of some trait on behavior which is highly related to the predicted behavior. Furthermore, your "best bet" will be a measure of past achievement on a related variable or present performance on a similar task.

What could we use to predict the slow readers' ability to answer the questions at the end of each chapter in the social studies text? What is highly related to this ability? Surely reading ability would be. If we had reading comprehension scores or estimates of reading level we might use them as predictors. This would be especially good if we knew what level of reading skill was necessary to read the text being considered and to answer the questions at the end of the chapters. Another possible predictor might be the students' past achievement on similar tasks. Perhaps one of the simplest ways to solve this particular problem would be to build a test which would give us a measure of present performance on a similar task. This should be easy. What we want to predict is how well the slow readers will be able to answer questions after they have read the chapters in the social studies text. So give them a single chapter (or some portion of one) to read, have them answer the questions at the end, and use these scores as predictions of how well they are likely to do on the rest of the text. Note the procedure being suggested: give students a sample of the kind of task you want them to be able to do and then use their performance on that sample task as a predictor of their performance on the total task. That procedure can be applied to a variety of predictive problems. For example we might wish to predict our students' abilities to solve problems by manipulating blocks, learning from lectures, perceiving spatial relations in designing landscapes, or learning clerical skills.

Step 2: Obtain Information on the Predicted Variable

In order to get an estimate of the relationship between two measures, you must have scores from *both* measures on the same group of people. Consequently you should have obtained these scores from some other group than those for whom you wish to make predictions. (What is there to predict if you already know the predicted score?) Usually this means that you will use the information you obtained one year to estimate the relationship between the variables and then you will use that to help you make predictions on subsequent years. For example, last year Mrs. George found out that those who did well on the "Arithmetic Fundamentals" unit also did well on the "Using Arithmetic Facts" unit. This year she will use this knowledge to help her predict which students might have trouble when they get to the "Using Arithmetic Facts" unit.

Step 3: Estimate the Relationship between Predictor and Predicted and Use the Estimate to Make Predictions

The estimate of relationship you make can be determined by a correlation coefficient or by an expectancy table. Both of these procedures are explained in Appendix A.

Rules for predicting future performance will usually take one or the other of the following forms:

1. If performance on the predictor variable is high, predict a high performance on the predicted variable.

This is a general rule based upon the principle that when variables are highly related to each other, performance on one can be used to predict performance on the other. When we do not have specific information about the relationship between the predictor and predicted variables, we must make our predictions on this very general level:

2. Use the average score of an appropriate reference group as the predicted score.

What this rule says very simply is this: locate individuals like the individuals for whom you are predicting; find out their average level of performance on the predicted variable; use that value as your prediction. For example, if, in the past, students in the top 25 percent of the class averaged a grade of B+ on a test in aerodynamics, predict a grade of B+ for those students who are in the top 25 percent of their class this year.

3. Use an expectancy table to predict the *probability* of succeeding at any given level.

This will undoubtedly be your most useful rule for accurate predicting. Whenever you do have previous information about the level of performance of a group of individuals on both the predictor and predicted variables, you can establish an expectancy table which will in turn serve as your rule for making predictions.

SUMMARY

1. Standardized tests are interpreted by comparing the raw scores to some referent. The scores which are a result of this comparison are called *derived* scores.
2. Derived scores which are norm-referenced are rank, percentile rank, standard score, deviation IQ, and grade-equivalent scores.
3. Criterion-referenced estimates from standardized tests are made by comparing an individual's test performance to a list of criteria (usually behavioral objectives).
4. Caution should be exercised when making criterion-referenced estimates because often there are only a few items measuring a given objective. When used as formative judgments, criterion-referenced estimates are valuable.
5. Standardized test scores are used to make two major types of predictions: (1) predicting general achievement and (2) predicting success in a specific area.
6. The following information is placed in standardized test manuals to help you interpret any results you obtain: (1) norm tables, (2) behavioral objectives or tables of specifications, (3) formulas for converting raw scores to derived scores.
7. When selecting a norm table, make certain the norm group is appropriate and that the testing upon which the table is based took place at approximately the same time of year that you tested your students.
8. To grade tests and assignments is to make estimative judgments. Common grading practices are grading on the curve, percentage correct grading, assigning percentile ranks, grading on an achievement continuum, and grading on a standard.
9. The following suggestions were made for assigning report card grades: (1) use grades as judgments of achievement only; (2) use an appropriate method for combining data; and (3) do *not* always combine all data.
10. Whenever you make judgments about typical performance, be especially aware of the type of referent you are making and the kind of comparison you make to that referent.
11. Classroom predictions can be made quite accurately if the relationship between the predictor and predicted variable is established. An expectancy table provides an especially useful way to estimate that relationship.

References

Bloom, Benjamin S.: "Learning for Mastery," *Evaluation Comment,* UCLA, CSEIP, nos. 1 and 2, May, 1968.

Lyman, H. B.: *Test Scores and What They Mean,* 2d ed., Prentice-Hall, Inc., Englewood Cliffs, N.J., 1971.

Suggested Reading

For an extensive coverage of the problems associated with assigning grades, see:

Terwilliger, James S.: *Assigning Grades to Students,* Scott, Foresman, and Company, Glenview, Ill., 1971.

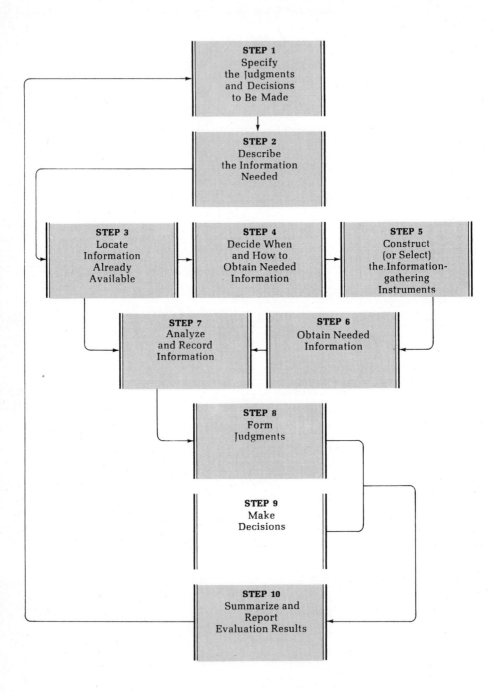

CHAPTER 8

Making Decisions

There is no more important reason for evaluation than this: Evaluation leads to better decision making. And there is no busier decision maker than the classroom teacher. If you can learn to take the judgments you have made from carefully obtained information and use those judgments to help you make better decisions, you will find for yourself the real value of evaluation in the classroom. This chapter was written to help you do that.

Note that this chapter has not been designed to make you a decision maker. Rather, it has been designed to help you learn to use judgments you have made to make *better* decisions.

Making decisions is something we all do every day. It is such a common task that we rarely think about how we do it. This chapter has been developed to help you think through the steps involved in decision making.

The idea behind this is not to make you change your decision-making strategies so much as it is to help you become aware of those you do use. Furthermore, it has been designed to serve as a guide when you are faced with important decisions. Many of the important decisions you will make as a teacher should be carefully, systematically worked through. However, you will find that no matter how carefully you carry out the decision-making process, you cannot make good decisions on the basis of faulty judgments. It is important, therefore, that you get into the habit of verifying the judgments you have made. Therefore,

---

The first goal of this chapter is to help you to do the following:

1. Verify judgments before using them in making decisions.

Furthermore, studying the material in this chapter should help you to

2. Become more conscious of the steps you take each time you make a decision.
3. Work through each step in the decision-making process systematically any time you have an important decision to make.

VERIFYING JUDGMENTS

The idea behind verifying judgments is not new to you. To verify something is to establish its truth. We frequently question the judgments of others. When we question someone's judgment, we show that we doubt the truth of that judgment. Consider the following examples:

Examples of Everyday Judgments and Responses Which Call for Verification

JUDGMENTS	RESPONSES CALLING FOR VERIFICATION
1. Don't go in there, the food is lousy.	1. It is? Did you ever eat there?
2. They have a great team.	2. Since when?
3. There is a 30 percent chance of rain tonight.	3. What's that based upon? The sky looks pretty clear to me.
4. He was a great President.	4. What did he do that was so great? If he was, why were we at war during most of his term?

If you look carefully at the right-hand column above, you will see that responses calling for the verification of judgments are essentially questions which call for evidence that the judgment is true. There are two steps you might follow when checking on the truth of judgments:

Steps to Take when Verifying Judgments

Step 1: Double-check the accuracy of the information upon which the judgment is based.

Step 2: Obtain empirical evidence of the truth of the judgment.

Step 1: Check the Accuracy of the Information

Throughout this book, you have been given a number of ways to check on the accuracy of information. Some of the ways were rather sophisticated (e.g., determining the standard error of measurement for a test). Some of the ways were logical and much more subjective (e.g., watching for clues to see if the test scores might contain error).

Now you need to ask the question: "Is the information as accurate as I am able to obtain?" If you have test scores which are completely inaccurate *and* you know that you can easily obtain other more reliable scores before you must make decisions, then you should probably decide not to use that information. On the other hand, if the information you have is highly inaccurate and you will not be able to obtain other information, you will then have to use the judgments in your decision making anyway.

If the judgments you have made (or the judgments you are using which someone else has made) are based upon information which is likely to be as accurate as you can get, go ahead and use these judgments in making decisions. If, on the other hand, the information upon which the judgments are made seems to be somewhat inaccurate, you have the following alternatives:

1. Wait until you can obtain more accurate information and then make new judgments. (This is an especially appropriate alternative when the decisions to be made are important and/or are irreversible.)
2. Go ahead and make the decisions but be ready to reverse them in case the judgments were less accurate than you thought.
3. Go on to step two, checking on the truth of the judgments by obtaining empirical evidence.

Step 2: Obtain Empirical Evidence

The general procedures for obtaining evidence about the truth of information were explained in Chapter 2. Basically, the same procedures should be followed here. First, form hypotheses about the behavior of those who were judged. Second, test those hypotheses, either confirming or rejecting them.

Form hypotheses on the basis of the judgment. The hypotheses we form should meet certain criteria if they are to be really useful in helping you to verify judgments.

Each time we form hypotheses which are designed to help us verify judgments, those hypotheses should meet the following criteria:

1. The hypotheses should follow logically from the judgments.
2. The hypotheses should be stated as expected outcomes.
3. The hypotheses should be observable and testable.

Let us examine a variety of judgments, in each case answering the general question: "If this judgment is true, what else could be expected?" The answers to this question should take the form of hypotheses to be tested. Suppose, for example, that Zelda was judged to have high math ability. On the basis of that judgment, you might hypothesize that she would do well on the math assignments given her in class. Another hypothesis we might make about Zelda's math performance is that she would score high on a math achievement test or a math aptitude test.

Notice that the hypotheses we formed were based upon logical expectations of Zelda's behavior. Given the judgment that she has a high math ability, these hypotheses made sense. We did not form hypotheses about her reading achievement or ability; we did not form hypotheses about her ability to get along with other students; we did not form hypotheses about how well she likes school; nor did we make hypotheses about how well she can write creative stories.

The judgment in the above example was of a very general nature. Consequently it was easy to derive testable hypotheses on the basis of that judgment. When judgments are made about more specific abilities, testable hypotheses are not quite as obvious. What would you hypothesize, for example, about a girl who was judged to have a good ability to discriminate among long and short vowel sounds?

First of all, one might expect this girl to be good at discriminating among the other sounds in the language. Furthermore, if she is good at discriminating among sounds, she is likely to be good at learning the correct pronunciation of words. Notice that these hypotheses are not only logically related to the judgment made but they are also stated as expected outcomes.

The above examples were judgments of aptitude or ability. Hypotheses can also be formed from judgments of achievement. Suppose we have a reading achievement score which places Sharon in the 95th percentile in reading comprehension. This judgment had been made on the basis of information from a standardized reading achievement test. Assuming that this judgment is accurate, we might hypothesize that Sharon will do well in her reading in school and her reading grades will be high. Furthermore, we might hypothesize that if she were given another standardized reading achievement test she would also score very high. We might also hypothesize that Sharon's grades will be high in many subject areas (particularly those where reading skills are crucial).

The above judgment of Sharon's achievement in reading was a norm-referenced judgment. What kinds of hypotheses could we make if we had a criterion-referenced judgment of achievement? The difference between these two kinds of judgments, you will recall, is that in the norm-referenced judgment you have a statement of the student's achievement as compared to her peers (or some norm group). A criterion-referenced judgment of achievement in reading would specify a particular *level* of achievement as defined by an achievement continuum in reading. Given this kind of information, we might be able to make some further hypotheses. First of all, it would be logical to expect that an individual who was judged to have reached a given level of achievement on some continuum would then be able to perform any of the behaviors described by the lower levels on that same continuum. Whenever a judgment has been made about the level of achievement in an area where behaviors have been hierarchically arranged, it is reasonable to hypothesize that a person, having reached some given level, will then be able to successfully perform those tasks which are prerequisite to that level. For example, being able to translate passages at a particular level of difficulty in the French language requires that the student has been able to successfully use certain rules of grammar as well as to have reached a given level of understanding of the French vocabulary.

Many of the judgments we make about students are judgments about their typical behavior rather than their maximum performance. This is especially true of the judgments we make about a student's attitudes, opinions, and personality traits. If we have made judgments about the behaviors in the affective domain, we can form testable hypotheses by answering the question: "Given these attitudes, judgments, or judged personality traits, what is the person likely to do?" Notice that this question refers to the typical behavior of the student. We are asking "How will an individual *typically* behave if he is judged to hold certain attitudes or opinions?" Suppose, for example, that it is our judgment that Peter hates geometry. On the basis of this judgment, we might hypothesize that he will frequently skip geometry class. Other hypotheses that we might make are: Peter will frequently turn his assignments in late, he will talk about how he hates doing the geometry work, he will find excuses to avoid doing work in geometry, etc.

EXERCISE 8.1

For each of the following judgments, write *at least* one hypothesis. Remember that the idea is to assume that the judgment is correct and then to seek an

answer to the question, "What else might be expected?" Compare your answer
to those of your peers and/or have your instructor look at them to see if you
are on the right track. Check each hypothesis to see that it meets the criteria
listed earlier.

1. *Judgment:* Sartan is a great judge of character.
   Hypotheses: He should be able to. . . .
2. *Judgment:* Wanda is the poorest speller in the class.
3. *Judgment:* Bob is a class leader.
4. *Judgment:* Fonda has an IQ of 147.
5. *Judgment:* This third grade class will have little or no trouble making the
   transition from manuscript to cursive writing.

We have suggested that in order to verify judgments which have been made,
one should form testable hypotheses and then check to see if those hypotheses
hold true. The way in which you form hypotheses differs slightly depending
upon the type of judgment you are trying to verify (estimates, or predictions).
We would offer the following suggestions for forming hypotheses about the truth
of each of these types of judgments:

Estimates.   An estimate is a value placed upon some general ability, level
of achievement, or personality trait. Therefore, in order to form hypotheses which
would help you to verify estimates, you should

1. Hypothesize that if the student were to be measured by the same or a similar test,
   he would be estimated to have the same general ability or level of achievement.
   Furthermore, if attitudes, opinions, personality traits, etc., were correctly estimated, those same attitudes, opinions, etc., would be displayed if he were
   measured again on the same or a similar measure.
2. Hypothesize that if the student were to try a variety of *specific* tasks which require
   the estimated general ability or level of achievement, he would be able to perform
   them. Furthermore, in a variety of situations the student should display behaviors
   which are characteristic of his estimated general attitudes, opinions, traits, etc.

Predictions.   A prediction places an expected value upon some future performance on a specific task. Therefore, in order to form hypotheses which would
help you verify predictions, you should:

1. Hypothesize that if the student were to be measured by the same or a similar
   measure, the prediction of future performance would be approximately the same.
2. Hypothesize that if you ask the student to perform a task similar to the predicted one, he will perform much as he would be expected to on the predicted
   task.

Notice that in all the above examples, the hypotheses have been worded
so as to suggest ways in which they could be tested. Testing them out is the final
step in verifying judgments.

Confirming or rejecting hypotheses. In order to test any hypotheses you have formed, you need to determine the following:

1. What is the expected outcome or behavior identified in the hypothesis?
2. What are the conditions under which that outcome is expected to occur?

The expected outcome indicated by any hypothesis should be easily identified. Consider this example: "When reading new material orally Duane should have little trouble sounding out unfamiliar words." What is the expected outcome in this hypothesis? Obviously, it is the sounding out of unfamiliar words.

Try another example: "John's score on another IQ test will also be below average." This time the expected outcome is below average performance on some other test.

If your hypotheses are properly formed, you should be able to identify the conditions under which the outcome is expected to occur. What are the conditions under which Duane is expected to have little trouble sounding out unfamiliar words? Obviously, the answer is "When reading new material orally." What is the condition under which John is expected to have an IQ below average? According to the hypothesis stated above, John is expected to have an IQ score below average on "another test of IQ."

EXERCISE 8.2

For each hypothesis, decide which words refer to the expected outcome and which words refer to the conditions under which the outcome is expected to occur.

1. *Judgment:* Alice scored average on the reading test.
   Hypothesis: Alice should score about average on another form of the same test.
2. *Judgment:* Eloise scored at the top of her class on the arithmetic achievement test.
   Hypothesis: Eloise will do better than anyone in the class on another arithmetic achievement test.
3. *Judgment:* Jim successfully completed the problems on page 75.
   Hypothesis: Jim will have no trouble with the similar problems found on page 78.
4. *Judgment:* Doug is highly creative, as indicated by a "creativity" test.
   Hypothesis: Doug will be chosen by his classmates as the "one who comes up with the most ideas." (A guess-who technique will be used).
5. *Judgment:* Freddie is a leader, according to the sociogram that was done.
   Hypothesis: Freddie will take over a small group discussion session if no leader is appointed.
6. *Judgment:* My observations suggest that the class is motivated and involved in its projects.
   Hypothesis: The class will continue to work on their projects when I leave the room.

If you look carefully at the hypotheses in Exercise 8.2, you will see that there are two conditions under which outcomes are expected to occur. The first three hypotheses in that exercise all call for conditions which are similar to those under which the information was obtained for the original judgments. For example, in the first hypothesis, Alice was expected to score about average *on another form* of the same test. In other words, the conditions under which this hypothesis was to be tested were the same as those under which the information for the original judgment was obtained. The only difference is that another form of the test is used.

In the second example, Eloise is to be tested on another test measuring the same thing. This is not another form of the same test but another test which is *similar* to the first one used. Contrast these conditions to the conditions under which the behaviors in hypotheses 4, 5, and 6 are expected to occur. Notice that in these hypotheses the conditions under which the outcomes are expected are quite different from the conditions under which the original information was gathered. In example 5, Freddie was judged to be a leader on the basis of information obtained from a sociogram. It was hypothesized on the basis of this judgment that he would assume a leadership role if given the opportunity.

When testing hypotheses by setting up conditions which are very similar to those under which the information was gathered for the initial judgment to be made, you are using a process of *replication.* When you replicate, you essentially form a judgment on the basis of information gained under approximately the same conditions under which the first information used for the first judgment was gained. *If the two judgments agree,* your hypothesis has been borne out and the original judgment is confirmed.

A second method of testing hypotheses is to compare judgments based upon two different kinds of information. This is a procedure which would be used in testing the hypothesis about Duane's word-attack abilities. The original information used to form the judgment about these skills was a word-attack test. The hypothesis that he would have little trouble reading orally is confirmed when you obtain supplementary information about Duane's abilities. This technique is called *supplementing.* An oral reading test is not the same as a test of word-attack skills, even though the two skills are probably highly related. An observation of Duane's oral reading skills provides a *different* kind of situation for obtaining information about Duane's word-attack skills. If he is proved to have little trouble reading, the hypothesis is borne out and the judgment is confirmed.

When you have confirmed the hypothesis which is made on the basis of particular judgments, you can feel more comfortable in making decisions based upon those judgments. When the judgments you have made are difficult to confirm, you should be more careful in your decision making. Furthermore, you should always be ready to alter or reverse any decisions made on the basis of unconfirmed judgments.

EXERCISE 8.3

There are two ways to confirm these hypotheses, replication and supplementation. For each of the judgments listed below, write one hypothesis which would replicate the information about which the judgment was made and one hypothesis which would supplement the information upon which the judgment was made.

1. *Judgment:* Jan has an IQ of 110 (Lorge Thorndike).
2. *Judgment:* Kamir will succeed in algebra (scored in top 10 percent of an algebra aptitude test).
3. *Judgment:* Joe cheats (was caught cheating on the playground).

MAKING DECISIONS

You are teaching math in seventh grade. The results from the midterm exam are computed. Most of the students obtain fairly high scores, but Marilyn's score places her almost 3 standard deviations below the mean. A close look at her test shows that she did well on some parts of the test, but she got all the long division problems wrong. All the evidence you have suggests that the test is reliable and that Marilyn's score is accurate. Consequently, you form the following judgment: "Marilyn does not understand long division." Next, you verify that judgment by taking Marilyn aside and questioning her about the concepts and procedures involved. She was unable to answer most of your questions. Now you must decide how to help Marilyn overcome this problem. How do you decide what to do?

If you think about the above problem for very long, you will realize that making a decision like this is quite involved. Decision making is a highly complex process (and yet we do it almost automatically). I believe that the better you understand this process of decision making, the more likely you will be able to make good decisions. This is probably most true when you take the time and effort to carefully arrive at an important decision by working systematically through the decision-making process.

Common Causes of Bad Decisions

Teachers indeed do have some specific decision-making problems. They are making decisions constantly and rarely have time to deal with a highly rigid model. Nevertheless, teachers frequently arrive at incorrect decisions because they use *no* systematic approach to decision making. It seems reasonable to believe that teachers' decisions would be more accurate if they could learn to avoid the following primary causes of faulty decision making.

Common Causes of Bad Decisions

1. Inadequate statement of objective
2. Too few alternatives considered
3. Failure to consider consequences
4. Failure to take into account your system of values
5. Faulty judgments used

Inadequate statement of objective.   A brief explanation of the above state-ments is in order. Many decisions are faulty because the decision maker did not know precisely what he wanted to occur as a result of the action he decided upon. For example, in the situation described earlier in this section, a number of things can be done to help Marilyn with her math. But, what do we want to happen when we help Marilyn? A clearly specified objective (in behavioral terms, please) will help you to select a course of action which is mostly likely to accomplish that objective.

Too few alternatives considered.   Another major cause of faulty decisions is the fact that too few alternatives are considered. For example, suppose that in trying to think of a way to help Marilyn, we only consider alternative sets of math assignments chosen from supplementary textbooks. We may be missing some alternative approaches which would better help Marilyn to reach the objective of being able to work long division problems which are appropriate for her grade level. We might, for example, wish to consider the alternative of programmed instruction, or private tutoring or. . . .

Failure to consider consequences.   A third reason for faulty decisions is the failure to consider the consequences of the alternative courses of action. What if we finally decide on a way to help Marilyn learn to do long division, but it turns out to take several weeks of extensive work and causes Marilyn to hate math?

Failure to account for your system of values.   A fourth reason for faulty decisions is the failure to take into account our system of values. It seems to be pretty clear that our system of values *does* affect the decisions we make, *whether we want it to or not.* The problems seem to come when we let this occur on a sub-conscious level. Our decisions are likely to be more rational if we make a con-scious effort to account for the values we hold.

Faulty judgments.   A final cause of poor decisions is poor judgments. If your judgments are faulty and you make a "right" decision, you are lucky. This is why I have stressed the importance of basing judgments upon sound informa-tion and then verifying the judgments *before* using them in decision making.

Steps in Decision-making Process

In the next few pages, the major steps involved in decision making will be outlined. These "steps to take" were developed to meet the following criteria:

1. *They must not be artificial.* They must be possible and *plausible.* That is, *they must work!*
2. *They must NOT be chronologically dependent.* We do not make decisions in a linear fashion, one step after another. We move back and forth in our minds working on first one element, then another.
3. *They must work for quick, in-the-hand decisions as well as slow, deliberate ones.*
4. They must allow the teacher to place the most value on those elements being considered which *he* personally feels are most important.

If you carry out the following steps each time you are faced with an instructional decision, you will be less likely to make the errors which commonly lead to faulty decisons. As you read about the decision-making process being proposed here, look for the points in the process where judgments enter in.

A Preview of the Steps to Take when Making Instructional Decisions

Step 1. *Specify your objective* (Determine what you want your action to accomplish).

Step 2. *Identify the possible alternatives* (and their probable outcomes).

Step 3. *Consider the consequences* of each course of action and its probable outcomes.

Step 4. *Choose the best alternative.*

Step 1: Specify your objective. Unless you know precisely what you want the chosen course of action to accomplish, you will find yourself fluctuating among alternatives, not knowing which to choose. When that happens, you either take an inordinate amount of time choosing and/or end up choosing the wrong alternatives. Make certain that when you do specify the desired outcome of your action, you phrase it in behavioral terms. This will help you to find out whether or not the desired outcome was reached (i.e., whether the alternative chosen was effective). The importance of this step will become increasingly obvious when you reach the final stage in the process. During that stage you will have to make some judgment about how well the alternative(s) might meet the stated objective. Remember our problem with Marilyn? We need to decide how to help Marilyn. Our objective is to help her to be able to successfully solve long division problems which are appropriate for her grade level.

Step 2: Identify the possible alternatives and their probable outcomes

Identify possible alternatives. Although this step is a rather obvious one, it is extremely important. Many "bad" decisions occur because all the possible alternatives are not considered. For example, suppose a teacher must decide what assignment to give the third graders who are having trouble dividing common geometric shapes into fractions. If the only alternatives under consideration are all of the teacher-teach-the-student variety, it is possible that the best alternative might not be considered. Perhaps the best alternative would be a discovery assignment. The students might use objects in the classroom to "discover" the classification of shapes. Or perhaps a fraction game would help the students understand. In any case, it is important that potentially good alternatives are not overlooked in decision making.

The number of alternatives that are possible and the nature of those alternatives varies depending upon the kind decision to be made. For example, when making selection decisions, there are only two alternatives: accept or reject. However, you must remember that in making selection decisions you are essentially deciding on the basis of one individual at a time. Suppose, for example, that an administrator (J. Smoon) is trying to select students for his program. Suppose further that he has room for only fifty students. Each time a student comes to him, Smoon must decide whether to accept or reject the student. The factors which influence acceptance or rejection may be rather involved. For example, the total number of selection decisions you have to make in a given situation may be important. If there are only fifty slots to fill and you have five hundred students to select from, the selection procedure will proceed differently than if you have one thousand students to select from. Furthermore, we might argue that there is still one more alternative (i.e., selection with certain restrictions). For example, an administrator decides to select a student into the program but places him on probation. That may seem like a third alternative, but it is technically the result of two decisions: (1) deciding to select the student and (2) deciding to place him on probation.

Whenever you are making selection decisions, it is important to remember how many individuals you have to select from and what the possibilities are for placing and treating those individuals once they have been selected. These considerations may in fact help you to decide in each individual's case whether or not they should be selected.

Placement decisions usually allow more alternatives than selection decisions. You will recall that a placement decision is one in which an individual is placed in a particular place in a sequence of events. An example of a placement in location is to place students in assigned class hours. Some are assigned to third-hour math class, some to sixth-hour, etc.

An example of placing students according to a time scale is to start some students on their arithmetic lesson on Friday and other students on Monday. Trying to decide when to begin a new unit in history is another example.

Placing students at some point in a sequence of events is illustrated by decisions to begin at a given page in a textbook or to start instruction at a given level of achievement. The number of placement decisions that can be made is limited to the number of places available, the number of points in an instructional sequence, or the number of points in the time line of interest.

Treatment decisions are those decisions in which you decide how to "treat" an individual or a group of individuals. The many instructional decisions a teacher makes daily fit into this category. Whenever the teacher asks, "Now what should I do?" "Which procedure should I follow?" "What kinds of assignments shall I give?" and similar questions, he is struggling with treatment decisions. It is in the area of treatment decisions where teachers must use the greatest amount of creativity in trying to come up with alternatives from which to choose. Those teachers who are able to think of the greatest number of viable alternatives to helping students reach a given objective, for example, are frequently the most successful teachers.

There are a number of things that can be done to be certain that you have not left out any important alternatives when making treatment decisions. I would make the following suggestions:

1. Begin with the first alternative that comes to mind.
2. Note the major characteristics of this alternative. Identify the *type of action* involved in the alternative, determine who the *doer of that action* is. Think about what or whom the *recipient of that action* is. *When is the action* supposed to take place? Finally, determine what the conditions will be when the action takes place.
3. Think about which of these major characteristics could be changed. Is it possible to change the type of action called for? Can the recipient of the action be someone or something different from the first alternative? Does it make sense to change the time of the action? Could the place of the action be changed?

It does not take one long to quickly go through all the possible alternatives, eliminating those which are not viable or workable. After this has been done, the alternatives which are left represent the possible alternatives from which you can select.

In our problem with Marilyn, some of the possible alternatives might be as follows:

Alternative 1: Give her assignments from supplementary textbooks (begin with short division problems and have her work through long division ones).

Alternative 2: Have her work through programmed, individualized lessons on division.

Alternative 3: Assign one of her peers the job of teaching her.

Alternative 4: Give her objects to manipulate and problems to work out. Guide her to discover the rules governing long division.

Alternative 5: Tutor her yourself after school.

Specify the probable outcomes of each alternative. What is the outcome of each alternative course of action? If _____, then _____? If this alternative is chosen, then what will result? If that one, then what will happen? Note that this step calls for the use of judgments. The probable outcome of each course of action is usually stated in terms of a predictive judgment.

If Marilyn does tutor herself after school, then she is *not likely to learn to solve long division problems.* If Marilyn does work through programmed lessons, she will have a *moderate chance of reaching the objective we set for her.*

If Tim enters the speech contest, then *he is likely to win.*

If Jane enters the speech contest, then she will *have a good chance of winning;* she will also probably get behind in her other schoolwork.

Recognizing the fact that specifying the probable outcome of any given alternative is essentially a predictive judgment, we can expand upon this notion. You recall that stating the probability of an event or outcome occurring is one way of making a predictive judgment. Another way is to indicate the proportion of times that a given level of performance will occur (remember the expentancy tables). What we are saying here is that rather than judging the probability of a single outcome occurring, we might specify a number of possible outcomes and indicate the probability of each of the various ones occurring. This is important when you consider the fact that some of the possible outcomes might be desirable and some of them might be undesirable. For example, we may specify that the probability of a student passing a course is 50 percent. This is based upon some judgment of his ability. However, we might also indicate that the probability of his getting higher than a D is only 25 percent, and the probability of his getting anything higher than a C is down to 5 percent.

Step 3: Consider the consequences of each course of action and its most probable outcome.   At this point we have a number of alternative courses of action. For each of these alternatives we have listed the possible outcomes and their probabilities of occurrence. Now, for each of the possible outcomes, some prediction must be made about the consequences of that outcome. In actual fact, we may consider only the consequences of the most likely outcomes rather than trying to list the consequences of every conceivable outcome. If an outcome is very unlikely to occur and if the consequence is only slight, we need not worry about it.

Suppose a given course of action is chosen from among a number of alternatives. Suppose, further, that the expected outcomes do occur. What would the consequences of those outcomes be?

Marilyn does receive help from her peers and she does reach the objective. What will be the consequences? Will she learn to rely on her peers for help in her other work too? Will she disrupt the rest of the class while she is learning?

Tim enters the speech contest and *does* win. What will the consequence of his winning be? Will Tim become a better person for this win? Will a win make him more confident in himself? Will this make him more enthusiastic about speech class?

Jane enters the speech contest and *she* wins. Will she find the win as rewarding as Tim? Will she tend to become conceited?

What about the consequences of the less probable but also possible outcomes? Suppose Tim does *not* win. What will the consequences be? Will he become discouraged enough to quit speech class? Will he be able to accept the loss and become a better person for it?

EXERCISE 8.4

Write out a clearly stated instructional objective (review Chapter 4 if you need to). Next, list a number of possible alternative courses of action to help you reach that objective. Finally, make some guess about the probable consequences of each course of action. Compare your answers with those of your classmates.

Step 4: Choose the best alternative. This last step involves bringing together in your mind (or on paper, when the decision is an extremely important one) everything you considered up to this point. You must now consider the alternative courses of action, their probable outcomes and possible consequences, *in light of some system of values.*

This step may sound a bit philosophical, but it is extremely practical. In the final analysis, our values play an important role in decision making. The weight we give to each alternative and the importance we place on each possible consequence depends upon our system of values. Do we value the individual more highly than the institution? Do we value time more than money? Do we value success more highly than attempts? The way in which we answer these and many similar questions tells us what our values are. Those things we consider most important will get the most weight in any choice among alternatives. We should be very aware of the values affecting our decisions.

Any time we make decisions, our choices are affected by our own value system. Whether we want them to or not, the values we hold *do* affect what we do. However, by bringing to a level of consciousness the values we do hold, we may more likely see how those values relate to the particular decisions we are trying to make.

The above discussion has highlighted the fact that there are many factors to consider when choosing one alternative course of action over another. We would suggest, therefore, that some way of systematically considering these factors would make decision making a more logical process. We will probably be less likely to miss an important factor if we consider the alternatives from each of three different points of view. These viewpoints are as follows:

1. The probability that the expected outcome will occur (a predictive judgment)
2. The similarity of that expected outcome to the desired outcome (an estimative judgment)
3. The value we place upon the possible consequences

The probability of occurrence.   One important kind of judgment we must make about *each* of the alternatives we are considering is essentially a predictive judgment. Based upon the information we have, what is the likelihood that the expected outcome of the alternative course of action will occur?

Suppose, for example, we are considering a number of possible ways to help Marilyn learn to successfully solve long division problems. For each alternative, we make some judgment about how we think it will work. Think of it this way: Where on some probability continuum would each of the alternatives lie?

Very low probability that the outcome will occur

Very high probability that the outcome will occur

Let us imagine that the following five alternatives that we discussed earlier are being considered as ways to help Marilyn:

Alternative 1: Give her assignments from supplementary textbooks (begin with short division problems and have her work through long division ones).

Alternative 2: Have her work through programmed, individualized lessons on division.

Alternative 3: Assign one of her peers the job of teaching her.

Alternative 4: Give her objects to manipulate and problems to work out. Guide her to discover the rules governing long division.

Alternative 5: Tutor her yourself after school.

Alternative 1 has some appeal because it will not take much work, but the probability of Marilyn reaching the objective set is fairly low.

Alternative 2 could work quite well except that Marilyn is not a very good independent worker. Predictive judgments: Alternative 2 has a moderate chance of succeeding.

Alternative 3 could work. Marilyn works well with her peers. Judge alternative 3 to have high probability of success.

Alternative 4 is an unknown. Marilyn has never done any discovery work for you yet. Let us predict a moderate level of success.

Alternative 5 should work extremely well. You know that with individual attention, Marilyn has an excellent chance of reaching the objective.

The above discussion suggests the following lineup of the alternatives along a "probability of the outcome occurring" dimension:

A_1	A_4 A_2	A_3	A_5

Very low probability   Very high probability

At this point, alternative 5 looks like a winner. Alternatives 2 and 4 cannot be distinguished. But there is more to be considered.

The similarity of the expected outcome to the desired outcome.   Another important dimension against which we must compare the alternatives is the "how well do the expected outcomes match the desired outcome" dimension. In other words, the question has now become: "Do the probable outcomes of each alternative match, to the same extent, the desired outcome as specified in your objective?"

Our objective was that Marilyn learn to work long division problems. How well do the expected outcomes of each alternative match this objective?

The expected outcome of alternative 1 should match almost perfectly with the desired outcome. The assignments proposed in this alternative all deal specifically with learning long division (beginning with the foundation in short division). Rate alternative 1 high on this dimension.

The programmed units we have available; they introduce the long division concepts and rules systematically and with very little "extra" information. Rate alternative 2 high on this dimension. Its expected outcome does look like the desired outcome.

Assigning a peer to teach Marilyn may work, but the outcome is likely to be somewhat different from what we expect. Her peer is not going to be as precise and will probably not "stick to the subject" as closely as the other alternatives. Rate alternative 3 fairly low on this dimension.

Alternative 4 offers a fairly good chance that Marilyn will learn some things about division. How many of the concepts and rules she will or will not learn from this procedure is difficult to determine. Rate alternative 4 low on similarity to the desired outcome.

Alternative 5 looks good again. If you tutor her, you will be able to devote all your energies toward the single objective you have in mind.

Let us add this similarity dimension to the probability-of-occurrence dimension and replot the alternatives. (See Figure 8.1.)

You can see now how the alternatives are shaping up. Although alternative 1 does not have a very good chance of succeeding, if it would succeed, the outcome would match the desired outcome very closely. Now alternatives 2 and 4 are clearly distinguished. They both have moderate chances of success, but alternative 2 is more likely to yield an outcome which *matches* the desired outcome. But, there is still one more dimension. That value system of ours must still be reckoned with.

Value of possible consequences.   At this stage in making a decision, we consider the consequences of our action and weigh those consequences in light of our system of values. Earlier (step 3) we considered the consequences of each alternative. But the time element is not critical (i.e., step 3 comes "earlier" in our

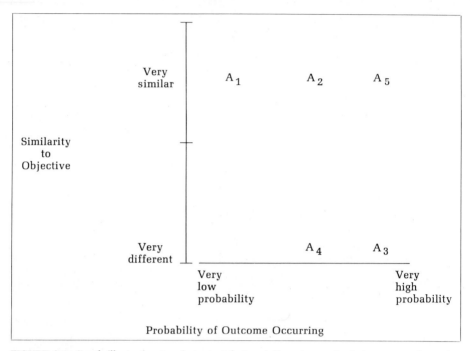

FIGURE 8.1. Graph illustrating two important factors influencing one's choice among alternative courses of action.

discussion and our thinking *about* decision making, but it may occur at different times for each alternative). The important thing to remember is that, somewhere along the line, you must consider the consequences of what you plan to do. Remember also that the action itself can have certain consequences (besides the fact that some learning outcome may occur) and the outcome of that action can have various consequences. As you consider the consequences of each alternative, you need to place some value on the alternative in light of how you judge its consequences. The alternative gets rated, then, on a good-to-bad scale depending on how you perceive the consequences. Let us try this out with out five alternative approaches to helping Marilyn.

Alternative 1 has a good chance of *not* succeeding. The consequences of Marilyn failing again are pretty bad. Furthermore, the action of this alternative (doing more problems in a book) will probably yield the following consequences: Marilyn will get bored and will dislike working problems out of math books. This alternative is not valued high at all. Give alternative 1 a rating near the "bad" end of the scale.

The second alternative has some chance for success, and the consequence of this outcome is that Marilyn may like math again. Furthermore, she will catch up. The programmed instruction is something new and Marilyn may respond well to it. Another consequence of alternative 2 is the fact that the teacher will not have to spend a lot of time with Marilyn and the rest of the class will not be held back. That is good, also. Rate alternative 2 toward the "good" end of the value scale.

Alternative 3 has some appeal because the teacher will not have to spend too much time with Marilyn. However, there are some risks involved. One highly likely consequence of Marilyn working with her peers is that they will disrupt the students nearby (they may even disturb the whole room). Rate alternative 3 about middle on a good-to-bad value scale.

Alternative 4 has fairly high value because the consequence of working with blocks, buttons, etc., may make Marilyn feel she is having fun in math again. If she does discover some rules "on her own" this could be a real boost to her self-concept.

The fifth alternative has a good chance of succeeding and should yield an outcome which closely matches the desired objective. However, it will take a lot of the teacher's time. The teacher and student will have to stay after school. Marilyn may resent having to stay after school. She may learn to dislike math and may feel she is being punished for not knowing how to work long division. Rate alternative 5 toward the bad side of the value scale.

In Figure 8.2, we have attempted to show you graphically what you do in your mind when you weigh all plausible alternatives by rating each alternative along the three dimensions just discussed. Alternative 2 looks like our best answer to Marilyn's problem, although that may not be the alternative we would have chosen before we "took everything into account." What we hope for is to

FIGURE 8.2. Representation of the kinds of judgments we make about alternative courses of action.

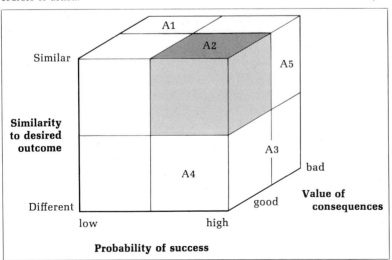

find an alternative that is high on all three dimensions (i.e., likely to result in an outcome which closely matches the desired objective and likely to be accompanied by "good" consequences). Alternative 2 makes it. Alternatives 4 and 5 both come close. They are worth considering as alternatives to fall back on if it looks like alternative 2 is not working.

Obviously, we do not have little three-dimensional cubes in our heads. But we can think in "three dimensions." That is, we can consider alternative courses of action along three dimensions, all of which are important when making a decision. The steps we take may not match the sequence we have proposed, and we probably do many of these things simultaneously. However, if you get in the habit of making certain you have set your objective clearly and considered all plausible alternatives, their outcomes and consequences, your decisions are likely to yield high returns in terms of improved instruction.

SUMMARY

1. Evaluation's real value lies in the aid it provides for decision making.
2. Good decisions cannot be made on the basis of faulty judgments. Therefore it is desirable to verify judgments before they are used in decision making.
3. Verifying judgments involves two steps: (1) double-checking the accuracy of the information upon which the judgment is based and (2) obtaining empirical evidence of the "truth" of the judgment.
4. There are two basic methods for testing hypotheses about judgments: (1) replication and (2) supplementation.
5. Bad decisions often occur because of one or more of the following faults: (1) an inadequate statement of objective was made, (2) too few alternatives were considered, (3) there was a failure to consider the consequences, (4) the decision maker did not take into account his system of values, (5) faulty judgments were used.
6. One approach to decision making proposes the following steps: (1) specify your objective, (2) identify the possible alternatives and their probable outcomes, (3) consider the consequences of each course of action and its probable outcomes, (4) choose the best alternative.
7. Unless you know *precisely* what you want the chosen course of action to accomplish, you will find yourself fluctuating among alternatives.
8. Many "bad" decisions occur because all the possible alternatives are not considered.
9. The probable outcomes of alternative courses of action should be stated in terms of predictive judgments.
10. The decision maker should also be aware of the *consequences* of a course of action and its probable outcome.
11. When making a final selection from among alternative courses of action, you should weigh each alternative on the basis of (1) the probability that the expected outcome will occur, (2) the similarity of that expected outcome to the desired outcome, and (3) the value you place upon the possible consequences.

Suggested Reading

The following book provides an excellent, in-depth discussion of the role of evaluation in decision making:

Stufflebeam, Daniel I., Walter J. Foley, William J. Gephart, Egon G. Guba, Robert L. Hammond, Howard O. Merriman, and Malcolm M. Provus: *Educational Evaluation and Decision Making,* F. E. Peacock Publishers, Inc., Itasca, Ill., 1971.

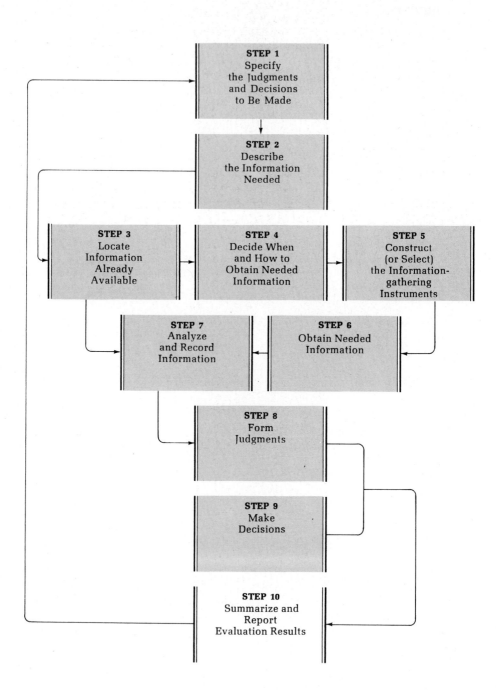

STEP 1
Specify
the Judgments
and Decisions
to Be Made

STEP 2
Describe
the Information
Needed

STEP 3
Locate
Information
Already
Available

STEP 4
Decide When
and How to
Obtain Needed
Information

STEP 5
Construct
(or Select)
the Information-
gathering
Instruments

STEP 7
Analyze
and Record
Information

STEP 6
Obtain Needed
Information

STEP 8
Form
Judgments

STEP 9
Make
Decisions

STEP 10
Summarize and
Report
Evaluation Results

CHAPTER 9

Summarizing and Reporting Evaluation Results

In the last two chapters you learned how to form judgments and use them in decision making. Now, the last step in the evaluation process is to summarize your evaluation results and report them to others. There are many people interested in the teacher's evaluation results. Students, parents, administrators, counselors, employers, and other teachers would all like to know how you judged each of your students and what decisions you made with regard to each one.

It is important that you learn to

1. Summarize the results of evaluation so that they can be used in producing evaluation reports.
2. Apply the general rules of reporting when producing both written and oral reports

---

THE RATIONALE FOR EVALUATION REPORTS

By assigning grades which indicate levels of achievement, teachers have for years been able to report the progress of the students to those who were interested. However, the report card and the traditional marking system have been challenged many times throughout the history of education. Time and time again, it has been argued that report card grades do not effectively report the progress of a student. Yet grades and the traditional report card still remain after years of being questioned and challenged.

The report cards of today are really not much different from those which were used many years ago. Some attempts have been made to make the report card somewhat more useful and understandable by those who must interpret it, and these changes will be discussed shortly. But why has the report card survived throughout all this challenge and criticism? There are at least two important reasons why the report card (or some form of reporting) is still used. First of all, there is a need for a precise, easily stored indication of pupil achievement and progress. This need is most keenly felt by administrators, for they have the problem of storing and retrieving vast amounts of information about many students. Anytime that you can reduce a student's progress in a given subject to a single number or a single letter, you have greatly reduced the task of storing and retrieving that information. So the administrative use of these grades has been an important influence to keep the grades as simple as possible. This simple, essentially numerical description of student progress is also useful for making predictive decisions. Report card grades have been found to be particularly effective predictors of future school achievement.

A second explanation for the continued use of report card grades may be that measurement experts have had some influence on the schools. In an attempt to make grades as precise and as accurate as possible, these experts have frequently emphasized the importance of test and measurement data. When these kind of data are used to compute grades, the grades tend to be more reliable. So, in the interest of reliability, grades are still being used as ways of summarizing and reporting student achievement. However, in the interest of reliability, the grading system has essentially lost much of its validity. There are many uses for evaluation reports to which the typical report card and the usual approach to grading simply do not lend themselves. The following list of uses for evaluation summaries and reports should serve as a guide when you prepare your own summaries and reports.

Uses for Summaries and Reports of Evaluation Results

1. They can provide information which serves as a basis for further judgment and decision making by students, parents, teachers, counselors, administrators, and employers.

2. They can provide information which clarifies the rationale behind the judgments and decisions which were made. This will be of further value when trying to evaluate the judgments and decisions we have made and/or when trying to defend our judgments and decisions to others.
3. They can provide information which helps to determine the cause of unplanned learning outcomes. A review of previous evaluation results can help us to identify the time and place where unplanned learning outcomes (e.g., bad attitudes, misinformation) began to occur.

Thus far, summaries and reports were treated as if they were the same. In fact, they both do provide the advantages cited above. But they are *not* the same. A report communicates the information included in the evaluation summary. Summaries of evaluation results provide the information for the report.

A teacher uses a *summary* as a way of finding out for himself what all his evaluation efforts have resulted in. He uses a *report* as a way of communicating to others what he has found out.[1]

SUMMARIZING EVALUATION RESULTS

It should be obvious that it is an impossible task to summarize the results of evaluation if no evaluation occurred or if the information the evaluation was based upon was almost nonexistent. As obvious as this may be, there are many teachers who approach the task of trying to summarize data (so they can fill out a report card, for example) without having any real data on hand to summarize. Sometimes this occurs because the teacher has not anticipated the judgments and decisions that were necessary and sometimes this occurs because the teacher failed to properly record the information used to make those judgments and decisions. This is why Chapter 6 so strongly stressed the need for a systematic approach to recording information.

The following steps to take should help you to produce a meaningful summary of evaluation results. This kind of summary can then be used as a source of information for written and oral reports.

A Preview of the Steps to Take When Summarizing Evaluation Results

1. Determine the purpose of the summary.
2. List the major decisions that had been made.
3. List the judgments which influenced those decisions.
4. Summarize the information used to make each judgment.

---

[1] It should be noted that rarely does a given report include everything from an evaluation summary.

Step 1: Determine the Purpose of the Summary

Before you begin to summarize your evaluation results, you should have clearly in mind who (or what) the summary is about, who the summary is for, and what it will be used for. By thinking this through very carefully and making a brief statement at the beginning of your summary to this effect, the summary will be much more meaningful and useful.

Who is the summary about?   Will this be a summary of evaluative information about a single student, about an entire class, or about some small group (e.g., a special reading group)? Or perhaps the evaluation summary will be about the teacher, about you and your attitudes toward your students or your effectiveness as a teacher.

The same information might very well be used to evaluate a particular student, a class of students, a set of materials, or the effectiveness of the teaching. However, the judgments and decisions made will differ depending upon whether it is the student, the teacher, or the program that is being evaluated. *So it is crucial, as you begin your summary of evaluative data, to indicate who or what your summary is about.*

Some summaries may be more limited in scope than others, and you may wish to specify the *particular* course, the *particular* subject matter, or *particular* problems that have arisen for which the summary is being compiled. For example, you may need to summarize all the evaluations that have been made about a particular approach to teaching science that you have been trying over the last few semesters. Or you may wish to have a summary of all the information about your elementary students' strengths and weaknesses in a given subject matter. If your summary is to be limited in some way, this should be stated so that you will not bring in unnecessary or inappropriate material.

Who is the summary for?   Sometimes summaries are made to serve quite specific purposes. For example, a summary may be completed to provide the teacher with information for a particular parent-teacher conference. A parent is concerned about his child's attitudes toward school. The child seems to pretend to be sick and the parent is concerned. The parent-teacher conference about this problem can be very enlightening. If the teacher has made certain judgments and decisions which may be pertinent to this problem, he could carefully summarize these and bring this summary to the conference with him.

When we ask the question, "Who is the summary for?" we really are asking, "To whom will the findings of the summary be reported?" Summaries are *always* made by the teacher for the teacher. However, the teacher will then use the summary for his own use or he will report *all or part* of the summary to others. The contents of the summary is determined at least in part by whom the findings will be reported to.

Who are the typical recipients of the information contained in evaluation summaries? Those to whom the teacher most frequently reports his findings include the following: students, parents, administrators, other teachers, and counselors.

What will the summary be used for?   There are two ways that this question can be interpreted: (1) What kind(s) of reports will be made with the findings? (2) What will the report(s) be used for?

There are many kinds of reports which the teacher may be called upon to make. The most common include report cards, letters, diagnostic reports, conferences, and phone calls. The specific procedures involved in each of these kinds of reporting will be discussed later in this chapter. No matter what kind of report is produced from an evaluation summary, one or the other of two basic uses is likely to be made of those results. The most common use is the formation of further judgments and decisions. If we have some idea about the kinds of judgments and decisions that will be made, that will help us decide what should be summarized and reported. Some of the kinds of judgments and decisions typically made from a teacher's reports (and/or summaries) are listed below.

Examples of Judgments and Decisions Which Might Be Made with the Help of a Teacher's Reports of Evaluation Results

1. Should Marietta be placed in a special education class?
2. Could George afford to miss several class periods in order to work on the school yearbook?
3. Which of the seniors deserves the "student of the year" award?
4. How long would it take this class to complete the work in the textbook they are now using?
5. Would Patricia make a good office secretary?
6. When should the unit on complex fractions begin?
7. Which of the students from the fifth-hour class would be most likely to succeed in an advanced algebra class?
8. Choose six students to represent the ninth grade in the freshman challenge quiz game.

The other common use of an evaluation summary is to assess the value and/or quality of the evaluation itself. By looking back over the judgments and decisions which were made (and the information upon which they were based), a teacher can get an idea of how well he has been evaluating. Also, the summary can be used to help the teacher *defend* the evaluation he has made. When someone questions the validity of a teacher's judgments or decisions, a good summary of his evaluation results would provide him with evidence of that validity.

Step 2: List the Major Decisions Which Were Made

Once you have decided on the purpose of a summary, the next step is to list the major decisions that have been made. The most convenient way to list decisions is from the most recent back to the earliest. Go back as far as necessary depending upon your reasons for the summary and upon the time span the sum-

Decision: Retain H. B. in third grade 5/25/72
Decision: Work with H. B. individually in math 2/10/72
Decision: Solicit parents' cooperation in having H. B. work on math and reading exercises 11/17/71

FIGURE 9.1. A list of decisions which ultimately led to the decision to retain a student in the third grade.

mary is intended to cover. By listing the decisions in this manner, you will be able to see at a glance the major events which occurred during the time span of the summary. Look, for example, at the list of decisions in Figure 9.1. Notice how easy it is to see the progress (or lack of it) of this particular student. Even more importantly, the final decision to retain the student is easier to defend when one sees the many kinds of things the teacher did to keep the failure from occurring.

Although the list in Figure 9.1 covers an entire year, there are only a few decisions listed. If you had to list every decision he made throughout the year, there would be time for nothing else. However, by keeping track of those critical decisions, those turning points in the instructional process, you will be able to assess your own course of action more readily.

Step 3: Indicate the Judgments Which Influenced Each Decision

Judgments, you will remember, are value statements about an individual which estimate or predict that individual's performance. These judgments are used for making decisions. Suppose, for example, a teacher has made the following judgments: "Johnny is reading two years below grade level," "Johnny cannot use phonetic rules," "Johnny has a poor sight vocabulary," "Johnny has an attention span which is relatively short for his age." These kinds of judgments would influence the decision to put Johnny in a reading group which moves more slowly and concentrates more heavily on basic reading skills. Notice the value of summarizing the data in this manner. If the teacher can turn to his record-keeping system and locate the judgments which were crucial in influencing major decisions, he will have evidence for the decisions he has made. Figure 9.2 presents the judgments that led to the decisions which were listed in Figure 9.1. Notice how the knowledge of these judgments helps you to understand more readily the decisions that were made.

Each of the judgments in Figure 9.2 could be questioned. Therefore it is also important to have a brief summary of the information that was used to make the judgments.

Step 4: Summarize the Information Used to Make Each Judgment

Obviously, every judgment that was made about every child could not possibly be recorded and summarized in an evaluation summary. However, those judgments which had an important influence upon major decisions should be recorded. In turn, those judgments should be well substantiated by appropriate information. It would help to know, for example, that a judgment about a student which says, "Mary has very low ability for learning French," is based upon accurate information. And it would also help to know exactly what information was used in making that judgment. Consequently, the summary might include such bits of information as test scores on aptitude tests in French, the grade for the first six weeks of elementary French, etc.

Figure 9.3 presents the completed summary sheet for the evaluation which led to the decision to retain Johnny in the third grade (see also Figures 9.1 and 9.2).

Notice how each judgment has been made on the basis of certain information. Look, for example, at the judgment, "Johnny reads far below his grade level." The parent is likely to understand much better the decision to hold Johnny back if he can be shown that the judgment about Johnny's inability to read is based upon sound, accurate information. Consequently test scores, information from checklists made while Johnny was reading orally, and other data have been summarized. This should help to validate the judgment that Johnny has low reading ability. By summarizing evaluation data in this way and keeping the summary

FIGURE 9.2 A list of judgments which influenced the decisions that were listed in Figure 9.1.

```
Decision:  Retain in third grade          5/25/72
     Judgment:  1.   Getting behind
                     each week
                2.   Almost two years
                     behind

Decision:  Work with H. B. individually in math
           and reading
     Judgment:  1.   Does not understand when
                     given group instruction
                2.   Can benefit from individual
                     situation

Decision:  Solicit parents' help
     Judgment:  1.   Extra work at home will help
                     H. B. to catch up
                2.   Support from parents will
                     reinforce what I'm doing
                     in school.
```

I. Decision: Retain in third grade   5/25/72
   A.   Judgment: Getting further behind each
       week.

      1.   Information: See summary sheet
         showing where he is working in
         relation to peers.

   B.   Judgment: Almost two years behind.
      1.   Information: See achievement test
         scores; also oral reading assess-
         ment completed 5/17/72.

II. Decision: Work with H. B. individually in
   math 2/10/72 and reading (plus keep on
   working with slow groups).

   A.   Judgment: Is not understanding group
      instruction well enough.

      1.   Information: Assignments given
         immediately after instruction (see
         H. B.'s folder).
      2.   Information: Observation during
         group discussion (see folder for
         rating scale results on partici-
         pation and checklist on number of
         questions answered over one week's
         time).

   B.   Judgment: Can benefit some from indi-
      vidual work.

      1.   Assignments done during individual
         sessions (see H.B.'s folder).

   Decision: Elicit parents' cooperation in
   having H.B. work on some math and reading
   exercises.

III. A.   Judgment:
                   etc.

FIGURE 9.3. A complete evaluation summary listing the important decisions, judgments, and information which led ultimately to the decision to retain a student in the third grade.

in front of you, you can confidently approach the task of preparing any report
which must be made (to parent, students, teachers, or administrators).

EXERCISE 9.1

1. Why should the purpose of the summary be decided before the summary is begun?
2. Why does it help you to know what reports are likely to be made from your evaluation summaries?
3. What are the three major kinds of information included in a summary?
4. How can an evaluation summary be of help when you are called upon to defend a decision you have made?

REPORTING EVALUATION RESULTS

The real value of summarizing data in the manner just described is that we can use this summarization for the preparation and completion of reports. The teacher is frequently requested to report the results of his evaluations. Sometimes these reports can be anticipated far in advance (report cards are due on a given date) and sometimes these reports are unexpected (a parent drops in after school and asks for a progress report on his child). Reports of evaluation results may be written or oral, formal or informal, for the benefit of the teacher only or for the benefit of others. However, no matter what format or purpose, any report should meet the following criteria.

A good evaluation report should

1. Provide all the information needed by those for whom the report is intended.
2. Be clear and easy to understand.

The following suggestions are made in order to help you prepare reports which will meet the above criteria.

Suggestions for Reporting Evaluation Results
1. State clearly what it is that is being reported.
2. Include a guide for interpreting the information in the report.
3. State the information to be reported as directly and as clearly as possible.
4. Report information in a form that will be most meaningful to the person receiving the report.
5. Where necessary, explain how the information led to the judgments and decisions which were made.

The above suggestions are appropriate for all kinds of reporting. As you read about each of the more common kinds of reports, keep these suggestions in mind. Occasionally check back to see how the rules for using each of the forms of reporting are really nothing more than specific instances of these more general suggestions.

We will first discuss the written forms of reporting (report cards, letters, and diagnostic reports) and then the oral forms (conferences and phone calls).

Report Cards

Undoubtedly more arguments, more committee meetings, and more hours of searching for improved formats have been spent in an attempt to arrive at a useful report card than have been spent in concern over any other form of reporting. Perhaps this is due to the fact that report cards have failed to really report all of the information which is useful to the parent and the student.

Generally speaking, the most common use of the report card is to report grades which are indications of achievement. These grades have traditionally been valuable predictors of future academic success (at least at the high school level and beyond). However, it is often valuable to report more than just achievement. Therefore attempts have been made in some report card formats to indicate effort expended, attitudes toward school, work habits, typical performance, and school citizenship. For the most part, these attempts to report more than grades for achievement have not been very successful. There are probably three major reasons for this lack of success: (1) teachers frequently have no real evidence for anything but achievement, (2) the format used for most cards does not lend itself well to the reporting of anything but grades, (3) grades have traditionally been considered *the most important* mark on the card and the other information is frequently ignored.

The value of report card grades. Grades are most valuable because they provide a way of reporting to others a value judgment that has been made. These judgments become useful to others in decision making. In other words, the value of grades lies in the fact that their main purpose is the reporting of judgments. James Terwilliger (1971) put it very succinctly:

> Specifically, the purpose of grading systems is to provide a systematic and formal procedure for transmitting value judgments made by teachers to the student and to others most directly concerned with his development and welfare. *These value* judgments provide a basis for making important decisions which are faced in the normal course of an individual's development in our society.[2]

The procedures for forming these judgments (i.e., for assigning grades) was explained in Chapter 7. It is important, it seems to me, for teachers to indicate on the report card what type of judgment the grades are based upon.

[2] Quote taken from *Assigning Grades to Students,* James S. Terwilliger. Copyright © 1971 by Scott, Foresman and Company, Glenview, Ill., 1971, p. 7. Reprinted by permission of the publisher.

JEFFERSON JUNIOR HIGH SCHOOL

COLUMBIA, MISSOURI

SCHOOL YEAR 197____ 197____

Name _____ Subject _____ H. R. No. _____

TO PARENTS AND GUARDIANS: Please examine all parts of this report thoroughly. We believe the ratings on citizenship traits as well as the subject grade and attendance record merit your careful study. Please feel free to confer with the teachers, counselors and principal concerning the welfare of your child. We very earnestly solicit your cooperation and help.

JOHN J. STOLT, Principal

CITIZENSHIP TRAIT RATINGS

1 — Exceptionally High; 2 — Superior; 3 — Average; 4 — Below Average; 5 — Low.

	1	QUARTERS 2	3	4
Industry, work habits: The good worker concentrates on his work and doesn't waste time. He plans his work well and carries out plans industriously and systematically.	☐	☐	☐	☐
Self-discipline, emotional stability: The well adjusted pupil controls his emotions, doesn't lose his temper and practices self-control at all times.	☐	☐	☐	☐
Dependability: The dependable pupil can be relied upon to do his work regularly and complete it on time.	☐	☐	☐	☐
Cooperation, courtesy: The cooperative pupil does his part cheerfully and works well with others. The courteous pupil is polite and well mannered. He shows regard for others.	☐	☐	☐	☐
Class participation: Desirable pupil participation contributes to constructive class discussion and establishing a wholesome classroom atmosphere.	☐	☐	☐	☐

SUBJECT GRADE

QUARTER	1	2	Sem. Avg.	3	4	Sem. Avg.	Credit
GRADE							
ABSENCES							

Explanation of grades: A = Excellent progress; B = Above average progress; C = Average progress; D = Below average progress; F = Failure to meet minimum requirements — no credit.

FIGURE 9.4. Example of a report card which includes space for grading achievement (reported as a letter grade) and for rating noncognitive measures on a 1 to 5 scale. Used with permission of the Columbia Public Schools.

Supplementary information on report cards.   There are a number of other kinds of information besides grades which can be reported on report cards. The use of checklists and rating scales allows the teacher to check off or rate a large number of behaviors (both cognitive and noncognitive) for each student. Figure 9.4 illustrates one such report card format. Achievement is indicated by letter grades, and other characteristics are rated on a 1 to 5 scale.

The most serious disadvantage to this kind of card is the fact that the noncognitive characteristics are rarely evaluated by teachers. Hardly ever does the teacher make a systematic attempt to get information which will allow him to make the judgments about the noncognitive outcomes he is asked to rate on this type of card. If a teacher is going to bother to evaluate noncognitive performance, it will have to be the particular noncognitive behaviors which he personally feels are most important. When a teacher himself establishes the affective goals for his students, he is more likely to believe in their value. Furthermore, he is more likely to try to do a good job of evaluating for their attainment. Figure 9.5 presents an example of the kinds of goals that a teacher might establish and take the time to evaluate. A report card designed to allow the teacher to rate these kinds of noncognitive goals might prove to be valuable indeed.

Just as the attainment of affective goals can be reported through the use of checklists and rating scales, so can cognitive and psychomotor ones. It is possible, for example, to supplement the grades by reporting performance through the use of checklists or rating scales. It is also possible to eliminate the grades altogether, replacing them with checklists or rating scales. An example of this kind of reporting can be found in Figure 9.6.

Notice that the final section in this report card is entitled "recommendations." It gives the teacher the opportunity to write terse statements about what can and/or should be done to help the student. In other words, this gives the teacher an opportunity to suggest possible decisions based upon the judgments reported on the card. It lets the teacher tie together all of the information reported for the parent and helps the parent see what the school is going to do next. Furthermore, the teacher can make a statement here about the student's ability to reach the goals which have not yet been reached and to indicate what the parent can do to help. Notice that the statements in this part of the report card

FIGURE 9.5. Examples of the kinds of noncognitive goals which teachers might establish for their own classes.

Kindergarten:	Willingness to accept correction (evidenced by attempts to correct problem).
Third grade:	Neatness of handwriting (other students can read what they write).
Seventh grade:	Appreciation of poetry (occasionally read poems on display and found in library books at back of the room).
High school:	Respect the right of others to study (maintain quiet, even if not studying themselves) during study time.

The following skills should all be mastered by the end of the semester. Each one that is checked has been mastered.

1st marking period	2d marking period	3d marking period	Skills
X			Correctly draws up project plans
	X		Selects appropriate materials
			Uses the following tools when appropriate and does so with skill:
X			Hand tools
X			Sander
		X	Saber saw
	X		Coping saw
	X		Drill press
		X	Lathe
		X	Finishes wood correctly
		X	Selects appropriate finish

Recommendations

On the basis of your progress to date, the following recommendations are offered:

1st marking period _____

_____

_____

2d marking period _____

_____

3d marking period _____

_____

_____

FIGURE 9.6. Reporting cognitive outcomes with checklists and rating scales.

should be kept extremely terse and any elaboration that is needed should be done in the form of a letter or through a parent-teacher conference.

By dividing a report card (or any type of progress report) into three major sections, three specific kinds of information can be reported.

Three Kinds of Evaluative Information Which Can Be Reported on Carefully Devised Report Cards

1. *Letter grades*—Judgments about the achievement of the student
2. *Supplementary information*—Judgments about the attainment of both cognitive and noncognitive goals
3. *Explanation of the above judgments*—and some suggested courses of action (recommendations)

These three sections would give the parent a fairly complete picture of the student's progress in school. Furthermore, they open the door to more in-depth reporting such as letters and parent-teacher conferences.

EXERCISE 9.2

Defend or refute each of the following statements:

1. Grades should be based entirely on achievement.
2. Achievement scores (even from the same subject) should not always be combined.
3. It is important to distinguish between "amount" achieved and "level" of achievement.

Letters

There have been a number of attempts in recent years to replace the report card with a formal letter written by the teacher to the parents. This is commendable because a letter can convey more information than a typical report card. Nevertheless, it is a lot of work for the teacher. Many students who are performing well, achieving up to ability, and reaching their goals within a satisfactory amount of time will have no need for a letter. All this information can be conveyed quite clearly on a report card such as the one described in the section above. However, there are a number of times when the report card cannot convey all the information necessary. Furthermore, there are times between marking periods when a letter would be an appropriate way of reporting information. It is often helpful to get cooperation from the home on certain problems that arise in the school. A very effective way to solicit this help is through the use of a letter.

The most important reason for using the letter as a form of reporting is that it can be an effective way to communicate special needs at special times.

Characteristics of a well-written letter. A well-written letter has certain characteristics. Whenever a report is made in the form of a letter it should have these characteristics.

A well-written letter used to report evaluation data is

1. Friendly yet somewhat formal, conveying the importance of the information it contains
2. Terse, coming quickly to the point, containing little superfluous information
3. Clear in its purpose, explaining exactly why it has been written
4. Complete in its explanation, describing the decisions which were made and the judgments and information the decisions were based on
5. Positive, even though some unpleasant information may need to be reported
6. Prescriptive, suggesting further action to be taken.

Steps to take when writing a letter. Following the steps listed below should help you to write letters which will have the above characteristics.

A Preview of Steps to Take When Writing a Letter

1. Specify the reason for the letter.
2. List the information to be included in the letter and arrange according to the format described above (decisions, judgments, information).
3. Write a first draft of the letter.
4. Put away for a short time and then revise.

Step 1: Specify the reason for the letter. This step must be taken *before the letter is even begun.* It should be eventually incorporated into the first part of the letter itself, but it should be written down first so it can be referred to while the letter is being written.

Is the letter being written because the teacher wants help from the parents (e.g., help in controlling the student's behavior)? Or is the teacher writing the letter because he wants to convey some information about the student (e.g., the student has shown a spurt in progress and the teacher wishes to thank the parents for the cooperation they have given in helping the student overcome difficulties)? Perhaps the letter is being written to an administrator to let him know that a student may be in need of special help (e.g., a request is being made for a battery of special individualized tests to be given). Whatever the reason for the letter, it must be clearly stated so that, as you begin to write, everything you say will relate directly to that purpose.

Step 2: List information to be included.   Generally, the following information should be included in a letter. First, the purpose of the letter and the decision which has been reached relative to that purpose. Secondly, the judgments which have been made about the student which relate to that decision. Third, the necessary evidence for the judgments (e.g., observational data, test scores, etc.) should be included. Fourth, you should include a prognosis about how well a student might do if given help in overcoming the problem. This is not necessary if the letter is written for the purpose of reporting good gains or a problem solved. But most letters are written for the purpose of seeking help or soliciting continued help from the parents. A prognosis should be included so that there is reason for the parent to carry out the recommendations, which are to be the last part of the information recorded in the letter.

Step 3: Write the first draft.   Once you know what information you wish to communicate and you have it arranged in an appropriate order, then the first draft of the letter should be written. Remember: this letter must communicate as simply and directly as possible if it is going to be effective.

Step 4: Put the letter away for a time and come back to revise it.   It is usually best to wait at least one night before revising your first draft. Your final draft should be typed neatly and present a good overall appearance when it is first opened. *Do not forget* to sign the letter.

EXERCISE 9.3

Write a brief letter to the parents of a fourth grade boy who seems to be losing interest in school. His grades have dropped and his reading achievement score is below average (last year's score placed him at the 84th percentile). You have decided to move him to a lower reading group. Make certain your letter meets the criteria discussed above.

Diagnostic Reports

Diagnostic reports are a rather formal way of presenting a great deal of diagnostic information which has been obtained about students. They include information about achievement, aptitude, and special problems related to health, psychomotor skills, personality traits, interests, social-emotional development, etc. They are usually used to report information to teachers who will be doing further work with students or to administrators who must make administrative decisions about where to place these students. These kinds of writeups are generally done by psychometricians or clinical psychologists, and one might wonder why a teacher needs to worry about how to construct them. However, clinical psychologists, counselors, administrators, and special education teachers are all becoming aware of the fact that a really thorough diagnosis of a student's problems should take into account all the diagnostic information that the classroom teacher can provide. Therefore, if the teacher can learn to follow the same careful rules for writing a diagnosis as those followed by clinical persons, the information that teachers report to these specialized persons may be easier for them to use.

The first thing to be presented in a diagnostic writeup is a clear statement of the problem that exists (i.e., the reason for the diagnosis).

This statement should be followed by all the information which is pertinent to the problem being diagnosed. The first kind of information that the teacher should report should be non-test information (e.g., observations, analysis of daily work, anecdotes, etc.). This information should be stated carefully so as not to present a biased picture. Whenever a judgment is made, it should be backed up with a summary of the information which led the teacher to make that judgment. Although in a diagnostic writeup of this kind judgments about the student's behavior are in order, the teacher should be cautioned against making statements of judgment which cannot be supported with substantial evidence. The teacher may also wish to include the academic history of the student and any indications of health problems or physiological defects which have been noticed.

Following a listing of all the non-test data, the teacher should include any achievement test scores. First of all, he should indicate the scores obtained on appropriate teacher-made achievement tests. These should be reported in standard scores or class rank. Next, any scores which the teacher has available from standardized achievement tests should be reported. The name of the test, along with a brief description of what it measures, should be included for both the teacher-made and the standardized test. Whenever possible, information should also be supplied about the validity and reliability of the tests.

After having reported achievement test scores, the teacher should report any aptitude measures that he has. First of all, scores from teacher-made tests which have been devised to indicate a student's specific skills or aptitudes for various subject matter should be reported. These should be followed by standardized aptitude scores. Include such things as general aptitude (e.g., an IQ) as well as specific aptitude for certain subjects (e.g., aptitude for math or for foreign language).

Scores from any specialized tests should be reported next (e.g., physiological measures, psychomotor skill tests, personality or interest inventories). Most of these specialized tests will have been given by psychometricians in individualized testing situations, and the teacher would not have access to this kind of information. However, occasionally a teacher may have such things as his own interest inventory, and this is the appropriate place to record that information.

After all the various tests and non-test data have been summarized by the teacher, he should then make some recommendations (*if* they are called for by the person requesting the diagnosis). For example, the teacher might recommend that a certain student be given special help or be referred for further testing.

Whatever the recommendation, it should arise naturally from the information which has been reported. Thus the final section of the report, which should include a summarization and defense of the recommendations, will be quite easily accomplished. Include in this last section of the report a very brief statement of the problem and the reason for the diagnosis. Follow this with a *brief* summary of the information and end with a terse statement of the recommendations.

EXERCISE 9.4

List the kind of data to be included in a diagnostic report. This outline (extracted from the above discussion) will serve to guide you whenever you need to produce such a report.

Conferences

Parent-teacher conferences are becoming ever more popular in the school because they offer a useful way of reporting a great deal of information in a relatively short time. Furthermore, they have an advantage over written reports because, in a conference with a parent, you know he is listening to what you are reporting. If you send a written report home, you are never really sure that he reads or understands it. The conference is a form of oral reporting, but it is more than simply a technique for reporting information. It is also a useful way to obtain information. So the conference becomes an information-gathering technique as well as a reporting technique. Therefore we might discuss briefly the major characteristics of conferences and indicate some of the steps that might help you to conduct a successful conference. This discussion will center around the parent-teacher conference, which is the most popular of all conferences used in schools today. But the general rules that will be discussed can be applied to other kinds of conferences also. One of the major problems of parent-teacher conferences is that the information reported is often *not accurate* and does *not fulfill the purpose* for which the conference was designed. Another problem with the parent-teacher conferences is that they take a great deal of time. Schools are often closed down for a full day or for several half-days so that conferences can be held. If a conference is well prepared, well executed, and carefully followed up, the time spent out of the classroom for the purpose of these reporting sessions is well worth it. However, if a conference is poorly conducted and is not efficient, then the inordinate amount of time it takes is certainly not worth the effort. A further problem with the parent-teacher conferences is that the parents whom the teachers need to see most frequently do not show up for conferences.

Despite these problems, the parent-teacher conference continues to be a popular and useful method of reporting the general progress of students to parents. Popularity of these conferences is much greater at the elementary level.

At that level there is greater concern for a variety of outcomes which are not directly related to learning content. It is at this stage in the child's educational development that he is learning to learn, learning to live with others his own age, developing some confidence in his ability, etc.

The very word *conference* implies more than just reporting—it implies conversation, a two-way flow of information, an exchange of ideas. Therefore teachers must be prepared to report *and* to be reported to. They should have available at the time of the conference a report that they can refer to as well as a questionnaire which will help them to obtain information. There are three major aspects of a parent-teacher conference that a teacher must consider: the preparation, the conference, and the follow-up.

Preparation for the conference.   The first thing you should do when preparing for a conference is check to see that you have all the materials you need. Use the following chart as a checklist.

A Checklist of the Materials Needed for a Parent-Teacher Conference

1. A summary of the evaluation which has been made about the student
2. A list of characteristics typical of the age group of the student being reported on
3. An outline of the school program
4. A list of the major goals for the year
5. A folder containing some examples of the student's work
6. A questionnaire to be used in obtaining information from the parents

---

An evaluation summary.   If you have a summary of the evaluations you have made about the student, you will undoubtedly be able to answer most questions the parent might have about the student's achievement. Furthermore, any decisions you made will more easily be defended if you have a summary of the information and judgments which led you to make them.

Information about characteristics of the student's peers.   It will help you to keep the evaluation report in perspective if you have available some information about typical aptitude, achievement, and behavior of the student's peer group. This information is to be seen as normative only and *not* as a standard to be held up as a goal to be reached by a given student.

An outline of the school program.   It is much easier to explain where a student has been, where he is going, and how well he is progressing if you have an outline of the school program in front of you. This outline should include brief descriptions of courses covered, options available, rationale for particular courses of study, etc.

A list of major objectives.   What was this student expected to accomplish so far this year? What is he expected to accomplish the rest of the year? What are his chances of reaching those goals? These and other similar questions will be easier to answer if you have a list of the major instructional goals (in observable terms, please) for the year.

Examples of student work.   A carefully selected sample of the student's work will convey more information to the parent than many verbal explanations could hope to. The samples of work should serve to illustrate the points you have to make in your diagnosis and should reinforce the need for any prescription you may feel is in order.

A questionnaire.   If you have a few questions written down to help guide you through your interview with the parent, you may very well gain more insight into your students during conference time than through any other information-gathering session. Do not allow the opportunity of a parent-teacher conference to go by without obtaining a picture of your student from his parents' perspective.

The conference itself.   The following suggestions should help you to conduct a relaxed, profitable conference. All your well-laid plans and carefully prepared materials will not help you at all if the atmosphere of the conference is unfriendly or if you discover too late that you have been discussing the wrong child.

Meet the parents with a smile.   If possible you should meet them at the door of the room. Introduce yourself, check on the parents name, and confirm the name of the child that you are about to discuss. This will give the parents an opportunity to correct you if you have made an error. Conferences have gone on for quite a while before either the parents or the teacher realized that the wrong child was being discussed.

Have comfortable chairs for parents to sit upon.   Often conferences are held with parents sitting on the tiny desks of their small children; this makes them uncomfortable and not in an appropriate position to talk seriously about their child's behavior. Also, it is helpful to have chairs available outside the room where the conferences are being held so that parents who may be waiting for their conference to come up have a place to wait comfortably.

Have parents seated where they can easily see test scores or student work.   Nothing is more frustrating then straining to see what the teacher is trying to talk about and not being able to (i.e., because it is too far across the desk or because there are a number of things piled on the teacher's desk which hide the material from view).

Speak clearly and distinctly.   It will be easy enough for you to be misinterpreted in parent-teacher conferences. Be certain to speak loud enough that you can be clearly heard.

Never guess. If a parent asks a question which you are unable to answer about a child, do not fake it. If you do not know the information, admit that you do not but indicate that you will find the answer to the question as soon as possible. Give credit to the parent for asking a good question rather than making him feel embarrassed for asking you a question that you could not answer. As soon as you put yourself on the defensive, the parent is likely to lose his belief in your ability to handle his child.

Listen and talk. Part of the time the teacher should listen to the parents. However, there is some information which needs to be reported and the teacher must have his time also. Furthermore, the parent will often ramble on, telling stories about his child or talking about other things that may be only slightly related to what is being discussed. When this occurs a teacher needs to shift the conversation as politely as possible to the particular aspects of the child being discussed.

Solicit the cooperation of the parents. The parents should feel that they have some part in the educational development of the child. This will help to more firmly establish the cooperation between the parent and the teacher.

Watch the time carefully. It is important that you do not run overtime. Do not keep the next parents waiting in line.

Dismiss the parents on a positive note. When the time is up you should politely ask the parents to leave. Leave them with a positive statement about their child's behavior.

Leave the door open for future conferences. Never end a parent-teacher conference without clearly indicating to the parents that they should feel free to contact you later.

Parent-teacher conference follow-up. The most often neglected and yet most important aspect of a parent-teacher conference is the follow-up after the conference is over. If the teacher has done a good job of obtaining information from the parents, this information ought to be recorded and placed in the student's file. Furthermore, the important decisions and recommendations should be recorded. These can be referred to in future conferences and can be used by the teacher in planning his lessons. This will help the teacher to carry out his part of the course of action. No one thing will kill the effectiveness of a parent-teacher conference more quickly than for parents who have been fulfilling their part of agreed upon action to find out that the school has not been doing its part.

Many schools ask the teachers to fill out forms which summarize the results of parent-teacher conferences. These are to be sent on to an administrator and sometimes they are also used for other teachers. When these forms are provided, you should keep a copy for your own files. Slip one copy into the student's folder and summarize any information in the beginning of your lesson plan book so you will not forget to carry out the agreed plan of action.

Another very important part of the follow-up of a teacher conference is an indication to the parents that the conference was in fact successful and that useful information was obtained. Sometime between the conference and the next time a report is due, you should drop a note or make a short phone call to the parents indicating that you are following up on the things talked about in the conference. Give a brief report on the progress being made at that time.

EXERCISE 9.5

1. Why is it important to prepare carefully for a parent-teacher conference?
2. What should you be doing during a parent-teacher conference?
3. What kinds of things should be done to facilitate a successful parent-teacher conference?

Telephone Calls

Perhaps without even realizing it, teachers do a great deal of reporting by telephoning. The potential for misunderstanding is greatest during telephone conversations. Most often, neither the parent nor the teacher is prepared for the call. The phone call is usually the result of some unusual or dramatic event. Emotions usually run high and things can easily get worse instead of better. However, when phone calls are handled carefully, they can be very useful for reporting data and for continuing to establish rapport and cooperation between the home and the school. Many of the rules for conferences might apply to telephone calls also. The teacher must remember that no number of telephone calls can substitute for a conference. Phone calls should be used to substitute for conferences only in extreme cases when parents simply will not or cannot come to the school for a conference.

Teacher-initiated calls. Telephone calls are useful as supplements to conferences. Let us examine briefly some general rules for initiating successful phone calls.

Call when the student is not at home. The student might be listening in on the conversation or might be able to catch enough of it even from hearing just the one side that all of the advantage of discussing ways of helping him could "go down the drain."

Keep the "bad" news to a minimum. Emphasize the positive. If there is a serious problem that needs to be talked about, a phone call should simply be a way of setting up a conference for more in-depth discussion of the problem.

Be prepared. Have notes at your side when you call (this is an advantage of calling the parents rather than waiting for them to call you).

Identify yourself. Whenever you phone a parent make sure you clearly identify yourself, indicating what student you are calling about and your reason for calling.

Find out who you are talking to. Make sure that you are talking to the parent and not an older sister or someone else in the house. Be alert to the fact that there may be other people listening (on the extension phone or on a party line). Because of the lack of privacy of most phone calls, it is obviously desirable for teachers to limit what is talked about to those things which are not quite so private. Reserve the face-to-face conference for those things which are of a personal nature.

Calls initiated by others. If someone else (e.g., parent, administrator, or employer) initiates the call, then there is one major overriding rule that the teacher should follow. It can be stated in one word—listen.

You should listen, striving to hear what it is that the parent has to say. Do not argue back. Show concern and understanding and try to find out why the parent called. Find out exactly what the problem or concern is. Almost all phone calls which are initiated by parents are made because the parent is either irritated or concerned. Sometimes parents will be upset and may display anger or may show evidence of illogical reasoning. These are things that the teacher might pounce upon in defense of his own position, but that is an unwise thing to do. The best way to handle this kind of situation is to listen carefully, let the parent talk himself out (he may feel better just for having done so). Next, find out exactly what the concern is. Finally, find out what evidence that parent has to support his concern.

Unless the questions being raised can be easily answered (perhaps because you anticipated they might be coming and were ready for the phone call), you should not try to answer them on the phone. Instead, you should arrange for a later phone call or a conference during which the problem can be discussed more fully. This will give you the opportunity to investigate the problem thoroughly, finding out both sides of the story where necessary. At the same time, this gives the parent and the teacher some time to calm down. When talk resumes teacher and parent are both likely to be more objective.

Telephone follow-up. Like conferences, telephone calls often should be followed up with a short note acknowledging the call and outlining the things that were talked about and the decisions that were made. This makes the parent feel that the call was not wasted. This will go a long way toward establishing very solid cooperation between the home and the school.

EXERCISE 9.6

1. What do you see as the major advantages and disadvantages to *(a)* parent-teacher conferences, *(b)* phone calls?
2. How can phone calls and conferences be used along with letters to effectively communicate with and seek cooperation from parents?

SUMMARY

1. There are at least two reasons why report card grades are still being used: (1) there is a need for a precise, easily stored indication of pupil progress, (2) report card grades, when based upon test data, tend to be more reliable than nonmeasurement forms of reporting.
2. Summaries and reports of evaluation results should provide information which is useful for (1) further judgment and decision making, (2) examining the rationale for the judgments and decisions that were made, and (3) determining the cause of unplanned learning outcomes.
3. A report communicates some or all of the information in an evaluation summary. A summary provides the information for an evaluation report.
4. Summarizing evaluation results involves the following steps: (1) determine the purpose of the summary, (2) list the major decisions that were made, (3) list the judgments which influenced those decisions and, (4) summarize the information used to make each judgment.
5. A good evaluation report should provide all the information needed by those for whom the report is intended and it should be clear and easy to understand.
6. A good report card should probably provide a way to report judgments about the cognitive and noncognitive performance of students and a way to provide an explanation of those judgments (including recommendations where appropriate).
7. A well-written letter reporting evaluation results should be (1) friendly yet businesslike, (2) terse, (3) clear in its purpose, (4) complete in its explanation, (5) positive, and (6) prescriptive.
8. A diagnostic writeup should include the following: (1) a clear statement of the problem which exists, (2) information pertinent to the problem being diagnosed (non-test information, achievement scores, aptitude scores, and scores from special tests), and (3) recommendations (when requested).
9. Conferences should follow the rules of good interviewing.
10. In preparation for a conference, you should check to see that you have (1) an evaluation summary, (2) information about the characteristics of the student's peers, (3) an outline of the school program, (4) a list of major objectives, (5) examples of student work, and (6) a questionnaire.
11. The follow-up to a parent-teacher conference is vital to the success of the conference. Record the important information gained and courses of action decided upon and send the parents a brief follow-up note.
12. Carefully handled phone calls can be useful for reporting data and maintaining rapport with the parents. Phone calls should be followed up with a short note and/or a scheduled conference.

Reference

Terwilliger, James S.: *Assigning Grades to Students,* Scott, Foresman and Company, Glenview, Ill., 1971.

Suggested Readings

Good discussions of grading and reporting can be found in the following texts:

Ahmann, Stanley J., and Marvin D. Glock: *Evaluating Pupil Growth,* 4th ed., Allyn and Bacon, Inc., Boston, 1971, chap. 15.

Ebel, Robert L.: *Essentials of Educational Measurement,* 2d ed., Prentice-Hall, Englewood Cliffs, N.J., 1972, chap. 12.

Mehrens, William A., and Irvin J., Lehmann: *Measurement and Evaluation in Education and Psychology,* Holt, Rinehart and Winston, Inc., New York, 1973, chap. 17. '

PART THREE

PROCEDURES FOR CONSTRUCTING OR SELECTING SPECIFIC INFORMATION-GATHERING INSTRUMENTS

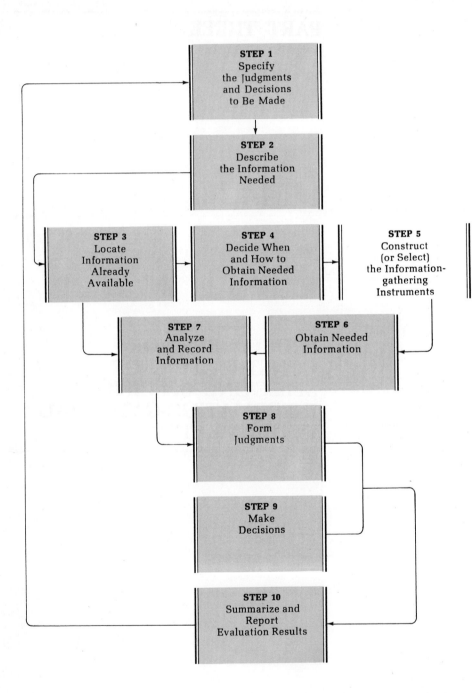

CHAPTER 10

Constructing Checklists and Rating Scales

Checklists and rating scales are useful tools for observing student performances and products. However, unless care is taken in constructing these tools, a great deal of instrument error will occur. Furthermore, the biases of the observer will be less likely to affect the results of observation when well-constructed tools are used.

This chapter has been written to help you learn to

1. Construct a checklist
2. Construct the major types of rating scales
3. Evaluate your checklists and rating scales

CONSTRUCT A CHECKLIST

By following the five steps discussed below, you should be able to produce check-lists that will be valid, reliable, and easy to use.

A Preview of the Steps to Take When Constructing a Checklist

Step 1. Specify an appropriate performance or product.

Step 2. List the important behaviors or characteristics.

Step 3. Add any common errors.

Step 4. Arrange the list of behaviors or characteristics.

Step 5. Provide a way to use the list.

FIGURE 10.1. A list of performances and important behaviors.

Playing a clarinet

.... Holds instrument properly
.... Has a satisfactory ambature
.... Uses correct alternate
        fingering where necessary
.... Checks the key signature
        and time
.... Counts correctly

Using a sewing machine

.... Plugs in the machine
.... Threads the machine
.... Checks needle
......   Threads the needle
.... Adjusts stitch length

Using the library

.... Uses *Readers' Guide to
        Periodical Literature*
.... Uses *Educational Index*
.... Uses card catalog
.... Uses bound volumes of
        journals
.... Uses unbound (recent)
        journals

Doing an Experiment

(Third grade)
.... Writes down what he is
        trying to find out
.... Gets equipment needed
.... Checks over procedures
.... Gets pad to write down
        results

*Using addition and subtraction to work out a
story problem in fourth grade math*

.... Decides what the problem is asking
.... Decides what information the problem provides
.... Writes a number sentence that fits the problem
.... Arrives at a correct solution

Step 1: Specify an Appropriate Performance or Product

Checklists are fairly easy to construct and use, but that is not a reason to use them. Make certain that the information you need about the performance or product you are evaluating is included on the list. Checklists provide you with "it's there—it's not there" kind of information. Ask yourself the following question about any performance you are evaluating: "Are there some behaviors characteristic of this kind of performance which are so important that it is valuable simply to know whether or not they occur?" If your answer is yes, then a checklist is an appropriate instrument to use.

A similar question should be asked about any product you wish to evaluate: "Are there some characteristics typical of this kind of product which are so important that it is valuable simply to know whether or not they occur?" Again, if your answer is yes, then a checklist is appropriate.

A few examples of performances and products which can be evaluated are presented in Figure 10.1. For each performance, *some* of the behaviors which might be used in a checklist have been listed. For each product, *some* of the characteristics which might be important have been listed.

Step 2: List the Important Behaviors or Characteristics

The examples in Figure 10.1 illustrate what you must do in this step. Let us take one of the performances listed there and complete the list of important behaviors for that performance:

Checklist of Skills Needed to Use a Sewing Machine

Before a student is allowed to use a machine on her own, she should be able to

Plug in the machine	Oil the machine
Thread the machine	Adjust the stitch length
Remove the bobbin	Use the foot control
Wind the bobbin	Properly position the material to be sewn
Insert the bobbin	
Remove the needle	Start the machine (insert needle into fabric first)
Insert the needle	
Adjust the tension	Stop the machine correctly (needle out of the fabric)

Step 3: Add Any Common Errors

It is important to find out not only if desirable procedures are being followed but also if undesirable ones are. For example, it may be important in rating a speech to find out whether or not a student uses gestures. It also may be important to find out if a student uses any *distracting* behaviors (e.g., saying "ah" or putting his hands in his pockets). Do not add too many undesirable traits. Add only those that are serious and very common.

Step 4: Arrange the List of Behaviors and/or Products

A checklist will be much easier to use if the behaviors to be observed are listed in the order in which they are likely to occur. If a product is being evaluated, then the characteristics should be arranged so that the examiner can begin at one place on the product and examine it systematically, part by part.

Step 5: Provide a Way to Use the List

There must be a convenient place to check each behavior as it occurs (or each characteristic present). The best way to do this is to place blanks along the side of the page on the left-hand margin next to each characteristic being checked. A check mark is made only when the characteristic described occurs. These same blanks can be used for putting in the number, indicating the place in the sequence where the characteristic occurred.

EXERCISE 10.1

Select some kind of performance that you are very familiar with. Produce a checklist that could be used in judging that performance.

CONSTRUCTING RATING SCALES

Rating scales have a definite advantage over checklists because they allow us to make systematic judgments about the degree to which a behavior or characteristic is present. A rating scale usually consists of a set of characteristics or behaviors to be judged and some kind of scale. The observer uses the scale to indicate the quality, quantity, or level of performance observed. The points along each scale represent different degrees of the attribute under observation. A set of directions tells the observer how the scale is to be used.

Example of Rating Scale for Rating Discussion Leaders

Directions: Rate the discussion leader on each of the following characteristics by placing an "X" anywhere along the horizontal line under each item.

1. To what extent does the leader encourage discussion?

Discourages discussion by negative comments	Neither discourages nor encourages discussion	Encourages discussion by positive comments

2. How well does the leader keep the discussion on the right track?

Lets the discussion wander	Only occasionally brings the discussion back on target	Does not let discussants wander from the main topic

3. How frequently does the leader ask controversial questions?

Never asks controversial questions	Occasionally asks controversial questions	Continuously asks controversial questions

4. How does the leader respond to inappropriate comments?

Ridicules the one who made the comment	Treats inappropriate comments the same as appropriate ones	Discourages inappropriate comments

Notice that the excerpts from the above rating scale help the observer to focus on specific, observable aspects of the trait being judged. Furthermore, if it is used on many students, they will all be judged from a common frame of reference. This provides objectivity and improves the reliability of observation—*if the scale is well designed.* The procedures outlined below have been written to help you design a good rating scale; but once it is completed, it can be used over and over. Systematically observing students is much easier with well-designed rating scales.

A preview of the steps to take will help you to see the relationship of each step to the others.

A Preview of the Steps to Take When Constructing a Rating Scale

Step 1. Specify an appropriate learning outcome.

Step 2. List the important characteristics of each outcome.

Step 3. Define a scale for each characteristic.

Step 4. Arrange the scales.

Step 5. Write the instructions.

Step 1: Specify an Appropriate Learning Outcome

There are many learning outcomes as well as outcomes of growth and development which can be judged with the use of a rating scale. Gronlund (1971, page 421) classifies them into three major areas: procedures, products, and personal-social development. Examples of outcomes which can be rated in each of these areas are listed below.

Examples of Outcomes Which Can Conveniently Be Measured by Using a Rating Scale

Procedures

Singing	Using a band saw
Playing an instrument	Solving a problem
Leading a discussion	Handwriting
Drawing a picture	

Products

An oil painting	A blueprint
A woodworking project	A typed memo
An outline	A jar of jam
A handwriting sample	

Social-Personal Traits

Friendliness	Generosity
Politeness	Extroversion
Honesty	Endurance
Patience	

Step 2: List the Important Characteristics of Each Outcome

This step is essentially the same as step 2 for constructing checklists. Carefully analyze each outcome and decide what is most important to the accomplishment of that outcome.

Deciding What Is Important to the Accomplishment of a Given Outcome

If the outcome is a procedure, ask "What important behaviors are exhibited by individuals who can successfully execute this procedure?"

If the outcome is a product, ask "What important features are characteristic of high quality products of this type?"

> If the outcome is a result of a personal-social development, ask "What important behaviors are most commonly associated with this personal-social trait?"

Below are specific examples of these general question types accompanied by some possible answers. Notice that each answer lists *only* those characteristics which are most important to the outcome being rated.

Examples of General Questions and Answers

What behaviors are exhibited by individuals who can successfully play tennis? They can:

Hit a forehand drive

Hit a forehand lob

Hit a backhand drive

Hit a backhand lob

Anticipate the opponent's next move

Place a ball accurately

Etc.

What important features are characteristic of good charcoal sketches of nature? They are:

Well composed

Contain bold as well as thin lines

Free, not stiff

Shaded so as to create a mood

Etc.

What important behaviors are usually associated with friendliness?

A ready smile

A readiness to speak

An interest in others

A willingness to meet others

A memory for names

Etc.

Step 3: Define a Scale for Each Characteristic

A scale defines an underlying continuum. A ruler is a scale used for judging the physical characteristic of length. The continuum defining length (which theoretically ranges from zero to infinity) is marked off in some meaningful units (inches, centimeters, etc.). Think of rating scales as rulers designed to measure the quantity or quality of certain characteristics. Whereas rulers are used to measure length, rating scales are used to measure such characteristics as participation, friendliness, smoothness, appropriateness, frequency, value, balance, beauty, and flexibility. Like rulers, rating scales should also be marked off in meaningful units. However, the units on a ruler are all of equal value, and the distances between the points are equal. This is *not* true of the points along a rating scale. Suppose, for example, we have constructed a scale for rating ability to stay with a task. Our scale might look like this:

Ability to Stay with a Task

1	2	3		5
Gives up at the first sign of any trouble	Gives up with a minimal amount of struggle	Keeps trying even though experiencing difficulties	Stays with the task after most would have quit	Never quits until told to by the teacher

All five points are drawn equidistant from each other, but in reality we do not know the significance of the difference between a rating of 1 and a rating of 2. Nor do we know how that compares to the difference between a rating of 3 and a rating of four. Is someone who stays with a task only after most would have quit (a 4 on our scale) twice as good at staying with a task as someone who gives up with a minimal amount of struggle (a 2 on our scale)? Obviously, we do not know. Maybe our scale would represent reality better if it were drawn this way:

1		2	3	4		5

Or this way:

	2	3		4	5

Or this way:

1	2		3	4	5

But we do not know which drawing best represents reality. Consequently, we might as well draw our scales *as if* all the points along them represented equal intervals. This is not to say that we should interpret them that way. Nor does it mean that we should not be concerned about this problem when constructing our scales. This problem is obviously a major source of error. Operating on the idea that it is better to try to prevent error from occurring than to try to cope with it later, we should define our scales as carefully as possible. The suggestions which follow may help.

Establish the extremes of the continuum. When attempting to define a scale, first describe the extreme ends of the continuum. If the characteristic you are measuring is most naturally rated in terms of frequency, then this is an easy task. Your scales would range from zero to infinity, never to always, rarely to very frequently, 0 to 100 percent, 0 to 15, etc.

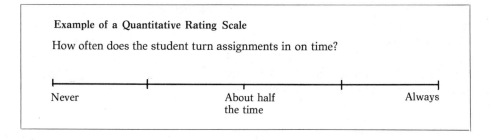

Example of a Quantitative Rating Scale

How often does the student turn assignments in on time?

Never   About half the time   Always

However, when the characteristic being measured is to be rated in terms of the *degree* to which it exists, the *quality* of performance, the *level* of development, the *quality* of product, or similar qualitative terms, then our task of defining the extreme ends is more difficult. Some sample scales of this kind are given below:

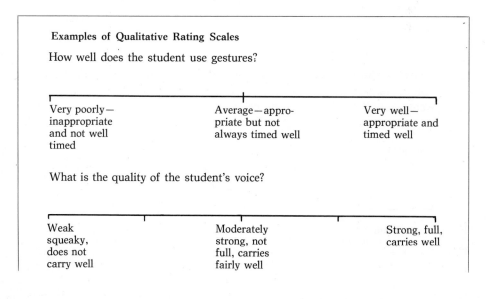

Examples of Qualitative Rating Scales

How well does the student use gestures?

Very poorly— inappropriate and not well timed   Average—appropriate but not always timed well   Very well— appropriate and timed well

What is the quality of the student's voice?

Weak squeaky, does not carry well   Moderately strong, not full, carries fairly well   Strong, full, carries well

Indicate the extent to which this drawing conveys a feeling of depth.

Appears to be flat, almost no perspective	Appears to have some depth, but lacks proper perspective	Looks quite realistic, like a good photograph; good perspective	Looks real, almost like a 3D photograph; excellent perspective

Notice that in each of the above examples, the descriptions at either extreme describe the worst and the best a person (or product) could possibly be. Take a hint from that! Whenever you are defining the extreme ends of a continuum designed to be used in rating a person, think of someone you know who exemplifies the negative or low end of the scale. Next, think of someone you know who exemplifies the positive or high end of the scale. Now describe each of those persons from the point of view of the characteristic being measured.

Example of a Rating Scale for a Personality Trait

HONESTY

Uncle Clem		The preacher "back home"
Always lies. Stretches every story out of proportion. Exaggerates to his own advantage.		Never lies, does not even "hide" the truth or twist it slightly. So honest it hurts.

This same procedure can be used when defining the ends of a continuum designed to rate products. Simply think of an "ideal" product and a "reject" or an "everything went wrong" product. Now describe each one.

Example of a Scale to Rate Products

A SALT AND FLOUR MAP

Severely cracked, poorly proportioned, inaccurate topography, sloppy		Smooth, well proportioned, neat, excellent accuracy of borders and topography

---

EXERCISE 10.2

Take time out to try applying what you just learned.

1. Define the extreme ends of a continuum designed to be used for rating a person's *trustworthiness* (or some other trait of your own choice).
2. Define the extreme ends of a continuum designed to be used for rating some product (e.g., soap carving, oil painting, diagram of a bridge construction, blueprint, map).

Describe the points between the extremes. Try to describe each point along the scale so that the difference in quantity and quality between any two points is approximately equal. Although it is not always possible to obtain equal intervals along the scale, it *is* possible to place the points along the scale in the correct rank order. Make certain, for example, that the behavior(s) descriptive of the fifth point on the scale *do* represent a higher-quality performance than the behaviors described at the third point. Examine your extremes and then try to describe two or three points representing behaviors (or features) which are not quite so extreme. Usually, it is best to divide a scale into an odd number of points (3, 5, or 7). This is the case when there is a netural point or a clear-cut midpoint between the two extremes. For this kind of scale, the first point to describe (after the extreme ends) is the midpoint.

Examples of Behavioral Rating Scales

COMMITMENT TO A CAUSE

Definitely against the cause	Neutral	Definitely for the cause

To what extent does this pupil play with other children?

Always plays with others	Plays with others about half the time	Never plays with others; always plays alone

---

You now have three points clearly defined (the two ends and a midpoint). This is often enough. Sometimes, however, you may wish to give the observer a little more guidance by describing a couple more points. Think of the low end of the scale and the midpoint as defining a separate scale and the midpoint and the high end as defining another separate scale. Next, try to describe the midpoints of each of these.

Example of a Behavioral Rating Scale

How well does this student participate in class discussion?

	Midpoint		Midpoint	

| Never partici- pates in class discus- sion. You would not know he was there. | Occasion- ally par- ticipates in discus- sion, but would rather listen than express his own views. | Partici- pates in class dis- cussion very well. Gives his own views and allows for the views of others. | Partici- pates freely — sometimes taking over. Does not always allow other points of view to be heard. | Dominates the class discussion. Will not tolerate the views of others. |

There are several ways to describe the points on a rating scale. The three most common types of descriptions are numerical, graphic, and descriptive. Sometimes combinations of these are used (e.g., descriptive-graphic). A numerical rating scale is simply a list of numbers keyed to descriptive labels which remain constant from one characteristic to the next. The observer circles the number which best describes the person or product being evaluated.

Example of Numerical Rating

Circle the numbers which best describe this individual's relationship to his classmates. Use the following key:

5 = excellent

4 = above average

3 = average

2 = below average

1 = poor

Numerical scales are also used when frequency of occurrence is being judged.

Examples of Numerical Rating for Frequency of Occurrence
How many times does the speaker say "ah" during a three-minute speech?

1 = less than 5

2 = 5 to 10

3 = 10 to 15

4 = 15 to 20

5 = more than 20

When describing points along a scale graphically, you draw a horizontal (or sometimes vertical) line and divide it into equal parts. Each dividing line is accompanied by a label describing that point on the continuum. The observer places an *x* anywhere on the line. This allows him to mark between two points, closest to the one he feels best describes the individual.

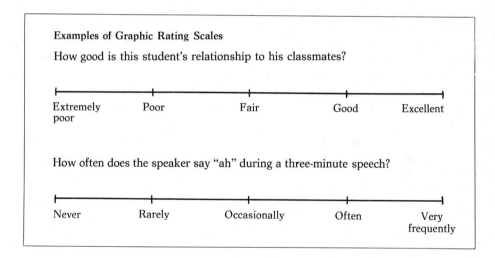

Examples of Graphic Rating Scales

How good is this student's relationship to his classmates?

| Extremely poor | Poor | Fair | Good | Excellent |

How often does the speaker say "ah" during a three-minute speech?

| Never | Rarely | Occasionally | Often | Very frequently |

A descriptive scale implies a more complete verbal description of the points along the continuum than the verbal labels used in the last two examples. Usually, a graphic arrangement is also used, producing a descriptive-graphic scale. Whenever you write a verbal description of points along a scale, be certain to be terse and to use behavioral, observable terms like those used in writing behavioral objectives (see Chapter 4).

Example of a Descriptive Rating Scale

How good is this student's relationship to his classmates?

Extremely poor; fights, argues, blames others, always wants his own way	Fair; has some friends, often tries to get his own way, has some fights	Excellent; has many friends, considers others first, helpful, almost never in an argument

The advantage of a numerical over a graphic scale is that it yields numbers (which are easier to record and which can be manipulated). The graphic scale, on the other hand, has an advantage because the traits being rated are more explicitly stated in observable terms.

Step 4: Arrange the Scales

For any given procedure, product, or personal-social trait, several scales will be used (one for each of the important behaviors or characteristics). If there is any logical arrangement for these scales, place them in that order (e.g., in the order of expected occurrence).

One other thing that must be considered when arranging the scales is the "direction" of each scale. A given scale can take any one of three directions. It can go from negative to positive:

Poor	Fair	Excellent

Or, it can go from positive to negative:

Excellent	Fair	Poor

Or it can go from strong (not necessarily positive) to neutral and back to strong:

Strongly disagree	Neither agree nor disagree	Strongly agree

Notice that to disagree is not necessarily negative. It depends what you are disagreeing with.

When the observer is marking a number of scales in a row, it is easier if they are always arranged in the same direction (e.g., negative to positive). However, with this arrangement it is easy to establish a response pattern (e.g., "This guy's pretty good, I'll mark all 4s") and just mark all down one side of the page, marking each scale about the same. If you think this will be a problem, it can be avoided by occasionally changing the direction of some of the scales (e.g., every so often, put in a positive-to-negative arrangement).

Step 5: Write the Instructions

Most often you will use your own scales, and you may feel that it is not necessary to write instructions to yourself. However, there may be opportunities for other teachers to use your scales. Furthermore, some of the scales you develop may be used by students. It is valuable, for example, to obtain student perceptions of the instructions, the textbooks, etc. Whether you use your own scale or some-one else uses it, it is important to have a set of instructions clearly specified. This will help reduce any error which might result from a misunderstanding of how the scale is to be used.

The instructions to the observer-rater need not be elaborate. However, they *must* contain the following information:

The instructions accompanying any rating scale should contain the following information:

1. A statement naming or describing the overall procedure, product, or trait being rated.
2. Directions on how to mark the scales.
3. Any special instructions (e.g., add any comments at the end or omit any characteristics you do not feel qualified to judge).

Examples of Instructions for Rating Scales

Rate the student's ability to present a convincing argument. Place an *x* any-where on the horizontal line below each of the characteristics of debaters. In each case place the *x* at the place which you think best describes this stu-dent's ability.

For each feature below, circle the number which best describes this oil paint-ing. Make any additional comments about the painting at the bottom of this page.

The above instructions will help you to produce paper-and-pencil rating scales for most instructional outcomes. These kinds of scales are the most popular and they yield analytical ratings (i.e., a given performance, product, or trait is analyzed and the most important characteristics are identified and carefully de-scribed).

Instead of trying to devise a series of descriptive scales which would define some attribute, one might produce product scales, using actual examples of products. These sample products could be used as examples illustrating each of the points along some scale. Ratings would be made by comparing the product being rated to the products at the various points along the scale.

Learn a lesson from a group of junior high art teachers who were trying to rate products produced by the seventh grade art classes. The products were creative wax sculptures, and they found it difficult to define the important characteristics. (Creativity would be one, but how would you describe the points along a scale of creativity except as "not creative at all" to "very creative"?) Although they could not always verbalize all their reasons, the three art teachers were in almost complete agreement as to which sculptures were the best, which the worst, and which "about average." Knowing that they would be having the next group of seventh graders do the same assignment, they decided to develop a product scale using the students' own work as models.

The first thing these teachers did was select the three best and the three worst sculptures. These would be used to anchor the ends of the scale. There is nothing magical about selecting three examples at each end; often one is enough. However, they felt that by selecting three very different but equally good creative pieces as "best" examples, they could demonstrate the fact that any particular form was not necessarily best. You see, they decided to use the product scale they were developing as concrete "behavioral objectives"—a demonstration to future students. By looking at the products on the scale, students could get a fairly good idea of what would and what would not meet the teachers' expectations.

You should be able to anticipate what they did next. They identified three "about average" sculptures as examples of the midpoint on the scale. Next, they identified some which seemed to fit about halfway between the "average" and the "best" and between the "average" and the "worst." Now they had a 5-point scale. Each point on the scale was represented by three actual, student-produced sculptures.[1]

The final touches were placed on the scale by writing brief descriptions of the examples at each point. In the descriptions, they tried to point out the "good" and "bad" features. To use this scale in the future, the teachers would simply take a piece of sculpture and compare it to the examples on the scale. If it looked most like those at position 2, it would receive a score of 2, if most looked like those at position 5, a score of 5, etc.

Think of the many "products" that students produce which could be much more easily and objectively rated if this kind of scale were available. Handwriting samples, art projects, woodworking projects, maps, term papers, and canned goods prepared in home economics class are but a few examples.

Although performance skills are somewhat more difficult to scale in this manner, some of them can be done this way. Suppose, for example, you wish

---

[1] Many times it is not convenient to keep the actual samples of student work. In that case, snapshots or slides can be taken and used instead of the actual objects.

to rate young musicians on the quality of their tone. Verbal descriptions such as "round and full" or "weak and listless" are useful but fall short of really describing the differences in tonal quality that can exist. By obtaining examples from students (and perhaps from some professionals, to define the upper ends) on audiotape, a series of recordings describing very poor to very good tonal quality can be produced. By producing these for voice and for each of the major instruments, a music department can build a library of rating scales which the students could use to rate their own tone.

EXERCISE 10.3

1. On the basis of what you just read, you should be able to complete the rating scales you began in Exercise 10.2. There you identified the extreme ends of a personality trait scale and a product scale. Now describe the points which lie between the extremes of these continuums.
2. Write a brief set of instructions for using one of the scales you devised. Make certain that all three important elements (as discussed above) are included.

EVALUATING CHECKLISTS AND RATING SCALES

The basic procedures for evaluating any information-gathering instrument were presented in Chapter 5. You will remember that we will want to find out if the instrument is valid, reliable, and easy to use. Two ways to do this were suggested: (1) before using an instrument, check it for obvious flaws, and (2) try the instrument out to see how well it works.

Checking for Obvious Flaws

The validity of a checklist or rating scale is determined to a great extent by which behaviors or characteristics were selected to be checked or rated. You want to be certain that you have chosen the most important traits or characteristics to be included in your instrument. An easy way to find out if you missed any important ones is to solicit the help of a friend or fellow teacher. Tell this person in general terms what you are trying to evaluate with your scale (e.g., contemporaneous speaking, ability to get along with others, a free-form art project). Next, ask this person to tell you what he thinks the important traits or characteristics are. Discuss any differences between his list and yours. Note that it is *your* scale. *You* know what you want to measure. Your friends' comments are not to be the final word. You must finally decide whether or not any suggestions your friend makes should be included. You solicit his help because he *may* think of some characteristics which you happened to forget. If he thinks of something you did not think of, you must still decide whether or not it is important.

As long as you have the cooperation of a friend, have him do one more thing for you. Ask him to read over the descriptions you have used to describe the particular behaviors listed on your checklist or placed on your scales. Now have him "translate" those descriptions into his own words. If some of your descriptions are ambiguous, your friend's translation may not sound like what you had in mind when you produced the instrument. Ambiguity, you will remember, is a major cause of unreliability. Rewrite any descriptions which may be ambiguous. Be clear and concise.

Finally, ask your friend to read the instructions and tell you in his own words what he would do if he were to use the instrument. Again, you are checking for ambiguity, a major source of unreliability. Clarify any parts of your instructions which are unclear.

Trying Out the Instrument

Use your instrument and, where possible, have others use it too. Take notes on any problems you had. Were there times you wanted to put something down but had no place to put it? Were there characteristics you did not get an opportunity to observe? Were the behaviors as described typical of those you observed? Did the performance move too fast for the number of ratings you had to make? These and many similar questions often arise as you use a checklist or rating scale. They signal problems with the instrument that could probably be corrected with a little rewriting.

Whenever you are trying out an instrument, you should keep a note pad handy so that you can jot down any questions which may arise or any problems which may occur. Sometimes there will not be time to make notes while you are using an instrument of observation. You may have to jot down your impressions *after* you have finished using the instrument. Therefore, it is advisable to plan to have extra time immediately after you have tried out an instrument of observation. Use this time to write down your impressions while they are still fresh in your mind.

Validity. There are a number of ways to check the validity of an information-gathering instrument (see Chapter 2). The most sensible way for the classroom teacher is to simply verify the information which the instruments yield. On the basis of the information obtained, what hypotheses would you postulate about the behavior of your students in similar situations? Watch your students in these situations and confirm or reject those hypotheses. If the hypotheses are confirmed, you have evidence of the validity of your instrument. If they are not confirmed, you do not have evidence of validity.[2] The following example illustrates this procedure.

[2] This procedure was discussed in more detail in Chap. 2 (pp. 53 to 55). You may wish to go back and review those pages at this time.

Having rated his students' performances on setting up an experiment, the science teacher wondered whether or not his ratings were valid. On the basis of the results he had obtained, he set up several hypotheses about how some of the students might be expected to behave if they were asked to set up a similar experiment. For example, he hypothesized that Jim would select the wrong equipment and would not establish the proper controls. It was hypothesized that Alice would set up her experiment correctly, but only after consulting with her classmates about many of the steps.

After the hypotheses were written down, the teacher gave the students another experiment to set up. He then checked to see if his hypotheses were confirmed or rejected. He found that most of the students performed as hypothesized, and so he felt that his rating scale was fairly valid.

The teacher in the above example had little trouble interpreting his findings. His students performed as predicted and thus he had evidence of the validity of his rating scale. Suppose, however, the hypotheses the teacher had set up were not confirmed. Now, how would the findings be interpreted? Would the teacher be correct in assuming that his scales were not valid? Not necessarily. Whenever the information obtained from two different instruments does not agree, there are a number of possible explanations. It is possible, for example, that one or the other or both of the instruments may be invalid; that is, measuring the wrong thing. It is also possible that one or the other or both of the instruments may be unreliable; that is, inconsistent. Furthermore, it is also possible that extraneous situational factors may cause inaccurate information to be obtained. These factors may affect either instrument during any given information-gathering session.

Two things should be apparent from the above discussion:

1. You should never make decisions on the basis of a single piece of evidence.
2. When trying to validate an instrument, make certain that the replicated or supplementary information to be used as a criterion is gathered with a valid and reliable instrument.

Reliability. It is highly unlikely that you will obtain valid results (as described above) if your instrument is not reliable. However, there is a major source of error in checklists and rating scales: scorer error. Chapter 2 describes the procedures for estimating scorer error, and you may wish to obtain an estimate of scorer reliability. The procedure is simple enough. Have two observers rate the same performances (or products) *at the same time.* You will need the simultaneous ratings of the two observers for several students. Now correlate the ratings of observer one with the ratings of observer two, using the formula found in Appendix A. The resulting correlation coefficient will be an estimate of the scorer reliability of your instrument.

EXERCISE 10.4

1. What three factors should a checklist or rating scale be evaluated on?
2. In your own words, describe the procedures for checking for flaws before an instrument is used.
3. How can the validity of an instrument be checked?
4. If an instrument has been shown to be valid (i.e., to yield valid information), will it likely be reliable? Why or why not?

SUMMARY

1. Checklists and rating scales are both useful tools for observing student performances and products.
2. There are five steps to take when constructing a checklist: *(a)* specify an appropriate performance or product, *(b)* list the important behaviors or characteristics, *(c)* add any common errors, *(d)* arrange the list of behaviors or characteristics, and *(e)* provide a way to use the list.
3. Checklists provide you with "it's there—it's not there" kind of information.
4. Rating scales allow us to make systematic judgments about the degree to which a behavior or characteristic is present.
5. The five steps to take when producing a rating scale are as follows: *(a)* specify an appropriate learning outcome, *(b)* list the important characteristics of each outcome, *(c)* define a scale for each characteristic, *(d)* arrange the scales, and *(e)* write the instructions.
6. Product scales can be constructed by using actual examples (or pictures of them) of student work.
7. The validity, reliability, and ease of use of your checklists and rating scales should be checked before you use them as well as after you use them. Any faults should be corrected before they are used again.

Reference

Gronlund, N. E.: *Measurement and Evaluation in Teaching,* 2d ed., The Macmillan Company, New York, 1971.

Suggested Readings

The following texts have particularly good chapters on the use of checklists and rating scales:

Ahmann, Stanley J., and Marvin D. Glock: *Evaluating Pupil Growth,* 4th ed., Allyn and Bacon, Inc., Boston, 1971, chap. 7.

Mehrens, William A., and Irvin J. Lehmann: *Measurement and Evaluation in Education and Psychology,* Holt, Rinehart and Winston, Inc., New York, 1973, chap. 12.

Stanley, Julian C., and Kenneth D. Hopkins: *Educational and Psychological Measurement and Evaluation,* 5th ed., Prentice-Hall, Inc., Englewood Cliffs, N.J., 1972, chap. 16.

Thorndike, Robert L., and Elizabeth Hagen: *Measurement and Evaluation in Psychology and Education,* 3d ed., John Wiley & Sons, Inc., New York, 1969, chap. 13.

More in-depth coverage of the problems involved in evaluating products and performances can be found in

Fitzpatrick, R., and E. J. Morrison: "Performance and Product Evaluation," in R. L. Thorndike (ed.), *Educational Measurement,* American Council on Education, Washington, D.C., 1971, chap. 9.

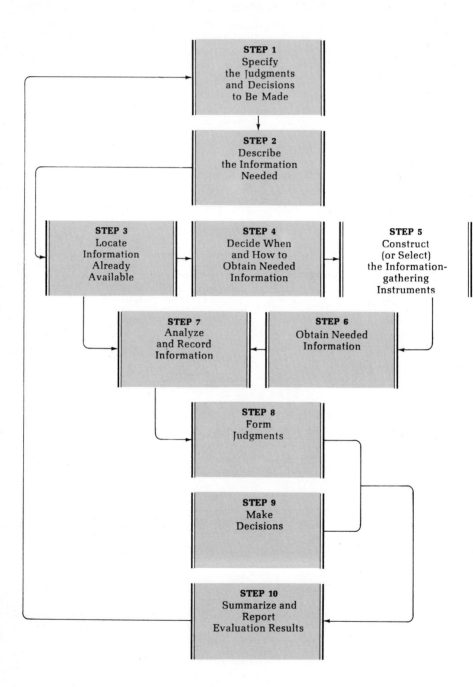

CHAPTER 11

Developing Questionnaires, Interview Schedules, and Sociometric Instruments

In Chapters 5 and 6, you read about the values of and the problems associated with inquiry. To be able to ask the right questions in the right way is indeed an art. Well-developed questionnaires and other tools of inquiry can help you to practice that art more successfully. Some basic suggestions for writing good questions were presented in Chapter 5. These suggestions will now be made more specific.

In this chapter you will learn how to
1. Construct questionnaires
2. Develop interview schedules
3. Construct sociometric instruments
4. Evaluate the instruments of inquiry

CONSTRUCTING QUESTIONNAIRES

Questionnaires are lists of questions written down so they can be systematically responded to. The major difference between a questionnaire and a test is that there are usually *no correct answers* to the questions posed in questionnaires. Questionnaires are primarily used to obtain opinions and attitudes rather than measures of achievement. The basic steps in questionnaire construction are listed below:

A Preview of the Six Basic Steps in Questionnaire Construction

1. Describe the information you need.
2. Write the questions.
3. Arrange the questions.
4. Provide a way to respond.
5. Write instructions.
6. Reproduce the questionnaire.

Step 1: Describe the Information to Be Obtained

There are three things that must be specified clearly from the beginning: (1) who or what you want opinions about, (2) whose opinion you are interested in, and (3) the type of information you are trying to obtain. You should already know this from the first stage in the evaluation process. Just double-check now to be certain that you do know exactly what information you need.

Assuming that questionnaires are to be used for obtaining opinions (and tests for obtaining knowledge), the first thing you should do is determine who or what you want opinions about. Your questions must clearly indicate the object of the opinion being called for.

A questionnaire should be designed so that it is appropriate for those who will be responding to it. If, for example, you want the opinions of your *students* about a textbook, you might ask entirely different questions than if you are seeking the opinions of fellow teachers. The questions in a questionnaire must be written at an appropriate reading level (keep the vocabulary and the sentence structure simple). Furthermore, you should ask about persons or things the respondents would know about and have an opinion about.

The type of information you obtain will differ according to the kind of opinion questions you ask. Suppose, for example, you want your students' opinions about the unit in English which dealt with studies of American dialects. Do you want to know about how effective the students perceived the unit to be? Or do you wish to find out how the unit affected their interest in the study of English? The kinds of questions you ask will differ according to the type of information you want.

Step 2: Write the Questions

Follow the suggestions given in Chapter 5. Write your questions as clearly and concisely as you can. Make certain that your questions are suited to those who must answer them. Write *every* question so that it will give you the *type* of information you need.

There are many types of questions which can be asked. The discussion in Chapter 5 highlighted some of them. The questions in a questionnaire can take the form of checklists or ratings scales (see Chapter 10 for details on construction), open-ended, fill-the-blanks, or choice-type questions (see Chapter 13).

There are some kinds of questions which are more appropriate for questionnaires than for tests. Although it is not exhaustive, a good representative list of these kinds of questions is provided by Brandt (1972). Each kind of question in his list is given below, along with a brief description and some examples to show how they can be asked.

Questions particularly useful in questionnaires.

Leading questions. Leading questions are used to open up a topic on which opinions are desired.

Examples of Leading Questions

What do you think about class discussions?

What do you think of the idea of having assemblies on Friday?

Comparative questions. Comparative questions force the respondent to make preferential judgments among content items.

Examples of Comparative Questions

Would you rather play ball or watch a good movie?

Which do you prefer, arithmetic or history?

Recall-of-past-event questions. These questions are used to find out how much the respondent remembers about a given event.

Examples of Recall Questions

What do you remember about the potato chip factory we visited?

What happened when we allowed our specimen to become contaminated?

Recall of past respondent behavior. These questions are useful for determining the kinds of behavior the respondent has previously engaged in. They can be used to first establish the fact that the respondent has behaved in a given way and then they can be followed by a question which asks if that behavior is typical.

Examples of Recall-of-Behavior Questions

What did you do first when you went in the library?

Can you remember any time that you copied from someone else's paper? Do you do that often?

Feeling questions. Feeling questions are used to obtain subjective, affective reactions to past or present events.

Examples of Feeling Questions

How do you feel about the new dress code in school?

How did you feel when you heard we would have to go to school on Saturday this week?

Cause-effect questions. These questions are used to find out the respondent's reasons for particular events or situations.

Examples of Cause-Effect Questions

Why did the president impose a price-wage freeze?

What makes students want to work hard for a teacher?

What-was(is)-there-about-it questions. These questions are used to get the respondents to cite additional details about their reactions, opinions, or happenings.

Examples of Questions about Reactions

What bothered you most about what happened?

What was it that made you go ahead and do that anyway?

"Would" questions. "Would" questions can help you to find out about the respondent's beliefs or standards.

Examples of "Would" Questions

If you were the teacher and that happened in your room, what would you do?

If you were Tom Sawyer and that happened to you, what would you do? Why?

"Should" questions. "Should" questions help you to find out about the respondent's beliefs about preferred and ideal actions and situations.

Examples of "Should" Questions

In your opinion, what should be the most important subject in school?

What do you really feel a class president should be like?

"Why" questions. These questions can be used for a variety of purposes. Most frequently they are used to probe for more detail. They also can be used to probe for reasons for certain beliefs:

Examples of "Why" Questions

Why do you think that the case should have been handled that way?

Why were the main characters in the play always covering up their actions? Do we do this too? Why?

Step 3: Arrange the Questions

Question arrangement, like all other evaluation activities, should be related to the *reason* for the evaluation. The four arrangements discussed below are commonly used.

General to specific. One way to arrange questions is to place the questions of a general nature first and then to add increasingly more specific questions, with the most specific questions placed at the end. This is a particularly useful arrangement when the reason for the questionnaire is to obtain opinions at various levels of generality. This procedure will also yield information that can be used to compare general opinions to opinions about specific instances.

Noncommittal to sensitive. It is usually best to begin with questions which do not call for a commitment on the part of the respondent. These first questions should be nonthreatening. Later, questions about topics the respondent is a bit more sensitive to can be asked.

Topical arrangement. Often the questions in a questionnaire can be grouped by topic or subtopic. This allows the respondent to consider all the questions about another topic. This arrangement usually makes it easier for the student to respond and helps him to be more consistent, because he expresses all his opinions about a specific topic within a short time.

Mixed arrangement. Sometimes you may want to find out if a student is consistent in his attitudes toward certain persons, places, or things. By mixing the questions up, it is a little more difficult for the student to remember how he responded to an earlier question about the same or a similar object. This reduces the possibility that he will spot any inconsistency in his answers and change some to produce an artificial consistency which may not reflect his true opinions.

Step 4: Provide a Way to Respond

When writing questions, the *type* of response to be made is decided. Now you must provide a *way* for the respondent to make his responses. The first thing to determine is whether the responses should be made on the questionnaire itself or on a separate answer sheet. It is usually easier for the respondent to respond right on the questionnaire, but it is easier to score if the responses are made on a separate answer sheet. If separate answer sheets are used, the same questionnaires can be used for several classes within the same semester or for the same class from semester to semester.

When open-ended responses are called for, allow sufficient space for the longest expected answer. When rating scales are used, make certain they are not crowded together, making them difficult to mark. When alternative responses are to be made, keep each alternative separate from the others and if separate, answer sheets are used to make certain the alternatives are labeled the same way on the answer sheet as they are on the questionnaire.

Step 5: Write the Instructions

Well-constructed questionnaires will yield poor results if the instructions are not equally well written. The instructions accompanying a questionnaire should contain two major elements: (1) a rationale for the questionnaire and (2) the procedures for using it.

In the rationale, the respondent should be given a legitimate reason why he should bother to answer the questions. This part of the instructions can be brief but should be believable.

Example of Questionnaire Introduction

This questionnaire is designed to obtain your opinions about this course. We want to find out how this course can be improved. We need to know where changes will be most helpful to the students.

When describing the procedures for responding to a questionnaire, you should not only tell the respondent how he is to respond but also inform him of any limitations you wish to place on the responses.

Example of Limiting Instructions

For each item, you are to choose the number, on a 1-to-5 scale, which comes closest to matching your perceptions of this course. *Remember:* We want to know how *you* feel, not what you think we want to hear.

If the procedures for responding are somewhat complex or if you have reason to believe that the students are unfamiliar with the type of responses you wish them to make, you should provide them with an example.

Example of Question

1. How difficult was this course for you?

| Much easier than most other courses I have taken | About as difficult as most other courses I have taken | Much more difficult than most other courses I have taken |

If you find this course to be much easier than most other courses, you would fill in no. 1 on the answer sheet provided. If it was somewhat easier than most other courses, then no. 2 would be appropriate. If it is slightly more difficult, then you should fill in no. 4 on your answer sheet, etc.

Finally, instructions should indicate whether or not the results will be held confidential.

Example of Instruction

Please do not sign your name. These responses are to be confidential.

Step 6: Reproduce the Questionnaire

When typing up a questionnaire make certain you use a format which is easy to read and does not crowd questions together in an attempt to save paper. Leave plenty of space between questions. Make certain there is more than enough room to respond.

Ditto or mimeograph procedures are both easy to use, but do not try to get more copies than the original will allow. If any pages are "faint" and difficult to read, the respondent will quickly tire of responding and will quit or respond more or less at random, just to get finished.

EXERCISE 11.1

1. How do the questions in a questionnaire differ from those in a test?
2. How can the arrangement of items in a questionnaire affect the answers you are likely to obtain?
3. What are the two main elements needed in the instructions for a questionnaire? What will be the effect of either element being left out?

SPECIAL TYPES OF QUESTIONNAIRES

There are two types of questionnaires that are particularly useful to classroom teachers: inventories and attitude scales. These two types of questionnaires are valuable for obtaining self-reports.

Inventories

The inventory provides a means of obtaining lists of interests, likes and dislikes, perceptions of one's own abilities, strengths, weaknesses, etc. The inventory is constructed by making a list (or several lists) of behaviors, opinions, interests, perceptions, etc. The individual is asked to check off those things which are representative of his own behavior, perceptions, or feelings.

Examples of Inventory Items

Check each of the following statements which are true of you.

I like school.

I would rather play ball than read a good book.

I enjoy listening to others read aloud.

I watch many different TV programs.

The rules for constructing inventories are essentially the same as those for constructing checklists (see Chapter 10). The interest inventory is an especially useful tool for elementary school teachers. An inventory of the various kinds of gamelike learning activities can help the teacher find out which activities the students will most likely enjoy. A checklist of types of books the students would like to read can help you make decisions about what to include in the library as well as decisions about which books to ask particular students to read.

Attitude Scales

Although attitude scale construction is difficult, teachers can produce some simple scales. These should be used with caution to provide information which is supplementary to that obtained through observation and informal interviews. Perhaps the easiest kind of scale to produce is the *Likert* scale. In this scale, a number of statements are presented to the respondent. He then indicates on a 5-point scale whether or not he agrees with each statement. The 5-point scale (which remains the same throughout the inventory) is shown in the following examples.

Examples of 5-point Scales

Textbooks are usually exciting

1	2	3	4	5
Strongly agree	Agree	Undecided	Disagree	Strongly disagree

This class is providing me with useful information

1	2	3	4	5
Strongly agree	Agree	Undecided	Disagree	Strongly disagree

The secret to producing useful scales of this kind is to write good statements to which the students can respond. The following guidelines should help you to construct usable Likert scales.[1]

Guidelines for Constructing Likert Scales

1. Each statement should be phrased in words which are familiar to the respondent. Use the language of the respondent, not the technical jargon of your own discipline. Also use simple sentence structure.

[1] For more complete instructions on how to construct attitude scales of a variety of types, see A. L. Edwards, *Techniques of Attitude Scale Construction,* Appleton-Century-Crofts, Inc., New York, 1957.

2. Each statement should express a *clearly positive* or a *clearly negative* attitude. Make certain that you have chosen statements that truly represent negative and positive positions. It may be helpful to try out your statements before including them in your instrument. Find persons who you know hold extreme positions (e.g., politically very liberal or very conservative) and see if they strongly agree or strongly disagree with your statements.
3. The final list of statements should include an approximately equal number of positive and negative statements.
4. Each statement should yield information needed. Do not present a statement "just because it would be interesting to see how the students would respond." Each statement should be clearly related to an attitude or opinion you need information about.

DEVELOPING AN INTERVIEW SCHEDULE

Interviewing is an inquiry *technique.* It is a procedure, not an instrument. The procedures to follow during an interview were discussed in Chapter 6. In this section, you will learn how to develop an *interview schedule.* An interview schedule is the instrument which guides the interviewer. A set of questions (essentially a questionnaire) is the heart of the interview schedule. Other elements in the interview schedule include a statement of the purpose of the interview, a set of guidelines for establishing rapport with the interviewee, an outline of the structure of the interview, a note indicating the time and place of the interview, and a space to write down notes during the interview.

An interview schedule is usually written out so that each of the elements listed above can be referred to as the interview is conducted. However, when preparing for short, less formal interviews, these elements need not be written down. Nevertheless, you should give some thought to each of these elements as you prepare to interview.

A Statement of the Purpose of the Interview

There are many reasons for conducting interviews. Some of the more common reasons were cited in Chapter 5. Having decided what you expect to accomplish in an interview, it is important to keep that goal in mind as you conduct the interview. It is very easy to get sidetracked in an interview. If the first thing on your interview schedule is a statement of purpose, it will serve as a reminder to you and you will be more likely to obtain the information you wanted. Specify first the primary purpose of the interview. Then ask yourself: "What kind of information can I most likely obtain from such an interview?" The questions you decide to ask during the interview will be determined in part by your answer to this question.

A Set of Guidelines for Establishing Rapport

A good interviewer can quite quickly establish rapport with the interviewee. Planning ahead, where possible, can help you to become effective in this first stage of an interview. The first thing you should do is identify some nonthreatening topics with which you can open the conversation. Next, figure out a way to make the purpose of the interview meaningful and acceptable to the interviewee. If, for some reason, the main purpose of the interview should not be made known to the interviewee (e.g., because he would feel threatened or be biased and thus not respond honestly and objectively), you should make up a pseudopurpose which seems plausible and legitimate. Third, establish sound, meaningful reasons why the interviewee should be completely honest. Also, provide convincing arguments that the information will he held in the strictest confidence and will not be used against the interviewee. Be ready to show how the information obtained can be used to help the interviewee.

A Set of Questions

After you have reminded yourself of the purpose of the interview and decided on a way to establish rapport, you are ready to develop a set of questions to be used. The rules for formulating questions for interviews are essentially the same as those we discussed in Chapter 5. An additional consideration must be kept in mind when questions are to be used in interviewing: they are to be presented to the respondent orally. This means that you must be certain that the questions are short and easy to understand. The respondent must remember the question you ask as he searches for a response. Think about how often you look back and reread a question on a test. You cannot do that in an interview. Use commonly understood words and do not phrase your questions in complex grammatical structures.

An Outline of How the Interview Will Be Structured

An interview can be successfully structured in several ways. The particular structure to be used should be determined by the purpose of the interview and the nature of the relationship between the interviewer and interviewee. Some interviews are very highly structured. The questions are almost all worked out in advance, a specific time and place is set aside, and the formal purpose is well specified. This highly structured interview is particularly good for communicating ideas and/or obtaining very specific information about particular topics.

The other extreme is the completely unstructured interview. Most of the questions are not formulated in advance and the interviewer "plays it by ear," letting one question lead to another. This kind of structure (or lack of it) is sometimes useful for obtaining very general information. Unexpected interests, attitudes, and opinions are often uncovered during such loosely structured interviews. Because of the informal, conversational tone of such interviews, they are good for opening up and keeping open important lines of communication. This type of interview is very good for situations where the interviewee feels threatened and is hesitant to talk.

Many interviews conducted by teachers fall somewhere between these two extremes. Usually, teachers have some idea about the kind of information they want, and so they formulate in advance *some* of the questions they wish to ask and fill in with other appropriate questions as the interview proceeds. The idea is to select several key questions and place them in the interview according to a predetermined plan. Each key question is designed to lead to related questions. The common ways to arrange key questions were discussed earlier in this chapter (see page 299).

Note on the Time and Place of the Interview

A brief note on when you plan on talking with Susan or John's parents or Liza's gym teacher will serve two purposes: (1) it will remind you of whom you are interviewing, when and where, and (2) when you record the information you obtain from an interview, you will know when it was gathered. It is easy to put off recording and filing interview notes. If you do delay this you will at least have a record of who was interviewed, when, and where.

A Space for Note Taking

During most planned interviews, you will want to take brief notes. Having a place available for this right on the interview schedule assures you that when the notes are filed away, the information about why the interview was conducted, with whom, in what way, etc. will not be lost.

EXERCISE 11.2

1. Explain the difference between the interview (a technique) and the interview schedule (an instrument).
2. What are the main parts of an interview schedule? How does each of these parts help you to minimize error in the information obtained during an interview?

CONSTRUCTING SOCIOMETRIC INSTRUMENTS

When information is needed about the social interactions within a peer group, sociometric techniques are extremely useful. Nominating devices and "guess-who" techniques are particularly useful for obtaining information about how individual students are perceived by their peers. Placement devices are valuable for obtaining information about the perceived relationships among the entire group of peers. This kind of information is actually in the form of peer *judgments.* These judgments are extremely valuable in helping the teacher to make placement decisions (and, to some extent, treatment decisions). Seating arrangements, committee assignments, and assignments for group projects all can be made more effectively with the aid of sociometric data. The goal of this section is to provide you with suggestions for constructing your own sociometric instruments.

Nominating Devices

Nominating devices are very simple. Typically, these devices present the individual with a situation which calls for him to choose one or more of his peers for a particular position or task. A typical nominating device used in elementary school classrooms asks each pupil to select the three classmates that he would like most to invite to a party. The instructions might read like this:

> Suppose you were going to have a big party at your house. If you could invite only three friends from this class, whom would you choose?

Notice that there are three main parts to these instructions: (1) a proposed situation (a party), (2) a position to be filled or task to be undertaken (friends to come to the party), and (3) rule(s) for nominating individuals for the position (choose three classmates). To construct a nominating device, you only need to draw up *clearly* written instructions which include these three elements and then decide how you will have the student respond. Thus there are four simple steps to constructing a nominating device.

Preview of Steps to Take When Constructing for a Nominating Device

Step 1. Set up a situation.

Step 2. Select a position to be filled or a task to be undertaken.

Step 3. Specify the rules for nominating.

Step 4. Decide how the individuals shall respond.

Step 1: Set up a situation. The situation can vary greatly (anything from a party to a group project in math), but it must have the following characteristics:

1. *It must be somewhat realistic* (e.g., a birthday party is realistic for third graders but not for high schoolers).
2. *It should be of interest to the individuals doing the nominating* (e.g., third grade boys are not very interested in dances but high school boys are).

3. *It should be familiar to the individuals doing the nominating* (e.g., a baseball game is familiar to almost all junior high students; a game of rugby to almost none of them).
4. *It should be described briefly.* (Do not go to great lengths to explain the details of the situation. Pick a familiar situation so that the typical details will be known to all.)

Step 2: Select a position to be filled or a task to be undertaken. The position (or task) must be one which is very familiar to everyone in the class. They should know what the consequences would be if someone filled the position (or took on the task). Obviously, we do not mean that the student should be able to perceive every conceivable consequence of his selections. But he should know something about the requirements for the position or task and how well those requirements would be met by those he nominates. Positions like the following meet this requirement: a "buddy" for a nature hike, a partner for a lab experiment, a person to help you with math, a leader for your discussion group.

Step 3: Specify the rules for nominating. The rule(s) for nominating should include the following elements:

1. Who may be chosen (e.g., all members of the class, including those absent today).
2. How many may be chosen (e.g., no more than four friends).

Sometimes you may wish to find out about the social interactions of a part of the class (e.g., a reading group). Most of the time, everyone in the class should be eligible to be nominated. Rarely should you allow students to nominate more than four or five persons for a given position or task. Interpretation becomes difficult after that.

Step 4: Decide how individuals will respond. In the lower grades, nominations are usually made orally, in a private interview with the teacher. In the upper grades the students can write down the names (or initials) of those they are nominating. This allows one to obtain information from the entire class at once. To make certain that no one is forgotten momentarily ("out of sight, out of mind"), an alphabetical list of all the classmates is often supplied. With younger children, class pictures can be posted on a board. The child need only point to the picture of the individual he is nominating. This helps those who have trouble reading and/or remembering the names of the class members.

EXERCISE 11.3

Write out a set of instructions for some sociometric device to be used at the grade level you teach (or hope to teach). Check to see that it meets the requirements discussed above.

"Guess-Who" Instrument

I am thinking of someone who is always helping others. Guess who?

I am thinking of someone who makes others laugh and feel good. Guess who?

The above statements are examples of the kind of item you would find in a guess-who instrument. It is used to help students judge their peers. The idea behind this kind of instrument is this: Peers often know the typical behavior patterns and the personality characteristics of an individual student better than the teacher does. By using the "guess who" instrument, the teacher can capitalize on this fact and obtain peer judgments. The procedure is simple. You merely present descriptions of typical behaviors or of common personality traits and then ask the individuals in the class to select classmates who best fit the descriptions. The secret here is to select appropriate behaviors or traits and then to describe them clearly and unambiguously. Constructing guess-who statements involves two steps:

Steps to Take When Constructing Guess-Who Statements

Step 1. Choose behaviors

Step 2. Describe the behaviors chosen

Step 1: Choosing Behaviors or traits.   This task is easy if you have descriptions of the judgments and decisions you expect to make as well as clearly defined statements of the information needed to make them. A first and most important question you must ask is, "Why do I need to know what a student's peers think of him?" If you cannot come up with a reasonable answer to that question (phrased in terms of judgments and decisions to be made), you should not use the guess-who technique. Some examples of the kinds of judgments and decisions which might rely on guess-who information are listed below. Read the list carefully and then try to think of some additional examples.

Examples of Judgments and Decisions Which Would Require Information from Guess-Who Procedures

JUDGMENTS

Who do the students perceive as most friendly, as leader, as best athlete, as most kind, etc.?

Who are the students that are seen by their peers as the least friendly, least athletic, etc.?

Which students are most and least popular?

DECISIONS

Who should be chosen as group leaders?

How should I arrange the classroom seating?

Which students should be asked to work as a team on small group projects?

How should the class be divided so that there will be two baseball teams that are somewhat equal in ability? Who should be chosen as captains?

Suppose we take some of the above judgments and decisions and try to determine the behaviors or traits that should be listed in a guess-who instrument. The behaviors or traits should be appropriate for the judgments and decisions to be made.

Examples of Guess-Who Questions

Judgment: Who do the students see as most friendly?

Traits or behaviors: Friendliness, smiles and is happy, helpful to others, etc.

Decision: Which students should be asked to work as a team on small group projects?

Traits or behaviors: Leadership, ability to follow, easy to get along with, cooperative, interested in others, etc.

Step 2: Describe the traits or behaviors.   After you select the traits or behaviors you are interested in, you simply need to describe them clearly enough so that the students will understand. Remember: These will be the statements to be used in the guess-who instrument. They should remind the students of one or more of their peers. They should be stated in *behavioral* terms.

Examples of Descriptive Statements

I am thinking of someone who talks to everyone.

Here is someone who is very quiet, rarely talking to anyone.

This person is always able to get the others to do what he wants.

> Who in this class can come up with the most original ideas?
>
> Here is a person that can hit a ball farther than anyone else in the room.
>
> If there was a math problem you could not work out, this student would be best able to help you.

Guess-who descriptions can be phrased both positively (this person is friendly) or negatively (this person is *not* friendly). Some teachers prefer to use only positive statements. Although this limits the information you will obtain, it does avoid the problems which could occur if the morale of the group is lowered because of the negative nominations. If there are good healthy relations among the students and the teacher, this is not likely to happen. If you feel that negative nominations could affect the group's morale, leave them out.

The guess-who technique can be used at virtually any age level. When it is used with very young children, you may wish to present it orally and let the child tell you his response (of course this means it must be done individually). With older children who read well, the statements can be handed out on mimeographed sheets and the names or initials of the nominees can be written right on the sheet below each statement. Students at the junior high age (or older) may find the guess-who element a little childish. These students can simply be instructed to choose those in the class who best fit each behavior described.

The instructions are quite simple, but they must be clearly communicated to the students. They should tell the student whom they may select from (e.g., the entire class), how many persons they can nominate for any given behavior (e.g., choose no more than two, or choose only one person for each statement), and how they are to indicate their choice (e.g., write down the name or initials of the person the statement reminds you of).

In the exercise below, we have produced some statements from a guess-who instrument to be used with fourth graders. These statements have been written to find out whom the students perceive as most cooperative. Some of the statements, for one reason or another, should probably not be included in the instrument. See if you can figure out which ones they are.

EXERCISE 11.4

The statements below were written for fourth grade level. They are supposed to measure perceptions of cooperativeness. Read each statement and mark it according to the following key:

OK = The statement is *appropriate* for this age level, describes cooperativeness, and is behaviorally stated.

NA = *Not appropriate* for this grade level (language too complex or example not appropriate for fourth graders).

NC = *Not* representative of *cooperativeness,* or lack of it (describes some other traits).

NB = *Not behaviorally* stated (vague and general, unobservable).

1. This person helps others as often as he (she) can.
2. Here is someone who always dominates rather than occasionally subordinating himself (herself) to the wishes of others.
3. Here is someone who enjoys playing games.
4. Who would be willing to change seats with you so you could see better?
5. This person understands others.
6. This person is always talking in class.
7. Here is someone who will help me get my car out into a busy street.
8. This person would let you take your turn early so you could start for home on time.
9. This person would rather make his own booklet than give in to the way the group wants to do it.
10. Who would be the first to volunteer their services for group experiments designed to further the cause of social integration?

Placement Devices

A placement device is another instrument for obtaining information about the social interactions among students. It consists of a diagram or drawing which pictures the scene of some group activity. The students are given this drawing and are told to "place" the group members where they think they might be found. Examples of this kind of technique can be found in Figures 11.1 and 11.2.

Notice that the diagrams are simple. You do not need to be an artist to produce one. Simple representations of objects can be drawn, as in Figure 11.2, or circles can be drawn without reference to any objects in the environment (Figure 11.1). A map of the room could be drawn, with squares representing the various objects. These squares could then be labeled. Figure 11.3 represents this approach and illustrates a placement device which can be used with high school students.

The information from these devices is not easily quantified, but interpretations can be made which will be useful supplementary information. This technique, like the nomination procedure discussed earlier, is especially useful for discovering those students who are the most (and the least) popular. By using these techniques, you can gain insights into who the loners in the class are and who the class leaders are. Social cliques can also be discovered. Various ways to interpret the information from these and other instruments of inquiry have been discussed in Chapter 7.

This Is Our Class in the Park

Where is everyone? Write each person's initials in one of the circles. Add circles where you need them and scratch out those you do not need. Everyone in the class is at the park. Put everyone somewhere on the diagram. A list of the names and initials of the class members has also been given to you. Refer to it as needed.

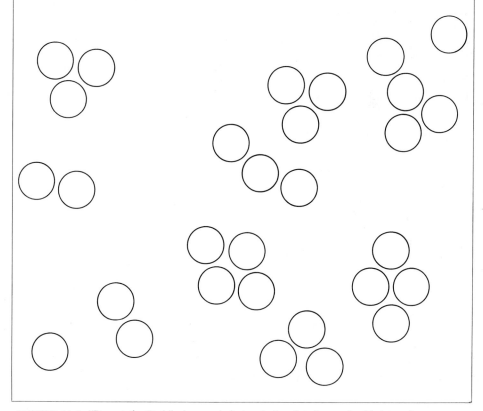

FIGURE 11.1. "Day at the Park" placement device designed to be used with later elementary or junior high students.

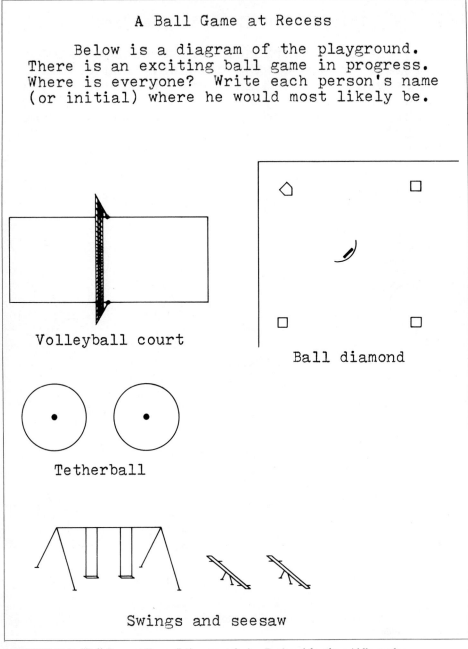

FIGURE 11.2. "Ball Game at Recess" placement device. Designed for the middle grades.

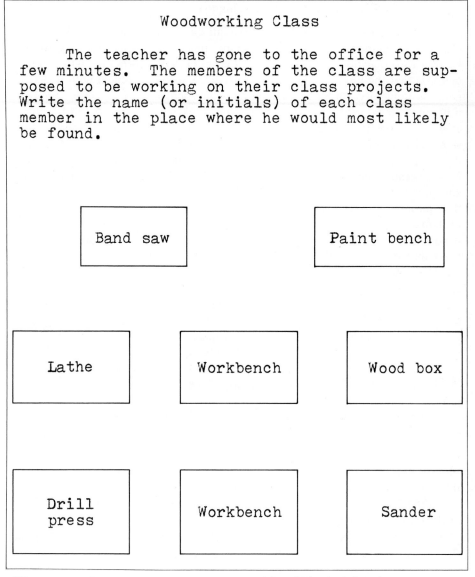

FIGURE 11.3. "Shop Class" placement device. Designed for a high school shop class.

EVALUATING INSTRUMENTS OF INQUIRY

When evaluating instruments of inquiry, you should follow the suggestions made in Chapter 5. Before you use your instrument, check it for obvious flaws and then try it out.

Common Flaws in Instruments of Inquiry

A list of questions is the heart of the questionnaire and the interview schedule. A very common problem with these instruments is inappropriate questions. Go over each question and ask yourself, "What kind of information will that give me?" "Is that the kind of information I need?" A second problem with questionnaires is ambiguity. Have someone tell you what each question is asking. Find out if he thinks it is asking the same thing you think it is asking. A third problem arises with questions which call for opinions. Opinions are formed on the basis of some referent (opinions are judgments, after all). Frequently, opinion questions do not specify any referent, and therefore there is no consistency from person to person because each chooses his own referent. For example, suppose you ask your students how well they liked the textbook being used. Before anyone can answer that question, he first asks, "Compared to what?" If a student compares the textbook to other textbooks he will make one judgment. If he compares it to the other materials used in the class (e.g., films), he will make a different judgment. Check to see that opinion questions specify some referent. For example, rather than asking, "Do you enjoy arithmetic?" ask, "How well do you like arithmetic compared to your other subjects?"

Problems arise with sociometric instruments when the situation is not appropriate for the age level of the students or is not realistic. Always check to see that the situation you have set up makes sense to the students. Ask some of the students if it seems like a natural, realistic situation to them. Sociometric devices can also fail to work properly if the instructions are not clearly understood. Double-check for ambiguity in your instructions.

Trying Out Instruments of Inquiry

One way to try out an instrument of inquiry is to use it on a small sample of students and then ask them about their answers. Find out why they answered the way they did. Find out what their answers mean to them. You will usually uncover any major problems with this technique.

Another useful way to find out if these instruments are doing what they are supposed to is to form judgments on the basis of the information you obtain and then verify these judgments. See Chapter 7 for the procedures for forming judgments and Chapter 8 to find out how to verify them.

SUMMARY

1. Questionnaires are lists of questions written down so they can be responded to. There are usually no correct answers and the primary purpose is to obtain information about the opinions and attitudes of individuals.
2. There are six steps in the construction of a questionnaire: (1) describe the information needed, (2) write the questions, (3) arrange the questions, (4) provide a way to respond, (5) write instructions, and (6) reproduce the questionnaire.

3. There are many types of questions which can be used to find out what a person feels about various topics. Choose the types of questions that will give you the information you need and then form each question clearly and concisely.

4. Four common ways to arrange questions are (1) general to specific, (2) noncomittal to sensitive, (3) according to topic, and (4) a mixed arrangement.

5. Instructions accompanying a questionnaire should include the following two elements (1) a rationale for the questionnaire and (2) procedures for using it.

6. Inventories are essentially checklists and are often used to find out about patterns of behavior or about the interests of students.

7. An interview schedule provides the interviewer with a set of guidelines. A good schedule will include the following parts: (1) statement of purpose, (2) guidelines for establishing rapport, (3) questions, (4) outline of the structure of the interview, (5) a note indicating time and place, and (6) space for note taking.

8. Nominating devices present the individual with a situation which calls for him to choose one or more of his peers for a particular position or task.

9. To construct a nominating device, you follow these steps: (1) set up a situation, (2) select a position or task, (3) specify the rules for nominations, and (4) decide how the individuals will respond.

10. A guess-who instrument presents descriptions of typical behaviors or common personality traits and asks the individuals to select peers who best fit each description.

11. Constructing guess-who statements involves two steps: (1) choosing behaviors and (2) describing those behaviors.

12. A placement device presents a picture or a drawing of the scene of a group activity. The students are asked to "place" the group members where they think each might be found.

13. To evaluate your instruments of inquiry, first look for common flaws (e.g., inappropriate questions, ambiguous instructions) and then try it out to see if it yields the information you expected it to.

Reference

Edwards, Allen L.: *Techniques of Attitude Scale Construction,* Appleton-Century-Crofts, New York, 1957.

Suggested Readings

For a detailed discussion of the problems of observation and inquiry, read

Brandt, Richard M.: *Studying Behavior in Natural Settings,* Holt, Rinehart and Winston, Inc., New York, 1972.

For further information on the art of asking questions, read

Hunkins, Francis P.: *Questioning Strategies and Techniques,* Allyn and Bacon, Inc., Boston, 1972.

Sanders, Norris M.: *Classroom Questions: What Kinds?* Harper & Row, Publishers, Incorporated, New York, 1966.

A good treatment of sociometric techniques is offered by

Gronlund, N. E.: *Sociometry in the Classroom,* Harper & Row, Publishers, Incorporated, New York, 1959.

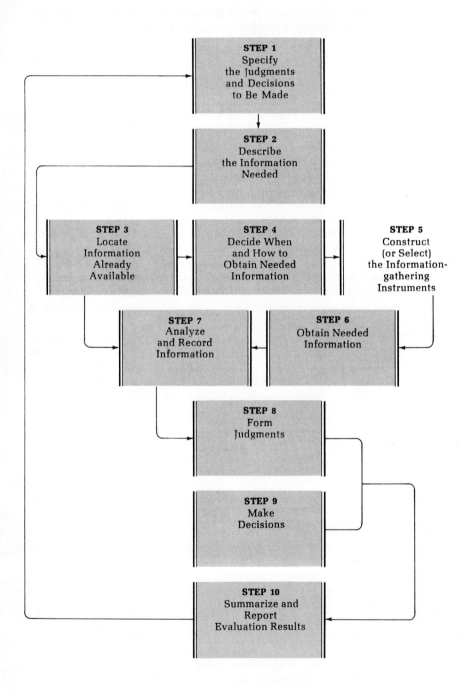

STEP 1
Specify
the Judgments
and Decisions
to Be Made

STEP 2
Describe
the Information
Needed

STEP 3
Locate
Information
Already
Available

STEP 4
Decide When
and How to
Obtain Needed
Information

STEP 5
Construct
(or Select)
the Information-
gathering
Instruments

STEP 7
Analyze
and Record
Information

STEP 6
Obtain Needed
Information

STEP 8
Form
Judgments

STEP 9
Make
Decisions

STEP 10
Summarize and
Report
Evaluation Results

CHAPTER 12

Designing Projects and Assignments

There is no greater source of information about student learning than the learning activities themselves. The daily work our students perform as they learn can provide us with invaluable information about how they are learning, how fast they are learning, how well they are remembering what they learn, how quickly they "catch on" to a new skill, etc. However, unless some attempt is made to systematically obtain this information, most of it will be lost. This chapter will help you in this regard.

> When you have finished this chapter, you should be able to design assignments and projects so that they can be readily analyzed for information about student progress.

Assignments are to help students learn. Assignments are also to help the teacher learn about what and how the students are learning. Assignments can serve both these purposes if they are well designed and carefully chosen. Whether you select assignments (from teachers manuals, workbooks, etc.) or design your own, they should have certain recognized characteristics if they are to provide you with useful information.

Assignments designed to provide the teacher with useful evaluative information should

1. Engage the student at some stage in the attainment of specific instructional goals.
2. Include complete instructions, clearly presented.
3. Be reasonable (i.e., within the students' capabilities).
4. Result in a performance or a product which could be readily analyzed, providing the teacher with information about what has been learned, how it has been learned, and what level of achievement the student has reached.

The following suggestions should help you to select useful assignments as well as to design your own. They are listed here as an overview. Each suggestion will then be discussed in detail.

Suggestions for Selecting and/or Designing Projects and Assignments

1. Decide what the student is supposed to learn from the experience.
2. Decide what information you wish to obtain about the student.
3. Determine what the students are to do.
4. Determine how the students are to communicate the results of what they have done.
5. Formulate the instructions to the students.
6. Establish the rules (and the rationale) for the analyses to be made.

SUGGESTION 1: DECIDE WHAT IS TO BE LEARNED

Every assignment you give should be designed specifically to help the student reach (or move toward) some instructional goal. That goal should be clearly specified in observable terms.

Examples of Goals Which Projects and Assignments Can Help Students to Attain

1. To list the five activities of plants as discussed in the textbook.
2. When given several samples of "unknown" plants, to be able to devise at least two different ways to classify them.
3. To write down the correct answers to the multiplication tables (through 10 × 10).

Often it takes several assignments to help a student reach a particular goal. When this is the case, you should state precisely how each assignment is to help the student attain the goal and you should decide exactly what the student should learn if he completes the assignment correctly.

Examples of Assignments Designed to Help Students Attain Particular Goals

Assignment for Goal 1, Above

1. Practice in writing the five activities of plants should help the student to remember them so that he will be able to write them without aid later.

Assignments for Goal 2, Above

1. Exercises in which students are to classify objects in as many ways as possible should help them to learn to look for various ways in which things can be classified.
2. This assignment (not yet clearly defined) should be designed so that the students will learn to identify the important distinguishing features of plants.
3. The students should be given practice classifying plants, devising as many schemes as possible on their own.

Assignments for Goal 3, Above

1. Writing each of the multiplication tables should help the student to be able to write them with no aids, making no errors.
2. Flashing the multiplication cards to each other should help the students to remember the "facts" over an extended period of time.
3. Counting by a counting number (e.g., 2s, 3s, 4s, 5s) both forward and backward on a number line can help the students to learn to describe the relationship between multiplication and division.
4. Working multiplication and division problems in pairs (e.g., 3 × 9, 9 ÷ 3) should help the student to transfer his knowledge of the multiplication facts to the solution of division problems.

Notice that the above examples represent a variety of learning outcomes. It is important for you to know as much as possible about the learning outcomes you expect from each assignment you give. The kind of learning, the level of learning, and the stage of the learning process all make a difference in what you should have the student do. It is valuable for you to find out what kinds of learning a particular student is having trouble with and at what stage in the learning process the trouble is occurring.

What Kind of Learning?

One obviously important consideration when designing assignments is the *kind* of learning that is to be expected. Learning outcomes are usually classified as cognitive, psychomotor, or affective. Even though most tasks do not represent pure measures of these categories, it is not too difficult to determine if a task is *primarily* cognitive, *primarily* psychomotor, or *primarily* affective (see Chapter 4).

What Level of Learning?

Another important consideration is the level of learning you expect your students to reach. This is especially important when sequencing assignments. It is extremely difficult for a student to complete an assignment calling for upper-level learning outcomes when he has not yet attained the prerequisite lower levels. Any of the popular taxonomies of learning can be used to describe the level of learning expected from a particular assignment (see Chapter 4). Gagné's taxonomy (Gagné, 1970) is especially useful because he describes the *conditions* under which learning at each level occurs.

A very useful technique to use when planning assignments is to develop achievement continua like those described in Chapter 2. Assignments can be designed to help you obtain information about how well a student has achieved at each point on an achievement continuum. Figure 12.1 illustrates this procedure. For each point on the achievement continuum, one or more assignments have been defined.

What Stage of Learning?

Most psychologists agree that learning occurs in three stages: acquisition, retention, and transfer (see, e.g., Travers, 1973). Assignments should be designed to help you obtain information about how well the student is learning at each of these stages. Sometimes a single assignment takes a student through all stages and sometimes many assignments may be needed to help the student through a single stage. At the risk of oversimplifying, we would describe the three stages as follows:

Acquisition stage. During this stage the student is learning new information. The

Continuum of achievement
for writing an explanatory passage

1	2	3	4	5	6	7
Able to develop an outline of topic to be covered		Writes acceptable topic sentence		Includes information to support topic sentences (in logical order)		Writes coherent passages with good paragraph transitions

Level 1 assignment: Select a concept from those listed on the blackboard and develop a brief outline of the important things which should be explained to make that concept clear.

Level 3 assignment: For each of the mini-topics, write a topic sentence which has all the characteristics that we talked about in class (also see page 103 in your text).

Level 5 assignment: List all the facts you can think of to support the following position: There are many times when . . .

Level 7 assignment: For each pair of paragraphs on your handout sheet, write a sentence that would "link" them together. Read about transition sentences in your text (pp. 108 and 109) before you begin.

FIGURE 12.1. Examples of assignments designed to help students reach various levels on an achievement continuum.

individual can do or say something at the end of acquisition that he could not do or say before he began (e.g., a child has studied a spelling word and can now spell it correctly).

Retention stage. During this stage, the newly learned information or skill is practiced so that it will be retained over a period of time. This stage is sometimes referred to as the *storage* stage because the learning acquired during acquisition is "stored" for future use (e.g., a child continues to practice the spelling word he learned so that he will remember it for the Friday spelling test).

Transfer stage. Often we store ideas in memory only to find it difficult to retrieve them and use them later. This ability to retrieve information and use it in a new situation (i.e., transfer it to new learning) seems to involve a variety of strategies but is also, obviously, dependent upon retention of the right information (e.g., a child uses her knowledge of how a word (train) is spelled to help her learn to spell a new word (drain).

There are four main reasons for you to know what stage(s) of learning is (are) being represented by a given assignment. First of all, each stage must occur in its proper order. This means that assignments designed to help students improve retention should be given *after* the information has been acquired and *before* assignments designed to help the student learn to transfer. (Yes, there are assignments which encompass all three stages, but even then the order in which the student goes through the stages is acquisition, retention, transfer.)

A second reason for knowing what stage of learning a student is in is that the requirements for learning differ from one stage to the next.[1] For example, the acquisition of new information generally requires more repetition, more practice with feedback, and more learning aids (visuals, mnemonics, etc.) to make the information meaningful. In order for long-term retention to occur, many opportunities must be given for repeating the correct response (overlearning). Transfer, on the other hand, occurs best when practice on many varied tasks is given. For example, having learned to use a ruler to measure length, the students are asked to measure a wide variety of items. This kind of practice will help them to successfully use a ruler to measure an object they had never measured before.

A third reason to distinguish among the stages of learning is the fact that the measurement requirements differ from one stage to the next. During the acquisition stage you should be looking for such things as the amount of time and effort expended in order to learn, the number of errors made, the kind of errors made, the strategies used by the student, etc. Retention should be measured at varying times after acquisition. You should look for the quality of the information retained and you should try to get some idea about how long it has been retained. In order to measure retrieval and transfer, you must set up a number of different conditions. For example, sometimes it is useful to know how retrieval as measured by a recognition method such as alternative response questions differs from retrieval as measured by a recall method such as open-ended questions. It is also important, when measuring for transfer, that the test present a *new* situation so that the student cannot answer correctly on the basis of memory alone.

Finally, you should be able to distinguish among the stages of learning because the information obtained about students at each stage is useful for making different kinds of judgments and decisions. For example, it is not fair to judge a person's math achievement on the basis of information obtained during the acquisition stage. Teachers frequently grade assignments which were completed *before* the students have acquired and retained. These grades are then used as part of the final report card grade reflecting achievement. However, suppose a student does poorly in the early stages of learning but catches on later and eventually learns well enough to transfer the information to a new situation with ease. Should that student be judged incapable (or less capable than his peers) because he had some trouble initially acquiring the information? Many good spellers struggle in their first attempts to spell a word. Numerous home run hitters failed miserably in their first attempts.

---

[1] The requirements during each stage also differ depending upon the kind and level of learning which is occurring. However, a discussion of these differences is beyond the scope of this book. Pointing out the *general* differences which exist from stage to stage should be enough to make you aware of the need to know at any given time what stage of learning a student is at.

It may be valuable for teachers to be able to say "Eloise acquires information slowly but retains it well," or "Fred acquires information rapidly but needs a great deal of review in order to retain it," or "Julie remembers almost everything you ask her to read but rarely can she transfer it to her relationships with her peers." Notice that the above judgments can lead to important instructional decisions (especially treatment decisions of the kind: "What kinds of assignments do I give those who acquire slowly?"). The judgments made in the early stages of learning are essentially formative judgments, whereas those made in the last stage are essentially summative judgments.

SUGGESTION 2: DECIDE WHAT INFORMATION YOU WANT TO OBTAIN

Much of the time you will want information about the students' progress toward *expected* learning outcomes. That is part of the reason for determining what the student is supposed to learn. Teachers usually find out whether or not the student could do an assignment. However, there is a great deal of other information that can be obtained by analyzing assignments. Some of the many kinds of information we can obtain are directly related to the expected learning outcomes but go beyond the simple "could-do-it" or "could-not-do-it" analysis. Examples of these kinds of information are given in the following outline.

An Outline of Expected Learning Outcomes Which Can Be Measured with Properly Designed Projects and Assignments

I. Information directly related to the expected learning outcomes
    A. Rate of acquisition
        1. Example: How many times did Gloria have to write her spelling words before she spelled them all correctly?
        2. Example: The number of times the students had to refer to the instructions before they could successfully conduct the experiments.
    B. Amount of information retained
        1. Example: How many of the theorems we studied did the students recall?
    C. Kind of information retained and used
        1. Example: The number of facts about *The Separate Peace.*
        2. Example: The number of inferences made from *The Separate Peace.*
    D. Kind of transfer situations successfully mastered
        1. Example: Using classification rules to classify unknown birds.
    E. Number of errors
        1. Example: Number of arithmetic problems wrong.
        2. Example: Number of parts incorrectly identified.
    F. Kind of errors
        1. Example: Number of addition and subtraction errors.
        2. Example: Number of important facts omitted from the defense of the two-party system.

G. Learning strategies
  1. Example: Utilized mostly original sources rather than secondary sources.
  2. Example: Began with several hypotheses and systematically tested each one.
H. Organizational strategies
  1. Example: Organized from general to specific.
  2. Example: Organized sequentially.

We have already discussed the importance of obtaining information about the unexpected results of learning activities (see Chapter 4). By analyzing the projects and assignments of our students, we can discover both good and bad *unexpected* outcomes. This information could then be used to make many instructional decisions (e.g., what should be done to correct this misconception? Should I slow down, giving the student more time? Should the students be given more practice?). Below is a continuation of the outline of kinds of learning outcomes that can be assessed with well-designed assignments.

An Outline of Unexpected Outcomes Which Can Be Measured with Properly Designed Projects and Assignments

II. Information about *unexpected* learning outcomes
  A. Information and skills not expected or planned for
    1. Example: When finding out the population of the major Midwest cities, what other information was gained *(a)* about those cities, *(b)* about other nearby cities, *(c)* about the states they were in?
    2. Example: When learning to use an electric drill was any information gained about *(a)* electricity, *(b)* hardness of materials, or *(c)* other tools used for making holes?
  B. Misinformation or bad habits learned
    1. Example: When studying the Rocky Mountain range, were any misconceptions formed (e.g., about the height of ranges in other countries, about the way all mountains have been formed, or about the Westward movement)?
    2. Example: When learning to form the manuscript letters, did anyone learn to form them neatly but with incorrect movements which could make cursive writing more difficult?
  C. Attitudes, opinions, and interests resulting from the learning activities
    1. Example: Did students learn how to multiply fractions *and* learn to dislike arithmetic?
    2. Example: Marie developed an interest in music theory because of her report on Beethoven's music.

Sometimes it is useful to obtain information from assignments which is completely unrelated to the goal of the assignment. Suppose, for example, you would like some information about how well your students *do* spell in a typical writing situation (as opposed to how well they can spell when given a spelling test). You could analyze the letters they write for Language Arts, the notes they take in history class, or the essay questions on their science exam. In each case you would count the number of misspelled words, obtaining a measure of typical rather than maximum performance. Giving an assignment for one purpose but analyzing it for another can give you information that will be valuable in making judgments about your students' typical behavior. Some examples of this kind of information are listed in the final part of this outline.

An Outline of Information Which Can Be Obtained from Projects and Assignments but Which is "Unrelated" to the Learning Outcome the Assignment Was Designed to Help the Students Reach

III. Information *unrelated* to the expected learning outcomes
   A. Communication skills
      1. Example: Penmanship.
      2. Example: Sentence structure and grammar.
   B. Interests
      1. Example: Johnny wrote five themes. Four of them were about baseball (the fifth, about football).
      2. Example: Peter did more extra credit assignments in social studies than in any other subject.
   C. Attitudes
      1. Example: An essay about the slavery at the time of the Civil War: Fargo, writing in the first person, revealed many of his own opinions.
      2. Example: Assignment in English—write a letter to a politician; analyze for topics discussed and positions taken on political issues.

EXERCISE 12.1

1. Why is it important for the teacher *as evaluator* to decide what the student is expected to learn from an assignment?
2. How is information about what the student is supposed to do in an assignment different from information about what he is expected to learn from it? How are these two related?

Determine What the Students Are to Do

No, this is *not* the same thing as determining what you want them to learn (or to be able to do). Here again, it is important to distinguish between learning activities and learning outcomes. The activities (e.g., projects and assignments) should be designed to *cause* the outcomes to occur, and therefore the activities should always be selected with the outcomes in mind. The question you must ask at this point is this: "What kind of assignment will help the students reach (or move toward the attainment of) the instructional goals which have been established *and will at the same time make it possible for me to obtain needed evaluative information?* We will discuss some of the major types of assignments, examining in each case (1) the kind of learning for which that type of assignment is best designed and, more importantly for evaluation purposes, (2) the kinds of information which can be obtained from an anlaysis of that type of assignment.

In Chapter 5 it was suggested that one useful way to categorize assignments is according to the stage of learning they are *primarily* designed to help the student with: acquisition, review (or retention), and transfer. Each of these will be discussed briefly. Keep in mind that this is not a book on instructional methodology. The kinds of assignments discussed here in no way represent a complete taxonomy of projects and assignments. Rather, the discussion here is designed to highlight some of the features of projects and assignments which are important when using these instruments for obtaining evaluative information.[2]

Acquisition assignments. Any assignment which is designed *primarily* to help students acquire new information or skills could be called an *acquisition assignment.* Many useful kinds of information can be gained from these assignments if they are carefully devised. Our ultimate goal for our students is that they will be able to transfer the information they learn to new situations. But, of course, there can be no transfer if the knowledge or skill is not acquired in the first place. There are three major questions acquisition assignments can help answer:

Three Questions Acquisition Assignments Can Help Us Answer

1. Did the students learn the knowledge or skill, i.e., did they reach the objective set for them?
2. How fast did the students acquire the knowledge or skills?
3. What kinds of errors did the student make during acquisition (and what misinformation did he acquire)?

When devising acquisition assignments to help you answer the above questions, you need to consider a number of problems which could cause your information to be in error. First of all, just because a student demonstrates to you that he has some information or has learned a skill, that does not necessarily mean he acquired that information or skill under your instruction and guidance. If you want to know what a student acquired during a six-week unit, for example, you

---

[2] *Projects* is a term sometimes used to denote long-range assignments (e.g., a term paper) or assignments involving the production of some object or display (e.g., a salt and flour map or a model of an African Bushman's village). The terms *project* and *assignments* are used somewhat interchangeably in this text. Both terms are used so that those who do distinguish between long-range and short-range assignments will realize that the concepts discussed here apply to both types.

need to know how much he knew *before* the unit began. Give a test or assignment prior to instruction to find this out.

A second problem arises when you try to find out how fast a student acquires learning. A rough estimate of acquisition rate is valuable as a predictor of how long it will probably take your students to reach particular kinds of objectives. However, it is very difficult to control the amount of time spent on an assignment. Even if all students work at the assignment at the same time (e.g., during class time), it is still difficult to tell who is actually working on the assignment the most number of minutes during a given time, such as a class period. This is not meant to discourage you from trying to get estimates of the amount of time spent on assignments; it is merely meant to help you to realize the potential source of error in this kind of information. Your estimates of acquisition rate will always be somewhat inaccurate. Nevertheless, data on the acquisition rate constitute important evaluative information. There is an important relationship between acquisition and retention which makes information on the acquisition rate particularly valuable. The longer it takes to acquire new knowledge or skill, the more practice and review it will take, *after it has been acquired,* to make certain that it will be retained.

Review assignments. Has the student acquired the information? If so, he will now need to review that material in order to be certain he retains it for longer than a day. Assignments designed to help the student review and practice can make the difference between students who take the newly gained knowledge and skills with them and those who forget that knowledge and skill. Periodic review assignments allow you to find out, at various times after acquisition, how much is being retained. Also, you will be able to obtain an estimate of how much review particular students need. The actual amount of review time needed is difficult to determine. However, by making norm-referenced judgments, you can find out which students are likely to need more review than others.

Another value of review assignments is that they can help you to spot unexpected learning outcomes early. Sometimes students pick up misinformation and bad habits when reviewing and practicing. Analyzing the students' review assignments will help you to notice these unexpected outcomes. If a student is going to be able to transfer information or skill to a new situation successfully, he must have learned that information or skill correctly in the first place.

It is important that you devise your review assignments so that the process the student uses to review is evident. For example, in math, make him show his work; in English composition, ask for outlines, notes, bibliography, etc.

Transfer assignments. Transfer assignments should provide the student with a *wide variety* of situations where he can try out his newly learned knowledge and skills. Carefully select the kinds of transfer situations you provide in these assignments so that you will be able to find out what a student can transfer and what he cannot transfer. By varying the conditions under which transfer is required you can find out under what conditions transfer of particular knowledge or skills does occur and under which conditions it does not occur.

Always give a review assignment just prior to a transfer assignment. You need to know what information and skills the student has retained before you can judge which ones transfer and which do not. If information has been forgotten, it obviously will not transfer to a new situation.

Determine How the Students Are to Communicate the Results

The nature of the students' response to an assignment determines to a large extent the kind of analysis that can be made and the kind of information the analysis will yield. Furthermore, it also determines the types of judgments and decisions that can be made with the information thus obtained. There are three important facets of the students' response to an assignment: the mode of the response, the length of the response, and the relative freedom to respond.

The mode of response. Should the results of a given assignment be communicated orally or in writing? Perhaps a performance (acting, singing, dancing, etc.) is more appropriate than the production of some object (e.g., a map, a drawing, a piece of sculpture). There are two criteria you should use to determine whether a given mode is appropriate. First of all, the mode used should be in agreement with the expected learning outcome—the objective of the assignment. For example, if you want the student to be able to write out the answers to the multiplication tables, then the assignment should call for that and not for just an oral recitation of them. Secondly, the mode of response called for should allow you to make the kind of analysis you wish to make. More detailed analyses can be made of products (samples of written work, sculptured objects, maps) than of performances (singing, acting, speaking). Products can be examined again and again, whereas performances occur and are finished.[3] Verbal performances (e.g., speeches) and verbal products (e.g., a prose passage) can be analyzed successfully with content analysis procedures. Observational techniques can be used to analyze nonverbal performances (e.g., dances) and nonverbal products (e.g., oil paintings).

The length of the response. The longer the response (i.e., the more work the student produces), the more likely you will have enough information to make a meaningful analysis. As you increase the amount of information you have on a student, you will *tend* to increase the reliability and validity of that information. You will remember from the discussion in Chapter 2 that this relationship between length and reliability and validity is dependent upon two important conditions: consistency and adequate sampling.

If you plan on analyzing an assignment (or series of them), it is important that the activities the student is involved in consistently call for the same type of response throughout. You must be certain that the characteristic you want information about (e.g., ability to solve particular types of problems) is in fact the characteristic you are getting information about—*throughout the entire assignment or set of assignments.* When attempting to lengthen an assignment, it is easy to add tasks which do not really call for the same skill the other tasks are

---

[3] Performances can be taped on audiotape or videotape and more detailed analyses can then be made. However, this is not always practical.

calling for. This must be avoided if any analysis of assignments is to be meaning-ful.

Equally as important as consistency is adequate sampling. For any given skill there may be several subskills. If you are to obtain a complete picture of a student's skill in a given area, you must be sure to get information about all the important subskills. Consequently, as you increase the length of an assignment (or instruct the student to make his response longer) be certain that the added length does not give you more information about *one* subskill or *one* aspect of a given behavior than it does about the others.

The relative freedom to respond. The amount of freedom the student is allowed when completing an assignment is an important variable in the analysis of that assignment. The effect of restricting student responses is to restrict the type of information you can obtain *and* the type of judgments you can make with that information.

Formulate the Instructions

All your good planning for well-designed experiments will be to no avail if your instructions to the students are unclear or inadequate. A good set of in-structions should very clearly specify what is to be done, how, and why.

Instructions for projects and assignments should include

1. A statement of what is to be learned.
2. A description of what is to be done (including any special instructions or limitations).
3. A statement of how the outcome of the assignment will be treated (i.e., how scored and what judgments and decisions will be made).

The learning outcome. Tell the student what he is supposed to learn. Why keep the expected outcome of an assignment secret? All too frequently, students set about to complete assignments without any real understanding of what they are supposed to learn from the experience. Notice, again, the distinction between the activity and the outcome. The student may know that he is supposed to com-plete a ten-page report on the new African nations (the learning activity) but have no idea about why he is to do the report (i.e., what he is to learn from doing it). Too often the students perceive assignments as things to be done "because the teacher wants them to be done."

At least two benefits accrue from telling the student what an assignment is supposed to help him learn. First of all, the student is more likely to want to do the assignment. The frequent cry, "Why do we have to do this stuff anyway?" might better be answered with a statement of an immediate, expected learning outcome than with a promise of future utility in the workaday world. The value of most assignments can be much more easily defended (and understood) in terms of what is to be learned than in terms of how that learning might serve some future purpose.

A second benefit of telling students what they are expected to learn is the fact that the students can more readily learn to evaluate their own progress. If a student understands what he is supposed to be learning from some assignment, he can more readily assess his own progress.

Student *A* is told to do all the problems on page 17 of his math book. He sees the pattern of responses being called for ("all these story problems are addition") and completes the assignment quickly, adding all the numbers in each problem. His assessment of his progress: "Finished very quickly, problems were easy, I know how to do these kinds of problems." On a subsequent test which includes several kinds of story problems, student *A* does very poorly. He is confused, frustrated, and angry at the teacher for making a "poor" test.

Student *B* is told that the story problems on page 17 are supposed to help him practice the procedures for analyzing a story problem and arriving at a solution. This practice is supposed to help him remember the procedures when he has to do this kind of problem again (e.g., on a test). He works out each problem conscious of the procedures he is following, trying to see how each problem calls for a specific use of a general rule. His assessment of his progress: "I know what process to use and it works for all the problems except no. 9. I can get the right answer but I don't see *why* it is the right answer. I'm not finished until I find out why." He goes to the teacher for help, learns how the general rule is to be applied in problems like no. 9, and then decides he is finished. On a subsequent test which includes several kinds of story problems, student *B* does very well. He is confident, happy, and eager to learn more math.

Unfortunately, student *A* is all too real and student *B* is merely a figment of this author's imagination. However, if we ever expect students to act more like student *B,* we must tell them what they are supposed to learn from the assignments we are having them do. The best way to do this is to phrase the outcomes in observable terms.

The learning activity.   Tell the student what he is supposed to do. Earlier,

---

Example of a Well-phrased Assignment

This writing assignment is supposed to help you learn to

1. Formulate well-constructed topic sentences
2. Write several statements supporting a topic sentence etc.

Do the problems on page 10. They will give you practice in using the addition facts to solve problems. This should also help you to remember these addition facts for later use.

you were urged to determine for any given assignment what it is you want the student(s) to do. Now you must communicate that to the students through the instructions you give them. In these instructions you must tell them what steps they must take and what the finished performance or product is to be like. Is there a due date? Are there any restrictions on the way the results are communicated — e.g., could a report be put on cassette tape rather than on typing paper? Is there any length restriction? Can the student solicit help? Are there any special sources that should be consulted? These and similar questions should all be answered in the instructions to the student.

The use of the results. Tell the student *how* you plan on using the results of an assignment. Do you plan on grading the assignment? Will the grade count toward the semester grade? Will you use the results to decide what assignment(s) to make next? What will you be looking for in the completed assignment? Are the results to be used to *help* the student or to *label* him? How will you judge a student's work? Will you compare it to that of his peers? Or will some other criterion be used? Will you compare a student's results with his own past performance? Whatever the use that will be made of the results of an assignment, the student has a right to know about it. Furthermore, if he sees some value in the intended use, he would be more likely to do his best to satisfactorily complete the assignment. This part of the instructions should be very carefully worded so as to be easily understood by *everyone* in the class. If a student makes errors on an assignment, we want to be certain that it is because he cannot do the work and not that he simply did not understand what was expected to him.

Establish Rules (and Rationale) for the Analysis to Be Made

In this last step in the development of assignments you must determine what kind of analysis you plan to make and why. The first thing to be decided is whether you will use observation or content analysis as your major information-gathering tool. Observation is particularly valuable for analyzing performances and nonverbal products. Content analysis is most useful for analyzing verbal communications (both oral and written). These decisions must be made before you give the assignment so that when the assignment is completed, you will know what to do with the results.

It is important to establish both the *rules* for analyzing an assignment *and* the *rationale* for doing so. The rationale should be nothing more or less than a statement of the judgments and decisions to be made with the information to be obtained from the analysis. Figure 12.2 is a facsimile of an assignment sheet designed for fourth graders. The teacher has written the following notes on his copy: instructions to be read to the students, a note on how the papers will be analyzed, and an indication of how the results will be used.

Notice that the instructions to the students tell why the assignment is being given, what the student is supposed to do, and how the teacher will use the results. The notes which follow the instructions will simply serve as guidelines for the teacher as he begins to analyze the papers that come in.

Name_____ Date_____

Write five sentences about things that happened
at school today. In each sentence draw a line
between the subject and the predicate.

Example:
Some of the boys│played touch football.

Instructions

We have been learning about the two main parts of a sentence:
the subject and the predicate. Now, I want you to write five sentences
about things that happened at school today. Make sure each sentence
you write has a subject and a predicate. After you have written
each sentence, draw a line between the subject and the predicate.
Use a different subject and a different predicate for each sentence
you write. Look at the example on your paper.

This assignment will help you to remember the two main parts
of a sentence. It will also give you practice in writing interesting
sentences. I will check your work carefully to make sure that
everyone writes good sentences and divides them correctly into
subject and predicate. If you do well, I'll know that you
understand how a sentence is divided into two main parts and we
can go on to find out how the predicate can also be divided into
parts. If anyone has trouble, I'll give you some extra help so that
you will understand how a sentence is divided before we talk about
how a predicate is divided.

The papers will be checked for the following:

____ incomplete sentences (missing subject or missing predicate)

____ incorrect division

____ between parts of noun phrase in the subject

____ between parts of the noun phrase in the predicate

____ between the main verb and the predicate noun phrase

Use of Results

No grades will be given - just encouraging remarks.
Errors will be noted in my own records and corrective
measures taken through individual or small group
instruction, further assignments, etc.

FIGURE 12.2. A writing assignment for fourth grade. Teacher's copy, upon which she has written
the instructions she plans to read to the students.

SUMMARY

1. There is no better source of information about student learning than the learning activities themselves.
2. Assignments designed to provide the teacher with useful evaluative information should: (*a*) engage the student at some stage in the attainment of specific instructional goals; (*b*) include complete instructions, clearly presented; (*c*) be reasonable; and (*d*) result in a performance or product which could be readily analyzed.
3. The following suggestions should help you to select or design projects and assignments which will be useful for obtaining evaluative information: (*a*) decide what the student is supposed to learn from the experience, (*b*) decide what information you wish to obtain about the student, (*c*) determine what the students are to do, (*d*) determine how the students are to communicate the results of what they have done, (*e*) formulate instructions to the students, and (*f*) establish the rules and the rationale for the analyses to be made.
4. The kind of learning, the level of learning, and the stage of the learning process are all important factors for determining what to have the student do. They also determine to some extent the kind of information you will be able to obtain about the learning outcomes.
5. Both expected and unexpected learning outcomes can be measured through the use of well-planned assignments. Sometimes it is also useful to obtain information which is not directly related to the expected learning outcomes.
6. A useful way to categorize assignments is the following: (*a*) acquisition assignments, (*b*) review assignments, and (*c*) transfer assignments. These categories emphasize the stage of learning the student is in at the time and help the teacher to find out at which stage the students are having trouble.
7. The mode of the response, the length of the response, and the freedom to respond should all be considered when deciding how to have the students communicate the results of their work.
8. Instructions for projects and assignments should include (*a*) a statement of what is to be learned, (*b*) a description of what is to be done, and (*c*) a statement of how the outcome of the assignment will be treated.

References

Gagné, Robert M.: *Conditions of Learning*, 2d ed., Holt, Rinehart and Winston, Inc., New York, 1970.

Travers, Robert M. W.: *Essentials of Learning*, 3d ed., The Macmillan Company, New York, 1973.

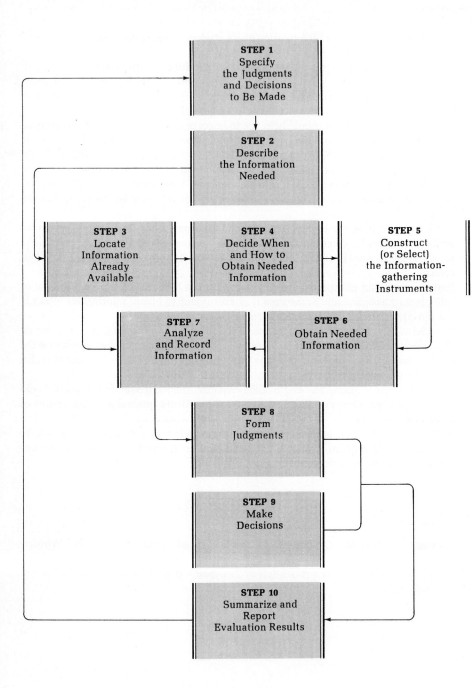

STEP 1
Specify
the Judgments
and Decisions
to Be Made

STEP 2
Describe
the Information
Needed

STEP 3
Locate
Information
Already
Available

STEP 4
Decide When
and How to
Obtain Needed
Information

STEP 5
Construct
(or Select)
the Information-
gathering
Instruments

STEP 7
Analyze
and Record
Information

STEP 6
Obtain Needed
Information

STEP 8
Form
Judgments

STEP 9
Make
Decisions

STEP 10
Summarize and
Report
Evaluation Results

CHAPTER 13

Constructing Teacher-made Tests

The procedures for constructing teacher-made tests are nothing more than specific instances of the general guidelines for constructing any teacher-made instrument (see Chapter 5). You will be able to produce high-quality tests if you follow the suggestions made in this chapter *and* if you strive to improve your tests by learning from your errors. The last section of this chapter will be particularly helpful because it provides you with techniques for evaluating and improving your tests.

In the first part of this chapter, the steps to take are presented. From start to finish, what do you do to produce a good test? This first section tells you. There are many types of items that can be used in teacher-made tests. Consequently, the item-writing step of test construction is enlarged upon in the second part of this chapter. There, step-by-step procedures are outlined for each type of item.

337

The information in the three parts of this chapter has been written to help you learn to

1. Determine what format to use for a given teacher-made test.
2. Write the items to be used in that test.
3. Write the necessary instructions to the students who will be taking the test.
4. Assemble the test.
5. Evaluate the test and its results.

Although there may be some slight differences in the way one constructs various kinds of test items, there are some general procedures which are useful no matter what type of test item(s) you plan on using. Before you begin to develop a teacher-made test, the steps in the preparation stage of evaluation should have been carried out. In other words, before you make plans for the construction of a *specific* test, you will have already identified the judgments and decisions you anticipate making. Furthermore, you will also have described the information needed. It is particularly important that a table of specifications has been developed or an achievement continuum has been constructed. Once you have completed this, you are then ready for the first step in developing a test: determining the format of the test.

DETERMINE THE TEST FORMAT

There are five questions that a teacher must answer at this point in test development:

1. What types of items should be used?
2. How many items should be used?
3. How difficult should the items be?
4. How should the items be presented?
5. How should the students respond?

What Types of Items Should Be Used?

A test is constructed from a number of items (questions or problems). It may contain all items of one type or a combination of item types. It is perfectly legitimate to use more than one type of item in a single test. How these items should be arranged and combined together to make a test which is easy to use will be discussed later.

There are numerous ways to categorize test items. The most popular classification scheme categorizes test items along two dimensions, the first according to the method of scoring and the second according to the freedom allowed in the students' responses.

Those tests which are scored objectively are called *objective test items* and those items which call for more subjective scoring techniques are called *subjective items.* For example, the true-false item is classified as an objective item because the answer is scored correct or incorrect according to the way the item has been keyed. If the teacher has decided that an item is true, then there is no room for subjectivity in the scoring. If the student has scored it true, he gets it correct; if he scores it false, he gets it incorrect. The essay test is the most common example of the subjectively scored item. In scoring an essay test, the teacher must make numerous subjective decisions about how close a student's answer is to some ideal answer; consequently the scoring is quite subjective.

A second way to categorize test items is according to the freedom that is allowed the student when making his response. Among the objective-type items, two types are usually identified: (1) selection items and (2) supply items. A selection item allows the student to select, from among some number of alternatives, the correct response. In supply-type items, on the other hand, the student must supply the correct response. Examples of the first type are the true-false, the multiple-choice, and the matching questions. The objective supply-type items are the fill-the-blank and the short-answer questions. The subjective essay items can also be classified along this dimension. Ahman and Glock (1971), for example, distinguish between a restricted-response essay item and an extended-response essay item.

The type of test item to be used is determined by four factors:

1. The level (and kind) of learning outcomes being measured
2. The way in which the results of the test will be used
3. The characteristics of the students taking the test
4. The time available for constructing, administering and scoring the test

As each of the types of test items is introduced, these four factors will be briefly considered. You will gain a fuller understanding of the similarities and differences among item types when you read the second section of this chapter (on how to construct specific types of items).

Matching. The matching item is best suited for obtaining information about a person's knowledge of facts. In particular, this type of item measures the ability of the student to associate two bits of information (e.g., a name and a date, a place and an event, a cause and an effect, a term and its definition). This type of item can be used successfully even with very young children. The only response the student needs to make is to draw a line between the matching terms or concepts. Matching exercises are easy to administer and score.

Examples of Matching Items

Select the terms on the left which match those on the right. You may use the terms on the right more than once.

1. True-false
2. Matching
3. Restricted essay
4. Extended answer
5. Short answer
6. Multiple choice

a. Objective, supply
b. Objective, selection
c. Subjective, restricted response
d. Subjective, extended response

Alternative response. The most common type of alternative-response item is the true-false item. A statement is made and the student must decide whether it is true or false. This kind of test item is best suited for obtaining information about simple learning outcomes. When direct recognition of true or false statements taken from the material which has been learned is used, we are measuring the lowest level of knowledge. However, true-false and other alternative-response questions can be used to obtain information at the understanding or application level fairly readily. For example, a person who understands concepts such as freedom or integrity or number sets would be able to identify examples and distinguish them from nonexamples. These types of items are more difficult to construct than it would seem, but when well-constructed, they can be used with almost any age group. These items are easy to administer and score.

Examples of Alternative-Response Items

1. True-false items are alternative-response items.
   a. True
   b. False
2. The gingerbread man finally got caught.
   a. Yes
   b. No
3. For each of the following pictures of interior design, decide whether or not it is an exemplar of contemporary design features. . . .

Multiple-choice items. The multiple-choice item is probably the most versatile item of the objective type. It can be used to obtain learning outcomes at almost any level, from the simplest to the most complex. However, if recall is an important factor, then multiple-choice is not appropriate. Furthermore, some upper levels of learning cannot be measured effectively by multiple-choice items (e.g., ability to organize data and ability to demonstrate a creative solution to a problem). Except for these few exceptions, multiple-choice items can measure almost any kind of cognitive learning outcome. Notice the variety in the examples given below.

Examples of Multiple-Choice Items

KNOWLEDGE LEVEL

1. Which one of the following types of items is usually considered a *subjective* item?
   a. True or false
   b. Essay
   c. Multiple choice
   d. Matching

ANALYSIS LEVEL

2. What part of speech is the underlined word in the following sentence? John *eagerly* played ball.
   a. Noun
   b. Verb
   c. Adjective
   d. Adverb

EVALUATION LEVEL

3. Which of the sketches drawn on the chalkboard portrays the best informal balance?
   a. Sketch 1
   b. Sketch 2
   c. Sketch 5
   d. Sketch 6

Good multiple-choice items are somewhat difficult to write, but they are well worth the effort. They tend to be very reliable, are easily administered, and can be quickly scored. If used with young children, this type of item should be kept short and simple.

Fill the blank.   The fill-the-blank item is a fairly common item used by classroom teachers. A statement is made and a word or phrase is left out and replaced with a blank or question mark. The student is then asked to fill in the blank with the appropriate word or phrase. This kind of item is an effective way to get at learning at the lower levels and measure fairly well the recall of specific facts. It is difficult to obtain understanding, application, analysis, and other upper-level, complex learning outcomes with this type of item. It is easily constructed, but if care is not taken, it can become difficult to score.

Examples of Fill-the-Blank Items

1. The Korean War began officially in the year ———————.
2. The first President of the United States was George ———————.

Short answer.   The short answer is very similar to the fill-the-blank item. It might be treated as a transition between the fill-the-blank item and the restricted-response essay item. In this kind of item a simple question is posed and the student is asked to supply a short answer (usually a phrase of one or two sentences). Like the fill-the-blank item it is restricted to the lower levels of learning, is fairly easy to construct, but can become a problem in scoring.

Examples of Short-Answer Items

1. What was the weather like when Jodi and Sue began their flight in their light plane?

————————————————————————

————————————————————————

2. Cite two ways in which test items can be classified.

————————————————————————

————————————————————————

Restricted-response essay.   The restricted-response essay does allow the student to show how much information he can recall from memory, but because the response is quite severely restricted, it is not very suitable for measuring such learning outcomes as those called for by creative problem solving, the development of an argument, or the defense of a position. The restricted-response essay is much more adapted to the recall of facts, the listing of events which occur, or the recall of steps to be taken in a certain procedure. This kind of item can be constructed fairly easily in a short time. If used with young children, an oral response mode should be used so that they are not penalized for a lack of writing skills.

An Example of a Restricted-Response Essay Question

List the ways in which installment loans differ from revolving charge accounts.

Extended-response essay. Extended-response essay items are very difficult to score objectively, but they do allow the student a great deal of latitude in his response. Consequently, creative skill, ability to organize and present original ideas, or the ability to defend a position or evaluate some product can be measured with this kind of item. Well-written extended-response essay questions are *not* easy to write.

An Example of an Extended-Response Essay Question

Suppose you are the manager of a large department store in a big city. Describe the kinds of optional credit plans you would offer your customers and discuss the economic repercussions of such options.

In reading the last few paragraphs, you should have noticed that the measurement of the lower-level learning outcomes is generally accomplished best through the use of the objective, selection-type items. As you move toward measuring the upper-level learning outcomes, it becomes necessary to use items which are a little more subjective and somewhat more difficult to construct and score. However, no matter what kind of item you use, it is extremely important that the item be well constructed and that it measure as directly as possible the learning outcome of interest.

How Many Items Should Be Used?

The number of items to be used is often determined by the amount of time available. In junior high and high school, the time is frequently limited to fifty-minute periods. However, if more than fifty minutes are needed, a test can usually be divided in half and each half can be given on a different day.

How many items can be answered in an hour? This question is very difficult to answer and requires some experience with the particular students involved as well as an understanding of the subject matter. Sometimes the rule of thumb "one multiple-choice item per minute" is used. But even this rule is subject to modification by the particular situation. If the students are slow readers, for example, then one item per minute is too many items. If the items are lengthy and require a great deal of thought, then this also may be too many items per unit of time. On the other hand, if the test includes many short, memory-type items, then one multiple-choice item per minute is an underestimate of the time it will take.

A most important factor related to the length of a test is the reliability of a test. The longer the test, the higher the reliability is likely to be. In the first stage of the evaluation process, you will have made some judgment about the importance of the decisions you anticipate making and about the accuracy of the information needed. Greater accuracy *tends* to come with greater length.

When making criterion-referenced judgments, you need to construct a test with enough items measuring each level of achievement as defined by the achievement continuum. In other words, not only must you be concerned about the total length of the test but also about the length of each part which measures the achievement of a different objective or level of achievement.

How difficult should the items be?   The major consideration in determining the difficulty level of a test is the kinds of judgments and decisions you plan on making. If you anticipate making selection decisions requiring norm-referenced judgments, the items should be at approximately the 50 percent level of difficulty. This means that about half of the students should get an item correct. Obviously, every item in the test will not be at exactly the 50 percent level of difficulty, but the average score for the test as a whole should be about 50 percent. When a test is at approximately the 50 percent level of difficulty, the scores spread out farther and allow you to make judgments about which student performed better than which other one. Notice that if the test is either too easy or too hard, the scores will tend to pile up at one end or the other of the continuum and it will not be possible to make distinctions among the performances of the many individuals whose scores will be identical or very close.

When criterion-referenced judgments are being made, the level of difficulty will vary according to the level of performance of the students and the amount of variation that exists among the students. If most of the students have reached a low level of performance, the test will appear to be easy. If most have reached a high level, it will appear to be difficult. If there is wide variation in the level of performance, the test will probably be at a moderate level of difficulty.

The test will probably appear to be easy when mastery judgments are being made because the majority of students are expected to perform at a high level of proficiency. When discrimination judgments are being made, a 50 percent level of difficulty would again be anticipated.

It should be noted that the difficulty of the test item is determined *only in part* by the level of performance that the student has reached. If the student does not know the materials well, the items will probably be difficult, and if the student does know the material well, the items will likely be easy. However, the difficulty of an item is also determined by how that item is written. A person who is very familiar with a given subject matter can write an item so difficult that most experts would get it wrong. He could also write an item covering the same material that would be so easy that someone knowing very little about the material could get it correct. The difficulty of an item can be manipulated by such things as the vocabulary used, the sentence structure used, and—in the case of multiple-choice items—the plausibility of the distractors (the alternatives which are not correct).

Probably the best approach to writing items is to try to measure as directly as possible each learning outcome. If you need to make a test more difficult (e.g., so you can make discrimination judgments), manipulate the difficulty by writing items over more complex learning outcomes. Do *not* manipulate the difficulty by using unnecessarily difficult vocabulary or sentence structure.

How Should the Items Be Presented?

Objective test items are usually presented in booklet form (typed and dupli-cated). Essay items can be duplicated or, in some cases, written on the black-board. However, test items can be presented orally as well as in written form.

Oral presentation is useful when the students are poor readers or have physical handicaps which make it difficult for them to read items from a booklet. Sometimes a tape recording or a record might serve as the stimulus for questions when a printed presentation would not be possible.

Test items are usually presented to an entire group of individuals at the same time. However, sometimes it is desirable to present a test individually (to one individual at a time). For example, by presenting the test to one student at a time, the teacher can get some idea about the process the student is using to answer the questions. This can be valuable information in subject matter areas requiring analytical skills, problem-solving skills, or the skillful use of logic and inquiry.

Most tests are given in the classroom, with books closed, and are carefully timed. Again, there may be times when the teacher will wish to break from the normal pattern and give a take-home test or an open-book test. Often, speed is not an important factor in the learning outcomes being measured. When this is the case, there is no need to time the test.

How Should the Students Respond?

Objective tests can be scored more easily if students respond on separate answer sheets. However, if this is not practical (students are too young or are handicapped), then other arrangements can be made.

Essay questions are usually responded to in writing, but an oral response can be valuable because a student can produce a much longer response in a shorter time. If the response is put on tape, it can be scored later. Of course, an oral response is more difficult to grade than a written one. Nevertheless, that disadvantage is somewhat overruled by the fact that you can get a lot of informa-tion in a short time and you can get that information from subjects whose writing skills are weak.

You can use virtually any test format which meets the needs of the situation as long as it also meets the following criteria:

Criteria for a Good Test Format

1. The students must be able to understand the questions.
2. The students must have time to think of the answer.
3. The students must have time to make an appropriate response.
4. The students must be capable of making the response called for (e.g., writ-ing out an answer)—though not necessarily the correct one.

EXERCISE 13.1

These multiple-choice questions are designed to help you test your understanding of the concepts presented so far in this section. Try to answer each one without looking back at the material.

1. You are trying to measure the *recognition* of many facts in as short a time as possible. You should probably use
    a. True-false items
    b. Fill-the-blank items
    c. Restricted essay items
2. "To match the names of authors with the poems they wrote." This objective should be measured with
    a. True-false
    b. Multiple-choice
    c. Matching
    d. Essay
3. Margaret Kolward wishes to select the three students who know the most facts about World War II. Should she use an objective test or a subjective one?
    a. Objective
    b. Subjective
    c. It really does not matter.
4. A history teacher was trying to find out what process his students go through in order to relate past events to current events. He should probably use
    a. Multiple-choice items
    b. Matching items
    c. Restricted essay items
    d. Extended essay items
5. All Miss Zoogler's fifth graders did poorly on an arithmetic test. Why?
    a. The test items were poorly written.
    b. The students had not learned the material.
    c. The teacher did a poor job of teaching.
    d. Any of the above could explain why.

WRITE THE ITEMS

Many books, pamphlets, and articles have been written about item writing. A few of the exceptionally well-written works are referred to in the list of suggested readings at the end of this subsection. Some of the techniques for item writing are founded in research studies, but most of them are simply the recommendations of successful item writers.[1] Nevertheless, the dos and don'ts of writing

---

[1] See Chap. 5 for a list of characteristics of good item writers.

each of the various kinds of test items can serve as useful guidelines, and a teacher learning to write test items would do well to follow them closely.

However, item writing is *not* a matter of merely applying a series of rules, "doing the dos" and "avoiding the don'ts." Rather, it is an art which requires the item writer to exercise judgment in the use of certain technical skills.

Item writing is essentially a task of producing items specifically designed for a given test that is specifically written to get a particular kind of information. The planning stage in the test-construction process helps the item writer to get started in the right direction. During that initial stage, the kind of information is determined and the general type of item best suited to obtaining that information is specified. Most classroom tests are designed to measure learning outcomes, and so the descriptions of the information needed usually take the form of a content-by-behavior table of specifications or a list of instructional goals arranged as an achievement continuum. Given an instructional goal and the general item type best suited to measure the attainment of that goal, what do you do next?

You will recall from Chapter 4 that an instructional goal has two major elements: (1) subject matter content and (2) a behavioral response to be made to that content. The next step, then, is to write an item which deals with the right subject matter content and which calls for a response which cannot be made correctly *unless* the person does in fact possess the behavior or skill identified in the instructional goal.

Consider the following instructional goal taken from the examples used in Chapter 4: "The third grade pupils should be able to write a personal letter, correctly placing the heading, greeting, body, closing, and the signature."

This instructional goal very explicitly states both the content and the expected behavior. The way to test this goal is to have the students write a letter and then check to see if they have correctly placed each of the parts of the letter. Notice that many kinds of test items could be written to measure the *general content* of this objective (i.e., the parts of a personal letter. . .). However, the student behavior called for is *correctly placing the parts when writing a personal letter.* Consequently, a test item asking the students to define the parts of a letter would be dealing with the correct subject matter content but would not be calling for the student behavior required in order to meet the instructional goal.

A well-written instructional goal usually specifies very clearly the expected behavior. This is why it is important when writing instructional goals to use verbs like *to write, to correctly place, to list, to describe, to draw, to identify,* etc. Our instructional goals are not always as explicit as this, however, and sometimes we must write items from a table of specifications, which also is usually less explicit. Suppose, for example, that one of the cells in a table of specifications for third grade simply calls for an understanding of the parts of a personal letter. A variety of different kinds of items could be written to measure this achievement. For example, a series of multiple-choice questions could be constructed in which definitions are given for each of the parts of the personal letter. The student is to select from among each definition the one which best defines the part described. If the item writer uses definitions which were not memorized in class, then the understanding level is being measured. If a student understands the concept of a heading, then he should be able to display that understanding by recognizing one which has incorrect content. The item writer might produce several examples of personal letter headings only one of which has the appropriate content, and he might then ask the student to select the one which is correct. This would be another way to measure the understanding of the parts of the personal letter.

So, a test item is supposed to obtain information about an individual's response to some defined content. Consequently, it should be designed so as to cause the individual being tested to make a particular kind of response—a response which, when examined, will provide the information needed about that individual. It would seem we have reached the logical end to the item-writing process when we have produced such an item. But that is not the case. The value of test scores lies not only in the kind of information they provide but also in the kinds of judgments and decisions which can be made with that information. The logic of item writing demands that test items be specifically designed so that particular kinds of judgments and decisions can be made.

Consider the following item taken from Gagné (1970, page 341).

Find the thickness of a pipe whose inner circumference is 9 pi and whose outer circumference is 21 pi.
(a) 12 pi
(b) 12
(c) 6 pi
(d) 6
(e) 3

This is a well-written item measuring the student's ability to solve a certain kind of geometric problem. The information obtained from the student's responses to problems of this kind can be very useful in making norm-referenced judgments. If we would like to know which students are most capable of solving these kinds of problems and which are least capable, then a test using this type of item would be appropriate. This item could probably be used effectively in a test given at the end of the semester for the purpose of making summative judgments. However, this would be a poor item to use when trying to determine how well the students are progressing toward the ultimate goals of learning how to solve various kinds of geometric problems. As Gagné has suggested, it is difficult to tell from this item exactly what the student is capable of doing. (In other words, this item would be of little value in making criterion-referenced judgments.) The reason for this is that the item is measuring two different principles at once. The first is the principle of relating circumference to diameter and the second is the rule that the outer diameter of a pipe equals the inner diameter plus twice the thickness of the pipe. If a student answers the item incorrectly, we do not know whether (1) he did not know the first principle, (2) he did not know the second principle, (3) he did not know either principle, or (4) he knew both principles but was unable to put them together to solve the problem. In order to make criterion-referenced judgments about the person's understanding of and ability to use each of the principles called for in the above item, separate items should be written measuring each principle and its use. These items used in conjunction with the above item would give you the information needed to make judgments about which particular skills the student had learned and which he had not. These kinds of criterion-referenced judgments are obviously extremely important in helping the teacher to make instructional decisions. If he knows exactly which concepts, which rules, and which bits of information a student knows and which he does not, the teacher can then plan the instructional activities accordingly. For instance, he can decide upon what assignment to give the student and what kinds of teaching activities he should engage in to help the student learn the things he has not yet learned. This is why the construction of an achievement continuum (see Chapter 4) is such an important prerequisite to the production of criterion-referenced tests. An achievement continuum will specify *all* the specific behaviors which are important to the proficient execution of some terminal behavior. By writing a few items for each specific behavior, the teacher will be able to get the information he needs to judge the level of achievement his students have reached.

WRITE THE INSTRUCTIONS

Writing the instructions to a test is simply a matter of answering this question: "What must a student know in order to correctly carry out the mechanics of taking a test?" Well-written instructions provide the student with the information he needs to take the test and they are clear, concise, and consistent.

The steps to writing good instructions were discussed in Chapter 5. You should follow those suggestions carefully. There are a few problems which frequently arise from poorly written *test* instructions. Suggestions for handling each of these problems are discussed briefly in the next few paragraphs.

Control the Reading Level of the Instructions

If instructions are to be clear to the students who must follow them, they need to be written at a reading/listening level which is commensurate with the students' ability. This means that you need to control the vocabulary level as well as the level of sentence complexity of the instructions. If you are teaching fifth grade, for example, the instructions you write should probably not be above third grade reading level. (If the *average* reading level of fifth graders is fifth grade, then many of the fifth graders will read below average—below a fifth grade level).

Provide Sample Problems

Most standardized tests include sample problems which are designed to help clarify the task and to help the examiner determine whether or not the students understood the instructions. Teacher-made tests might profitably copy this procedure from standardized test producers. Of course, sample problems are a waste of valuable testing time if the task is one which is very familiar to the students or is very simple. But sample problems can greatly clarify instructions when the task is complex or when it is one the students are not familiar with. Sample problems should illustrate the task procedures but should pose questions which would be easily answered by anyone taking the test. If you can be reasonably certain that someone knows the answer but still gets the problem wrong, then you may be able to assume that he does not understand what he is expected to do.

ASSEMBLE THE TEST

Once you have the items written and the instructions clearly specified, you are ready to put the test together. The difficult part of test construction is over when you have reached this step. However, if a test is not reproduced in a clear, uncluttered format or if the items are not properly arranged, your test results may not be as valid and as reliable as they could have been.

Select the Items to Be Used

Item writing is a difficult task which requires time and effort. It is therefore usually best to write items well in advance and to write more items than you will need. By recording these items in some systematic fashion (e.g., writing each item on an index card) you will be able to select from among all the items you have written those which seem to give you an adequate sample of the objectives being measured. Occasionally you may also wish to use some items which have been written by others (e.g., those provided by the teacher's manual accompanying the textbook). Consequently, you should have some systematic way of evaluating the items and making your final selection of those to be used in any given test. Five questions should be asked about each item:

1. Is the item unambiguous and free from irrelevant clues which may give away the answer?
2. Is the item measuring an appropriate learning outcome as directly as possible?
3. Do the final items (as a group) provide an adequate, representative sample of the learning outcomes being measured by the test?
4. Is there any overlap of the items which would allow the student to obtain the answer to one item from information supplied in another item?

It is valuable for you as the teacher to examine each of the items, make your selection, and then arrange the items in the approximate order you anticipate using them. After this it would be helpful to give the items to a fellow teacher who might review them for you, using the same criteria that you used in your selection. In seeing the items while they are still on index cards, this fellow teacher will feel free to critique them and will feel less reluctant to suggest the elimination of any item.

Reason for the test: *In this section put down the judgments and/or decisions you will be making and some statement of the knowledge area being measured. Whenever possible attach to this form a list of objectives being measured or a table of specifications.*

Instructions to the reviewer: *In this section you merely make a brief statement indicating the procedures to be followed when critiquing the items (e.g., sort into three piles - good, acceptable, unacceptable), or "for each criterion" an item fails to meet, place a number above that item which corresponds to the number of the criterion as listed below.*

Criteria for judging <u>each</u> item:

   1. Measures a particular learning outcome (as specified by the list of objectives or the table of specifications)

   2. Unambiguous

   3. Free from clues which give the answer away

   4. Clear writing style

   5. Vocabulary and sentence structure simple enough for the grade level

FIGURE 13.1. Sample form for evaluating teacher-made test items.

In order for a fellow teacher to adequately critique your test items, he needs to know why you are giving the test, what kind of information you expect to get from the test, how that information is to be used, and what criteria you think are important for assessing the individual items. Consequently, it is useful to have a standard form which you can give the teacher and which you can also use. This form could contain a statement of the reason for the test, a set of instructions to be used, and a list of criteria against which each item can be checked. Figure 13.1 presents an example of one such form. Whether or not you use this exact form is not important. However, it is important to use some systematic approach to the evaluation of test items as well as the final listing of items so that you will get uniform judgments from those making the critique.

Another source of information about test items is previous item analysis data. This information would be available only on items which have been used before. If an item worked well before and the conditions have not changed dramatically, it should work well again. It is desirable, therefore, to use a good test item more than once, and good teachers often develop a "pool" of items. From this item pool a good test can be built. The rationale behind item analysis and the step-by-step procedures for conducting such an analysis will be discussed later.

Arrange the Items Logically

It is generally agreed that the items must be arranged in a logical order and not haphazardly. First of all, items of various types should be grouped together so that the student does not have to change his type of response from one item to the next. This means that you put all the true-false items together, all the multiple-choice items together, and all the essay questions together. It is usually appropriate to put the simpler item types such as true-false or short-answer first and the more complex items later.

A second rule of thumb for arranging items is to arrange them from easy to difficult. The rationale behind this is that by having the easy items at the beginning of the test, the students who have more trouble will not get discouraged so quickly and are more likely to maintain a positive attitude toward responding to the test. Another factor is that the slower students (if they work methodically from the first to the last question) may struggle with some complex questions they are unable to answer at the beginning of the test and may not ever get to easier questions which they could answer. This would unnecessarily penalize them, for they should at least have the time to finish those items which they do know.

Another useful way of arranging test items is according to the way the material was covered during instruction. All the items which deal with a given topic and concept could be grouped together, and then those measuring the next concepts studied are grouped, etc. This allows the students to think about the particular group of concepts and ideas that were studied at one time and are related.

One final way of arranging items in a test is according to the level of learning as defined by one of the taxonomic approaches we examined in Chapter 4. Suppose, for example, that for a given content area we had questions which asked for factual material that must be memorized, others which called for an understanding of concepts, and finally questions which dealt with the understanding of principles and the application of those principles to problem solving. Because these levels of learning seem to be hierarchical in nature, what will normally happen is that the student will answer correctly those questions at a certain level until he reaches a level beyond which he is incapable of responding. When this happens, you can tell what level of performance and sophistication the student has reached by simply looking at his score. This is a valuable way of arranging items in a criterion-referenced test. Results from this kind of test could be used to make formative judgments.

Finalize and Insert the Instructions

Before finalizing a test, you should double-check to make sure that the instructions are very clear. Having clearly written instructions, you should then place these instructions at the beginning of each section of the test when items are grouped according to item types.

Provide a Way for the Student to Respond

Having decided on the instructions for the students, you must now provide the students with a way to make the responses you have asked them to make. The objective tests are usually more efficiently handled with a separate answer sheet. Machine-scored answer sheets and printed answer sheets are available for standardized tests. Teacher-made tests can also utilize these kinds of answer sheets, and they can be very easily made by the teacher. In Figure 13.2 there is an example of one format which can easily be typed on a ditto master and run off. Notice that the answer sheet includes a space for the student's name as well as other relevant information. Next, there is provision for each item to be answered. This answer sheet was designed to be used with a test which included true-false and multiple-choice items. Sometimes the students are asked to respond with short-answer and essay items, and you may then want them to respond on the test booklet itself.

Determine the General Layout

If a test is jam-packed together on a page, typed in single spacing, and highly cluttered, it is difficult for the student to take. Tests should be typed neatly and should be spaced on the page so that the items are uncluttered. The responses in multiple-choice test items, for example, should be typed so that each choice begins on a new line.

Examples of Multiple-Choice Questions

Poor: The first President of the United States was
    (a) Abraham Lincoln *(b)* George Washington *(c)* Eleanor Roosevelt
    (d) Andrew Jackson

Improved: The first President of the United States was
    a. Abraham Lincoln
    b. George Washington
    c. Eleanor Roosevelt
    d. Andrew Jackson

Name _____ Date _____

Subject _____ Class period _____

	T	F					T	F			
	A	B	C	D	E		A	B	C	D	E
1.	0	0	0	0	0	11.	0	0	0	0	0
2.	0	0	0	0	0	12.	0	0	0	0	0
3.	0	0	0	0	0	13.	0	0	0	0	0
4.	0	0	0	0	0	14.	0	0	0	0	0
5.	0	0	0	0	0	15.	0	0	0	0	0
6.	0	0	0	0	0						
7.	0	0	0	0	0						
8.	0	0	0	0	0						
9.	0	0	0	0	0						
10.	0	0	0	0	0						

FIGURE 13.2. Example of a teacher-made answer sheet.

Provide Alternate Forms

One final consideration is that of alternate forms. If the students are sitting very close together in the same room so that it is difficult *not to cheat* and virtually impossible not to see the responses on a neighbor's answer sheet, then it is usually wise to use alternate forms of a test. Probably one of the best ways to devise these alternate forms is to make slight rearrangements of the order in which the items are presented. If you are using an easy-to-hard item arrangement, you can take the first couple of easy items, change them around, and do this on down so that the items are not arranged exactly the same but that they do follow the same general easy-to-hard sequence. If you have items of different types, you might consider the possibility of starting one group with multiple-choice items and the next group with true-false items, etc. It is usually not valuable to reverse the order of the items, however, as this will put the more complex types of items first and the simplest types of items last. This is normally an undesirable arrangement.

Reproduce the Test

Whenever possible, tests should be typed and duplicated via a "ditto" or mimeograph process. If you do produce a test in handwriting, make certain it is legible. Always run off a few more copies than you need, so that if there are any unclear or smudged copies, you will not have to use them.

EXERCISE 13.2

Write brief answers to each of the following questions. Do not quote directly from the text; use your own words and examples.

1. What are the important characteristics of a good test item?
2. What are the major things which should be included in the instructions accompanying a test?
3. List four or five things which can happen if a test is not carefully assembled and reproduced.

HOW TO WRITE SPECIFIC TYPES OF ITEMS FOR TEACHER-MADE TESTS

MATCHING

The matching exercise simply presents two lists to the student and asks him to match each item from one list with an item from the other list.

Example of a Matching Exercise

Match the words in column *A* with the correct part of speech in column *B*. Some of the parts of speech must be used more than once.

A	*B*
1. the	*a.* Noun
2. house	*b.* Adjective
3. tall	*c.* Determiner
4. John	*d.* Adverb
5. an	
6. quickly	
7. boat	

The items in column *A* are typically called *premises* and those in column *B* are called *responses*. A single premise and its correct response could be considered a test item (each correctly paired premise and response usually counts as one raw score point). Notice, however, that a single item is of no value by itself. There must be a number of items which are similar in certain ways, so that the student is forced to discriminate among the various premises and responses in his attempt to form the correct pairings.

In a well-designed matching exercise, the same kind of relationship holds for each of the premises and responses in the exercise. For example, all pairs might be characterized by the relationship between a term and its definitions.

Example of a Matching Exercise Testing the Ability to Match Terms and Definitions

For each term in column *A*, select the statement in column *B* which best defines it. Record your choice on the line preceding the question number. There are more definitions than you will need. Do not use any definition more than once.

A	*B*
_____ 1. split-half reliability	*a.* An estimate of the degree of correlation between alternate forms of a test.
_____ 2. coefficient of stability	*b.* An estimate of the relationship between two measures of the same person
_____ 3. coefficient of equivalence	*c.* A measure of the internal consistency of test results
_____ 4. concurrent validity	*d.* An estimate of the correlation between the results of two different measures obtained at approximately the same time
_____ 5. predictive validity	*e.* An estimate of the correlation between the results of some measure and the results of some criterion measure obtained at a later date
	f. An estimate of how well a hypothetical construct is measured
	g. An estimate of the correlation between the results of two administrations of the same test given at different times

---

Other kinds of relationships which could be measured with a matching exercise are

Cause and effect (nicotine in the blood — contraction of the blood vessels)

Inventor and invention (Edison — the incandescent bulb)

Author and work (Jane Austen — *Pride and Prejudice*)

Event and its date (signing the Declaration of Independence — 1776)

Object and its function (pulley — lifting weights)

Problems and solutions (reduce the boiling point of water — create a partial vacuum)

Symptoms and ailment (cough, congested nasal passages — common cold)

Examples and categories (horse — noun)

A common criticism of the matching exercise is that it can be used to measure only simple learning outcomes (e.g., the memorization of names and dates). However, a careful look at the above list should convince you that this is not true. If, for example, the problems and solutions presented to the student are different from those they studied, you could get a measure of the student's problem-solving ability. Or suppose you wish to test the student's understanding of a classification scheme. The premises could be classified objects, and the responses could be the names of the categories in the classification scheme.

Perhaps the biggest drawback to the matching exercise is the fact that during the construction of such an exercise it is easy to deviate from the table of specifications or the instructional goals you are trying to measure. Suppose, for example, you are trying to find out if the students know the dates of the really significant events in the scientific revolution. If the list is fairly short, you may find it necessary to add items covering less significant events. This could result in an exercise which would be measuring the memorization of events *not* included in your original test plan.

Steps to Take When Constructing a Matching Exercise

The steps to take when constructing a matching exercise follow closely the general rules for constructing test items which were discussed earlier.

A Preview of the Steps to Take When Constructing Matching Exercises

Step 1. Decide what is to be measured.

Step 2. List the premises and responses to be used.

Step 3. Add distracting responses (or premises).

Step 4. Arrange the items.

Step 5. Write the instructions.

Step 1: Decide what is to be measured. In this first step you must determine three things:

1. The content of the premises and responses
2. The kind of relationship which exists between them
3. The level of learning required to make the responses

These three things should be clear from the table of specifications or from the achievement continuum you are using to guide your evaluation procedures. Suppose, for example, we have constructed a table of specifications for a fifth grade English test like the one in Table 13.1.

A matching exercise could be constructed to measure any or all of the cells in this matrix. The premises could, for example, be patterns or statements of the transformation rules. The corresponding responses would then be examples of the parts of speech, examples of the basic sentence patterns, or sample sentences which would result from certain transformational rules. If the particular premise-response combinations included in a matching exercise are the same ones studied in class or used in the textbook, then the level of learning being called for is the memorization level. If, on the other hand, the responses present examples which are new to the students, then the application level would be measured.

Step 2: List the premises and responses to be used. Although this step is usually very simple (e.g., listing the important events and their dates), it is sometimes difficult to think up good premises and responses. This is especially true when you are trying to measure upper-level learning outcomes or complex relationships (e.g., the application of principles governing cause-and-effect relationships). If you do have trouble coming up with a good list of well-worded premises and responses, you might try the following procedure: First, write simple declarative statements which represent important examples of the kind of relationship you are trying to measure.

TABLE 13.1

Table of Specifications for a Fifth Grade English Test

	Memorization	Application	Totals
Parts of speech	10	20	30
Basic sentence patterns	15	25	40
Transformational rules	10	20	30
Totals	35	65	100

Examples of Declarative Statements

A penetrating finish applied to open-grain wood produces an open-pore, close-to-the-wood finish.

Boiled linseed oil applied to unfurnished wood tends to darken the finish.

Applying stain to wood can cause the grain to be deemphasized.

Applying a sealer coat "ties down" the stain and filler.

Next, break these statements into two parts (the subject and the predicate). These will become your premises and responses.

Examples of Statements Broken Down

SUBJECT	PREDICATE
A penetrating finish applied to open-grained wood	produces an open-pore, close-to-the-wood finish.
Boiled linseed oil applied to any un-finished wood	tends to darken the finish.
Applying stain to unfinished wood	can cause the grain to be deemphasized.
Applying a sealer coat	"ties down" the stain and filler.

The above subjects and predicates could be used as premises and responses, but they are more complex than they need to be. It is usually best to simplify the wording.

Examples of Premises and Responses

PREMISE	RESPONSES
Penetrating finish on open-grained wood	produces an open-pore finish.
Boiled linseed oil on any unfinished wood	tends to darken the finish.
Stain on unfinished wood	can deemphasize the grain.
A sealer coat	"ties down" the stain and filler.

Step 3: Add distracting responses (or premises). A good matching exercise should have *approximately* 50 percent more items in one column than in the other. This makes it more difficult to get items correct merely through a process of elimination. Usually the list of responses is made longer by adding distracting responses. For example, to the responses in the exercise on wood finishing, we might add these distractors:

> tends to lighten the finish.
>
> covers up blemishes.

Notice that neither of these responses matches the premises to be used, but they may *distract* someone who does not know the material well and cause him to produce a mismatch (thus demonstrating that he does *not* know the material well).

  Sometimes it is convenient to have fewer responses. This would be the case when a single response would match several premises. For example, the response *adverb* would be correct for the premises *quickly, increasingly,* or *very.* The response *noun* would match many premises (e.g., *house, car, dog*).

  It is usually best to keep the shortest list of items (either premises or responses) to no more than seven or eight and no fewer than four.

  Step 4: Arrange the items. Arrange the premises and responses in such a way that it will be fairly easy for the student to sort through the responses in search of a match. First of all, this means that if one set of terms is shorter, it *usually* should be placed in the response column. Furthermore, if there is any way to arrange the items within the response column so that it would be easier to scan them, they should be arranged that way (logically, chronologically, alphabetically, etc.). Finally, the column of premises should be arranged randomly.

  Step 5: Write the instructions. Each matching exercise must be accompanied by a set of instructions which clearly indicates the kind of relationship that exists between the premises and the responses. This provides the student with a basis for matching. If this basis for matching is not clearly specified, it could lead to ambiguity and confusion.

  Let us apply the procedures in steps 4 and 5 to the premises and responses we developed for the test on wood finishing. Our completed exercise should look something like this:

Examples of Test Instructions

Match each wood-finishing procedure in column 1 with the result from column II that it will most likely produce. A result may not be used more than once. There are more results than you need. Only one result should be used for each procedure. Place the letter of the result on the line next to the procedure which would most likely cause it.

I

_____1. Penetrating finish on open grained wood
_____2. Boiled linseed oil on any unfinished wood
_____3. Stain on unfinished wood
_____4. Sealer coat

II

a. "ties down" the stain and filler.
b. covers up blemishes.
c. tends to lighten the finish.
d. tends to darken the finish.
e. can deemphasize the grain.
f. produces an open-pore finish.

Key Points to Remember When Constructing Matching Exercises

Material in a given exercise must be homogenous.

The kind of relationship between the premises and the responses must be clearly defined.

Keep the lists of items brief (shorter list, seven or less).

There should be approximately 50 percent more items in one column (either more premises or more responses)

Although this is difficult, matching exercises *can* be constructed to measure upper levels of learning.

It is not necessary for you to remember all the steps to take when constructing a particular kind of test item. You can look them up and follow them as you work at it. However, it is a good idea to try to put to use what you have read as soon as possible. Consequently, you should try to work each exercise in this chapter as you come to it in your reading.

EXERCISE 13.3

Construct a matching exercise in some subject matter area you are familiar with. Follow the steps outlined above. When you have finished, subject it to the criticism of your instructor or your classmates and colleagues.

ALTERNATIVE RESPONSE

The alternative-response item confronts the test taker with two alternatives. A statement is made or some stimulus is presented (e.g., a picture or diagram) and it is to be judged as true or false, as an example or a nonexample, as a fact or an opinion. The true-false item is an alternative-response item which is used frequently by classroom teachers. There are at least two reasons for the popularity of true-false items: (1) they *seem* to be easily constructed and (2) they *seem* to be useful for obtaining a lot of information in a short time. If these reasons were well founded in fact, they would make the use of true-false items tempting indeed. However, really good true-false items are difficult to construct. It is hard to produce items which are clearly true or false. Furthermore, those statements which *are* clearly true or false are often either so easy most students would get them correct or so trivial they are not worth using.

The idea that a lot of information can be obtained in a short time with true-false items is also misleading. The true-false item is limited almost entirely to the lowest levels of learning, and therefore only a narrow range of subject matter can be effectively measured with this type of item. Furthermore, when you take into account the problem of guessing, the advantage of being able to ask many questions in a short time almost disappears. When there are only two alternatives, the student has a fifty-fifty chance of getting an item correct by chance alone. If he is a good test taker, he will be able to pick up clues to the answers in the way the items are phrased (it is difficult to construct true-false items which are free from clues that could give away the answer). This means that in order to get a fairly reliable measure despite this error due to guessing, a *very* large number of items must be used. *But*—it is extremely difficult in most subject matter areas to find large numbers of clearly true or clearly false items. Consequently, the probability of obtaining reliable measures of anything but the most simple learning outcomes is very slim.

Notice that it is *difficult* to make norm-referenced judgments with the results of alternative-response items because high reliability is needed, and that is difficult to achieve with this type of item. However, criterion-referenced judgments are *virtually impossible* to make with results from this type of item. Criterion-referenced judgments are made on the basis of responses to small groups of items. Each group measures a given behavior or given level of performance (usually a single behavioral objective). Guessing causes the results of any given item to be highly unreliable and therefore useless for making sound judgments. Suppose, for example, a high school shop teacher gives a test measuring the student's knowledge of the function of the various parts of the machines used in the shop. What can he tell from a student's responses? If a student gets the two or three true-false items about a given machine all correct, the teacher is not sure if he really knows the functions of that machine or if he made a couple of lucky guesses.

True-false and alternative-response items have very limited value because of the disadvantages cited above. However, there may be some few learning outcomes which seem most naturally and most directly measured with this type of item. When this is the case, go ahead and use this type of item, but follow the rules for constructing such items very carefully. You must make these items as reliable as possible.

Although an entire true-false test is rarely justified, it would seem reasonable to place a few items within a larger test. However, they should be carefully written to measure worthwhile learning outcomes.

Steps to Take When Constructing True-False Items

Ebel (1971) has ably defended the use of true-false items, and he offers some valuable suggestions for writing them. Ebel suggests that true-false items can be written in three steps:

Ebel's Three Steps to the Construction of True-False Items

Step 1. Direct attention to an important segment of knowledge.

Step 2. Select a worthwhile proposition to test.

Step 3. Convert the proposition into a test item.

Step 1: Direct your attention to an important segment of knowledge. By the time you have reached the test construction stage, you should have already determined what information is important for your students to know. The content dimension of a table of specifications should serve to direct you to a particular segment of knowledge. Ebel presents the following paragraph as an example of a potentially important segment of knowledge.[2]

Sample Segment of Knowledge

An eclipse occurs when the light from one astronomical body is partially or totally cut off by another. In a solar eclipse the moon blocks off the sunlight by coming directly between the earth and the sun. In a lunar eclipse, the earth's shadow falls across the moon, cutting off the sunlight ordinarily reflected from the moon's surface.

Step 2: Select a worthwhile proposition to test. According to Ebel, a proposition should have these three characteristics:

1. It should be essential to a command of the segment of knowledge being tested.
2. It should be defensible as being true.
3. It should be obviously true only to those who have a good grasp of the segment of knowledge being tested.

[2] This sample paragraph as well as the examples of propositions and true-false statements derived from it were taken from Robert L. Ebel, *Essentials of Educational Measurement,* © 1972, pp. 173–175. By permission of Prentice-Hall, Inc., Englewood Cliffs, N.J.

Ebel offers the following proposition as an example taken from the segment of knowledge quoted above:

Sample Proposition

An eclipse is caused by the shadow of one body in the solar system falling on another.

Step 3: Convert the proposition into a test item. The test item is essentially a restatement of the proposition. It can be a true version or a false version of the original proposition. In fact, Ebel suggests that true-false items be written in pairs (a true version and a false version of a proposition). The true version is a restatement of the proposition and the false version is a plausible-sounding contradiction of a true statement. He offers five suggestions for restating propositions. Below are the five suggestions, along with a true and a false version of the sample proposition quoted above.

Suggestion 1: Restate the Essential Idea in Different Words

TRUE VERSION	FALSE VERSION
When some of the light from a star like the sun to a planet like the earth is blocked by some other body like the moon, an eclipse is said to occur.	When light from a star like the sun is reflected from a planet like the earth onto some other body like the moon, an eclipse is said to occur.

Suggestion 2: Restate a Part of the Original Idea

TRUE VERSION	FALSE VERSION
All eclipses involve shadows.	If light rays could not be bent, eclipses could not occur.

Suggestion 3: Relate the Basic Idea to Some Other Idea

TRUE VERSION	FALSE VERSION
An eclipse of the moon can occur only when the moon is full.	An eclipse of the moon can occur only when the moon is new.

Suggestion 4: Develop Implications of the Basic Idea

TRUE VERSION	FALSE VERSION
Prediction of eclipses requires information on the orbital motions of the bodies involved.	Prediction of eclipses requires information on the inclination of the earth's axis.

Suggestion 5: Infer the Effect of Different (Even Impossible) Circumstances

TRUE VERSION	FALSE VERSION
If there were no luminous astronomical bodies like the sun, eclipses would not be observed.	Eclipses cannot occur in the presence of luminous stars.

Steps to Take When Constructing Other Alternative-Response Items

It is somewhat easier to construct other types of alternative-response items because false versions of the statements need not be contrived. If you follow the four steps discussed below, you should have little trouble producing usable alternative-response items.

Preview of Steps to Take When Constructing Alternative-Response Items

Step 1. Select an appropriate learning outcome.

Step 2. List examples representative of each alternative.

Step 3. Select the examples to be used.

Step 4. Write the instructions.

Step 1: Select an appropriate learning outcome. The learning outcomes best measured by this type of item are those which call for an ability to distinguish between two alternatives (e.g., fact or opinion; correct or incorrect) or to classify into one of two categories (e.g., long vowels and short vowels; transitive verbs and intransitive verbs). Examine the following examples of learning outcomes which could be efficiently measured with alternative-response items and try to think of similar outcomes in the subject area with which you are most familiar.

Examples of Learning Outcomes Which Can Be Measured with Alternative-Response Items

To distinguish between fact and opinion

To determine if a sentence (or short passage) is written in emotive or non-emotive language

To identify examples of carnivorous animals

To determine whether or not a musical scale has been properly executed

When given a sample of wood and a finishing procedure, to determine whether or not the procedure would be appropriate

When given data and conclusions drawn from the data, to decide if the conclusions are supported by the data or not

When given a syllogism, to determine whether or not the conclusion is justified

To distinguish between an objective that is behaviorally stated and one that is not

Notice that some of the examples are not verbal (e.g., musical scales). There are many learning outcomes of this type, and we should be willing to try to test them. It would not be too difficult, for example, to produce a recording of musical scales being played properly and improperly by different instruments. These could be played one at a time as the students judged them.

Step 2: List examples representative of each alternative.   Draw a line down the center of a single sheet of paper forming two columns, one for each of the alternative categories. Now label the categories and write down as many examples as you can think of which clearly represent each category.

Example

ACIDS	BASES
Storage battery liquid	Baking soda
Tomato juice	Lye
Orange juice	Ammonia
Grapefruit juice	Washing soda
Lemons	Lime water
Cabbage	Milk of magnesia
Alum	Borax
	Sodium hydroxide

Step 3: Select the examples to be used. Once you have listed as many examples as you can think of which clearly represent each of the alternative categories, you then need to select those to be used as test items. Go back over your lists and cross out any examples which are not suitable because they are too usual, too obvious, or for some reason not really representative of the category. If only a small number of examples remain, then select a representative sample of them to be used as test items. Use an approximately equal number of examples from each category.

Step 4: Write the instructions. The instructions for alternative-response items must contain two important bits of information:

1. The rationale for the alternative categories
2. Directions for indicating the answer

The rationale for the alternative categories serves as the basis upon which the students must make their selections. If this rationale is not clearly specified, ambiguity will result and the test will be highly unreliable.

Some sample instructions are provided below. Try to identify the two major pieces of information they provide for the student.

Sample Instructions for Alternative-Response Test Items

1. Below is a list of animals. If you think an animal is carnivorous, place a "c" on the line next to that animal. If you do not think it is carnivorous, place an "n" next to it.
2. For each of the following statements, decide whether or not it contains emotive language. If you think a statement does contain emotive language, write "yes" before that statement. If you think a statement does *not* contain emotive language, write "no" before that statement.
3. Fill in choice *a* on your answer sheet for each bird that you think migrates. For each bird that does not migrate, fill in choice *b* in the appropriate place on your answer sheet.

Some learning outcomes require the student to respond to a number of items in light of some "given." For example: when *given* a syllogism . . . , when given data . . . , when given a set of facts . . . , when given a map . . . , etc. When this is the case, you must produce the necessary given and then list examples representing the two alternatives of interest.

Example of Alternative-Response Exercise

Read the following paragraph, and for each underlined noun, decide whether it is functioning as a subject or an object. If you think a noun is functioning as a subject, place an "s" on the line in front of it. Place an "o" before each noun you think is functioning as an object.

The boys[1] in the back row began to cut up. They threw paper[2] wads at the girls and hid their textbooks[3] in the closet. The teacher[4] scolded the boys[5], but they continued to get into trouble. Soon the principal[6] came and gave the boys[7] a lecture[8]. They listened carefully. When he finished they decided not to get caught next time.

_____1. boys
_____2. paper wads
_____3. textbooks
_____4. teacher
_____5. boys
_____6. principal
_____7. boys
_____8. lecture

The sample exercise was designed to measure the following learning outcomes: When given a paragraph or two, you should be able to distinguish between the nouns functioning as subjects and those functioning as objects.

True-false and other alternative-response items are limited in the kinds of learning outcomes they can measure. The problems associated with these items usually occur when someone tries to measure learning outcomes which do not naturally lend themselves to a two-choice format. You can successfully use these kinds of items if you use them *only* when appropriate, if you follow the steps for construction outlined above, and if you heed the additional suggestions offered below.

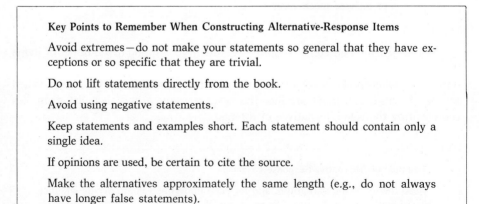

Key Points to Remember When Constructing Alternative-Response Items

Avoid extremes—do not make your statements so general that they have exceptions or so specific that they are trivial.

Do not lift statements directly from the book.

Avoid using negative statements.

Keep statements and examples short. Each statement should contain only a single idea.

If opinions are used, be certain to cite the source.

Make the alternatives approximately the same length (e.g., do not always have longer false statements).

EXERCISE 13.4

Select three or four of the learning outcomes used in the examples on page 366 and construct a true-false or other alternative-response item for each outcome you select. Have your work checked by your instructor or get together a small group of your classmates and critique each other's papers.

MULTIPLE CHOICE

The multiple-choice item consists of a stem, a correct alternative, and distracters (incorrect alternatives). The stem is designed to present a question or a problem as concisely as possible. The answer to the question posed in the stem is called *the correct alternative.* Other plausible but incorrect answers are called *distracters.*

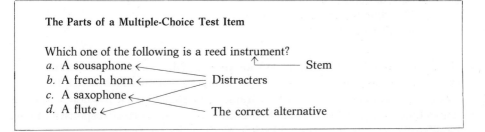

The Parts of a Multiple-Choice Test Item

Which one of the following is a reed instrument? — Stem
a. A sousaphone
b. A french horn — Distracters
c. A saxophone
d. A flute — The correct alternative

Well-written multiple-choice items can be used to measure a wide variety of learning outcomes. They are best suited for measuring at the understanding, application, and analysis levels of Bloom's taxonomy but can be used to measure outcomes at all the levels. To obtain objective, reliable information about the students' ability to apply information to a new situation is difficult. However, a teacher who has mastered the art of writing multiple-choice items has a much better chance of getting that information than one who has not. Multiple-choice items work best when each part of the item is designed carefully to do the job it was intended to do.

The Stem

The stem of the multiple-choice item presents the question or problem to the student. When he reads it, he should know exactly what the problem is *and* what frame of reference should be used to arrive at the solution. Examine the following stems:

The acids. . . .

Abraham Lincoln was nominated for President of the United States in . . .

The first example obviously meets neither of the criteria for a good stem. It is not clear what the problem is nor what frame of reference is to be used when trying to answer it. The second stem is a little better. We have an idea about what is being asked but we still are not sure of the appropriate frame of reference. Chicago, 1860, the Republican convention, the North, and three ballots are all possible answers. Now one would hope that the alternatives supplied in the item would clear up this ambiguity. There would be no problem, for example, if the choice were: *a.* Detroit, *b.* New York, *c.* Washington, *d.* Chicago. However, because the test constructor does have a single problem clearly in mind when he writes an item, he may not notice the fact that more than one alternative could be correct depending upon the frame of reference used when answering. Look at the following item, for example.

Poor Example of a Multiple-Choice Item

Nouns. . . .
*a. serve as subjects and objects
  b. are action words
  c. modify other words

Notice that *a* is keyed as the correct alternative. Obviously, the test constructor expects the answer in terms of the *most common way* in which nouns function. However, a student with a different frame of reference (what *possible ways* can nouns function?) would conclude that both *a* and *c* are correct responses (nouns modify other words in phrases like *baseball bat, butterfly net, fire extinguisher,* etc.). And how about the student who uses some of the more creative writers as his "frame of reference"? Phrases like *poppin' pills is livin' dangerously,* or *motorcycling weds power and pursuit,* or *brawls fashion brawn and brain* would lend pretty weighty evidence to the argument that nouns can be "action" words. Of course, all this is corrected with a better stem:

Improved Example

What is the most common way in which nouns function?
*a. As subjects and/or objects
  b. As conveyors of action
  c. As modifiers of other words

A better stem would also improve the question about Lincoln that was discussed earlier.

Improved Stem

In what city was Abraham Lincoln nominated for President of the United States?

---

or

> Abraham Lincoln was nominated for President of the United States in the year. . . .

The Alternative Responses

The stem has presented the problem. Now come the "multiple choices." One of the choices (the correct alternative) is considered to be a better solution to the problem than the other choices (the incorrect alternatives). The alternatives should *reinforce* the work of the stem. After reading the alternatives, the examinee should be all the more sure of the nature of the problem and the frame of reference that should be used when selecting a solution. *All* the alternatives, incorrect as well as correct, should flow smoothly and naturally from the stem. The uninformed, poorly prepared examinee should see all the alternatives as plausible solutions to the problem presented in the stem. Item-writing experts frequently offer the following suggestions as aids to attaining this goal:

Suggestion 1: The alternatives should follow grammatically from the stem. Consider the following items:

POOR	IMPROVED
The saber saw can be used	The saber saw can be used
a. without electricity	*a.* without electricity
b. to cut scrolled lines	*b.* to cut scrolled lines
c. is faster than a band saw	*c.* to cut wood faster than a band saw
d. was invented before the jigsaw	*d.* only to cut wood

In the poor version, the first two alternatives follow grammatically from the stem, but distracters *c* and *d* do not. It is obvious, therefore, that neither *c* nor *d* is the correct alternative. Notice how this has been corrected in the improved version. Now examine another example:

POOR	IMPROVED
Bitsy's favorite instrument was a	What was Bitsy's favorite instrument?
a. oboe	*a.* An oboe
b. flute	*b.* A flute
c. organ	*c.* An organ
d. trombone	*d.* A trombone

Again, in the poor version, two of the distracters (*a* and *c*) are not plausible because they do not follow grammatically from the stem. The improved version corrects this problem. Notice also that the stem stated in question form does a better job of presenting the problem to be answered.

Suggestion 2: The alternatives should be homogeneous.

They should be of approximately the same length.

POOR	IMPROVED
Why are silicone insulations used on the electrical cables in airplanes? 1. Silicone insulation is cheaper. * 2. Under normal operating conditions the insulation on an electric wire must remain flexible at temperatures from −80 to 350° F. Silicone insulation meets these conditions. 3. Silicone insulation insulates better. 4. Silicone insulation can be repaired more quickly.	Why are silicone insulations used on electric cables in airplanes? 1. Silicone insulation is cheaper to install. * 2. Silicone insulation remains flexible under severe temperature changes. 3. Silicone insulation insulates better with a thinner coating. 4. Silicone insulation can be more easily repaired if damaged in flight.

They should all have the same grammatical structure.

POOR	IMPROVED
During recess the Jasper brothers played *a.* baseball * *b.* in the barn *c.* football *d.* tricks on each other	During recess the Jasper brothers played *a.* behind the school * *b.* in the barn *c.* near the oak tree *d.* in the street

They should all include similar terminology.

POOR	IMPROVED
Which one of the following foods is the best source of quick energy?	Which one of the following foods is the best source of quick energy?

1. Fats	1. Fats
2. Water	2. Water
*3. Glucose	*3. Sugar
4. Starch	4: Starch

They should be equally plausible to someone not knowing the material. Ebel (1972, page 205) offers an excellent example of an item whose distracters are as plausible as the correct alternative (unless you know the right answer):

Example of Plausible Distracters*

To what did the title of Broadway musical *Top Banana* refer?

1. The dictator of a Central American country.
2. The warden of a penitentiary.
*3. The leading comedian in a burlesque.
4. The president of a large fruit company.

* Used by permission of publisher.

Steps to Take When Constructing Multiple-Choice Items

There is probably no "best" method for writing multiple-choice items.[3] However, by following the steps outlined below, you should be fairly successful in producing good items.

A Preview of the Steps to Take When Constructing Multiple-Choice Items

1. Analyze the learning outcome to be measured.
2. Write the stem *and* the correct alternative.
3. Write plausible distracters.
4. Arrange the distracters and the correct alternatives.
5. Check for ambiguity and irrelevant clues (revise if necessary).

Step 1: Analyze the learning outcome to be measured.   The task which faces the person trying to answer a multiple-choice question is a task of choosing among several alternatives. Consequently, the first thing you need to do is decide whether or not the learning outcome you are trying to measure can be demonstrated through a process of choosing among alternatives. If the learning outcome calls for the *recall* of certain facts or the *production* of some product, the "choosing among alternatives" would *not* be an appropriate task to measure the outcome. On the other hand, if the learning outcome calls for *selecting* the most efficient

---

[3] See the additional readings at the end of this chapter for a number of good sources which explain how to write multiple-choice items.

of several plans, then choosing among alternatives *would* be an appropriate task. There are many other learning outcomes where it is not quite so easy to tell if choosing among alternatives is an appropriate measurement task or not. A good way to proceed is to eliminate all those outcomes which could obviously *not* be demonstrated through a choice-among-alternatives format and then try to answer this question about those outcomes which remain: "*How* can this skill be demonstrated through a multiple-choice format?" Rewording this question may make it easier to answer: "For a given learning outcome, what kind of alternative choices should be expressed to the student taking the test?"

EXERCISE 13.5

For each of the following learning outcomes, decide what kind of alternative choices should be posed to the student taking the test:

1. Should be able to identify the correct spelling of 90 percent of the 100 most commonly misspelled words
2. Should be able to select the best procedure for removing a given type of stain from clothes
3. Should be able to identify the date of important events in the Spanish-American War
4. Should be able to select from among a number of examples the one which best illustrates a violation of the right to a fair trial
5. When given a description of a teacher's attempt to estimate reliability, should be able to identify the *type* of reliability being estimated

---

But suppose you are not working from behaviorally stated goals which clearly define both the content and the expected response to that content. This same kind of analysis can be applied to a table of specifications. Remember that one dimension of the table indicates the content or subject matter and that the other indicates the level of learning expected. Although some levels of learning are more readily measured by multiple-choice items than others, some outcomes at each level are measurable with these kinds of items. Table 13.2 presents the levels of the cognitive domain from Bloom's taxonomy. At each level I have indicated the kinds of alternatives which would allow one to measure that level of learning. For example, in order to measure objectives at the knowledge level, it would be appropriate to present the student with alternative *definitions* to choose from. Alternative *names, dates, facts, events, devices,* and *styles* could all be used.

If the knowledge level is being measured, then the alternatives should be presented in approximately the same wording and format in which they were learned. At the comprehension level, on the other hand, the alternatives must be stated "in other words." That is why Table 13.2 calls for alternative *restatements, illustrations, rearrangements,* etc. If a person has reached the application level, he should be able to distinguish between a correctly formed *generalization* of some

TABLE 13.2

Representative Kinds of Alternatives to Be Used When Measuring Each of the Levels in the Cognitive Domain

Level of Learning (Cognitive Domain)	Kinds of Alternatives to Be Presented	
Knowledge level	Definitions	Dates
	Facts	Properties
	Events	Styles
	Names	Devices
Comprehension level	Illustrations	Interpretations
	Restatements	Rewording
	Rearrangements	
Application level	Applications	
	Generalizations	
	Restructurings	
	Extensions	
Analysis level	Analyses	Parts
	Elements	Themes
	Assumptions	Arrangements
	Relationships	Patters
	Structures	
Synthesis level	Concepts	Plans
	Taxonomies	Communications
	Schemes	Inventions
	Discoveries	
Evaluation level	Judgments	Performances
	Flaws	Products
	Strengths	Weaknesses

idea, theory, or concept and an incorrectly formed one. He should recognize an appropriate *application* of some principle and be able to distinguish it from some inappropriate one. The synthesis level is perhaps the most difficult level to measure with multiple-choice questions. Typically it calls for the student to pull together disparate knowledge and skills and *produce* some new idea, product, or communication. The best that can be done with the multiple-choice format is to find out if the student can *select* the *concept, taxonomy, invention,* or *discovery* which best represents a synthesis of given bits of information. The evaluation level can be fairly easily measured by presenting alternative performances or products and having the student select the "best" according to certain criteria. Also, a single product or performance can be presented along with alternative *strengths, weaknesses, flaws, previous judgments,* etc. The student must then select the alternative he feels represents the best evaluation of that performance or product.

    Step 2: Write the stem and the correct alternative. The stem presents the question and the correct alternative presents the answer. The answer should follow logically and grammatically from the stem. One of the best ways to make certain this occurs is to write the stem and the correct alternative at the same time. If the stem is to be stated in question form, then write the question and, right below it, the correct answer.

Example of Multiple-Choice Question

Elmer has a white car. His friend Gordon has an identical car except that it is black. Both cars must sit in the hot sun for an hour. Which of the following statements best describes what will happen?
a. Elmer's car will get hotter than Gordon's.
b. Gordon's car will get hotter than Elmer's.
c. Both cars will be the same temperature.

After you have written the correct answer, read it carefully. Could it be stated more clearly? Is it clearly the best answer that could be given? Are there any qualifications or exceptions to the answer? When the answer to all of these questions is no, you are ready to write the distracters.

Sometimes a bit of knowledge is being tested which lends itself to the incomplete-stem format.

Example of Statement for Incomplete-Stem Format

The angle of reflection equals the angle of incidence.

In this kind of situation a complete statement is made and then divided into two parts: the incomplete stem and its completion (the correct alternative).

Examples of Stems with Completions

The angle of reflection equals/the angle of incidence.
Your body uses protein mainly to/build new cells.

When constructing this kind of item, it is crucial that you split the statement so that most of the information is in the stem and the stem is meaningful (i.e., the kind of alternative needed to complete it is clear). Notice that when a statement is incorrectly divided, the alternative becomes lengthy, it is difficult to think of distracters, and the problem is not clearly stated in the stem.

Incorrect Division into Stem and Alternative

Your body/uses proteins mainly to build new cells.

Many communities/add fluoride to their water supply because they find that it prevents tooth decay.

Correct Division into Stem and Alternative

Many communities add fluoride to their water supply because they find that/ it prevents tooth decay.

or

Many communities add fluoride to their water supply because they find that it prevents/tooth decay.

Step 3: Write plausible distracters. The distracters will "make" or "break" a multiple-choice item. They usually fail because they do not seem plausible (even to the uninformed) or they do not follow logically from the stem. This often occurs because the item writer has failed to keep the stem in mind while writing the distracter. Each distracter must be written specifically to answer or complete the stem. Item writers often get so involved in making each distracter "look like" the correct alternative that they forget the stem completely. Examine the following alternatives:

    a. Wild flowers
    b. Wild zebras
    c. Wild cranes
 d. Wild buffalo

The correct alternative is asterisked. Notice how similar each distracter is to the correct alternative. However, look what happens when we put the stem in place:

Which one of the following animals is most clearly in danger of extinction?

    a. Wild flowers
    b. Wild zebras
    c. Wild cranes
 d. Wild buffalo

Now, some of the distracters are obviously wrong. Since *a* and *c* are not animals, they could not be correct.

Of course, when you are creating a distracter, you cannot completely ignore the correct alternative and the other distracters. All the alternatives (correct and incorrect) should be very similar. Always check for this characteristic after an item has been written.

Good Example: Alternatives Similar	Bad Example: Alternatives Dissimilar
Which of the following animals is most clearly in danger of extinction? *a.* Elephants *b.* Lions *c.* Zebras **d.* Buffalo	Which of the following animals is most clearly in danger of extinction? *a.* The Siamese cat *b.* Black Angus cows *c.* Alligators **d.* Buffalo

Step 4: Arrange the distracters and the correct alternative. This is very simply accomplished. If there is some logical (or chronological) arrangement inherent in the alternatives, then arrange them accordingly:

Example of Numerical Arrangement

How many cups are there in one quart?

a. 2	*c.* 6
b. 4	*d.* 8

Example of Chronological Arrangement

When did the United States declare its independence?
a. 1776
b. 1778
c. 1780
d. 1786

Example of Alphabetical Arrangement

Which state joined the union last?
a. Alaska
b. Georgia
c. Hawaii
d. Texas

However, there is often no logical reason for arranging the alternatives in any special order. Then you should randomly arrange them so that the correct alternative occurs at each position approximately the same number of times throughout the test.

Step 5: Check for ambiguity and irrelevant clues. Once you have completed writing an item, make certain that it is free from ambiguity and that there is nothing in the item itself that would give the answer away. Only those who know the material should get the answer correct. Remember that a good multiple-choice item will have the following features.

Features of a Good Multiple-Choice Item

1. It will measure a learning outcome which can be measured through the selection of alternatives.
2. The stem will present a single problem clearly, concisely, and unambiguously, and it will contain as much of the item as possible.
3. The alternatives should be homogeneous and should follow logically and grammatically from the stem.
4. The correct alternative should be a better response to the stem than the distracters.
5. The distracters should be plausible but incorrect (or not as good as the correct alternative).

EXERCISE 13.6

Write a few multiple-choice items in a subject area you are familiar with. This will be good practice now and will serve to help you remember the rules you just read. Try to write at least one item to measure each of the following levels of learning: knowledge, comprehension, application, analysis.

Check your items against the criteria for good multiple-choice items. Find someone who is an expert in the subject matter of your items. Ask him to answer the items. If he answers incorrectly, ask him why he chose the answers he did. It could be that your items are ambiguous. If so, correct them.

FILL THE BLANK

The fill-the-blank item is very common, very simple, *and highly limited.* It should be used only when *recall* of factual material is being measured. The fill-the-blank item is truly simple in design. It is essentially a true statement with some word (or very short phrase) missing.

Example of a Fill-the-Blank Item

The details of regulating air transportation are handled by the _____ _____ board.

However, it is not as easy to construct as it might appear. A common practice is to lift some statement verbatim from a textbook and then replace an important term with a blank. This, of course, produces a highly artificial situation. (How often do we go around "filling in the missing word"?) Furthermore, this procedure leaves you with an item that is usually trivial, calling for a purely rote-memory response.

Steps to Take When Constructing Fill-the-Blank Items

A much better way to construct a fill-the-blank item is to follow the three steps for producing true-false items (except that only true versions of a proposition need be written).

Step 1: Direct your attention to an important segment of knowledge.

Step 2: Select a worthwhile proposition to test.

Step 3: Convert the proposition into a test item (follow Ebel's suggestions but remember that only a true version is needed for fill-the-blank items).

Now go one step further.

Step 4: Take the true version of an important proposition and replace a key term with a blank.   Let us try that with one of the true versions taken from Ebel's proposition about eclipses:

When some of the light from a star like the sun to a planet like the earth is blocked by some other body like the moon, a(n) ————————————— is said to occur.

When you are finished, make certain that only one answer correctly fills the blank. Notice what happens, for example, if we use another true version of the same general proposition:

All eclipses involve ————————————

This is a bad item because many things could fit the blank (e.g., two bodies, light, movement).

Key Points to Remember When Constructing Fill-the-Blank Items

1. Do not lift statements directly from the book.
2. Leave only important terms blank.
3. Keep items brief.
4. Limit the number of blanks per statement to one or two.
5. Try to keep the blanks near the end of the statement.
6. Make certain that only one term fits each blank.

EXERCISE 13.7

Now construct two or three fill-the-blank items which measure the *recall* of *important* information. Check to see that only one possible response will fit in each blank. Ask some of your peers to try to think of responses which might correctly fill the blanks. If too many possibilities exist, reword the item. If a "wrong" answer could be readily defended, ambiguity is probably the culprit and rewriting is needed.

SHORT ANSWER

The most common and perhaps the most justifiable use of the short-answer item is to measure the ability to solve arithmetic problems, manipulate mathematical symbols, and balance equations.

Examples of Short-Answer Questions

If pencils cost 7 cents each, how much will three pencils cost?

If $\underline{} + 12 = 5$, then $\underline{} = ?$

Short-answer items can also be used to measure learning outcomes of the "be able to list . . ." variety.

Examples of Short-Answer Listing Questions

List at least five tools which utilize an axle.
List, in order, the first fifteen Presidents of the United States.
What are the three main branches of government in American Democracy?

Short-answer items are not particularly difficult to construct. However, if you are not careful when writing these items, you can produce items that are highly ambiguous. Examine the item below and the two alternate versions.

ORIGINAL

In the story that you just read, what was in the car that was red?

ALTERNATE 1

In the story you just read what was in the red car?

ALTERNATE 2

In the story you just read what red object was in the car?

Which alternative version conveys the meaning of the original item? Only the writer of the original item knows. Either alternative could be what was meant. How does the poor student respond to the original item above?

The problem of ambiguity can often be avoided if you follow these suggestions for constructing short answer items:

Suggestion 1: Ask Only Those Questions Whose Answers Are Naturally Very Brief

Poor: What causes the weather to change?

Better: What will probably happen to the temperature in mid-America if the wind changes from southwest to northwest?

Suggestion 2: Be Brief and Direct (Do Not Use Flowery Language)

Poor: The various governmental powers are distributed among the three branches of our government. The power associated with which branch has been vested in Congress?

Better: Which branch of government is associated with the power invested in Congress?

Suggestion 3: Measure Only One Concept at a Time

Poor: What makes agriculture so difficult in Spain and what mineral deposits does Spain have which are mined in abundance?

Better:
1. Why is it so hard to raise crops in Spain?
2. What mineral deposits are found in Spain?
3. Which minerals are mined in abundance in Spain?

Suggestion 4: Clearly Specify the Nature of the Response to Be Made

Poor: Name Spain's leading cities. (leading in what way?)

Better: Name Spain's five largest cities.

Poor: What are your teeth good for?

Better: List the things you can do with your teeth.

Poor: At what temperature does water boil?

Better: At what temperature does water boil? Give answer in Farenheit at sea level.

EXERCISE 13.8

Write two or three short-answer items of your own. Make certain that they
a. measure only a single concept.
b. are stated unambiguously.
c. can be answered in a word, phrase, or at most a couple of sentences.

ESSAY

An essay item gives the student a great amount of freedom to respond. It gives him an opportunity to "show what he knows." Creativity, organizational ability, and the ability to synthesize and evaluate can all be measured efficiently with the essay item. However, because of the student's freedom to respond, it is extremely difficult to score the results of essay tests. This subjectivity in scoring reduces the reliability. In order to partially overcome this problem, the test constructor can limit the amount of freedom. The more freedom to respond is limited, the more reliable the results will *tend* to be. Essay tests can vary along a continuum which we might define as the freedom-to-respond continuum. If we were to construct a rating scale to reflect this continuum, our first step would be to define the extreme ends.

The one extreme would be characterized by essay items with clearly defined restrictions. The students would be given definite limits in terms of either amount of time or number of words (or lines, paragraphs, or pages). Furthermore, the topic to be written about would be clearly defined. (e.g., use only the information given in the movie we viewed yesterday) and sometimes the format would be determined (e.g., list, outline, write in complete sentences).

The other extreme would be characterized by essay items which are very

general and which place virtually no restrictions on the way the student is to respond. Picture it this way:

A Freedom-to-Respond Continuum

Tight
restrictions
placed upon
the student's
response

Virtually
no restrictions
placed upon
the student's
response

Some authors (see, for example, Ahmann and Glock, 1971, and Gronlund,
1971) divide essay items into two types: restricted-response and extended-response. Restricted-response items would be those which would fall closest to the
restricted end of the above continuum and extended-response items those which
would fall closest to the no-restriction end. This dichotomy does highlight the
two extreme types of essay questions. However, it can be misleading, because
essay items do not fall neatly into two categories but really lie along a continuum
like that described above. Essay items *tend to be* restricted or *tend to be* nonrestricted. Examine the essay items in Figure 13.3. Notice how the responses called
for vary from highly restrictive to virtually no restrictions at all.

There is no value in describing the above continuum and subsequently

FIGURE 13.3. Essay items varying along a freedom-to-respond continuum.

Highly
restricted

List the four suggestions discussed in this text for writing
short-answer tests.

Outline the events which, according to the text, led up to
the Depression of the thirties.

Somewhat
restricted

Describe the short-answer test, and list the steps in the
process or constructing one.

What events led up to the Depression of the thirties? What
part did each event play in causing the Depression?

Some
freedom

Discuss the short-answer tests (including construction
procedures).

Discuss the cause and effect of the Depression of the
thirties. Include in your answer documented evidence of
your position.

A great
deal of freedom

Discuss teacher-made tests.

Write four or five pages about the Depression of the
thirties.

using it to describe essay items *unless it makes a difference*—unless there is some *practical* significance in the amount of freedom which is allowed in the students' response. The important questions to ask are

1. How does the kind of information obtained vary as the freedom to respond varies?
2. How do the kinds of judgments and decisions vary as the freedom to respond varies?
3. How do reliability and validity vary as freedom to respond varies?
4. How does the usability of an item vary as freedom to respond varies?

Let us try to answer each of these questions in turn. The lower levels of learning (e.g., recall of facts, understanding, specific application) are more readily measured with questions which restrict the student's responses. As the freedom to respond increases, the level of learning most appropriately measured rises. Less restricted items tend to be more appropriate for measuring general application, analysis, synthesis, and evaluation.

As you allow a student more freedom to respond as he pleases, you tend to get better measures of creativity and originality. Furthermore, the more response freedom there is, the more information you can obtain about a person's thinking *process*. Restrictions tend to define the process to be used in answering the question, and you get a good picture of specific knowledge recalled. Freedom-to-respond items tend to make it difficult for you to get a clear picture of the students' specific knowledge. However, this type of item does allow you to see more clearly how the student analyzes, organizes, or synthesizes that knowledge.

The more freedom there is to respond, the more difficult it is to make norm-referenced judgments. When everyone is "doing their own thing," it is difficult to make meaningful comparisons among the students' responses. If you wish to make norm-referenced judgments, you must restrict the students' responses so that you can be certain that every person is interpreting and responding to each question *in the same way*. Restricted-response items are generally more useful for making important decisions because they tend to be more reliable. However, many instructional decisions made *first of all* for the good of the individual and the improvement of his learning can be aided greatly by information from essay items which allow a great deal of freedom to respond.

The more restricted an essay item, the more reliable the results are likely to be. The more freedom allowed in responding, the less reliable the results tend to be. This does not mean that just because an essay item restricts the student's responses that it will be reliable. Nor does it mean that just because an item allows a great deal of freedom, the results will be unreliable. However, other things being equal, the less restrictions, the less objectivity and the less reliability.

But what about validity? Validity cannot be ascertained until you first ask "Valid for what?" As a valid measure of recall of facts, the restricted items are best. On the other hand, nonrestricted items generally yield more valid measures of upper-level learning and creativity.

Restricted items tend to be easier to give, easier to take, require less time to take, and are easier to score. As you increase the amount of freedom allowed in the responses, you tend to make the item more difficult to administer and score. Also, as the student is allowed more freedom to respond, he will find it more difficult and more time-consuming to answer. Restricted items are usually a little more difficult to construct. However, well-written nonrestricted items must also be carefully constructed.

Steps to Take When Constructing Essay Items

Essay items, then, can measure a variety of things, depending upon the amount of freedom allowed in the response. Consequently, the thing to do when writing an essay item is to decide what information you need, what judgments and decisions you plan on making, and how reliable the results must be. Then you can decide how much freedom to respond you should allow. The complete step-by-step procedures for writing essay items are previewed below.

A Preview of the Steps to Take When Constructing Essay Items

Step 1. Decide what information you need and what judgments and decisions you plan on making with that information.

Step 2. Determine the amount of freedom to respond which will be allowed.

Step 3. Write the question so that it clearly indicates the nature of the problem being posed and the amount of freedom allowed in the response.

Step 4. Construct a model answer.

Step 1: Decide what information you need and what decisions you plan on making.   This step is simply a review of the first couple of steps in the evaluation process. At this point you are selecting from among the needed information and anticipated judgments and decisions those which you have decided to measure with essay items.

Step 2: Determine the amount of freedom to respond.   We have already discussed the important considerations when deciding how much freedom to allow the student in responding. Another way that one could approach the task would be to ask, "What restrictions should I place on the response or the responses to be elicited from the students?" The following ways to limit essay questions should prove useful to you when you are trying to control the freedom the student has when making his response.

Types of Restrictions Which Can Be Placed upon Responses to Essay Questions

1. Limit the topic (e.g., "Discuss *only* the effect on the auto industry").
2. Limit the length (e.g., "No more than two pages").

3. Limit time (e.g., "Write for approximately ten minutes on each of the questions").
4. Limit sources to be used (e.g., "Discuss only the causes specified in your text").
5. Limit the style of response (e.g., list, outline, diagram).

Step 3: Write the question. Note carefully that there are two important elements in an essay question: (1) a clear statement of the problem and (2) a precise description of the type of response desired (i.e, the amount and the kind of freedom allowed in the response). The following examples of essay items include a statement of the problem and a description of the type of response desired.

Examples Illustrating the Two Important Elements in Essay Items: A Clear Statement of the Problem and a Description of the Type of Response Expected

High School Government

Should governments maintain social welfare programs? Answer yes or no and then defend your position in one to three pages. Include in your response a discussion of at least three alternative types of programs and describe the effects each type is likely to have on the recipients of the program.

Eighth Grade Health

Why should we eat a variety of foods from each of the four food groups? Write down the most important function of the foods found in each group. Also describe in a sentence or two how we would be likely to feel with no variety in the food we eat.

Consumer Economics (First Course)

Define a negotiable instrument. Answer in no more than half a page. Include in your answer the essential elements of a negotiable instrument, and at least two examples of negotiable instruments.

Step 4: Construct a model answer. To write an answer to your own essay questions would not be too difficult. However, to write a *model* answer is something else. A model answer must serve as a key for scoring. The responses of the students are compared with this model answer and judged as to how well they match the model. This means that the model must meet certain criteria.

First of all, a model answer should clearly spell out the major content to be included in the answer. What terms should be included? What are the concepts which should be in the answer? If the question calls for the solution to a problem, what solutions will be acceptable? What principles should be included as an indication that the solution was not arrived at by guessing? In highly restricted items the content can usually be defined by a simple listing of all the terms.

Example of a Restricted Essay Item: Model Answer

This example includes part of the scoring key (model answer) which describes the content which students should include in their answer.

Question: Choose eight of the most abundant elements in the earth's crust and for each one give its name, its chemical symbol, and indicate whether or not it is a mineral.

Content expected in answer: eight of the following ten:

Name	Symbol	Mineral?
oxygen	O	No
silicon	Si	Yes
aluminum	Al	No
iron	Fe	No
calcium	Ca	Yes
sodium	Na	Yes
potassium	K	Yes
magnesium	Mg	No
titanium	Ti	No
hydrogen	H	No

In the items with a great deal of freedom to respond, the content might vary from answer to answer. In this case the kind of content which would be acceptable should be identified (e.g., definitions, premises, conclusions, research support, or examples of actual situations).

Example of a Scoring Key for an Essay Question Which Gives the Student a Great Deal of Freedom to Respond

Question: Discuss the important events connected with the growth of trade in America. Begin at the close of the War between the States and conclude with the present day.

Scoring Key: The following should be included in each answer:

1. A statement of the scope of the answer (e.g., foreign as well as domestic, laws and policies as well as innovations).
2. A selection of important events (at least five). Each event to be (*a*) described; (*b*) shown to have an impact on American trade (evidence must be given for this); and (*c*) placed in proper chronological order (with approximate date or dates if possible).

Secondly, a model answer should specify important organization features which should characterize a student's answer. In many cases, the answer to an essay question should be presented in a certain manner. Perhaps the materials should be presented in a particular order, as when explaining the procedures for filing a petition or the steps to take when writing a term paper. Sometimes an essay question may call for certain evidence to be brought forth to support a given position. Is the position clearly stated? Is the evidence appropriately chosen? There are many ways to organize an essay (logically, chronologically, from most to least important, pro and con positions, etc.). When the organization of the answer is important *(and only then),* the model answer should include those features.

Finally, a model answer must not "show off" the author's writing style. Anyone reading a model answer should be able to immediately locate the important elements of that answer. Remember this: The students' responses will all be written in different styles and, from answer to answer, different words may be used to say the same thing. You must be able to recognize those "things" that are the same as those in the model answer even though they may be worded differently or written in different styles. A student whose level of vocabulary and style of writing is much like the teacher's should not get a high score *unless* he has the right answer (i.e., the important elements must be there and, where important, they must be organized properly). On the other hand, a student with a style of writing far different from the teacher's should not get penalized *unless* he has an incorrect answer (i.e., the important elements are missing or important organizational features are absent).

A model answer, to be useful must

1. Indicate the major content (terms, concepts, principles, relationships, etc.) that should be treated in the answer
2. Specify any important organizational features that should characterize the answer (e.g., treatment of events in proper sequence, building a logical argument, citing of appropriate examples)
3. Be written so that the important elements of the answer are not hidden in an eloquent writing style

EXERCISE 13.9

1. Write a fairly restricted essay item and its model answer. Check with your instructor or your peers to see if they feel your question is well stated and your model answer meets the criteria discussed above.
2. Now do the same for a question which gives the students a little more freedom to respond.

HOW TO JUDGE THE QUALITY OF A TEACHER-MADE TEST

Perhaps the best way to find out if your test is any good is to have your students take it. If you learn to be critical of each test you produce, noticing the problems which occur when it is used, you will learn what needs to be corrected the next time. Gradually, as you gain experience and *learn from that experience,* you will become a good test constructor. It is crucial, then, that you learn how to judge the quality of your own tests. In the following discussion we will concentrate on those things you can do to judge the quality of test *results* (and, by inference, the quality of the test itself). This is done by giving the test and seeing what happens. Do not forget, however, that you should also judge the quality of the test *before* you use it. Suggestions for doing that have been made several times in the last few pages.

The information you get about the quality of your test results can help you to be more realistic about the judgments you make with those results. Furthermore, it can help you to get an idea of any problems involved in your test construction procedures. This should help you become a better test constructor more rapidly. Finally, information about the quality of your test results can help you to select test items to be used again. The four major ways to judge the quality of a classroom test are previewed below.

Four Ways to Judge the Quality of a Classroom Test

1. Watch for clues.
2. Analyze the items.
3. Check the validity.
4. Check the reliability.

Watch for Clues

This subtitle should look familiar to you. In Chapter 2, the strategy of watching for clues which would indicate that a test's results might be in error was discussed. Here, we are particularly concerned about those clues which will help

TABLE 13.3

Clues to Errors Commonly Found in Teacher-made Tests

Common Errors	Clues
Emphasis placed on wrong topic	Imbalance of items measuring a given concept or topic.
	Students complaint: "You measured things we didn't study."
Ambiguous items	Lack of agreement in responses of better students.
	Negative or low item discrimination index.
	Student complaint: "If you think of it this way, it could be answered 'A'."
Items difficult to read (i.e., unnecessarily difficult vocabulary and sentence structure)	Question are very long.
	Students asking lots of questions during the test.
	Students taking longer than expected to respond.

you to discover errors in the test itself. Table 13.3 lists the kinds of errors most commonly found in the teacher-made test. For each type of error, we have indicated some of the clues which might lead you to suspect that type of error exists.

Notice that the clues are only *indications* that the test may be in error. Whenever you notice any of these clues, you should examine the test carefully to see if there is any further evidence of error. The procedures discussed below can help you to pinpoint the kind of error(s) in your test more accurately.

Analyze the Items

Item analysis is a systematic procedure designed to give you very specific information about each item in your test. The information it provides can help you in a number of ways.

Item analysis can

1. Help you to identify poorly written items
2. Provide you with information that can help you to improve an item for future use
3. Give you a rough estimate of the internal consistency of your test

Item-analysis procedures are designed primarily for use with objective tests. (They are especially valuable for analyzing multiple-choice items.) If objective tests are not returned to the students, the items can usually be safely retained for use with future classes. This makes item improvement possible, and over a period of time a teacher can build a pool of well-written items. He can then draw from that pool when constructing a test. Highly reliable teacher-made tests can result from this strategy.

The logic of item analysis.   The major goal of item analysis is to find out how well the individual items in a given test are working. In other words, we analyze items to find out if they are doing what they are supposed to do. Is an item doing its job well? That is the important question to be answered.

What is an item supposed to do?

We have said before that each item in a test is supposed to help that test accomplish its main purpose: *to find out what the student knows or is able to do.* A given item, then, is designed to find out whether or not the student knows some specific bit of information. Consequently, if an item is working well, those students who *do* know the information being tested by the item should get it correct. Conversely, those students who do not know the information should get it wrong. The procedures for obtaining evidence about how well an item is doing its job follow logically from the above discussion. All one needs to do is find a group of people who know the material being tested and a group who do *not* know the material being measured. Ideally, everyone who knows the material should answer the items correctly and everyone who does not know the material should answer the items incorrectly. Let us explore this idea more fully as we discuss the actual procedures involved in item analysis.

The discrimination index.   We might say that an item works well when it discriminates well. A good item should discriminate between those who know the information (or have the skill) being measured and those who do not. We could obtain evidence about how well an item discriminates in the following way:

1. Identify a group of individuals who know the material well (call them *the top group).*
2. Identify a group of individuals who do not know the material at all (call them *the bottom group).*
3. Have both groups attempt to answer the items.
4. Compute the proportion of each group getting the item correct.
5. Find the difference between the proportion of the top group getting the item correct and the proportion of the bottom group getting the item correct (call this a *discrimination index).*

Picture it this way:

The proportion of the top group getting an item correct	minus	The proportion of bottom group getting an item correct	equals	A discrimination index

Now the problem is to identify the top group and the bottom group. The usual procedure is to define these groups on the basis of their total test scores. In other words, those who did best on the test as a whole are considered to be most knowledgeable about the material being tested and those who do most poorly on the test as a whole are considered to be the least knowledgeable. Those who do best make up the top group, whereas those who do most poorly are labeled the bottom group. Measurement experts generally agree that the best estimate of item discrimination is obtained when the high group consists of those students who scored in the top 27 percent of the class *on the test being analyzed* and the low group is identified as those who score in the bottom 27 percent of the class *on the test being analyzed.*

Suppose, for example, we have given a test to 100 students. Those 27 students who scored highest on the test would be called the high group. Those 27 students who scored lowest would be called the low group. After we have identified the high and low groups, we would take the following steps for each item in the test:

1. Find out what Proportion of the 27 students in the high group got the item correct.
2. Find out what proportion of the 27 students in the low group got the item correct.
3. Obtain the difference.

If, for example, 100 percent of the high group (27 out of 27 students) got item 1 correct and 46 percent of the low group (17 out of 27) got the item correct, then the discrimination index would be 0.54. We could write this as a formula in the following way:

$$H - L = DI$$

The *H* in the above formula stands for the proportion of the high group getting the item correct, the *L* for the proportion of the low group getting the item correct, and the *DI* stands for the discrimination index.

Constructors of standardized tests usually consider items having a discrimination index of 0.40 or better to be quite satisfactory. Items with a discrimination index of below 0.20 should probably be discarded or reworked. Items with a negative discrimination index (e.g., −0.41, −0.32, −0.10) are items which were answered correctly by more persons from the low group than from the high group. A negative discrimination index suggests that an item was either miskeyed or is highly ambiguous. This kind of item lowers the reliability of the test as a whole.

The difficulty level. Another indication of an item's quality is its difficulty level. If an item is part of a mastery test, you would expect the items to be quite easy. In a test designed to measure knowledge *prior* to instruction, the items will all be quite difficult. If you anticipate making norm-referenced judgments, you will want the test to discriminate clearly among students who have reached different levels of achievement. In order to obtain maximum discrimination, the items should be moderately difficult.

The difficulty level *(DL)* is easily computed. You simply determine what proportion of all the students taking the test got an item correct. If all got the item correct, the difficulty level would be 1.00; if half of the students got an item correct, the difficulty level would be 0.50; if 10 percent of the students got an item correct, the difficulty level would be 0.10, etc. Note that the easier the item, the higher the difficulty level. This is because the difficulty level is determined by the proportion of those getting the item *correct.*

The above procedures for computing the discrimination index and the difficulty level are time-consuming. In order to get the discrimination index, for example, the teacher must prepare a form on which he tallies every response made by every student in both the top and bottom thirds of the class. In other words, for two-thirds of the class (top and bottom thirds) the teacher must copy down all the answers to all the questions. As you might guess, teachers rarely do an item analysis of their own tests. When such an analysis is made on the basis of only a few students, as is often done, the results are not highly accurate anyway.

Teachers can save a great deal of time and energy by doing a show-of-hands item analysis right in class. This type of analysis yields slightly less accurate results. However, any item analysis done on teacher-made tests will be somewhat inaccurate anyway because of the small number of students used in the analysis (twenty-five to thirty is the typical classroom size). Consequently, I would recommend the show-of-hands method described below. It is easy enough that you can do it fairly regularly yet accurate enough that you can get some evidence about your item-writing skills. Furthermore, it can help you to quickly spot really bad items. A full item analysis for a fifty-item test can be completed in fifteen to twenty minutes of class time.

A Preview of the Steps in a Show-of-Hands Item Analysis

Step 1. Arrange the papers in rank order.

Step 2. Divide the papers into two equal groups.

Step 3. Pass out papers to the class.

Step 4. Choose a scorekeeper.

Step 5. Count the responses from a show of hands and record the data.

Step 6. Note any "bad" items.

Step 7. Examine the bad items carefully.

Show-of-hands analysis. You can obtain useful item-analysis data in a relatively short time right in the classroom. Simply follow the steps outlined below. These steps are based on short-cut procedures for obtaining item analysis data described by Paul Diederich in a small pamphlet called *Short Cut Statistics for Teacher-Made Tests* (see the suggested readings at the end of this section for information on where to obtain this useful pamphlet).

Step 1: Arrange the papers. After you have scored all the papers, arrange them in descending order from the highest score to the lowest.

Step 2: Divide the papers into two groups. Now, beginning from the highest score, count down to the middle of the pile, thus dividing the pile of papers into two equal groups. The one group will include the papers of the students scoring in the top half of the class (the top group), and the other group will be the papers of those in the bottom half (the bottom group). If there is an odd number of papers, keep out the middle paper and do not use it in the analysis.

Step 3: Pass out the two groups of papers. You want to make it easy to count the number of correct responses made by each group (those in the high and those in the low). The best way to do this is to pass out the papers from the top half to one side of the room and the papers from the bottom half to the other side of the room. In order to maintain the privacy of each individual's performance, you can have the students put code numbers rather than their names on their papers. The teacher should have a record of each student's code number so that the scores can be properly credited.

Step 4: Choose a scorekeeper. Someone should be appointed to count the number of correct responses in each group and to record the data obtained for each item. If there is an odd number of students, there will be someone without a paper (because you eliminate the middle paper from the analysis), and he can be chosen as scorekeeper. If there is an even number of students, the teacher can serve as scorekeeper.

Step 5: Count responses and record the data. Once all the papers have been passed out, explain to the students that you are trying to discover how well the test helped to find out whether or not they knew the material. Explain to them that when you call out the item number, everyone holding a paper that has that item correct should raise his hand.

Call for item 1. The scorekeeper counts the number of hands raised in the high group (e.g., 10), calls out the count, and records it below item 1 on an extra copy of the test. He then counts the number of hands raised in the low group (e.g., 4), calls that number out, and records it next to the first number.

Now you have the number of "highs" who got the item correct (e.g., 10) and the number of "lows" who got the item correct (e.g., 4). Adding these two numbers together will give you the total number getting the item correct (e.g., $10 + 4 = 14$). Converting this total to a proportion (dividing by the number of papers in the analysis) will give you a difficulty level ($14 \div 28 = 0.50$). Notice that you can tell by the total number of students getting an item correct whether it is very easy or very hard, and it is therefore unnecessary to figure the proportion of students getting an item correct. You should question only those items that deviate a great deal from what you expected. Items that are too easy or too hard should be questioned *unless* they were purposely designed that way.

Now subtract the number of lows getting the item correct from the number of highs getting it correct (e.g., $10 - 4 = 6$). This difference gives you a kind of discrimination index. Notice that it is computed as the difference in the *number* of persons from each group getting the item correct rather than the proportion from each group getting the item correct. Consequently, you must interpret this index a little differently than you would the discrimination index described earlier.

Record the difficulty level for each item next to the number of lows getting the item correct, and record the discrimination index next to the difficulty level. You will now have four numbers for each item. Always record them in the order described above and you will not have to bother to label each number. The first number will be the number in the high group getting the item correct. The second number will be the number of persons in the low group getting the item correct. The third number will be the difficulty level (i.e., the total number of persons getting the item correct). The final number will be a discrimination index computed as the difference in the *number* of persons from each group getting the item correct.

Examples

1. Which one of the following words is a collective noun?
   a. Hobby
   b. Herd
   c. Hat
   d. Harold
      10, 4, 14, 6
2. Which store was the original 5- and 10-cent store?
   a. Mattingly's
   b. Kresge's
   c. Sears
   d. Woolworth's
      6, 5, 11, 1

Step 6: Note any bad items.   Quickly take note of any bad items that are much easier or much harder than you expected them to be. You may wish to discuss these with your students. Remember, an item may be too easy because the right answer is obvious and not because the students really understand the material.

Next, mark any items which do not discriminate well. Use the following rule of thumb as a guide.

> The high-low difference should exceed 10 percent of the total number of papers in the analysis.

Before you begin an analysis, divide the number of papers to be analyzed by 10 and round off to the nearest whole number. The resulting number will serve as a criterion for judging the discrimination index of each item. If the high-low difference exceeds this number, it is discriminating satisfactorily. If it is equal to or less than this number, you should examine the item further to see what, if anything, is wrong with it.

For example, suppose there are 27 papers to be analyzed. Dividing by 10 and rounding off to the nearest whole number, we get 3. Therefore *for this analysis* we should question any item with a high-low difference with three or less.

Step 7: Examine the bad items more carefully. The first thing to do is to discuss the "bad" items with the class. The students may be able to offer numerous reasons why an item was too easy, too hard, or nondiscriminating. Below is a list of some of the common faults of items which can be discovered through a class discussion.[4]

Common Faults of Items Frequently Noticed by the Students Taking a Test

1. A rare exception may make an otherwise correct response incorrect (or an incorrect one correct).
2. An item question (or stem) can be interpreted in more than one way.
3. An item has been miskeyed.
4. An item asks for information the students had not had an opportunity to learn.
5. An item measures trivia.

Besides a general class discussion, a more in-depth analysis can be made to find out why an item may be bad. Diederich (1964) offers the following suggestion based upon the show-of-hands technique described above:[5]

---

[4] Students are not always correct in their analysis of a test item. Do not automatically accept their complaint as legitimate, but always be willing to consider their complaint.

[5] From *Short-cut Statistics for Teacher-made Tests* by Paul B. Diederich. Copyright 1960, 1964, by Educational Testing Service. All rights reserved. Reprinted by permission.

Second Stage of Item-Analysis

There may be a few items in a test that turned out to be too easy, too hard, or, for no apparent reason, did not discriminate satisfactorily, and class discussion does not reveal anything wrong with them. If there is time, these may be subjected to a second stage of item analysis, which is too laborious and time-consuming to apply to more than a few items. For these few items, one asks how many in the high group and then how many in the low group *(a)* omitted the item and *(b)* chose each response. Results like the following may indicate what is wrong:

	Omit	Responses				
		1	2	3	4	5
High	0	11	9	0	0	0
Low	0	14	4	2	0	0

The right answer, response 1, is indicated by a line between the highs and lows who chose it. Three more lows than highs chose it, hence its index of discrimination is −3. Why? The figures for response 2 suggest an answer.

This response was too attractive to the high-scoring students. Perhaps they thought response 1 was too obvious. They suspected a trap; then they figured out some interpretation of response 2 that they could defend as the right answer. If so, discussion should reveal what interpretation they gave to response 2, and it can be revised in a way that does not permit this interpretation. At the same time, responses 4 and 5 might be made a shade more plausible but still definitely wrong, because in their present form they were wasted; nobody chose them.

EXERCISE 13.10

A show-of-hands item analysis is fairly easy to do. However, if you do not understand why it is to be done or if you do not know how to interpret the results, it is a waste of time. To check your understanding, answer the following questions:

1. An item analysis is performed in order to find out
   a. How easy (or how hard) the items were
   b. Which items are contributing to the internal consistency of the test as a whole
   c. How well each item discriminates
   d. All of the above
2. Which item is the easiest?
   a. Item 1: difficulty level = 0.50
   b. Item 2: difficulty level = 0.75
   c. Cannot tell without further information
3. Which item is the most difficult?
   a. Item 1: discrimination index =0.50
   b. Item 2: discrimination index =0.75
   c. Cannot tell without further information

4. At what level of difficulty is the "potential" level of the discrimination index at its highest?
   a. 0.10
   b. 0.30
   c. 0.50
   d. 0.80
   e. 0.90

Using a show-of-hands technique, Mrs. Sullern obtained the following data on the first five items in a history test. Thirty-nine students took the test. Complete the information for items 3 through 5 and then answer questions 6 through 11.

Item-Analysis Data

Item	Number high	Number low	Total	High-low difference
1	10	5	15	5
2	19	19	38	0
3	16	6	22	____
4	4	15	____	____
5	14	10	____	____

5. Which item is the easiest?
6. Which item is the hardest?
7. Which item is the "best"?
8. Which item is a negative discriminator?
9. Which items should be examined more closely?
10. Which items are OK?
11. What number should the high-low difference *exceed* for satisfactory discrimination?

Check the Test's Validity

The most important kind of validity for teacher-made tests is content validity. You will recall from Chapter 2 that content validity is assessed by carefully examining tests, item by item, to determine if the items individually and collectively are measuring what they are supposed to. Ideally, you will have a clearly defined set of instructional goals or a well-developed table of specifications which you can use as a guide when analyzing your test. You should try to decide which specific objective or which cell in the table of specifications is being measured by each item in the test. If an item does not clearly measure a specific objective, it is not a valid item for that test. If a test includes a large number of items which do not measure specific objectives, the test will have very low validity.

Invalidity can also occur because there are specific objectives (or particular cells in a table of specifications) which are not measured at all. If there are large numbers of unmeasured objectives, the test will have low validity. It should be noted, however, that a test designed for norm-referenced judgments does not need to measure *every* "objective" if it measures a fairly representative sample of them. On the other hand, if criterion-referenced judgments are to be made, every single objective must be measured (in fact, best results occur when several items are used for each objective).

Check the Test's Reliability

One indication that a test is internally consistent (reliable) is the fact that most of the items have high discrimination indexes. For most daily tests and quizzes, this is all the evidence you will need. However, there may be some occasions when you will wish to know rather precisely what the reliability of your test is. Then it would be appropriate to compute an internal consistency coefficient using the KR-21 formula explained in Appendix A. Below are some of the situations for which you might wish a reliability coefficient.

Situations for Which Reliability Coefficients Would Be Useful

Anytime an important decision rests upon the evidence of one or two tests (e.g., to pass or fail a student).

When a report card grade or mark of final achievement (i.e., an important summative judgment) rests upon one or two tests.

Whenever you need a standard error of measurement as an estimate of the amount of error in an individual's score (see Chapter 2 for an explanation of the standard error of measurement and Appendix A for instructions on how to compute it).

Whenever you plan on "standardizing" one of your tests (as you might do if you were going to use the same pretest each semester).

Evaluating Criterion-referenced Mastery Tests

A special problem arises when you try to evaluate criterion-referenced mastery tests. Because you expect most students to master the material they are being tested on, there will be very little variance in the test scores. Without this variance, traditional reliability estimates cannot be made and the item-analysis procedures

TABLE 13.4

A Portion of an Item-Response Chart for a Criterion-referenced Mastery Test on Weather Maps*

OBJECTIVES →	KNOWS BASIC TERMS												
CONTENT AREAS →	Pressure		Temperature		Humidity		Wind		Clouds			Fronts		
ITEMS →	1	2	3	4	5	6	7	8	9	10	11	12	13	14
John Able	+	+	+	+	+	+	+	+	−	−	−	+	−	−
Mary Baker	+	+	+	+	−	−	+	−	+	−	−	−	+	+
Henry Charles	+	−	+	+	+	+	−	+	−	−	+	+	−	+
Joe Darby	+	+	+	+	+	−	+	+	+	−	−	+	+	−
Betty Frank	+	+	+	+	+	+	+	+	+	−	+	−	+	−
Bill Jones	+	−	+	+	+	+	−	+	−	−	−	−	−	−
Louise Kerr	+	+	+	+	+	+	+	+	+	−	+	−	+	+
Kathy Mann	+	+	+	+	+	+	+	+	+	−	+	+	+	−
Douglas Smith	−	−	−	+	+	−	+	−	−	−	+	+	−	−
Frances Young	+	+	+	+	+	+	−	+	+	−	−	+	−	−

* Reprinted with the permission of Macmillan Publishing Co., Inc., from *Criterion-Referenced Tests for Classroom Instruction*, p. 45. Copyright © 1973 by Norman E. Gronlund.

described above do not work well. Gronlund (1973) suggests that the teacher make a record of the student responses to each item, grouped according to the objectives they measure. You simply list the students' names along the left side of a piece of paper and the items (grouped by objectives) along the top. Then you simply put a *plus* sign for each item a student answered correctly and a *minus* sign for each item a student missed. Table 13.4 presents an example of part of such a record. When too many students miss an item, the item is bad *or* that concept was not learned (the instruction was bad).

Further information can be gained by administering the same test *before* and *after* instruction. Charting the responses for both pretests and posttests can help you judge the quality of your items. An example of this kind of chart is found in Table 13.5. This table was adapted from Gronlund (1973), who deliberately distorted the results to illustrate several basic patterns of response.

Item 1 in Table 13.5 is an ideal criterion-referenced mastery item. No one got it correct before instruction, everyone got it correct after instruction. The instruction and the test item were both good. Item 2 was answered correctly by everyone both times. Either the item was too easy or it represents an objective that did not need to be taught. Everyone missed item 3 on both tests. Either the item was bad or the instruction was ineffective. Item 4 would indicate a bad item or instruction that confused students and caused them to "unlearn" or forget that which they once knew.

TABLE 13.5

A Portion of an Item-Response Chart Showing Correct ($+$) and Incorrect ($-$) Responses before and after Instruction*

ITEMS	1		2		3		4		5	
PRETEST (B) POSTTEST (A)	B	A	B	A	B	A	B	A	B	A
Jim Hart	−	+	+	+	−	−	+	−	−	+
Dora Larson	−	+	+	+	−	−	+	−	+	+
Lois Trent	−	+	+	+	−	−	+	−	−	+
Donna Voss	−	+	+	+	−	−	+	−	−	+
Dick Ward	−	+	+	+	−	−	+	−	+	+
Bob West	−	+	+	+	−	−	+	−	−	−

*Reprinted with the permission of Macmillan Publishing Co., Inc., from *Criterion-Referenced Tests for Classroom Instruction*, p. 46. Copyright © 1973 by Norman E. Gronlund.

The first four items in this chart illustrate extreme findings. Rarely will *all* the students respond the same way on a given item on both tests. However, when item responses have trends which look like those illustrated in the first four items of Table 13.5, you can make similar interpretations to those made above. Item 5 illustrates a more normal pattern of responses. Although not everyone improved with instruction, most students did. This pattern of responses indicates a good item and good instruction.

SUMMARY

1. You should not begin to construct a test until you have completed the first four steps in the evaluation process.
2. The first step in test construction is to determine the format of the test. This means that you must decide *(a)* what types of items should be used, *(b)* how many items should be used, *(c)* how difficult the items should be, *(d)* how the items should be presented, and *(e)* how the students should respond.
3. The type of test item you decide to use is determined by four factors: *(a)* the level (and kind) of learning outcomes being measured, *(b)* the way in which the results will be used, *(c)* the characteristics of the students taking the test, and *(d)* the time available for constructing, administering, and scoring the test.
4. A test should include enough items to measure a representative sample of the outcomes being measured.

5. The level of difficulty of a norm-referenced test should be about 50 percent. For criterion-referenced tests, it will vary. Mastery tests usually have a very low level of difficulty.

6. Tests can be presented orally or in written form, in class or at home, with books opened or closed. The presentation of test items should be made in a way that will make it easy for the students to respond.

7. Response modes should be selected to make it easy for the student to respond and to give you the kind of information you need.

8. Item writing is an art which requires skill in the use of item-writing techniques.

9. A test item must deal with the subject matter content and the student's expected response to that content as defined by behavioral objectives or a table of specifications.

10. Test instructions should provide the student with the necessary information for him to take the test. They should be clear, concise, and consistent.

11. Before assembling a test, check all the items to make certain that they are well written and that together they will provide an adequate sample of the learning outcomes being measured.

12. Arrange items logically so that the test will be easier for the student to take and easier for you to score.

13. The test should be laid out, typed, and reproduced so that it is easy to read.

14. To construct a matching exercise, follow these steps: *(a)* decide what is to be measured, *(b)* list the premises and responses to be used, *(c)* add distracting responses (or premises), *(d)* arrange the items, and *(e)* write the instructions.

15. When constructing true-false items, *(a)* direct your attention to an important segment of knowledge, *(b)* select a worthwhile proposition to test, and *(c)* convert the proposition into a test item.

16. When constructing other alternative-response items, *(a)* select an appropriate learning outcome, *(b)* list examples representative of each alternative, *(c)* select the examples to be used, and *(d)* write the instructions.

17. To write multiple-choice items, *(a)* analyze the learning outcome to be measured, *(b)* write the stem and the correct alternative, *(c)* write plausible distracters, *(d)* arrange the distracters and the correct alternatives, and *(e)* check for ambiguity and irrelevant clues.

18. The steps to take when writing fill-the-blank items are: *(a)* direct your attention to an important segment of knowledge, *(b)* select a worthwhile proposition to test, *(c)* convert the proposition into a true version of the true-false item, and *(d)* take this true statement of an important proposition and replace a key term with a blank.

19. Well-written short-answer items require that you *(a)* ask only those questions whose answers are naturally very brief, *(b)* are brief and direct, *(c)* measure only one concept at a time, and *(d)* clearly specify the nature of the response to be made.

20. The steps to take when writing essay items are: *(a)* decide what information is needed and what judgments and decisions will be made, *(b)* determine the amount of freedom to respond which will be allowed, *(c)* write the question so that it clearly indicates the nature of the problem being posed and the amount of freedom being allowed in the response, and *(d)* construct a model answer.

21. There are four ways to judge the quality of a classroom test: *(a)* watch for clues, *(b)* analyze the items, *(c)* check the validity, *(d)* check the reliability.

22. Item analysis can help you to identify poorly written items, provide you with information that can help you to improve an item for future use, and give you a rough estimate of the internal consistency of your test.
23. A show-of-hands item analysis takes only a few minutes of class time but gives you fairly accurate indexes of difficulty and discrimination.
24. Criterion-referenced mastery tests cannot be evaluated with the traditional procedures. Charts showing the pattern of responses for each item provide valuable item data for evaluating these tests and the instruction which preceded them. Pre-post instruction analysis is especially helpful for evaluating mastery tests.

References

Ahmann, J. S., and M. D. Glock: *Evaluating Pupil Growth: Principles of Tests and Measurement,* 4th ed, Allyn and Bacon, Inc., Boston, 1971.

Deiderich, Paul B.: *Short-cut Statistics for Teacher-Made Tests,* 2d ed, Educational Testing Service, Princeton, N.J., 1964.

Ebel, Robert L.: *Essentials of Educational Measurement,* Prentice-Hall, Inc., Englewood Cliffs, N.J., 1972.

Gagné, Robert M.: *The Conditions of Learning,* 2d ed., Holt, Rinehart and Winston, Inc., New York, 1970.

Gronlund, Norman E.: *Preparing Criterion-Referenced Tests for Classroom Instruction,* The Macmillan Company, New York, 1973.

Suggested Readings

Besides those listed above, the following measurement texts also include good chapters on test construction:

Gronlund, Norman E.: *Measurement and Evaluation in Teaching,* 2d ed., The Macmillan Company, New York, 1971.

Marshall, Jon C., and Loyde W. Hales: *Classroom Test Construction,* Addison-Wesley Publishing Company, Inc., Reading, Mass., 1971.

Mehrens, William A., and Irvin J. Lehmann: *Measurement and Evaluation in Education and Psychology,* Holt, Rinehart and Winston, Inc., New York, 1973.

Stanley, Julian C., and Kenneth D. Hopkins: *Educational and Psychological Measurement and Evaluation,* 5th ed., Prentice-Hall, Inc., Englewood Cliffs, N.J., 1972.

Thorndike, Robert L., and Elizabeth Hagen: *Measurement and Evaluation in Psychology and Education,* 3d ed., John Wiley & Sons, Inc., New York, 1969.

For excellent examples of test items in a variety of subject matter areas, see Part Two of the following work:

Bloom, Benjamin S., J. Thomas Hastings, and George F. Madaus (eds.): *Handbook on Formative and Summative Evaluation of Student Learning,* McGraw-Hill Book Company, New York, 1971.

Some of the issues in criterion-referenced measurement are discussed in:

Popham, W. James (ed.): *Criterion-Referenced Measurement,* Educational Technology Publications, Englewood Cliffs, N.J., 1971.

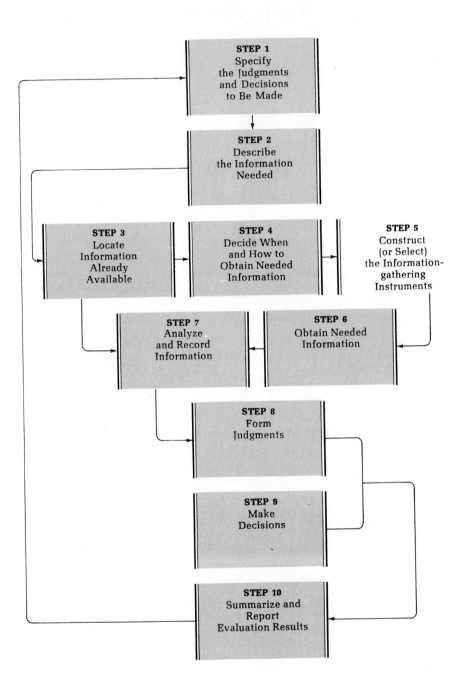

CHAPTER 14

Selecting Standardized Tests

Step 5 in the evaluation process involves constructing (or *selecting*) the particular information-gathering instrument you plan on using. If, during the first part of this step, you decided that a standardized test[1] should be used, then you need to select a particular standardized instrument from among the multitude of available ones. This chapter has been written to help you learn how to do that.

Standardized tests have been used regularly for years in virtually every school system in the United

---

[1] Throughout this chapter the author will follow the common practice of referring to all standardized information-gathering instruments as standardized tests. Keep in mind that some standardized instruments are not *tests* in the true sense of the word. For example, personality measures are really inventories, but they are often referred to as tests.

States. Actually, they have probably been misused as often as they have been correctly used. And because of the many instances of the misuse of standardized tests, they have been the object of a continuous debate in educational circles for the past several years. Many of the issues in this debate would be resolved rather quickly and much of the misuse of these tests would cease if the test users would come to a better understanding of what these tests are and what they should be used for.[2]

Consequently, in the first section of this chapter, the major types of standardized tests will be described and the kinds of judgments and decisions which can be made with them will be indicated. In the second section, step-by-step procedures for selecting a standardized test will be explained.

This chapter should help you to meet the following objectives:

1. When given a set of anticipated judgments and decisions, you should be able to indicate which type(s) of standardized tests would be appropriate.
2. You should be able to describe the use of each type of standardized test.
3. When given a description of an educational situation (including a list of decision areas), you should be able to take the necessary steps to select appropriate standardized tests.
4. When given a statement of the kind of information needed about a standardized test(s), you should be able to identify the important sources where that information could be located.

Notice that we will not be discussing *specific* standardized tests. It would be highly impractical to deal with each one of the many hundreds of tests presently being published. A few of the better tests of each type could be considered, but this has been done in numerous other texts which have emphasized standardized testing. Some of these texts are annotated in the list of suggested readings at the end of this section.

STANDARDIZED TESTS: WHAT AND WHY

What Is So Different about the Information They Provide?

In Chapter 5 a standardized test was defined as an instrument designed to obtain many kinds of information under standardized conditions. Usually a table

---

[2] See the suggested readings at the end of this chapter for references concerning some of the issues being presently debated.

of norms accompanies the test. The information obtained from a standardized test has the following three characteristics: (1) it is clearly defined, (2) it has known parameters, and (3) it has been obtained under ideal conditions. Let us examine each of these in turn.

It is clearly defined. Standardized tests are designed to clearly measure some specified behavior or set of behaviors. The planning stages of standardized-test construction are very elaborate. In aptitude tests, for example, the construct being measured is very carefully defined. In achievement test construction, subject matter experts and test construction experts work together to produce a highly elaborate table of specifications defining exactly how many items should be measuring specific behaviors or particular bits of knowledge. The information obtained from a standardized test is related very clearly and directly to a table of specifications, a set of objectives, or a carefully defined theoretical construct. Most of the time, when you obtain information from a standardized test, you know quite specifically what kind of information you have. Examine, for example, the descriptions of some of the constructs being measured by the Differential Aptitude Test. These are direct quotes from the test manual and illustrate how precisely test publishers try to define what they are measuring.

> The *Verbal Reasoning* test, as its name implies, is a measure of ability to understand concepts framed in words. It is aimed at the evaluation of the student's ability to abstract or generalize and to think constructively, rather than at simple fluency or vocabulary recognition.
>
> The *Numerical Ability* test is a measure of the student's ability to reason with numbers, to manipulate numerical relationships, and to deal intelligently with quantitative materials. It teams with the *Verbal Reasoning* test as a measure of general learning ability.
>
> The *Space Relations* test is a measure of ability to deal with concrete materials through visualization. There are many vocations in which one is required to imagine how an object would look if made from a given pattern, or how a specified object would appear if rotated in a given way. This ability to manipulate *things* mentally, to create a structure in one's mind from a plan is what the test is designed to evaluate.[3]

Some standardized achievement tests (especially those designed to allow criterion-referenced judgments) offer even more explicit descriptions of what they are measuring. Below are some of the objectives being measured by the TABS (Tests of Achievement in Basic Skills) Mathematic Skills test. These objectives are quoted directly from the *Examiner's Manual* (level C). These are only selected objectives. There are sixty-four objectives being measured by this test at this level. Each one is as explicitly stated as those quoted.

---

[3] These excerpts were taken directly from the *Fourth Edition Manual* for the Differential Aptitude Tests, forms L and M (Bennet, Seashore, and Wesman. Reproduced by permission. Copyright 1947, 1952; © 1959, 1963, 1966, 1968, by the Psychological Corporation, New York, N.Y. All rights reserved.

Examples of TABS Objectives*

1. A student must correctly add three four-digit whole numbers.
4. A student must correctly divide a four-digit whole number by a two-digit whole number and represent any remainder as a common fraction.
14. Given a sequence of three common fractions, the student must correctly determine the lowest common denominators for the fractions.
40. Given two dimensions of a rectangle, the students must correctly determine its areas; or given one dimension and the area, the student must correctly determine the other side.
54. The student must correctly identify any base 10 (decimal) number in its expanded form.

These objectives were taken directly from the TABS *Examiner's Manual* (level C).

*James C. Young and Robert R. Knapp, "Mathematics Skills Examiner's Manual," *Tests of Achievement in Basic Skills,* Educational and Industrial Testing Service, San Diego, Calif., 1972, pp. 3 and 4. Used by permission.

Information from standardized tests has known parameters. In the process of standardization, these tests are given to large samples of individuals differing in age, grade, socioeconomic status, geographic location, etc. The results which are obtained are carefully analyzed and numerous parameters are calculated (e.g., average performance of each age group). Each of these calculations serves as an estimate of the results you might expect to get if you gave the test to a similar group of individuals under similar conditions. Some of the most helpful parameters are listed below.

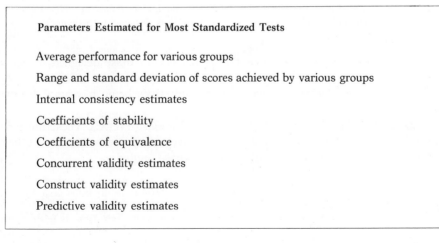

Parameters Estimated for Most Standardized Tests

Average performance for various groups

Range and standard deviation of scores achieved by various groups

Internal consistency estimates

Coefficients of stability

Coefficients of equivalence

Concurrent validity estimates

Construct validity estimates

Predictive validity estimates

Information from standardized tests is obtained under "ideal conditions." Publishers of standardized tests do everything in their power to make certain that testing conditions will be "ideal" each time the test is used. Directions are very explicitly stated, sample problems are supplied, instructions for timing are given, and suggestions are made for providing a pleasant "climate" and establishing appropriate motivation. You might gain some appreciation for the trouble publishers go through in an attempt to provide for ideal conditions by reading the following excerpts from the manual accompanying the Iowa Tests of Basic Skills.[4]

Advance Arrangements

1.   **Seating.** If there is any choice of rooms in which the tests may be given, adequacy of writing space, freedom from crowding, and adequacy of lighting are the major factors to be considered. Remember that the pupil must have room to handle an open $8\frac{1}{2}'' \times 11''$ booklet and a separate answer sheet, and that in taking Tests A-1 and A-2 he also must have room for scratch paper. Desks or tables should be used in preference to tablet armchairs wherever possible, and should be cleared of all other materials. During the testing the pupils should be separated as much as the seating arrangement of the room allows. A seating arrangement that discourages copying is better than warning against copying.

2.   **Pencils.** The pupils should be told in advance to come provided with two soft (No. 2) black-lead pencils and an eraser. (If IBM 805 answer sheets are to be scored by machine, the sheets must be marked with electrograph pencils.). . . .

Time Schedule for Administering the Tests

The entire battery of tests will require about five hours to administer, four hours and thirty-nine minutes of which is actual working time. It is recommended that the tests be given on four consecutive days: Tests V and R the first day, Test L the second day, Test W the third day, and Test A the fourth day. They may be given on four consecutive half-days, but such a full schedule of testing may tire the pupils unduly. Under no circumstances should they be given in a single day.

If several grades in a building are being tested, . . .

Distributing and Collecting the Test Materials

Be certain that you distribute the appropriate answer sheets to your pupils. If the same answer sheet is to be used in more than one test session, you may wish to formulate a plan to facilitate returning the pupils' answer sheets. . . .

If you are administering the tests to a large group, you will require the assistance of one adult proctor for every 30 pupils beyond the first 30. In this case, before the first testing. . . .

Timing the Tests

It is essential that time be kept accurately. A watch with a second hand will do for this purpose; a stop watch is even better. If you are using an ordinary watch, make a *written* note (in the spaces provided in this manual) of the exact time at which you start each test.

---

[4] Excerpts quoted below were taken directly from the *Teacher's Manual* accompanying the Iowa Tests of Basic Skills (Lindquist and Hieronymous, Houghton Mifflin Company, Boston, 1964, pp. 4–6). Used by permission of the publisher.

Preparing the Pupils for the Tests

It is extremely important that the pupils know why they are taking the tests and what use will be made of the results. Pupils must be stimulated to earnest effort if the potential values of the testing are to be realized.

It is wise, therefore, to schedule a short session a day or two in advance of testing in which the nature and purposes of the testing are discussed. To assist you in doing this, the pupil's report folder "How Are Your Skills?" has been prepared.

The above quotes are only *excerpts*. The full set of instructions is even more explicit. These quotations were taken from the general directions. The manual also provides instructions for each subtest. Included in these specific instructions are precisely worded directions which the examiner is to read verbatim.

What Kinds of Decisions Can Be Made with the Results?

Administrative decisions.   The main administrative decisions which rely heavily on the results of standardized tests are grouping decisions. Decisions about how to group students for instruction are the kinds of placement decisions which call for measures of aptitude as well as measures of achievement. At most colleges (and most private schools), selection decisions are standard procedure. These decisions can be made more accurately with standardized-test results. Sometimes administrative decisions related to the promotions and awards given to students can be aided by information from standardized tests. Some administrative decisions about teachers (e.g., what kinds of teaching assigments to give individual teachers) could be made easier with standardized-test scores. However, standardized-test scores should not be used in making decisions about promotion, tenure, or merit pay of teachers. As a measure of student achievement, tests are valuable. But there are too many factors besides the teacher which may cause that achievement to be at the level it is. Consequently, you cannot safely say that x amount of achievement is due to x degree of teaching quality. Decisions related to curriculum change, to the selection of appropriate textbooks, to the allocation of time, space, and money all can be made easier with standardized-test information. Of course, that should only be a *part* of the information used as input into the decision-making process. The effectiveness of a particular textbook for example, might be ascertained by using standardized achievement scores as well as information from teacher-made tests covering the material which that textbook was supposed to cover.

Counseling decisions.   Most decisions made by school counselors are related to educational and vocational guidance problems. Decisions about a choice of college or a choice of career can certainly be aided by the use of aptitude and past achievement information as well as by the information about a student's interests and attitudes. Furthermore, decisions about whether a student needs special clinical or educational help can best be made if some information is available about his personality, his interests, and his attitudes as well as about the amount of success he is having in school as defined by a standardized achievement test.

Instructional decisions. Although teachers rarely use standardized-test results to help them make instructional decisions, this *is* a decision area where these results could be extremely helpful. Below is a list of a few of the many questions which represent instructional decisions which could be made with the benefit of standardized-test results.

Questions Representing Instructional Decisions That Could Be Aided by Standardized-Test Results

1. Should I assign this supplementary text?
2. How fast should we move through this material?
3. How many reading groups should I have?
4. Which students should serve as coordinators for the research groups?
5. How much review of math concepts should I do?
6. When should I begin moving into an explanation of basic algebra concepts?
7. Shall I begin the preprimers next week?
8. Should the tenth graders be given less grammar and more literature?
9. Should I use a discovery approach? How much guidance should I give?

Why Should a Given Type of Standardized Test Be Used?

Let us examine a little more closely the kinds of situations which would call for the use of each of the major types of standardized tests.

Achievement tests. Most educational judgments and decisions center around student achievement. An achievement test is a test designed to measure a person's present level of knowledge, performance, or skill. It is designed *primarily* for making estimative rather than predictive judgments. Of course, predictions can be made from achievement data, but that is not the primary purpose of these kinds of tests. There are a wide variety of standardized achievement tests. You must learn how to select those which will give you information best suited for your particular needs. However, it should be remembered that standardized achievement-test results should *supplement, not replace* the results of teacher-made tests.

The diagnostic achievement tests are particularly valuable for helping a teacher make judgments about the particular areas of strength and weakness of individual students. When these areas of strength and weakness are identified, the teacher can then provide the appropriate learning experiences (treatments) for each student. Of course, this information from standardized tests should be supplemented with information from teacher-made tests, classroom observations, and the analysis of assignments.

A less obvious value of standardized achievement test scores is their value to the lesson-planning activities of the teacher. An achievement test given at the beginning of the school year can provide valuable information to the teacher in building his lesson plans. By examining the scores of the class as a whole for each of the various subject matters, the teacher can often get clues about the level of achievement his students have reached. He can then design his lesson plans so as to strengthen those areas for the class as a whole. Small subgroups of students who have common areas of weakness can often also be identified early in the term through the use of standardized achievement tests.

Another valuable although not so common use of standardized achievement tests scores is program assessment. By comparing the average score of the class *across* subject matters, the teacher can find areas of the program or curriculum where there are particular strengths and weaknesses. It is not uncommon, for example, for an elementary teacher to find that his students have performed well above the national norms on all of the subtests of the Iowa Basic Skills Test except for the map-reading section. This information can be useful to the teacher because it helps to point to an area in his program where greater emphasis could be placed the following year.

Although it is unwise for administrators to use standardized-test results as a way of assessing a teacher's effectiveness, these results can be used by the classroom teacher himself. Because the teacher knows what goals he has set for his students, he can compare these goals to those measured by the standardized test. Where there is a good correspondence, he should expect his students to do well on that portion of the standardized test (assuming they have at least average aptitude). If the goals he has set for his students do not match those being measured by the standardized test, then that portion of the test is an inappropriate measure. Of course there are a number of other variables which could affect the outcome of a student's performance on a standardized test besides the variability of teaching effectiveness. The level of aptitude of the student, the particular kind of material being taught, and the local objectives of the particular teacher all will affect the outcome. But the *teacher* is more aware of these variables than anyone else in the school system. By taking these variables into consideration, he can usually make fairly sound judgments about how effective his teaching has been.

Aptitude tests. An individual's *aptitude* for some task *predicts* how well he will perform that task. The major use of aptitude test results is in making predictive judgments. All kinds of decisions rely on predictive judgments and consequently on information about aptitude. If I am to select certain individuals for a given task (e.g., earning a college degree), I need to know what each one's relative aptitude for that task is. In order to place a student properly in an educational program, I must know what aspects of that program he has the most aptitude for. In giving assignments to individuals (treatment decisions), I must consider their aptitude for the task I am about to assign.

When a teacher asks, "Is Jeremiah working up to capacity?" he is asking for a judgment to be made which calls for an estimate of achievement *compared to* an estimate of aptitude.

When a teacher wonders whether a mathematics text will be too difficult for the tenth graders, he wonders about the aptitude of those students.

When an employer tries to decide whom to hire as production manager, his decision must be made, in part, on the relative aptitudes of those applying for the job.

When a counselor is faced with the task of deciding who should take general math, his task is easier if he knows the students' algebra aptitude scores.

Aptitude tests are valuable (though often misused) in most educational decision making. Individuals cannot be accurately assessed, educational programs cannot be appropriately evaluated, and teaching cannot accomplish its goals without the aid of estimates of aptitude. Standardized aptitude tests provide an important portion of those estimates.

Measures of typical performance. Measures of typical performance include personality inventories, interest inventories, and measures of attitudes and opinions. It is easy to see why these are referred to as measures of *typical* performance. A person's personality, for example, is not so much determined by how well he can respond to others as it is by how well he *typically does* respond to others. Likewise, interests and attitudes are characterized by typical rather than maximum performance. Sometimes these measures are referred to as noncognitive measures (although the noncognitive category could also include measures of psychomotor skills). We are all aware of the importance of noncognitive factors in learning. When someone is interested in a task, he tends to stick to that task longer and work harder at it. Our interests affect our performance in school, at play, and on the job. Furthermore, our interests are important when we choose a course of study, a vocation, or a career. An individual's attitudes are closely related to his interests. Attitudes also affect what we choose to do and how well we do it. Attitudes, like interests, tend to change fairly often, and so it is difficult to obtain information which is stable enough to be used over an extended period of time. Personality traits are somewhat more stable, but they are difficult to measure reliably. The value of these measures to the classroom teacher is minimal. Sometimes the results of an interest inventory can help the teacher to more successfully individualize his instruction but usually a formal, standardized instrument is not needed to get the kind of general information about student interests that the teacher needs.

The most important reason for the typical performance measure is to obtain information about particular students who are having problems. A counselor and teacher, working together, can often help a student through some rough spots in his development *if* they can get some indication about the nature of the problem. Standardized, noncognitive measures considered along with cognitive measures can help provide some evidence. Many times the results of these tests given in school will indicate the necessity for more thorough evaluation by a trained psychologist or psychiatrist. Most of the time, however, these results simply serve to help the teacher and counselor to guide the student into those educational and vocational experiences where he is most likely to succeed.

EXERCISE 14.1

Take a moment to review what you have just read. Keep your answers brief, and they will be useful to you for later review of this material.

1. List the three characteristics which are unique to standardized tests.
2. Cite at least four administrative decisions which can benefit from the results of standardized tests.
3. In what two major decision areas within the realm of counseling are standardized tests helpful?
4. There is an assessment problem for which standardized achievement tests are *not* appropriate. What is it?
5. Name two noncognitive measures which are important in learning and which are frequently obtained with standardized tests.

STANDARDIZED TESTS: HOW TO SELECT THEM

The multitude of standardized tests which are available to teachers measure a wide variety of abilities and behaviors. Consequently, the task of selecting a particular test which best meets your needs can be complex and time-consuming. The remainder of this chapter is designed to help make that task easier for you by describing the step-by-step procedures one should follow when selecting a standardized test.

In order to be successful in obtaining the test which best fits your needs, you must know what to look for in a test and where to go to find it. Three factors are generally considered to be the most important characteristics of a good standardized test: (1) validity—i.e., the test should yield the kind of information you must have in order to make the judgments and decisions you expect to make; (2) reliability—i.e., the test should be as free from measurement error as possible; and (3) practicality—i.e., the test should be easy to use and not too costly. It is often assumed that this kind of information can be fairly readily obtained by examining the tests and their manuals and by checking some reliable source for critical reviews. It is usually further assumed that one simply examines those tests which provide the major type of information needed (e.g., achievement, aptitude, or personality) and selects the test which is most valid and most reliable. Then, if there are practical considerations (e.g., high cost) which would make that test undesirable, one would select the next-best test.

For a number of reasons, it is not that simple. There is no "best" test of achievement. There is no single aptitude test which is "better" than all the rest.

A test, or for that matter an entire testing program, should be selected to best meet the needs of those who will use the test results. A test which best meets the needs of one school may not be useful at all to the personnel in another school.

Whether a committee is developing a testing program for an entire school system or an individual teacher is selecting a single test for use in his class, the process of test selection is essentially the same. It should be a process which begins with a statement of needs and moves through an organized search for a test to meet those needs. The following steps provide such an organized approach.[5]

The four major steps in standardized-test selections are as follows:

1. Define your needs.
2. Narrow your choice.
3. Obtain and examine the test materials.
4. Make your final choice.

Following these steps fairly rigorously will help you to obtain those standardized tests which are best suited to your purposes. Each of these steps will be discussed in some detail. A thorough understanding of the process of test selection will help you not only in the selection of tests but also in determining the potential value of a test already in use in your school.

Step 1: Define Your Needs

There are a number of things which should be considered when deciding what to look for in any standardized test (or, for that matter, in any testing program). To make certain that you do not miss any of the important considerations in the test selection, you should begin your selection process by answering the following three questions:

1. What information is needed?
2. How much error can be tolerated?
3. What practical limitations will be encountered?

What information is needed? No two tests yield exactly the same information about the person to whom they are administered. Consequently, if you can describe with enough precision the kind of information you need, you will be better able to select from among the many standardized tests the one which best meets your needs. We have already indicated that standardized tests are usually

---

[5] These four steps were first suggested by Gronlund (1965, 1971). The details of each step have been modified somewhat to fit the principles established earlier in this text, but the basic procedures were spelled out by Gronlund.

grouped under the headings of achievement tests, aptitude tests, and measures of typical performance. However, to simply indicate that an aptitude measure is needed or that achievement scores are desired is not enough.

Suppose the teachers in an elementary school decide they need to find out about how much their pupils have achieved. More particularly they want to know if their pupils learned what they were supposed to. The most precise statement of the information they need would be a list of the terminal instructional goals for each subject matter at each grade level. If this is available, the few most promising tests can be examined carefully to see how well the items in each subject matter subtest measure these instructional goals. Besides this comparison of test items to instructional goals, other considerations can help in the test selection. If the level of learning emphasized in the teacher's goals is known, test selection is easier. Some achievement tests measure mostly memorization of facts. Others tend to emphasize the acquisition of concepts and application of rules. If the instructional goals were at the upper level of a taxonomy of learning, then the test should not measure just memorization of facts. If, on the other hand, instructional goals were mostly factual in nature, then the test used should be designed to measure facts. For traditional instructional goals, certain standardized tests should be selected. For more progressive goals, other tests would likely be more appropriate.

Although aptitude tests may seem to be much more alike than achievement tests, it quickly becomes apparent that this is not the case. Therefore a description of the *kind* of aptitude information needed will also help. First of all, a gross distinction can be made on the basis of whether general aptitude or aptitude for a specific task or content area is needed. Suppose a measure of scholastic aptitude is needed. Would not almost any intelligence test do? Do not all intelligence tests measure approximately the same thing? The answer here is no, because there are many differences in what is being measured by the various intelligence tests that are available. As you know, the kind of information needed depends on how that information is going to be used. If you are trying to predict future academic performance, one kind of aptitude test is needed. If you are trying to get a potential for learning ability, that requires a different kind of test. The immediate use of all test data is to serve as a basis for judgments. The types of judgments to be made determine some of the test characteristics that will be important. For example, if predictive judgments are to be made, predictive validity and test-retest reliability (or alternate-form reliability with time between the testing) are the technical considerations of importance. If judgments are to be made about an individual's achievement in one subject matter compared to his achievement in another, then an achievement battery is probably more useful than a single achievement test.

The ultimate use of evaluative data is in decision making. Different kinds of decisions require different kinds of tests and test data. Administrative decisions are usually made about all or most all of the students. Therefore tests which can be given to many students in a fairly short time and at a relatively low cost

TABLE 14.1

Characteristics Needed in a Standardized Test Which Is to Be Used for Making Particular Types of Decisions and/or Judgments

TYPES OF DECISIONS AND JUDGMENTS FOR WHICH STANDARDIZED-TEST DATA WILL BE USED	CHARACTERISTICS NEEDED IN THE STANDARDIZED TEST
Decisions	
Administrative	National and local norms, high predictive validity.
Counseling	Nonthreatening, variety of norms available, high predictive validity.
Instructional	High content validity, local norms, items keyed to objectives, internal consistency.
Research	Construct validity usually very important, fairly high reliability needed, alternate forms frequently needed.
Selection	Well-defined norms; high predictive validity, test-retest reliability, general aptitude and achievement.
Placement	Aptitude and achievement scores for specific topics, concurrent and predictive validity important, standard error of measurement for each grade level.
Treatment	Criterion-referenced (keyed to instructional goals and specified criteria), measure of local objectives, local norms, norms for different times of the year.
Judgments	
Estimates	Concurrent and construct validity are crucial; both general and specific aptitude and achievement desirable.
Predictions	General and specific aptitude; predictive validity must be very high.
Norm-referenced	Well defined norms; norms which match the group being judged; high reliability (especially test-retest) and high validity.
Criterion-referenced	Keyed to objectives; match local objectives closely; high content validity; high statistical reliability and validity, although desirable, not necessary.
Formative	Measures of classroom objectives; easily scored and interpreted so results can be obtained quickly.
Summative	General as well as specific achievement.

are chosen. A high school decides to group all its students into high, middle, and low ability groups for English and math. Every student must be tested. The testing should probably occur every year at every grade level. Individual tests would be impractical if not impossible to administer. Instructional decisions, on the other hand, sometimes require individually administered tests. For example, in making assignments to her students in remedial reading, Mrs. George is required to make an in-depth diagnosis of each student's problems. This kind of in-depth diagnosis can usually be done most effectively with individually administered tests. Table 14.1 further illustrates the fact that particular characteristics are needed in a test if it is to fulfill particular needs (i.e., when the results are to be used in making particular kinds of judgments and decisions).

How much error can be tolerated?   You will recall from Chapter 2 that validity and reliability coefficients are estimates of freedom from error and are used to compute estimates of the *amount* of error you are likely to make in judgments and decisions about an individual. The standard error of measurement (computed from a reliability coefficient) estimates how far an obtained score is from a true score. The obtained score, when properly interpreted, serves as the basis for judgments. For example, when a raw score from an intelligence test is converted to an IQ, a numerical description is obtained that is essentially a judgment about how intelligent that person is. The standard error of measurement tells us approximately how much error there is in that judgment. The standard error of estimate, on the other hand, indicates approximately how much error occurs when we make predictive judgments. The more reliable and the more valid a test is, the smaller will be the standard error of measurement and the standard error of estimate respectively. This means that the error in the judgments we make will be smaller. Consequently, the answer to the question, "How much error can be tolerated?" is determined to a large degree by the importance of the judgments and—more importantly—the subsequent decisions that will be made. The more important the decisions, the smaller the amount of error that can be tolerated and therefore the greater must be the validity and reliability. Suggestions for determining the importance of decisions were presented in Chapter 3 (pages 69 to 70). When the anticipated judgments and decisions are far-reaching and relatively permanent, the most valid and reliable tests available should be used. By being aware of the probable effects of the judgments and decisions that are to be made, you will be better able to determine how important it will be to obtain the test which is most valid and reliable.

However, you already know from our discussion in Chapter 2 that there is no single "best" estimate of either validity or reliability. There are different kinds of validity and reliability estimates. The importance of a particular validity or reliability estimate is determined by the kinds of judgments and decisions you plan on making with the results of the test.

What practical limitations will be encountered?   An obvious factor which may limit which test you can use is your budget. When you consider the quantity and the quality of the information you get for your dollar, most standardized tests are quite reasonable. Nevertheless, some tests are more expensive than others and when standardized tests are used often and for large numbers of students, the cost can add up surprisingly fast. You should know, before you begin your search for a test, how much money has been budgeted. When figuring the cost of a test, do not forget the cost of scoring and recording results.

Another factor which may limit your use of standardized tests is the school personnel. Many of the standardized tests can be administered and interpreted by teachers and even clerical workers who have been trained in their use. However, some standardized tests, especially those administered individually, require that a specially trained psychologist or psychometrist administer and interpret them. Although most of the larger test publishers try to exercise some control over who may purchase tests, it is difficult and costly to check on the qualifications of each purchaser. Schools placing orders for tests are seldom questioned except when trying to purchase a complex test designed to be used only by clinical psychologists who are trained in their use. The test *user* is under obligation to restrict his use of tests to those which he is qualified to give. Complete guidelines for those using tests can be found in the *Ethical Standards of Psychologists* (American Psychological Association, 1968). If you are in doubt about whether your school has the personnel qualified to use any given test, check these *standards* and write the publisher asking for a statement of the qualifications needed to use the test.

Most academic achievement tests can be safely used by teachers if they carefully follow the instructions in the manual. Group-administered aptitude tests, interest inventories, and some group-administered personality inventories can be used by persons having a good grasp of the principles of measurement and evaluation and some understanding of the principles of psychology, guidance, and statistics. However, most personality tests should not be administered or interpreted by teachers. Individually administered tests and tests of a clinical nature should be only used by those whose education and training is appropriate for the particular test being used. For example, a master's degree in psychology or a closely related field and an appropriate amount of training in the use of the specific test would be needed for the Stanford-Binet, the Wechsler Scales, or the Illinois Test of Psycholinguistic Abilities.

A final practical consideration is scheduling. When and how often will a test be used? Suppose an achievement test is to be given each fall. If the standardized achievement test being considered does not include normative data which was also gathered in the fall, no meaningful norm-referenced judgments can be made. If a student is given a test in September, it would not be fair to compare his score with students who took the test in May, after having nearly completed the course work for that year. Many publishers collect normative data at different times throughout the year so that there will be an appropriate set of norms for the test user no matter when he plans on giving the test.

How often do you plan on giving a test? Suppose you would like to get two or three measures of achievement throughout the year in order to keep track of the students' progress. It is important not only to have appropriate norms for the different times throughout the year but also to have different forms of the test available. If the same form is used several times, a student will be able to remember from one testing to the next what the questions were and how he answered them. Thus much of the obtained score would be a reflection of how much he remembered from time to time rather than of how much progress he was making.

Step 2: Narrow Your Choice

Having clearly defined your needs so that you are aware of the kinds of information needed, how accurate that information must be, and what the practical limitations are, you can then begin a search for an appropriate test.

Deciding on a specific type of test. By reviewing the first few steps in the evaluation process, you will know what kind of information you need. It will be relatively easy to decide whether you want a measure of aptitude, achievement, or typical performance. But to narrow your choice to a specific kind of test within each of these categories is a little more difficult. This task will be easier if you see it as simply a series of decisions you must make. Each decision brings you to a new decision point, and, as you choose among alternative types of tests, you finally narrow your choice to a very specific type. At that point, you are ready to find out what tests of that type are available. We have diagrammed this "narrowing" process in Figure 14.1. Examine it to get an overview of the decision points involved and then read the discussion which follows. It is designed to acquaint you with the important considerations at each decision point.

Aptitude. If a measure of aptitude is what you need, then the next decision you must make is between tests which measure general scholastic aptitude (most of these are referred to as intelligence tests) or some special aptitude (e.g., creativity, music aptitude, or aptitude for algebra). Scholastic aptitude tests and in-

FIGURE 14.1. Selection of a standardized test. A "narrowing down" process: making decisions at several points.

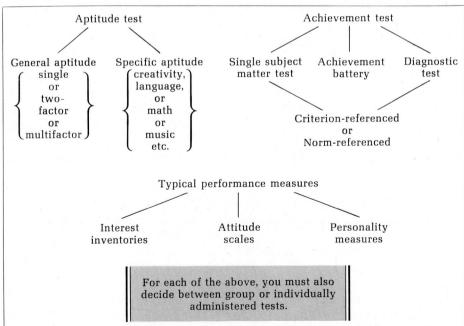

telligence tests are designed to *predict* academic achievement. Note that they generally do *not* claim to be measures of innate ability to learn. They *do* claim to predict the grades an individual is likely to attain in most educational settings.

The many scholastic aptitude tests can be further divided into single-factor and multifactor tests. The single-factor tests yield a total score (usually called IQ) which is supposed to be a measure of general ability. There are also two-factor tests which yield two scores, one presenting *verbal* ability and the other a *nonverbal* ability. The nonverbal ability measures are either *nonlanguage* scores (an understanding of the language is not required) or *performance* scores (obtained from tests where the examinee is asked to manipulate objects in an attempt to complete an assigned task). Multifactor aptitude tests provide scores of many aptitudes. Usually a total score, which is supposed to be a measure of general aptitude, is also provided. General aptitude tests come in two varieties: group-administered and individually administered tests. Group tests can be used by persons with limited training. They are easy to administer, score, and interpret. Furthermore, they are inexpensive and can be given to large groups of students at one time. Individually administered tests tend to be more reliable. They also provide the examiner with insights into the test-taking behavior of the examinee. They must be administered individually by trained personnel and are expensive and time-consuming to administer.

Achievement. If an achievement test is needed, you must first decide whether to use a single subject matter test, an achievement battery, or a diagnostic test. Achievement batteries are the most popular because achievement in several areas can be tested in a relatively short time and self-referenced judgments can be made (i.e., an individual's performance can be compared in one subject matter to his performance in another). The single subject matter tests are longer and tend to be more reliable than the subtests of the batteries. Furthermore, they can be chosen to more carefully match the teacher's own instructional goals. Suppose, for example, a battery is selected because the math portion is a good measure of the classroom objectives. It is highly likely that the other subject matter areas will not match the classroom objectives so well. Using single tests of each subject matter, the teacher can select each subject matter individually, matching each test as closely as possible to his instructional goals. The diagnostic tests are designed to measure specific areas of strengths and weaknesses in a given subject matter area. For the most part, they are limited to reading and mathematics. To be most helpful, a diagnostic test should be criterion-referenced (keyed to an achievement continuum which has been defined in terms of behavioral objectives). Most are not. More of these will be appearing on the market, however, as the techniques for constructing and standardizing criterion-referenced tests become more refined.

Typical performance. If measures of typical performance are needed, a choice must again be made. The alternatives are interest inventories, attitude scales, or personality measures. Interest inventories are most useful for helping students find out what kinds of interests they have and how these interests relate to various vocations and/or educational pursuits. Some interest tests are keyed to vocations and others to educational pursuits. Still others are keyed to free-time activities. If attitudes are to be measured, you must decide if you are after general attitudes (e.g., open-minded versus close-minded) or if you wish to measure more specific attitudes (e.g., political attitudes, attitudes toward religion, attitudes toward minority groups, etc.). Personality tests are usually individually administered and teachers are generally not qualified to give them. Some are clinically keyed to abnormal personality traits (e.g., paranoid, schizophrenic) and some are keyed to more normal personality traits (e.g., aggressive, outgoing). Another way to classify these measures is according to the type of instrument being used to obtain the information. Some use a rating-scale technique (e.g., the examinee indicates which of several behaviors are typical of his behavior). Others use a projective technique (e.g., an inkblot is presented and the examinee tells the examiner what he sees, thus *projecting* his personality onto a non-meaningful stimulus).

The next few paragraphs explain three other schemes for classifying standardized tests. As you read about these classification schemes, take note of the fact that each classification makes it possible for a different kind of judgment or decision to be made. And herein lies the genius of so many different types of tests. Each type is best designed to yield information which is most useful for making particular kinds of judgments and decisions.

Group versus individual.   Standardized tests are often classified as group tests or individual tests. Group tests are designed to be given to large groups of individuals at a time. They usually require the examinee to be able to read and are frequently highly loaded on verbal activity. They are generally good predictors of academic achievement. Individual tests are designed to be given to one individual at a time. They are time-consuming and costly to give but usually very reliable. Norm-referenced judgments can be made with both types. However, group tests have the advantage if selection decisions are to be made from those judgments, because it is economical to give group tests to large numbers of individuals. If judgments of progress are to be made, group tests are better because they usually come in two or more forms and can be administered quite frequently. Institutional decisions are normally based on group tests, whereas individual decisions are frequently made on the basis of individualized test results. Many aptitude tests are individual tests, but most achievement tests are group tests. The diagnosis of problems is best accomplished with individual tests. These tests often yield information about the thinking *process* of the examinee as well as about the *"product"* he produces. Group tests, on the other hand, are most useful in screening large numbers of individuals, but they generally yield a "number-right" score rather than a description of the thinking process.

General versus specific.   Another way in which standardized tests are classified is along a general-to-specific dimension. Some tests are designed to get a general overall impression of ability or achievement (e.g., the general intelligence tests and the achievement batteries). Other tests are designed to obtain information about highly specific abilities or achievements (e.g., algebra aptitude and algebra achievement tests). The more general the test coverage, the more useful it will be for judging a person's overall performance and general academic potential or accomplishment. However, if your decisions call for judgments about specific skills, specific tests must be used.

Content versus process.   A third way to categorize standardized tests is according to whether they are content-oriented or process-oriented. Content-oriented aptitude tests rely on measures of a person's knowledge of certain content (e.g., how many foreign words does he know?). Process-oriented aptitude tests, on the other hand, try to obtain measures of a person's skill in a given area (e.g., how quickly can he learn a given list of foreign words?). Achievement tests can also be categorized in this way. Some of them (e.g., the Stanford Achievement Test, tend to ask more content questions, and others (e.g., the Iowa Test of Basic Skills) try to ask questions requiring the use of *skills* which should have been learned. A content-oriented geography test, for example, would ask questions about the locations and geographical characteristics of certain areas. A process-oriented geography test, on the other hand, might test various map-reading skills. The different uses of these two types of tests are obvious: if you are judging process or skills learned, you use a different kind of test than if you are judging content or knowledge gained. Furthermore, the process tests *tend* to measure more upper-level learning outcomes and the content-oriented tests *tend* to measure lower-level learning outcomes.

Finding out what tests are available.   Eventually, you will want to carefully examine specimen sets of those tests which seem most likely to meet your needs. First, however, you need to find out what tests are available that are designed to give you the kind of information you need. There are two main sources of information which will help you to find the available standardized tests: Buros's *Tests in Print* (Buros, 1961) and the test publishers' catalogs.

Buros's *Tests in Print* is a comprehensive listing of the published tests used in education, psychology, and industry. This index gives the title of the test, grade levels for each test booklet, publication dates, special features about the tests, types of scores provided, and the names of the authors and publishers. Also, a reference is made to the reviews of these tests in Buros's *Mental Measurements Yearbooks,* which we will discuss shortly.

For the most up-to-date information about available tests, you will need to consult the publisher's catalog. These catalogs will give you brief descriptions of the tests, telling you what is being measured, what the test results might possibly be used for, and what age and grade levels the tests are designed for.

Furthermore, practical features such as cost, administration time, etc., will be described. Of course, the publishers' catalogs are designed to sell tests. Consequently it is most important that you examine the critical reviews of any test, no matter how appealing the description in the publisher's catalog.

Obtaining more complete information. *Tests in Print* and the catalogs from the publishers will give you only brief descriptions of the tests available. Nevertheless, these sources can help you eliminate any tests which clearly do not meet your needs. The next step in narrowing your choice is to obtain more complete information of those tests. You will want information about the cost, ease of administration, the scoring and interpretation, availability of norms, the number of forms available, and other general information. Furthermore, you will want information about the strengths and weaknesses of a particular test. This last bit of evaluative information is not available in the *Tests in Print* or the publishers' catalogs. A most valuable source of this kind of information is Buros's *Mental Measurements Yearbook* (Buros, 1938, 1940, 1949, 1953, 1959, 1965, 1972). These yearbooks are published periodically and contain careful descriptions of standardized tests and critical reviews of each test. The reviews are written by specialists who have expertise in measurement and in the general content area measured by the test being reviewed.

Besides these valuable reviews which describe the major strengths and weaknesses of a test, the yearbooks include a bibliography of journal articles which have been written about each test. By locating and reading these articles, you can obtain still further informative and evaluative information about those tests which appear to be most promising. A final feature of the yearbooks is their relationship to *Tests in Print.* For each test located in *Tests in Print,* a reference is made to the reviews in the yearbooks. Thus, you can first locate the tests in *Tests in Print* and then turn to the corresponding reviews in the *Mental Measurements Yearbook* for more complete information and critical reviews.

The other major source of evaluative information about tests is professional journals. Many of the important journal articles can be located through the bibliography in the yearbooks. Other articles can be located by referring to the *Psychological Abstracts* and the *Education Index.* These two references abstract journal articles from virtually all major journals in psychology and education. The journals which are most likely to contain test reviews are *Educational and Psychological Measurement, Journal of Educational Measurement, Journal of Consulting Psychology,* and *Personnel and Guidance Journal.*

Narrowing the list to a few tests. With the information from the sources we have just described, you should be able to produce a relatively short list of tests which appear to be what you need. It is important to note that the selection process thus far has been essentially a process of elimination. Using the sources described above, you should eliminate all but a few tests. Specimen sets of those tests which seem most promising should then be obtained and examined closely before a final choice is made.

Step 3: Obtain and Examine Specimen Sets

Now that you have narrowed your choice to a few tests which seem to best meet your needs, the next step is to examine the test materials themselves. This step will provide you with much information available no other way and will allow you to completely and carefully compare the tests on the basis of how well they fit your needs. A test must measure what it is you want measured, be of high technical quality, and be easy to administer, score, and interpret. All reusable parts should be durable and the accompanying manuals should be helpful and understandable.

Obtaining specimen sets for examination. A specimen set can usually be obtained at a very low cost from the publishers. Send for your sets well in advance of the time you will need to make your test selection, because it takes time for the tests to arrive in the mail (usually two to six weeks), and a thorough examination also takes time. Specimen sets can often be found in a nearby college or university or within the school system's main administrative offices. However, the relatively low cost of specimen sets make them a good investment. Having your own specimen sets allows you to examine them at your leisure. If you do purchase a specimen set, keep it securely guarded, just as you would any standardized test. Copies of the tests or questions on the tests should not be placed in the hands of those who may later take the test.

What will you get if you order a specimen set from a publisher? Most specimen sets of standardized tests contain the following: a test booklet, answer sheets (when not a part of the test booklet), scoring keys, examples of pupil and class record sheets, and a manual (or set of manuals).

Standardized test booklets are either consumable or reusable. With a consumable booklet, students mark their answers in the test booklet itself and the booklet is then scored and consequently consumed in the process of being used. A reusable booklet is usually more sturdily constructed, often spiral bound, and is to be used over and over again. The student is specifically asked not to make any marks in this kind of test booklet. Instead, he marks his responses on a separate answer sheet. Answer sheets provided with standardized tests are designed either to be hand- or machine-scored. When they are to be machine-scored, a special kind of pencil is sometimes required. However, most machine-scored answer sheets now require the use of an ordinary number 2 pencil. Answer sheets vary a great deal in the ease with which they can be used. Sometimes the spaces for students' responses are very close together and very difficult to follow.

Scoring keys used for hand-scoring should be durable and easy to use. Many publishers now use transparent plastic keys. These are very durable and allow the scorer to spot items where the student marked more than one response.

Many standardized tests include a record-keeping system. This system will usually include a chart for tallying the responses of all the students in a given grade. This allows you to see how a particular class has done and is also the first step in the development of local norms, an important procedure which was discussed in Chapter 6. Some test manufacturers will also include a system for recording the scores of individuals and will even make provisions for keeping track of individual scores from year to year.

Each standardized test should be accompanied by at least one manual, which should include the information on how to administer, score, and interpret the test. Often the test publisher will produce a teacher's manual, giving instructions for administering and scoring the test, and a separate manual called an administrator's or technical manual. This technical manual will include statistical data on the validity and reliability of the test, descriptions of the norms, and other important technical information. Sometimes the teacher's manual will include one section for interpreting the scores, and then a more technical explanation of score interpretations will be included in the technical or administrator's manual. It is imperative that any interpretations be in line with the statistical and technical information supplied by the test publisher. Sometimes diagnostic interpretations may be suggested which in fact are not warranted on the basis of the technical information.

Examining a specimen set.   There are at least three major steps that should be followed when examining a specimen set. First of all, you should obtain an overview of the contents and then examine the test itself very carefully. Finally, you should examine the test manual or manuals in an attempt to obtain information about the quality of the test being considered. Let us consider each of the steps in turn.

An overview.   When first obtaining a specimen set, it is a good idea to look the contents over carefully and check to see how attractive and durable the materials are. Materials should hold up well, be easy to handle, and be easy to read. You should be able to find your way through the explanatory information easily, and the instructions to the students and examiner alike should be distinct, clear, and concise. The scoring keys should be easy to use and the record-keeping system should require a minimum of computation and detailed procedures.

The test should have obvious physical features such as easy to read pages which turn easily and lie flat. If the test is nonconsumable, it should be particularly durable. Besides these physical considerations, a test should include easy to follow instructions, and the examples used should be very clear as to the kind of response the student will be required to make.

The test itself.   After you have examined the test booklet, you should examine the test item by item. As you read each item, ask yourself, "What bit of knowledge, what skill, what learning outcome is being measured by this item?" This is especially important if the test is an achievement test. When selecting an achievement test, you will be interested in knowing how well the test items measure your instructional goals. If your instructional goals are explicitly stated in a form like that described in Chapter 4, then you can place these goals before you while you examine the test. For each item, try to decide whether or not it measured any of your instructional goals. The greater number of your instructional goals the test items seem to measure, the more useful the results of the test will be. This item-by-item, goal-by-goal analysis is the best way to establish the content validity of a test.

Some publishers are beginning to include a content-by-behavior description of the test items in their standardized tests. These are usually included in the teacher's manual. If these are provided, the task of making a thorough content validity study is much easier. After checking a few items to see that the publisher's description of what is being measured is accurate, you can then compare that description to the description of what you wish to measure (i.e., your list of instructional goals). As we witness the publication of more criterion-referenced tests like the TABS (Tests of Achievement in Basic Skills), we will undoubtedly find the publishers beginning to list in observable terms the instructional goals being measured — along with an indication of which items are measuring which goals. This should make the selection of achievement tests easier.

A particularly useful way to familiarize yourself with a standardized test is to take the test. Begin by reading the instructions word for word. Do exactly as the instructions tell the student to do. Try out each example and then work through the test, timing yourself carefully. When you have finished, score your test, interpreting your score just as you would that of your students. This role-playing procedure will help you to see how smoothly the mechanics of taking the test are likely to go. Furthermore, it will give you an opportunity to examine each question individually. As you try to answer each question, look not only for what is being measured but for how it is being measured. Look also for any possible ambiguities that might signal poorly written items and potential unreliability.

The manual. The manual accompanying a standardized test should include a wide range of important data. In an attempt to see to it that the standardized test manual will include all the information a user will need, a joint committee of members from the American Psychological Association, the American Educational Research Association, and the National Council of Measurement in Education have produced a set of standards for educational and psychological tests and manuals. These standards have been published by the APA and are available for $1 (American Psychological Association, 1966). I would recommend that every school system place this small booklet in its library as a reference source for teachers and members of test selection committees. Let us briefly examine the major considerations in this publication's standards. No test publisher is obligated by law to follow these standards and therefore, even though a test is commercially produced, it may not have a good manual. However, if a test manual meets the standards described below, you should have the information you need to make your final decision about whether or not to use a test. The standards established by this committee are categorized under the following headings:

1. Dissemination of information
2. Interpretation
3. Validity
4. Reliability
5. Administration and scoring
6. Scales and norms

A brief explanation of each of the categories will give you an idea of the kinds of things which measurement experts feel are important in a standardized test.

The first topic treated by the standard's committee is dissemination of information.

The APA standards make it very clear that it is the responsibility of the publisher to produce a manual or set of manuals which will make available to the test users all the information he needs in order to make appropriate interpretations of the test. A second important point under the topic of dissemination of information is that information about a test gets outdated very quickly, and therefore the manual should be kept up to date. Such things as social conditions, job definitions, and educational pressures change very dramatically, and therefore the interpretations of the scores on a number of tests must also change.

The interpretation of test results (the second topic in the standards) is extremely important. If the score is misinterpreted, judgments and decisions based upon that score will also be inaccurate. It is therefore extremely important that test manuals should supply whatever materials are necessary to make interpretations of the test results meaningful. This frequently takes the form of records to be filled out for both the group and the individual. Furthermore, information should be supplied about the purpose and applications for which the test is recommended. If it takes specially trained persons to administer or interpret the test, this should also be indicated.

Validity is the third topic of concern. A test manual should report the validity of a test for each type of judgment for which the test is recommended. If a test is designed primarily to help the test user to make judgments of a predictive nature, then predictive validity should be carefully established. On the other hand, if the test's primary concern is to yield information about a person's past achievement, then content validity is most important. If predictive or concurrent validity is reported, then measures of the criterion which were used should be carefully described. Furthermore, with the criterion-related validity reports, information should be made available describing the sample used in the validity study and the conditions under which the testing was done. The test user can then judge whether or not the reported validity is pertinent to his situation. Furthermore, any statistical analysis which may have been used to estimate criterion validity should be reported in clear, meaningful terms.

The third kind of validity which the standards suggest should be reported is construct validity. This kind of validity is important if interpretations of the test are to be made using the results as a measure of a theoretical variable. Therefore it is important that the manual distinguish between interpretations made on the basis of the theoretical construct used in the test construction and the interpretations arising under other theories. For example, if a test is supposed to measure the construct of anxiety, then the test manual should distinguish its definition of anxiety from other possible definitions.

Next to validity, the test user is concerned about the reliability of the test. The APA standards suggest that reliability refers to the accuracy (consistency and stability) of measurement, and that this is an important consideration when using a test and interpreting the results obtained from it. You will recall from the discussion in Chapter 2 that there are a number of sources of error and that various reliability estimates attempt to account for these different sources. Therefore it is important that a variety of methods for estimating reliability be used and clearly described in the manual. If no evidence of reliability has been obtained, the manual should clearly state that. The test user can then judge whether or not this is a test he would want to use.

If reliability estimates or estimates of the errors of measurement are reported, the manual should also specify the procedure used to obtain those estimates. Furthermore, a description of the sample of persons taking the test should be provided. Such things as the maturity of the group, the variation in ability in the group, the attitude of the group toward the test, etc., can be important in the size of the estimates of reliability which have been obtained. If reliability measures were obtained on a highly heterogeneous group and a test user is planning on using the test on a homogeneous group, he cannot expect the same kind of reliability as that reported by the test manual. If more than one form of the test is produced, then evidence of the comparability of alternate forms should also be included. If a test is designed to measure some general homogeneous trait, then evidence of the internal consistency of the test should be made available. Often a test is to be used for predictive purposes or to compare a person's performance over time. In such cases, test-retest reliability is crucial; every effort should be made to obtain this reliability estimate and report it carefully in the manual.

A fifth area of concern is that of administering and scoring the test. The directions for administration should be clear, easily followed, and an exact duplicate of the directions used when the test was standardized. Likewise, scoring procedures should be presented with a maximum of detail and clarity so as to reduce the likelihood of scoring error.

The final topic covered by the standards committee is scales and norms. Scales and norms refer to the way in which the scores are reported and the group for which the norm-referenced judgments can be made. It is extremely important that the manual should describe exactly the kinds of scales being used, so that interpretation of the test can be made accurately. The norms must be carefully described so that the test user can determine whether or not the norm group is characteristic of the group for whom he will use the test. The norms should be up to date and appropriate to the purpose(s) of the test. Furthermore, norms should be reported in terms of standard scores or percentile ranks. The manual should contain enough detailed information about the kinds of scores being reported and the reference group on which the test was normed so that proper interpretation of the scores can be made.

Step 4: Describe the Major Characteristics of the "Final Contenders"

In the first step of this selection process you define your needs. In step 2 you narrow the choice to a few tests which seem to come closest to meeting these needs. Then, in step 3, you obtain specimen sets and carefully examine each one. Now you will summarize what you found out in steps 2 and 3. This should help you to highlight the important similarities and differences among these "final contenders." If you can describe the major characteristics of each of these tests, you will then be able to compare them to each other as well as to the needs which you outlined in step 1. Some standard form for recording all the things you find out about each test should help you to be certain that all the necessary data about each test have been obtained. This will make the final test selection easier. No matter what format you decide to use when summarizing the data you have obtained about a test, it should include the information outlined in Figure 14.2.

Step 5: Make Your Final Selection

At this point in the selection process, you have a statement of the characteristics needed in a test as defined by your needs and a statement of the characteristics of the few tests which seem best to meet those needs. The final selection is made by comparing the list of your needs to the descriptions of the tests being considered. There will rarely if ever be a perfect match. Furthermore, one test may meet some of your needs best but may not meet some of your other needs very well. There is, therefore, no easy solution to the problem of deciding between two or three tests which will come very close to matching your needs. When you arrive at a point in the selection process where choosing one test rather than another

FIGURE 14.2. Information which should be included in any summary sheet used to describe a standardized test.

    I. Identification
       A. Title of test
       B. Authors
       C. Publishers
       D. Date of publication
       E. Date of latest revision (and if not the same, date of standardization)
    II. Purpose served
       A. Type of information being measured (aptitude, achievement, interests, etc.; speeded or power)
       B. Kinds of judgments which can be made from the results (norm-referenced/criterion-referenced; estimative/predictive; survey/diagnosis)

III. Cost factors
    A. Per-pupil cost for booklets and answer sheets
    B. Cost of scoring and recording (especially if machine-scored)
    C. Administration time
IV. Options available
    A. Type of scoring (hand or machine)
    B. Number of forms available
    C. Age and/or grade levels covered
    D. Type of test booklet (consumable/nonconsumable)
    E. Types of scores available
 V. Validity
    A. Validity—for the total test and any subtests or part scores for each age or grade level
       1. Content validity (evidence available)
       2. Concurrent validity (size of coefficient(s) and appropriateness of criterion measures)
       3. Predictive validity (size of coefficient(s) and appropriateness of criterion measures)
       4. Construct validity (logical and empirical evidence)
       5. Standard errors of estimate
    B. Reliability—for the total test *and* subtests or part scores for each age or grade level
       1. Consistency over a period of time (size of coefficient and time between administration)
       2. Consistency between forms
       3. Internal consistency (KR formulas, split-half coefficient)
       4. Consistency among examiners (necessary for tests where options are available to the examiners, as in many individually administered tests)
       5. Standard error of measurement
    C. Norms
       1. Type (grade equivalent, percentile, stanines, etc.)
       2. Characteristics of the population sampled (age, socioeconomic status, geographic location, size of sample, etc.)
VI. Practical features
    A. Overall impression of materials (well arranged, easy to read, eye appealing, etc.)
    B. Durability of materials
    C. Administration (How easy is it to give; how easy to take?)
    D. Scoring (Is the scoring unnecessarily complex?)
    E. Interpretation (How easily can the scores be interpreted? Are the charts easy to read?)
    F. Recording (Are provisions made for recording both individual and class data easily?)
    G. Reporting (Are there procedures for reporting the results to others? Are they flexible?)
    H. Adequacy of the manual (Can you easily find all the information you need to administer, score, and interpret the test?)

merely becomes a process of trading one set of advantages for another, you must decide which advantages are most important to you.

The above procedures are particularly applicable for selecting specific tests or test batteries. It should be noted, however, that tests are often selected as part of a larger schoolwide testing program. A testing program usually includes tests of aptitude and achievement as well as tests of interests and/or attitudes. A testing program can be developed following the same process described above: define your needs and then select the tests to meet those needs.

One further consideration should be kept in mind when developing a testing program: *remember that all the tests in a program should work well together.* This means that they must yield complementary information about the students, not overlapping or redundant information. It means also that, together, they should not take an inordinate amount of testing time. If possible, the tests should be chosen so that they do not all have to be given at the same time of the year.

Fuller explanations of the problems involved in developing a full testing program can be found in some of the annotated sources listed at the end of this section.

SUMMARY

1. A standardized test is an instrument designed to obtain many kinds of information under standardized conditions. A table of norms usually accompanies the test.
2. The information from standardized tests (1) is clearly defined, (2) has known parameters, and (3) has been obtained under "ideal" conditions.
3. There are many administrative, counseling, instructional, and research purposes for standardized test results. Particular types of standardized tests are better suited than other types for given purposes.
4. Achievement tests are designed to measure a person's present level of knowledge, performance, or skill. They are designed *primarily* for making estimative judgments.
5. Aptitude tests are designed to measure a person's aptitude for performing some task. They are designed *primarily* for making predictive judgments.
6. Personality inventories, interest inventories, and attitude and opinion scales all obtain information about a person's typical performance. These noncognitive measures provide valuable additional information about how an individual might perform in the classroom as well as in other settings.
7. There are four steps to take when selecting standardized tests: (1) define your needs, (2) narrow your choice, (3) obtain and examine the test, (4) make your final choice.
8. There are four major sources of information about standardized tests: Buros's *Tests in Print,* Buros's *Mental Measurements Yearbook,* the tests publishers' catalogs, and journal articles (referenced in *Psychological Abstracts* and *Education Index*).
9. Send for specimen sets well in advance of the date on which you will need to use the test. Examine specimen sets carefully for practical features, content validity, and reliability.
10. *Standards for Educational and Psychological Tests* is a small booklet filled with information about what to look for in a standardized test.

11. When you have narrowed your selection to a few tests, carefully summarize the information you have about each one and then decide on one that best meets your needs.

References

Burros, O. K. (ed.): *The 1938 Mental Measurements Yearbook,* Rutgers University Press, New Brunswick, N.J., 1938.

———: *The Nineteen-Forty Mental Measurements Yearbook,* Rutgers University Press, New Brunswick, N.J., 1940.

———: *The Third Mental Measurements Yearbook,* Rutgers University Press, New Brunswick, N.J., 1949.

———: *The Fourth Mental Measurements Yearbook,* Gryphon Press, Highland Park, N.J., 1953.

———: *The Fifth Mental Measurements Yearbook,* Gryphon Press, Highland Park, N.J., 1959.

———: *The Sixth Mental Measurements Yearbook,* Gryphon Press, Highland Park, N.J., 1965.

———: *The Seventh Mental Measurements Yearbook,* Gryphon Press, Highland Park, N.J., 1972.

French, John W., and William B. Michael: *Standards for Educational and Psychological Tests and Manuals,* American Psychological Association, Washington, D.C., 1966.

Gronlund, N. E.: *Measurement and Evaluation in Teaching,* 2d ed., The Macmillan Company, New York, 1971.

Suggested Readings

The following texts give excellent coverage to a wide variety of standardized instruments:

Anastasi, Anne: *Psychological Testing,* 3d ed., The Macmillan Company, New York, 1968.

Cronbach, Lee J.: *Essentials of Psychological Testing,* 3d ed., Harper & Row, Publishers, Incorporated, New York, 1970.

Mehrens, William A., and Irvin J. Lehmann: *Measurement and Evaluation in Education and Psychology,* Holt, Rinehart and Winston, Inc., New York, 1973.

Thorndike, Robert L., and Elizabeth Hagen: *Measurement and Evaluation in Psychology and Education,* 3d ed., John Wiley & Sons, Inc., New York, 1969.

APPENDIX A

Statistics

Using the test scores found in table A.1 as your source of information about the seventh graders' science scores, answer the following questions:

1. How is Mary Yordell doing compared with her classmates?
2. Was Jim Gelperly's test 3 score any better than his score on test 1?
3. How well did the class as a whole perform on the first test?
4. Which test was the most difficult? Which was the easiest?
5. On which test were the variations among the individual scores the greatest? How big was that variation?
6. Is there any relationship between how well a student did on the first test and how well he is likely to do on the fourth one (i.e., how well could we have predicted a person's fourth test score if we knew what his score on test 1 was)?
7. Which test is most reliable (i.e., internally consistent)?

TABLE A.1

Test Scores for a Seventh Grade Science Class

Name	TEST NUMBER				
	1	2	3	4	5
1. Albern, Mary	62	15	97	27	20
2. Atoo, Peter	59	14	97	8	20
3. Bampy, Sue	61	16	98	31	32
4. Bertrap, George	63	13	96	27	20
5. Bokett, Elmer	67	20	98	30	32
6. Bykor, Cordell	68	12	95	7	21
7. Coplie, Jill	17	19	97	29	21
8. Cot, Willie	28	8	92	8	19
9. Dermi, Hortense	64	15	96	27	20
10. Elkom, David	39	14	96	29	19
11. Gelperly, Jim	59	12	95	5	19
12. Guzzle, William	39	14	95	28	20
13. Hoosky, Sarah	66	12	94	3	16
14. Hymk, Fred	40	14	95	8	19
15. Juppy, Helen	60	15	96	26	15
16. Lardell, Randy	29	16	98	29	28
17. Lexi, Harold	62	15	96	20	17
18. Lodussy, Dot	43	14	95	9	16
19. Nordcle, Debbie	63	19	96	22	19
20. Pullup, Connie	63	16	95	9	18
21. Racy, Mark	41	18	96	24	18
22. Reilip, Doug	62	17	95	23	17
23. Solpez, Todd	42	18	98	28	21
24. Tame, Lorrie	43	17	97	27	18
25. Tenner, Justine	29	15	96	11	18
26. Twizky, Sheri	55	17	97	27	18
27. Yordell, Mary	63	14	95	10	18

The above questions represent but a small sample of those which might be asked about the information found in a teacher's record book. You undoubtedly found them somewhat difficult to answer. However, these kinds of questions *can* be answered. The secret is in learning to arrange and describe such sets of scores as those found in Table A.1. This section has been designed to help you do just that. More specifically, the explanations and formulas in this section should help you to meet the following objectives:

When given a set of scores you should be able to

1. Produce
   a. A frequency distribution

      b. A histogram
      c. A line graph
  2. Compute
      a. Mean, median, and mode
      b. Range, quartile deviation, and standard deviation
      c. Correlation coefficient
      d. Reliability coefficient
      e. Standard error of measurement and standard error of estimate

Furthermore, when given any one of the statistics described above you should be able to

  3. Explain what it means, so that someone who has not studied statistics could understand you.

Frequency Distributions

One of the first things that can be done to make sense out of a set of scores is to arrange them in order from high to low (see Figure A.1). You can see that the lowest score on the test was 17 and the highest was 68. Furthermore, the score of 17 was way below the others (the next-highest score was 28). Something else you should notice from this arrangement is the fact that a number of students received the same score and that there seems to be some tendency for the scores to group together. This grouping tendency can be seen more clearly if we arrange the scores into groups and count the number of persons with scores falling in each grouping. We grouped these scores so that we would have six groups, each group including a 10-point spread of scores (see Figure A.1).

There are a number of elaborate schemes for figuring out how many groups to have, but two rules of thumb should be all you will need for working with classroom data.

  1. Divide the score into no less than six and no more than twelve groups.
  2. The spread of scores within each group should be equal (e.g., 15–19, 20–24, 25–29, etc.).

The idea is to group the scores so that it is easiest to see how they distribute themselves (i.e., where they tend to "cluster" and where they tend to "thin out"). When you group scores in this way and then count the number of persons whose scores fall within each grouping, you have produced what statisticians call a *frequency distribution* (see Figure A.1).

Histograms

The information displayed in a frequency distribution can also be put into graph form to help give a clearer picture of the way a group of scores are distribu-

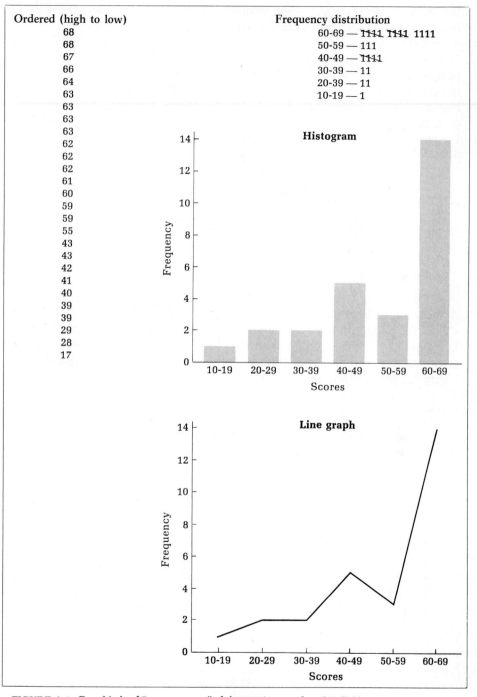

FIGURE A.1. Four kinds of "arrangements" of the test 1 scores found in Table A.1.

ted. Suppose we place the score groupings (sometimes called steps) along the horizontal axis of a graph. Along the vertical axis we will place the frequency of occurrence (i.e., how many individuals scored at each step in the distribution). Now, if we draw a bar up from each step to a height which equals the number of people scoring at that step, we will have a "picture" of the frequency of scores at that step. Do this at each step and you have a *histogram* or *bar graph.* (See Figure A.1.) By comparing the height of the bars from step to step in the distribution, we can get a relatively good picture of the way the scores are distributed. For example, in test 1, we can see that the largest frequency (fourteen persons) occurred at the highest step (score range: 60–69).

Would you say that this was a fairly easy test?

The lowest frequencies were for the lowest steps (only three people scored below 30 and only five below 40).

Would you say that there were a few students who did much more poorly than their classmates?

Line Graphs

The *line graph* presents essentially the same information as the histogram. A line is drawn from the middle of the top of each bar. You can see the relationship of the histogram to the line graph by comparing these two kinds of graphs in Figure A.1. The line graph provides us with the same information as a histogram, but it gives a little clearer picture of the overall shape of the distribution. Figure A.2 presents line graphs of all five tests found in Table A.1.

FIGURE A.2. Line graphs of tests 1, 2, 3, 4, and 5 from the data in Table A.1.

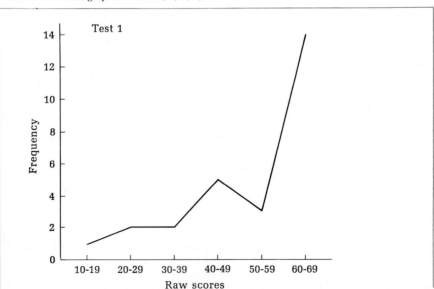

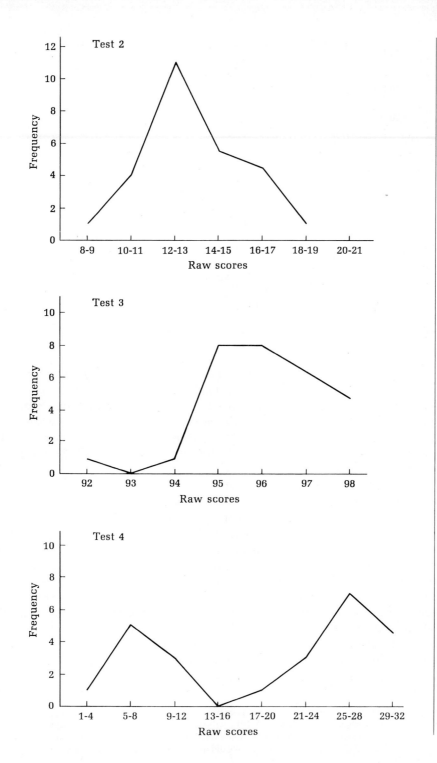

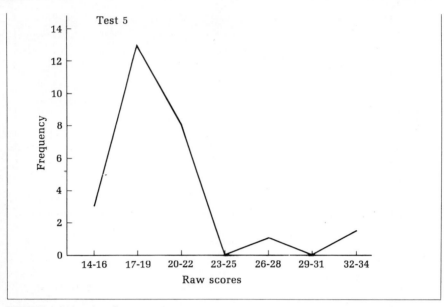

FIGURE A.2 *(continued)*

Can you tell from the graphs which test was hardest? Which was easiest?

Hint: Ignore the raw scores. The number of items correct does not mean much if you do not know how many possible points there were. You should be able to tell from the general shapes of the curves that tests 3 and 4 were generally easier than tests 1 and 5. We make that judgment because the scores tend to pile up on test 5 down at the low end (sixteen students scored below 20). Test 5 seems to be a difficult test.

What else can you tell about test 4? It is easy for most people, but there seems to be a small group who scored very low (nine students scored below 13).

What other differences are there in the shapes of these distributions? What do these differences tell us about the tests? The scores tend to pile up (or cluster) near the middle of test 2 and near the low end on test 5. Test 2 seems to be of moderate difficulty and test 5 of greater difficulty. You are beginning to see how the shape of a distribution tells us something about the test that was used.[1] Now compare these two tests to test 1: where do the scores tend to cluster in these tests? The scores from tests 1 and 5 tended to cluster near the ends (test 1 near the high end and test 5 near the low end), and those from test 2 tended to cluster near the middle. These three shapes are specific examples of more generalized shapes. They are important enough to have names. The shape of the distribution for test 1 is called a *negatively skewed curve*. It is called this because the tail of the dis-

---

[1] You should note that when we say a test was easy we simply mean that most students scored high. We are not sure (without further evidence) if the subject matter was easy, the test questions easy, or the students very bright and knowledgeable. Some verification of the judgments made on the basis of such scores would likely resolve this problem. We did discuss the verification of judgments in Chap. 8.

tribution (that end where the frequency trails off) curves toward the low (or negative) end (the scores tend to cluster *away* from that negative end). The more generalized form is usually pictured as a smooth curve (see Figure A.3). The shape of the distribution for test 5 is skewed in the opposite direction. It is called a *positively skewed curve*. Positively skewed curves are characterized by the fact that the tail of the distribution is on the positive end and the scores tend to cluster *away* from that end. The generalized form of a positively skewed distribution is a reverse image of the negatively skewed one (see Figure A.3).

The shape of test 2 is more symmetrical, with the scores clustering toward the middle and with the tails at both ends looking very much alike. An idealized curve which has these characteristics (and more) is called the *normal curve*. The normal curve is bell-shaped and is symmetrical (one half is a mirror image of the other). We will discuss this curve in more detail later. For now, note its general shape (Figure A.3).

Now compare the graph of test 3 with the graphs of all the other tests (see Figure A.3). Notice that the students are bunched up more tightly in test 3 than in

FIGURE A.3. Three generalized shapes of distribution.

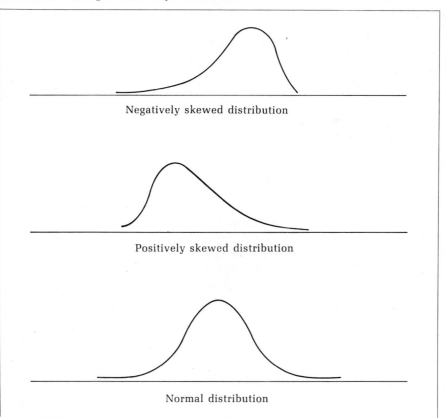

Negatively skewed distribution

Positively skewed distribution

Normal distribution

any of the other tests. Only 6 points separate the lowest from the highest score (98—92 = 6). Compare that with the others. For example, in test 1 there are 51 points separating the top and bottom scores (68—17 = 51). In some of these distributions the scores are spread out much more than in others. Which situation allows you more easily to make norm-referenced judgments?

When scores are spread out, there are not as many individuals obtaining the same score. Consequently more distinctions can be made. If everyone scored the same, you could not make any norm-referenced comparisons. If many individuals receive the same score, you drastically reduce the number of comparisons you can make. Norm-referenced judgments require a distribution of scores that is fairly well spread out.

We are about to shift from a discussion of graphic descriptions of data to a discussion of numerical descriptions of data. Before we do, however, we want you tô understand clearly that *we are not shifting topics.* We are still concerned with describing data. Our goal is still the same: to figure out ways that will help us to compare the performances of groups *and* the performances of individuals within a group. In other words, we are still seeking ways to make sense out of sets of scores like those found in Table A.1.

The shift in our discussion is simply a move to a more precise descriptive system than that offered by graphic representations. The problem with graphic descriptions is that they do lack precision and the descriptions are too general (e.g., the scores tend to pile up near the high end). Furthermore, it is a pretty inefficient system that requires you to draw a picture every time you wish to make sense out of a set of scores.

However, some useful information about the way scores distribute themselves can be discovered by examining graphic descriptions of sets of scores. Two facts are especially apparent:

1. Scores tend to cluster together around some point in the distribution.
2. Scores vary a great deal in how much they spread out from that cluster.

This tendency for scores to cluster together is called *central tendency* and is an extremely important characteristic of score distributions. Shortly, we will learn how to describe that tendency numerically. Following that discussion we will learn how to arrive at numerical descriptions of the amount of variation in a set of scores (these descriptions are referred to as *measures of dispersion*).

EXERCISE A.1

1. What is a frequency distribution?
2. How does a histogram help you to better understand test results?
3. What is the relationship between a histogram and a line graph?

NUMERICAL DESCRIPTIONS

Central Tendency

There are many ways to define the center of a distribution. The most common are (1) the mode, (2) the median, and (3) the mean.

The mode. If we define the center of a distribution as that point about which the scores tend to cluster, then it makes sense to define the most popular score as the center. In fact, wherever we find a score which occurs *more frequently* than any other score, we will find other scores clustered around it in a distribution. We call that most popular score the mode. The mode is the simplest to compute (but the least stable) of all the measures of central tendency. The mode is the center of a distribution of scores in much the same way as a model is the center of attraction in a crowd of people.

The median. The median divides a distribution of scores into two equal halves. Half of the scores fall below the median and the other half fall above the median. Examine the following distributions:

A	*B*
1, 3, 3, 4, 5, 7, 9	15, 17, 18, 19, 20, 21, 23, 24

The median in distribution *A* is 4. There are three scores below 4 and three scores above it. The median in distribution *B* is 19.5. Four scores fall below 19.5 and four scores fall above 19.5. Compare distributions *A* and *B*. Distribution *A* has an odd number of scores. Consequently a score (in this case 4) falls on the median. Distribution *B* has an even number of scores. Consequently the median is the point halfway between the two middle scores. No score falls at the median in a distribution with an even number of scores. The median is a *point* in the distribution that divides that distribution in half. Sometimes a raw score falls on that point and sometimes not.

The computation of the median is basically very simple. You merely rank the scores from high to low and count up to the midpoint.[2] The specific steps to take are listed below.

How to Calculate the Median

Example *A.* Given: an *odd* number of ungrouped scores — 19, 16, 8, 12, 15

1. Rank them high to low accordingly — 19, 16, 15, 12, 8

---

[2] When the median falls somewhere in a group of tied scores (e.g. 3, 7, 8, 8, 8, 9, 10, 11, 13), the procedures described above will not yield a median which is perfectly accurate. However, the correction for these tied scores involves more work than it is worth for the classroom teacher. These procedures will yield medians which are accurate enough for classroom use.

2. Count up from the bottom until you have counted off half the scores (i.e., 15).
   Two scores are above 15.
   Two scores are below 15.

Example *B*. Given: an *even* number of ungrouped scores — 8, 13, 6, 14, 16, 10

1. Rank them high to low — 16, 14, 13, 10, 8, 6
2. Count up from the bottom *halfway between the two middle scores.*
   The two middle scores are 10 and 13
   Calculate as follows:
   $$\frac{10-13}{2} = 11.5$$

The mean. The mean is the most commonly used measure of central tendency. Whenever an average is reported, everyone assumes that it is the mean (even though the median and mode are also "averages"). The mean is frequently referred to as the *arithmetic average,* and almost everyone knows the arithmetic computation: you simply add up all the scores and divide by the total number of scores. We express this in a formula as follows:

$$\bar{X} = \frac{\Sigma X}{N}$$

In this formula the letter X with a line over it is called X bar and stands for the mean; the Greek letter sigma (Σ) stands for "the sum of"; the letter X stands for a single score; and the letter N stands for the total number of scores. Consequently we read this formula as follows: "The mean is equal to the sum of the scores divided by the total number of scores."

Calculating the mean

a. 7,3,2,5,6,7,8	*b.* 16,32,17,18,39,49
7	16
3	32
2	17
5	18
6	39
7	49
8	6 $\underline{\mid 171}$ = 28.5*
7 $\underline{\mid 38}$ = 5.4*	

*Notice that, like the median, the mean is not a score but a point in the distribution (a score does not usually fall at the mean).

Why three measures of central tendency? Each of the measures of central tendency describes the center of a distribution from a different perspective. You should choose to use that measure which will allow you to describe most appropriately the data you have.

For example, if you are interested in identifying the most frequently occurring score (or the most common level of response), the mode should be used. However, the mode is very unstable. If you have several samples of data drawn from the same population, you will probably obtain widely varied modes from one sample to the next. This means that estimative or predictive judgments based upon the mode are likely to be grossly in error.

When you need a highly stable measure of central tendency, you should use the mean. From sample to sample (within a given population), the mean varies less than any other central tendency measure.

Although the median is not as stable as the mean, it is a valuable measure of central tendency for classroom use. It is relatively easy to compute and it divides the scores into two equal groups (that is an easy "center point" to visualize). It is the best measure of center when the distribution is highly skewed.

EXERCISE A.2

1. Given: 7, 13, 13, 15, 18, 19, 21
   Compute: *a.* Mode
   b. Median
   c. Mean
2. Briefly describe each of the three measures of central tendency.

Dispersion

Earlier we suggested that there are two important ways to describe a distribution of scores: (1) by describing its central tendency and (2) by describing the amount of variation in the scores. The measures of variation are also called *measures of dispersion.*

Range. The simplest measure of dispersion is the range. It is an indication of the distance between the extreme scores. The range is computed by subtracting the lowest score from the highest score.[3]

Range = high score − low score

Example *A:* 7, 8, 9, 11, 15, 18; range = 18 − 7 = 11
Example *B:* 52, 54, 55, 58, 60, 68; range = 68-52 = 16

---

[3] In some texts the range is given as the highest score minus the lowest score plus one ($H - L + 1$).

The range has great appeal as a measure of dispersion because it is easy to compute and it "makes sense." In order to find out how far a set of scores is spread out, you merely look how far the extreme scores are spread apart. However, the range is unstable. It is affected by extreme scores and can be very misleading. Compare the following distributions:

Distribution *A*: 15, 16, 18, 19, 19, 19, 21, 22, 24, 25, 27, 30.

Distribution *B*: 15, 15, 15, 16, 16, 16, 17, 17, 19, 20, 20, 20.

The range is exactly the same for both the above distributions ($30 - 15 = 15$). The scores in distribution *A* are, in fact, spread out over a 15-point range. However, in distribution *B*, 11 of the 12 scores are within a 5-point range ($20 - 15 = 5$). Because *only* the extreme scores are used to compute the range, it is a very misleading measure of the spread in any highly skewed distribution.

Quartile deviation.

Problem: Extreme scores affect the size of the range and make it difficult to interpret.

Solution: Ignore the extreme scores!

Actually, it is not quite that simple. But that *is* the basic idea behind the quartile deviation. Suppose that, instead of computing the range over the entire distribution, we compute the range over the middle only. By doing this, any extreme scores will not affect our results. Let us try this with distributions *A* and *B* (above). First we will divide these two distributions into quarters.

Distribution *A*: 15, 16, 18,   19, 19, 19, 21, 22, 24   25, 27, 30
                                  ↑ first quartile   ↑ third quartile
Distribution *B*: 15, 15, 15,   16, 16, 16, 17, 17, 19,   20, 20, 20
                                  ↑ first quartile   ↑ third quartile

We have isolated the middle 50 percent of the scores. The point which separates the first quarter from the middle is called the first quartile. The point which separates the last quarter from the middle is called the third quartile. Now, the question is, "What is the range between the first and third quartiles?" To answer this question, we subtract the first quartile from the second quartile. Because the quartiles (like the median) are points on the continuum, they do not always fall at points occupied by scores. That is the case in these distributions. The third quartile (Q_3) for distribution *A* falls between 24 and 25 (24.5). The first quartile (Q_1) for this distribution falls between 18 and 19 (18.5). Subtracting Q_1 from Q_3 we get 6 (24.5 − 18.5). This range between Q_1 and Q_3 is called the interquartile range.

Dividing the interquartile range by 2 gives us what is called the semiquartile range—or, more simply, the quartile deviation. The formula for the process we just went through is

$$\text{Quartile deviation} = \frac{Q_3 - Q_1}{2}$$

Applying this formula to the data from distribution A we get

$$QD = \frac{24.5 - 18.5}{2} = \frac{6}{2} = 3$$

And doing the same for distribution B gives us a quartile deviation of 2.

$$QD = \frac{19.5 - 15.5}{2} = \frac{4}{2} = 2$$

A comparison of the quartile deviations of distributions A and B gives us a clearer picture of the differences in dispersion between the two distributions than does a comparison of the two ranges (the range of distribution A is 15 and of B is 5).

Standard deviation. The quartile deviation is a useful measure of dispersion if the distribution is skewed and if the median is the measure of central tendency being used. However, when the mean is the measure of central tendency being used, the standard deviation is a more appropriate measure of dispersion. The standard deviation is essentially a measure of how the scores are spread out from the mean rather than how much spread there is between the extreme scores (or between the quartiles). This "spread from the mean" notion is very useful for a number of statistical problems. For example, it is useful when trying to pinpoint the location of a particular score within a distribution. When trying to interpret a score, one of the first things we do is ask, "What was the average?" In other words, we want to know if the score is above or below average. Suppose that Gary has a score of 80 and the mean is 75. Gary's score is 5 points above the mean. But is that far above the mean or is it very close to the mean? In order to answer this question we need some standard distance from the mean to use as a guide (as a referent, if you will). The standard deviation serves that purpose and is computed as follows:

First, compute each score's deviation from the mean. Next, square each of these deviations. Then sum their squared deviations and divide by the number of individuals for whom we have scores. This gives us an average squared deviation from the mean, which is called *variance* and is very useful in many statistical manipulations. However, it is of little value to the classroom teacher. Variance is not stated in the same size units as the raw score. Rather than deviation from the mean, it is stated in terms of squared deviation from the mean. Therefore our final step is to take the square root of the variance. This yields the standard deviation. The formula looks like this:[4]

$$SD = \sqrt{\frac{\Sigma\,(X - \bar{X})^2}{N}}$$

The formula reads like this: "The standard deviation is equal to the square root of the sum of the squared deviations from the mean divided by the number of individuals."

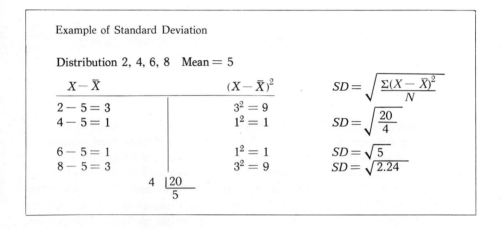

Example of Standard Deviation

Distribution 2, 4, 6, 8   Mean $= 5$

$X - \bar{X}$	$(X - \bar{X})^2$	$SD = \sqrt{\dfrac{\Sigma(X - \bar{X})^2}{N}}$
$2 - 5 = 3$	$3^2 = 9$	
$4 - 5 = 1$	$1^2 = 1$	$SD = \sqrt{\dfrac{20}{4}}$
$6 - 5 = 1$	$1^2 = 1$	$SD = \sqrt{5}$
$8 - 5 = 3$	$3^2 = 9$	$SD = \sqrt{2.24}$

$$4\,\overline{\big|\,20\,}$$
$$5$$

---

1. What are the characteristics of each of the following: range, quartile deviation, standard deviation?
2. Given: 2, 2, 5, 7, 8, 8, 9, 10, 10, 10, 12, 13
   Compute: *a.* Range
   　　　　　 b. Quartile deviation
   　　　　　 c. Standard deviation

MEASURES OF RELATIONSHIP

Correlation

The correlation coefficient is the basic statistic used in the computation of reliability and validity coefficients. The correlation coefficient is also important in most prediction systems. While formulas for computing the correlation coefficient will be provided, it is more important that you understand the statistic

---

[4] If you have a calculator available, you may find it more convenient to use the following formula:

$$SD = \sqrt{\frac{\Sigma X^2}{N} - \left(\frac{\Sigma X}{N}\right)^2}$$

well enough that you will be able to interpret it when you find it used in test manuals and research articles.

The basic notion. *Correlation* is a statistical term used to indicate a special kind of relationship between two sets of scores. Whenever we have two sets of scores *for the same individuals,* we can estimate the correlation between them. When two sets of scores *do* correlate, the scores covary. In other words, *as the scores on one measure increase, the scores on the other measure tend to increase or decrease in a uniform way.* Putting this in everyday language, we find that for two correlated measures, your performance on one will be reflected by your performance on the other. If they are positively correlated, you will do well on one if you do well on the other; if you do poorly on one, you will do poorly on the other. A *positive correlation* means that a high performance on one task will be associated with a high performance on the other. In other words, *when the scores on one measure increase, the scores on the other will tend to increase.* A *negative correlation* means that a high performance on one measure will be associated with a *low* performance on the other. In other words, *when the score on one measure increases, the scores on the other will tend to decrease.*

Let us examine several sets of scores which have been artificially arranged to illustrate the concept of correlation (Table A.2).

TABLE A.2

Scores Artificially Arranged to Illustrate the Concept of Correlation

Student	Test *A*	Test *B*	Test *C*	Test *D*
1	10	18	30	28
2	20	20	28	20
3	30	22	26	26
4	40	24	24	22
5	50	26	22	30
6	70	30	18	18

Tests *A* and *B* illustrate a perfect correlation. As the scores on test *A* increase, the scores on test *B* increase *in a uniform manner.* Notice that for every 10-point difference between students on test *A,* there is a corresponding 2-point difference between those students on test *B* (it does not matter what the size of this difference is as long as it is uniform throughout the distribution). Suppose we plot this data in graph form. We will put the test *A* scores along one axis and the test *B* scores along the other. Then we will place one dot on the graph for each student. Each dot will be placed at the point where his two scores intersect (see Figure A.4). The graph in Figure A.4 is called a *scatterplot.* A scatterplot provides us with a picture of how two sets of scores correlate. In this illustration you should notice the following: (1) all the dots lie on a straight line (this is the way a *pefect* correlation looks) and (2) the straight line *rises* diagonally from left to right (that is the way a *positive* correlation looks).

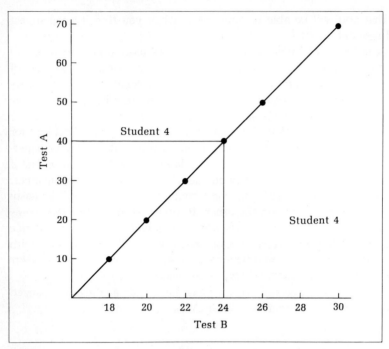

FIGURE A.4. Graph of tests A and B (Table A.2.).

FIGURE A.5. Scatterplot of scores for tests A and C.

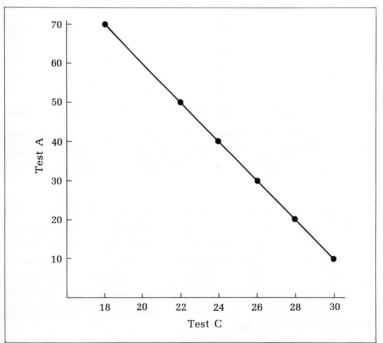

From the above discussion you can probably guess that a perfect negative correlation will look like this: (1) all the dots will lie on a straight line and (2) the straight line will *fall* diagonally from left to right (as one measure increases, the other will decrease, as in Figure A.5).

Now take a look at what a zero correlation looks like. There is no covariance among the scores. There is no way you can tell from the performance on one test what a student's performance will be on the other. (See Figure A.6.)

We rarely find perfect correlations in the things we measure in education (or anywhere else in the natural world, for that matter). What does a correlation look like that is not perfect (but greater than zero)? Examine the scatterplots in Figure A.7. Try to decide what a high correlation looks like compared to what a low correlation looks like. What is the difference between a scatterplot illustrating a negative correlation and one illustrating a positive one?

There are a number of things you can learn from the scatterplots in Figure A.7. First of all, you can see that the *linear* (straight line) function of correlation is obvious. Even though the dots are scattered [see (*a*)], they tend to lie along a straight line. Secondly, you will notice that the more the dots are scattered, the less the size of the correlation. Finally, there are at least two kinds of patterns which can yield a zero correlation: (1) a random scatter of the dots as found in (*h*), and (2) a curvilinear (curved) scatter as in (*g*). This "curved" relationship described in (*g*) illustrates the fact that a *zero correlation* simply means that *no*

FIGURE A.6. Scatterplot of tests A and D.

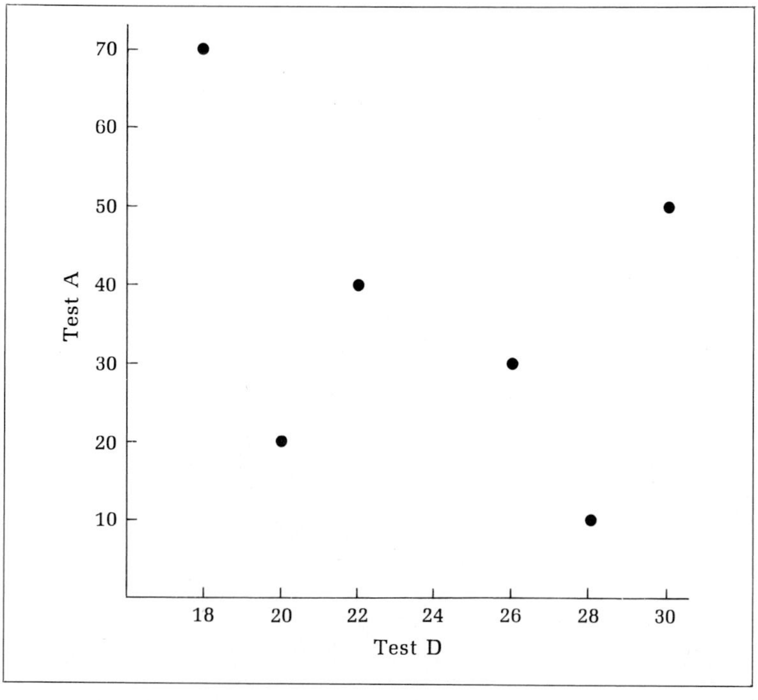

FIGURE A.7. Scatterplots illustrating various degrees of correlation.

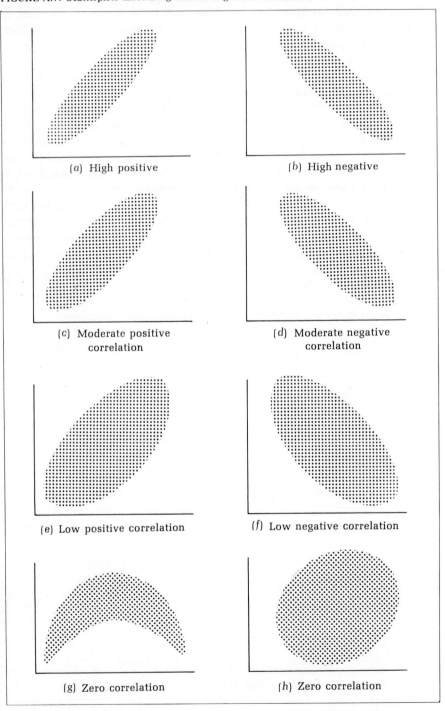

(*a*) High positive

(*b*) High negative

(*c*) Moderate positive
correlation

(*d*) Moderate negative
correlation

(*e*) Low positive correlation

(*f*) Low negative correlation

(*g*) Zero correlation

(*h*) Zero correlation

linear relationship exists. It is possible that a relationship which is not a linear one exists between variables.

Below is a summary of the important things you should know about correlation. Study these carefully and then read on to find out how to compute the correlation between two measures.

1. A correlation coefficient indicates only *linear* relationship (or lack of it). It is possible to have a zero correlation between two variables that are related in some way other than in a linear fashion.
2. The correlation coefficient is only an *estimate* of the correlation which actually exists.
3. The strength of a correlation is indicated by the size of the correlation coefficient and has *nothing* to do with the sign (+ or −). A plus sign simply tells you that the correlation is a positive (direct) relationship. The minus sign tells you that there is a negative (inverse) relationship between the two measures. Correlations of −.87 and +.87 are of exactly the same strength.
4. Correlation does *not* imply cause and effect. For example, there is a high correlation between the preacher's salaries in small Midwestern towns and the amount of beer consumed in those towns. No cause and effect is implied. Probably an increase in the economy would cause increases in both preacher's salaries and in the consumption of beer.

How to compute correlation estimates. There are a number of ways in which the correlation between two measures can be estimated. One of the easiest is to obtain a rough estimate of the size (and direction) of a correlation by constructing a scatterplot. This procedure was discussed above. Widely scattered dots indicate low correlation. High correlations are exemplified by narrow bands of dots (review Figure A.7).

Another fairly easy way to estimate the size of a correlation is to estimate a "tetrachoric" correlation. Diedrich (1964) explains how to do this in his little pamphlet entitled *Short-cut Statistics for Teacher-Made Tests* (pages 34 to 36). Here are the steps to take:

Steps to Take When Computing a Tetrachoric Correlation

Step 1. Rank-order the students on the basis of their scores for test 1. Draw a line through the list at the median.

Step 2. Repeat step 1 for test 2.

Step 3. Count the number of students whose names appear in the top half of *both* lists.

Step 4. Divide the number you obtained in step 3 by the total number of students taking both tests. (This gives you a percentage of the students scoring in the top half on both tests).

Step 5. Find this percentage in Table A.3 and note the corresponding correlation coefficient.

TABLE A-3

Tetrachoric Correlations Corresponding to the Percentage of Students Scoring in the Top
Half on Both Measures Being Correlated*

Percent	r	Percent	r	Percent	r	Percent	r	Percent	r
45	.95	37	.69	29	.25	21	−.25	13	−.69
44	.93	36	.65	28	.19	20	−.31	12	−.73
43	.91	35	.60	27	.13	19	−.37	11	−.77
42	.88	34	.55	26	.07	18	−.43	10	−.81
41	.85	33	.49	25	.00	17	−.49	9	−.85
40	.81	32	.43	24	−.07	16	−.55	8	−.88
39	.77	31	.37	23	−.13	15	−.60	7	−.91
38	.73	30	.31	22	−.19	14	−.65	6	−.93

* From *Short-cut Statistics for Teacher-made Tests* by Paul B. Diederich. Copyright © 1960, 1964, by Educational
Testing Service. All rights reserved. Reprinted by permission.

The estimate of correlation arrived at through the above procedures is accurate enough for most classroom uses of the correlation coefficient. However,
if you have a calculator available for your use, the Pearson product moment correlation coefficient can be computed without too much effort. The following
formula is fairly easy to use.

$$r = \frac{N\Sigma XY - (\Sigma X)(\Sigma Y)}{\sqrt{[N\Sigma X^2 - (\Sigma X)^2][N\Sigma Y^2 - (\Sigma Y)^2]}}$$

This formula is not so formidable as it first appears. You need only five
pieces of information (with some calculators you can get all five at once):

ΣX (sum of the raw scores for test 1)

ΣX^2 (sum of the squared scores for test 1)

ΣY (sum of the raw scores for test 2)

ΣY^2 (sum of the squared scores for test 2)

ΣXY (sum of the cross products of the raw scores of tests 1 and 2)

These five pieces of information and N (the number of students, *not* the
number of scores) are to be put into their proper places in the formula and the formula is then to be worked out.

Reliability

Reliability can be estimated in a number of ways (see Chapter 2). Test-retest
reliability is estimated by computing the correlation between the students' scores
on the first testing with the same students' scores on a second testing.

A split-half reliability can be computed by dividing a test into two halves
(usually the odd-numbered items versus the even-numbered items). The two

halves are then scored separately and the correlation coefficient between the two halves is computed. Because this coefficient will be an estimate of only half of the test, you must make one more computation: using the Spearman-Brown correction formula below, correct the size of the coefficient you obtained.

Spearman-Brown Formula for Correcting Split-Half Correction Coefficients

$$r_{xx} = \frac{2r_{\frac{1}{2}\frac{1}{2}}}{1 + r_{\frac{1}{2}\frac{1}{2}}}$$

r_{xx} = reliability of total test

$r_{\frac{1}{2}\frac{1}{2}}$ = reliability you obtained by correlating half of the test with the other half

Example: Suppose your split-half correlation is .60. The reliability will be .75.

$$r_{xx} = \frac{2\,(.60)}{1 + .60} = \frac{1.20}{1.60} = .75$$

The split-half reliability can be used for essay tests as well as objective tests. Suppose, for example, you have given a six-question essay test. Obtain separate scores for each half (e.g., the first, third, and sixth questions). Next compute a correlation coefficient for the split halves. Finally, correct this coefficient with the Spearman-Brown formula.

If you are computing the reliability of objective tests (each item is right or wrong) you can use the Kuder-Richardson formula 21 for estimating internal consistency. A simplified version of this formula as adapted from Diedrich (1964) is presented below. Once you have obtained the mean and standard deviation of an objective test, you can compute its reliability in a few minutes.

Simplified Kuder-Richardson Formula 21

$$r_{xx} = 1 - \frac{\overline{X}\,(K - \overline{X})}{K(SD)^2}$$

$\overline{X}$ = mean

K = number of *items* in the test

$(SD)^2$ = variance (standard deviation squared)

Example: $\overline{X} = 60$; $SD = 5$; $K = 70$ items

$$r_{xx} = 1 - \frac{60\,(70 - 60)}{70\,(5)^2}$$

$$r_{xx} = 1 - \frac{60(10)}{70(25)}$$

$$r_{xx} = 1 - \frac{600}{1750}$$

$$r_{xx} = 1 - .34$$

$$r_{xx} = .66$$

OTHER MEASUREMENT CONCEPTS

There are a number of other statistical concepts which were discussed throughout this text. The computational procedures for those most important to measurement will be presented here.

Derived Scores

In Chapter 7 several derived scores were discussed. This section will tell you how to compute them. Refer back to Chapter 7 for an explanation of their meanings.

Percentile rank. A percentile rank indicates the proportion of students who fall at or below a particular score. Thus, to compute a person's percentile rank, you simply find out what percent of the students taking the test scores ranked lower than he did. If there are no tied ranks (more than one person receiving the same score) the computation is easy: divide the number of students who scored lower than a particular score by the total number of students who took the test and multiply the result by 100 [(number below a given score ÷ total number of scores) × 100].

Example—Percentile Score

David has a raw score of 90. Twenty-one students scored below 90. There are 30 students in the class.

$$\frac{21}{30} \times 100 = .7 \times 100 = 70\text{th percentile}$$

If there are tied ranks, then the procedure is to count the number of students scoring below a given score plus half of the students scoring at that score. Now divide this number by the total number of students and multiply by 100.

Example—Percentile Score

Four students receive a raw score of 80. Seven students scored below 80. There were 30 students in the class.

$$[(7 + 2) \div 30] \times 100 = [9 \div 30] \times 100 = 30\text{th percentile}$$

Standard scores. The basic standard score is the z score. It is essentially a ratio of the individual's deviation from the mean to the standard deviation. It is computed by subtracting the mean from an individual's raw score and dividing the result by the standard deviation.

Example — Standard Score

Joan received a raw score of 35. The mean was 25 and the standard deviation was 5.

$$z = \frac{X - \bar{X}}{5.0}$$

$$z = \frac{35 - 25}{5} = \frac{10}{5} = 2$$

When a distribution of scores has been converted to z scores, the mean of the z score distribution is zero and the standard deviation of this distribution is 1. You can see why this is. If a person's raw score is equal to the mean, his z score will be zero because he will deviate zero points from the mean. Anyone who deviates 1 standard deviation from the mean (above or below) will get a z score of 1 (plus or minus). For example, suppose Joan in the above example had a raw score of 20. Subtracting the mean from 20 (20 — 25) leaves her with a —5 deviation from the mean, which, when divided by the standard deviation of 5, gives her a z score of —1. The 1 tells us she is 1 standard deviation unit from the mean, and the minus sign tells us she is below the mean.

Some people find it convenient to transform the z score into a score which does not have negative numbers. They feel that it is too easy to misinterpret a negative score or a score of zero (a z score of zero is right at the mean, but it is too easy to think of a zero as none correct). The most popular transformed standard score is called a Z score[5] and is computed using the following formula:

Formula for a Z Score

$$Z = z(10) + 50$$

This transformation will give you a distribution having a mean of 50 and a standard deviation of 10. Other transformations can be made by arbitrarily deciding on the size of the desired mean and standard deviation. You then simply multiply the size of the desired standard deviation times each z score and add to it the size of your desired mean [e.g., $z(100) + 500$].

[5] If the distribution of scores is normal this score is referred to as a T score.

Throughout all this calculation, the size and shape of the raw score distribution is not being disturbed. All we are doing is changing the name of the scores. It is rather like converting feet to yards or inches to centimeters. We do not disturb the measurements we have taken; we simply convert them to different size units. The standard scores simply report data in standard deviation units rather than raw score units.

The Normal Curve

The normal curve is a mathematical model which represents the way in which many human characteristics are distributed. It is a bell-shaped curve which is symmetrical (one side of the curve is a mirror image of the other). In a normal distribution, the mean, median, and mode all fall at the same point. Because the normal curve is precisely defined, it is possible to compute the proportion of scores falling under any area of the curve. This is illustrated in Figure A.8. This figure also helps you to see the interrelationship among the various derived scores. You can see that in a normal distribution approximately 68 percent of the individuals are included within 1 standard deviation of the mean (34.13 percent 1 standard deviation below and 34.13 percent 1 standard deviation above the mean). This means that approximately 68 percent also fall between -1 and $+1$

FIGURE A.8. The normal curve and various derived scores.

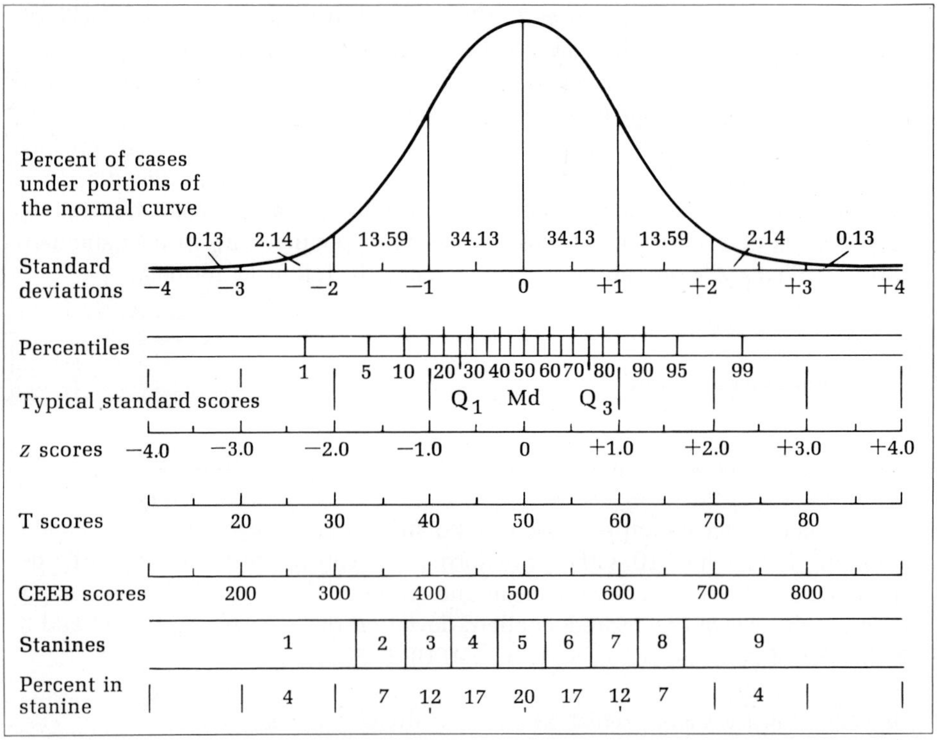

z scores, between T scores 40 and 60, and between College Entrance Examination Board (CEEB) scores of 400 and 600. Almost no one deviates more than 3 standard deviations from the mean.

Standard Error

In Chapter 2, we discussed the standard error of measurement and the standard error of estimate. The former estimate is the error we make in obtaining a raw score and the latter estimate, the error we make when using that score to predict some other measure. The formulas for computing these measures are given below:

The formula for the standard error of measurement looks like this:

$$Sem = S_x \sqrt{1 - r_{xx}}$$

The formula sounds like this: "the standard error of measurement is equal to the standard deviation of the test times the square root of 1 minus the reliability of the test."

The formula computes like this:

$$Sem = 10\sqrt{1 - 0.64}$$
$$Sem = 10\sqrt{0.36}$$
$$Sem = 10\ (0.6)$$
$$Sem = 6$$

The formula for the standard error of estimate looks like this:

$$Sy.x = Sy \sqrt{1 - r^2_{xy}}$$

The formula reads like this: the standard error of estimate (literally this reads: the standard deviation of y, given x) is equal to the standard deviation of test y times the square root of 1 minus the square of the correlation between tests x and y.

The formula computes like this:

$$Sy.x = 15\sqrt{1 - 0.60^2}$$
$$Sy.x = 15\sqrt{1 - 0.36}$$
$$Sy.x = 15\sqrt{0.64}$$
$$Sy.x = 15\ (0.8)$$
$$Sy.x = 12$$

The Expectancy Table

Expectancy tables provide a way to describe the relationship that exists between two measures (e.g., between aptitude and achievement). Expectancy tables provide one way of estimating the validity of a test. If a test measures the same thing as some other test, you would *expect* high scores on one to be associated with high scores on the other, etc. Expectancy tables are also very useful tools for helping you to make estimative and predictive judgments. An expectancy table is easy to produce. It is simply a matter of recording the data you have from two measures in such a way that the relationship between the two measures is highlighted. The steps to take are previewed below:

Steps to Take When Producing an Expectancy Table

1. Determine what kind of relationship you are interested in finding out about.
2. Select two sets of scores to plot and group them into convenient groups.
3. Place the possible scores on one test along one axis and those of the other test along the other axis.
4. Count the number of persons falling in each cell of the matrix.
5. Convert the numbers in the cells to proportions.

Let us work out a problem together. Suppose we want to be able to predict a student's success in conducting the experiments he will be assigned in the second unit of study in eighth grade science. We hope to be able to use his test scores on the test for the first unit as predictor (that is step 1); the relationship of interest is that between first-unit test scores and success in the conducting of second-unit experiments. The sets of scores to be used is obvious in this case: scores on the first-unit test and average grades on the second-unit experiments (Table A.4).

Now we need to group these scores. Suppose we group the first-unit test scores into the following categories: 0 to 20 percent correct; 21 to 40 percent correct; 41 to 60 percent correct; 61 to 80 percent correct; 81 to 100 percent correct. The grades on the experiments could simply be A through E. The next step is to place these along each axis of a matrix. The predictor scores (first-unit test scores) are traditionally placed along the vertical axis and the predicted scores (average grade on the experiments) along the horizontal axis (see Table A.5).

Now we need to fill our matrix in. Of course, we have to keep track of the scores on the first-unit test and then, *after* the experiments are completed, record those grades for the same students. These are the data recorded for you in Table A.4. The data in this table are simply transferred to the matrix by placing tally marks in the correct cells. The matrix is presented in Table A.5. Notice that there were five people who scored between 81 and 100 percent on the first-unit test (Sue, Gerry, Amy, Jill, and Doug). Four of them got an A average on their experiments. One of them (Amy) got a B average. In row two of the matrix in Table A.5, the second-unit grades are tallied for the six students who scored between 61 and 80 percent on the first-unit test. Two of these students received A's; two got B's;

TABLE A.4

Scores for Unit 1 Test and Grades on Experiments for Unit 2

Name	Unit 1 Test Score, Percent	Unit 2 Grade
Amy A.	85	A
Sarah A.	65	C
George B.	70	C
Eloise B.	73	B
Mary C.	59	C
Sue C.	89	A
Tom D.	53	D
Harold D.	19	E
Elmer D.	28	E
Todd E.	67	A
Carol F.	45	C
Sue G.	38	D
Terry J.	80	A
Wanda K.	72	B
Mary K.	56	C
Jill L.	92	A
Gary L.	55	C
Fred L.	37	C
Gerry S.	87	B
Forrdell S.	39	D
Wally T.	54	B
Mark T.	58	C
Cindy T.	60	B
Doug. W.	86	A

TABLE A.5

Expectancy Table Showing the Relationship between Unit 1 Test Scores and Unit 2 Grades (Number of Students per Cell)

Unit 1 Test Scores, Percent	AVERAGE GRADE ON EXPERIMENTS IN UNIT 2				
	A	B	C	D	E
81–100	1111	1			
61–80	11	11	11		
41–60		11	⊥⊥⊥⊥	1	
21–40			1	1	11
0–20					1

TABLE A.6

Expectancy Table Showing the Relationship between Unit 1 Test Scores and Unit 2 Grades (Proportion of Students per Cell)

Unit 1 Test Scores, Percent	AVERAGE GRADE ON EXPERIMENTS IN UNIT 2				
	A	B	C	D	E
81–100	0.80	0.20			
61–80	0.33	0.33	0.33		
41–60		0.25	0.625	0.125	
21–40			0.25	0.25	0.50
0–20					1.00

and two got C's. You can see from this table that the higher the first-test score, the better the chances of getting a good grade on the second unit. This is evidence of the predictive validity of the first-unit test.

The last step calls for us to convert the cell totals to proportions. (See Table A.6.) This is done row by row. For example, in row one, there are a total of five students (these are the ones scoring between 81 and 100 percent on the first-unit test). Four out of five (0.80) got an A average on their experiments. One person (a proportion of 0.20) got a B. So in the first two cells of the top row we would place 0.80 and 0.20, respectively. What would go in the first cell of the second row down? Two out of the six who scored in the 61 to 80 percent range got A's on their experiments. That is a proportion of 0.33.

The number of students represented in this table is relatively small and the proportions might not be very stable. If we could combine the results from several classes in the same school or the results from three or four years in a row, we would have a more stable relationship and our predictions would be more accurate.

Expectancy tables like these can be used to validate judgments, to estimate the validity of a test, and to make classroom predictions.

EXERCISE A.4

Review the basic concepts discussed in this appendix by computing the following for the data found in Table A.1:

1. Test 1: mean, median, mode, range, quartile deviation, standard deviation
2. Test 2: reliability
3. Correlation between test 1 and test 2
4. Expectancy table predicting test 4 from test 3

References

Diederich, Paul B.: *Short-cut Statistics for Teacher-Made Tests,* 2d ed., Educational Testing Service, Princeton, N.J., 1964.

Suggested Readings

The following introductory texts provide well-written explanations of basic statistical concepts:

Downie, N. M., and R. W. Heath: *Basic Statistical Methods,* 2d ed., Harper & Row, Publishers, Inc., New York, 1965.

Franzblau, Abraham N.: *A Primer of Statistics for Non-Statisticians,* Harcourt, Brace & World, Inc., New York, 1958.

Weinberg, George H., and John A. Schumaker: *Statistics: An Intuitive Approach,* Wadsworth Publishing Company, Inc., Belmont, Calif., 1962.

A fun-to-read paperback that will also help you to understand statistics better is:

Huff, Darrell: *How to Lie with Statistics,* W. W. Norton & Company, Inc., New York, 1954.

If you prefer a programmed text, try one of these:

Amos, Jimmy R., Foster Lloyd Brown, and Oscar B. Mink: *Statistical Concepts: A Basic Program,* Harper & Row, Publishers, Inc., New York, 1965.

Gorow, Frank F.: *Statistical Measures: A Programmed Text,* Chandler Publishing Company, San Francisco, 1962.

Gotkin, Lassar G., and Leo S. Goldstein: *Descriptive Statistics: Programmed Textbook,* John Wiley & Sons, Inc., New York, 1967, vols. 1 and 2.

APPENDIX B

Answers to Exercises

CHAPTER ONE

1.1 (1) *b.* (2) Information, judgments, decision making. (3) *a.* (4) *c.* (5) *b.* (6) *b.* (7) *b.* (8) *a.*

CHAPTER TWO

2.1 (1) Typical errors within the test are ambiguous items, items measuring information not covered in the course, and vocabulary that is unnecessarily difficult. (2) Typical errors within the testing situation include disturbances during testing, unclear instructions, scoring errors, and recording the score incorrectly. (3) Typical individual errors are due to taking a test when sick, having an "I don't care" attitude, and lack of test-taking ability.

466

2.2 (1) *c*. (2) *d*. (3) *a*. (4) *b*. (5) *a*. (6) *c*. (7) *a*. (8) *d*.

2.3 (1) Validity indicates how appropriate information is for making particular judgments and decisions. (2) Valid for what? (3) Because there are different uses of evaluative information (and different uses for tests). (4) *Concurrent:* estimates of a specific ability or performance; *predictive:* predictive judgments; *construct:* estimates of general ability.

2.4 (1) Judging the value of tests; computing the standard error of measurement and the standard error of estimate. (2) The two methods of estimating measurement error are both based on the fact that there are several identifiable sources of error. Watching for clues is a more subjective procedure but allows you to obtain an estimate prior to as well as during and after testing. Empirical evidence can be obtained only after the data have been collected, but it gives you a more objective, more accurate estimate. When very important judgments and decisions are being made, you will want an accurate estimate of error and should obtain empirical evidence. Most often, teachers will need only subjective estimates of error, like those obtained by watching for clues.

CHAPTER THREE

3.1 (1) Decision. (2) Judgment. (3) Judgment. (4) Judgment. (5) Decision. (6) Judgment. (7) Judgment. (8) Decision. (9) Decision.

3.2 (1) Selection. (2) Selection. (3) Placement. (4) Treatment. (5) Placement. (6) Selection. (7) Treatment. (8) Treatment. (9) Selection. (10) Assignment.

3.3 (1) Prediction. (2) Estimate. (3) Estimate. (4) Prediction. (5) Estimate. (6) Prediction. (7) Prediction. (8) Estimate. (9) Prediction. (10) Prediction. (11) Estimate. (12) Estimate.

3.4 (1) All three are formed by comparing information to some referent. They differ in the particular kind of referent used. (2) Because the objectives serve as statements of expected performance and provide the referent for making criterion-referenced judgments. Without a clearly defined referent, accurate judgments become difficult to make.

3.5 (1) Estimate, norm-referenced, deviation. (2) Prediction, self-referenced, deviation. (3) Estimate, criterion-referenced, master. (4) Estimate, norm-referenced, mastery. (5) Prediction, norm-referenced, deviation. (6) Estimate, criterion-referenced, mastery.

CHAPTER FOUR

4.1 (1) What is the information about? What kind of behavior is to be observed? How specific must the information be? How accurate must the information be? (2) Cognitive, affective, psychomotor. (3) Unexpected. (4) The cost of obtaining it. (5) When the needed information is carefully described, it is easier to decide when and how to obtain that information.

4.2 *The main objections to objectives are as follows:* they take a great deal of time and effort to construct; they hamper the process of individualizing instruction; they curtail spontaneity; they often specify trivial goals. *These objectives can be answered:* objectives for an entire course do not need to be developed all at once; good objectives are becoming more readily available; with clearly defined objectives, individualizing can be geared toward individual approaches to reaching the same goal. Spontaneity can be most effectively capitalized upon when an ultimate goal is kept clearly in mind; trivial goals, like trivial objective test items, represent a misuse of a worthwhile technique. *The major use of objectives are as follows:* guides for lesson planning; guides for selecting, constructing, and using evaluation techniques; guides for summarizing and reporting evaluation results; guides for learners when deciding when and how to study.

4.3 (1) *b.* (2) *a.* (3) *b.* (4) *b.* (5) *c* and *d.* (6) *c* and *d.* (7) *a* and *c.* (8) *d.*

4.4   1. *Subject Matter*   *Student Response*
   a. Multiplication tables   Repeat through 12×12
   b. Plot of short story   Select
   c. Names of notes in treble clef   Write

2. *Condition*   *Minimum level of performance*
   a. Given a description of five   Making no errors
       experiments
   b. Given a completed business letter   Identify at least twelve of the fifteen
                                                        components
   c. Given descriptions of six games   Correctly name five of the six
       which were taught

3 through 6. Check your goals against the criteria specified in Chapter 4 and have your instructor or your peers check your work.

4.5 (1) Describe the subject matter content and student responses expected; produce a content-by-behavior matrix; and indicate the proportion of items needed for each cell. (2*a*) The population is the knowledge or skill being tested. (2*b*) By defining the major characteristics of the knowledge or skill area.

4.6 Check your response with your instructor and/or peers.

CHAPTER FIVE

5.1 (1) *Advantages:* No need to obtain instruments and collect data yourself; data are immediately available so judgments and decisions can be made without delay. *Disadvantages:* Data are often outdated and inaccurate. (2) Do they fit the description of the information needed? Are they accurate? Can they be used to help make the specific anticipated judgments and decisions?

5.2 (1) *a.* (2) *d.* (3) *d.* (4) *c.* (5) *b.* (6) *b.* (7) *d.* (8) *a* and *c.*

5.3 (1*a*) *Observation:* versatile, somewhat subjective. (1*b*) *Inquiry:* subjective but highly useful for obtaining student perceptions. (1*c*) *Analysis:* invaluable for keeping track of learning progress and discovering incorrect procedures.

(1*d*) *Testing:* objective, highly efficient, but somewhat limited in the kinds of outcomes which can be measured. (2) A technique is a general procedure (e.g., inquiry). An instrument refers to a specific tool to be used (e.g., a questionnaire). (3) Kind of information needed; importance of judgments and decisions to be made; when the judgments and decisions must be made.

5.4 (1) Because in every case the idea is to obtain the right kind of information as accurately as possible, and the same basic sources of error affect all information-gathering instruments. (2) Knowing the subject matter well helps you to be able to relate everything to the reason you are evaluating and also to obtain an appropriate sample of knowledge; holding to particular educational values helps you to keep goals in their proper perspective; understanding those taking the tests will help you to write clear, unambiguous items. Skillful use of item-writing techniques will help you to produce clear, unambiguous, and valid items. (3) All can be learned.

CHAPTER SIX

6.1 (1) Observer bias. (2) Concentrate on the observable aspects of the specific behavior under observation; avoid generalizing your impressions; "hide" the identity of the authors of any products being rated. (3) "Halo" effect; personal response tendency; logical error. (4) So you do not unnecessarily influence the behavior of those being observed. (5) Because unusual behavior may not be representative of the individual's general behavior pattern (unless unusual behavior is typical of a given student). (6) *Advantages:* forces comparisons and provides good data for norm-referenced judgments. *Disadvantages:* Time-consuming, subjective.

6.2 (1) *Problem 1:* Respondent's "I don't care" attitude. *Solution 1:* Convince respondent that the questionnaire is worthwhile. *Problem 2:* Respondent doesn't understand how to fill out questionnaire. *Solution 2:* Provide clear instructions and double-check to see that respondents are responding correctly. *Problem 3:* Respondents feel threatened. *Solution 3:* Put respondents at ease. (2) Be ready, establish rapport, provide guidance to respondent, make certain the information is accurate, and know when to quit.

6.3 Do not analyze everything in depth; skim first, then analyze in more detail; save samples of work for later perusal; analyze quickly as the students are working.

6.4 (1) Good test administration involves having all needed materials ready and on hand, providing clear instructions, handing out materials systematically, monitoring the test taking, collecting the tests, and carefully scoring them. (2) Because test administration is a major source of measurement error. Typical errors due to poor test administration occur because of misunderstandings, cheating, big differences in length of time particular students have to work on the test, scoring errors, etc.

6.5 (1) Because it is important to make certain that available information is valid, reliable, and up to date. (2) Judgments are based upon information about student performance. Information describing the *conditions* under which that performance occurred is supplementary and serves to help you make more accurate judgments. (3) To compare the performance of his students from year to year; to help him make more meaningful norm-referenced judgments; to help him make predictions of future performance.

CHAPTER SEVEN

7.1 (1) A person's rank indicates his position relative to some reference group, such as a class. (2) Percentile rank indicates a person's rank in terms of percentage of individuals who score at the same level or lower than he does. (3) A standard score reports the individual's score in terms of how far he deviates from average. The deviation is reported under Deviation Units. (4) Deviation I is an IQ score which indicates how far the student's performance deviates from those the same age on an IQ measurement. (5) The grade-equivalent score indicates how far a student deviates from the average performance of students in his same grade. (6) Criterion-referenced interpretation scoring is accomplished by comparing the person's performance to some specified criterion.

7.2 (1) Grading on the curve is a norm-referenced judgment involving comparison of a student's performance to some theoretical distribution of scores. This often causes problems because students do not always perform as expected. Many classrooms contain many above-average students or many below-average students, and it is difficult to justify spreading students out whose basic performance is very much alike. (2) Correct scores are essentially deviation judgments in which the individual score is reported as a deviation from 100 percent correct. The problem with this type of score is that the only referent is the test itself, and because tests vary so much in difficulty level, it is virtually impossible to make any meaningful judgments on the basis of this type of score. (3) Grades as percentiles are essentially norm-referenced judgments in which the person's score is compared to how well others have done on the same test. The score is reported in terms of the percentage of students who have scored at that same level or lower. This type of score has many advantages, but it is sometimes confused with the percentage-correct score. (4) Grading on an achievement continuum is essentially a criterion-referenced judgment and involves comparison of the student's performance to the specified levels of performance found on an achievement continuum. The difficulty with this kind of scoring is that an achievement continuum must be carefully specified in behavioral terms before the information is obtained and judgments are made. (5) Grading on a standard is also a criterion-referenced judgment and involves specifying a particular level of performance which is to serve as a standard against which each individual's performance is judged. Obviously it is somewhat difficult to establish standards which are realistic, but if this can be done, grading on a standard is a particularly appealing procedure. (6) Grading on a standard scale is much like the grading on an achievement continuum. It is a criterion-referenced judgment which is made by comparing an individual's performance to several standards which have been arranged along a continuum. The problem again is one of specifying levels of performance which serve as standards along the scale.

7.3 (1) The advantage of keeping report card grades as measures of achievement only is the fact that achievement is more easily and accurately measured than other aspects of school behavior. Furthermore, if effort, personality, social development, and other student characteristics are to be graded, they probably should be reported separately. (2) Grades from tests and assignments should not be averaged when the subject matter is highly cumulative and you are interested primarily in the student's final level of achievement. (3) Formative, criterion-referenced judgments are judgments made *while* the student is learning, whereas summative judgments refer to those judgments made *after* the student has had sufficient opportunity to reach some instructional goal. These two kinds of judgments are alike in the sense that they both use performance criteria as the major referents.

CHAPTER EIGHT

8.1 Check your hypotheses against the criteria specified in Chapter 8 and compare your answers to those of your peers.

8.2 (1) *Outcome:* average score; *condition:* on another form of the same test. (2) *Outcome:* better than anyone; *condition:* on another arithmetic achievement test. (3) *Outcome:* will have no trouble; *condition:* on similar problems found on page 78. (4) *Outcome:* chosen by his classmates as one who comes up with the most ideas; *condition:* on a guess-who technique. (5) *Outcome:* will take over a small group discussion; *condition:* if no leader is appointed. (6) *Outcome:* the class will continue to work; *condition:* when I leave the room.

8.3 Check the results of this exercise with your instructor and/or your classmates.

8.4 Compare your answers with those of your classmates and double-check the text for appropriate ways to state the objectives and alternative courses of action.

CHAPTER NINE

9.1 (1) The purpose of a summary should be cited before the summary is begun, so that you will know ahead of time what you anticipate including in the summary and will know where to look for what information. (2) It helps to know what reports are likely to be made from your evaluation summaries because you can then include only the material which will be relevant to those reports. (3) The decisions which have been made, the judgments which influenced those decisions, and the information used to make each judgment. (4) By providing you with a written record of the judgments on which your decisions were based as well as the major information that led you to make those judgments.

9.2 The three items in this exercise call for you to defend or refute a number of statements. Make certain that your defense is based upon sound information and logic and not upon personal bias. Check your answers with your instructor and/or your peers.

9.3 Your letter should include a list of decisions which were made relative to this boy's achievement and the judgments and information upon which those decisions rested. Make certain that your letter meets the criteria discussed in this chapter.

CHAPTER TEN

10.1 through 10.3 Compare your work with that of your peers. If possible, try out your checklist to see if it works well. Will two or three people using it to rate the same product or performance arrive at similar ratings?

10.4 (1) Validity, reliability, ease of use. (2) Be certain that the most important behaviors are to be judged (ask a friend to help you decide); check to see that there is no ambiguity and that all descriptions are stated in observable terms; check on the clarity of the instructions. (3) Read it to determine if it is measuring what you want it to; try it out; verify the information it yields. (4) Yes, because an unreliable instrument is not likely to yield valid information.

CHAPTER ELEVEN

11.1 (1) Questionnaires more frequently contain questions which have no correct answer (they call for opinions, attitudes, interests, etc.). (2) Threatening questions too early can put the respondent on the defensive. Inconsistency can easily be guarded against if a mixed arrangement is not used; confusion may result if questions are not arranged by topic. (3) Rationale; procedures for use. Without appropriate rationale, the users may not take the questionnaire seriously and the results will be in error. Without procedures for their use, questionnaires are often answered incorrectly or important parts may be omitted. Again, the result is error.

11.2 (1) The interview refers to the activity—the *process* of inquiry, the inquiry itself. The interview schedule is a plan of action designed to lend structure and organization to the interview. (2) A statement of the purpose of the interview will help you and the interviewee to "stay on track" and help you to obtain valid information; guidelines for establishing rapport will assure more open and honest responses; questions established ahead of time are more likely to be less ambiguous than questions thought up during the interview; an outline of the interview schedule will help you to get the information you need and to avoid spending too much time obtaining information you do not need; a note on time and place will help you to avoid embarrassing situations which may cause the respondent to become uncooperative. Space for note taking makes it easier to write down information immediately so you do not forget it.

11.3 Ask your instructor and/or your peers to check your instructions for clarity.

11.4 (1) OK. (2) NA. (3) NC. (4) OK. (5) NB. (6) OK. (7) NA. (8) OK. (9) OK. (10) NA.

CHAPTER TWELVE

12.1 (1) Because it is difficult, if not impossible, to find out how well a student is learning unless you know what he is expected to learn. (2) The phrase "what the student is supposed to do" refers to learning activities, whereas the phrase "what the student is supposed to learn" refers to learning outcomes. The activities are designed to help the student *reach* the outcomes.

CHAPTER THIRTEEN

13.1 (1) *a.* (2) *c.* (3) *a,* because objective tests *tend* to be more reliable. (4) *d.* (5) *d.*

13.2 (1) It clearly, unambiguously measures very specific information about *particular,* expected behaviors. (2) Everything needed to take the test: type of responses called for, time limits, scoring criteria, etc. (3) Students can get incomplete tests; items may be difficult to read; students may become fatigued from trying to read poor reproduction; confusion can result and raise student anxiety.

13.3 through **13.9** Compare your work to that of your peers and/or ask your instructor to check it.

13.10 (1) *d.* (2) *b.* (3) *c.* (4) *c.* (5) 2. (6) 1. (7) 3. (8) 4. (9) 2, 4, 5. (10) 1, 3, 11. (11) 4.

CHAPTER FOURTEEN

14.1 (1) They provide information which is clearly defined, has known parameters, and has been obtained under "ideal" conditions. (2) Grouping students; selecting students for special classes; determining who will get scholarships; deciding who are eligible for class officers; etc. (3) Educational and vocational guidance. (4) Assessing teacher effectiveness. (5) Interests and opinions.

APPENDIX A

A.1 (1) A chart showing how many persons obtained each score. (2) It provides a picture of the way the scores distribute themselves. (3) They both describe the same basic data.

A.2 (1*a*) 13; 15; 15.1. (2*a*) The mode is the most frequently occurring score; the median divides a distribution into two equal halves; the mean is the arithmetic average.

A.3 (1) *Range:* unstable, easy to compute. (2) *Quartile deviation:* deviation from the median, good for highly skewed distributions. *Standard deviation:* deviation from the mean, highly stable. (2*a*) 11. (2*b*) 2. (2*c*) 3.37.

A.4 (1) 51.37, 63, 63, 51, 11.5, 14.64. (2) KR 21 $= .22$ (3) $L^{r3,5} = .58.$ (4)

Test 3

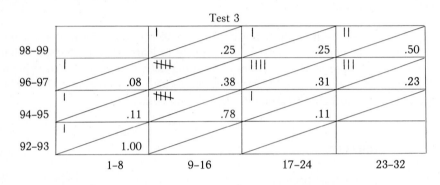

Index

Index